B. C. Bloomfield

An author index to selected British 'little magazines' 1930-1939

Mansell
1976

© 1976 B.C. Bloomfield

Mansell Information/Publishing Limited
3 Bloomsbury Place London WC1A 2QA England

ISBN 0 7201 0542 0

Text set in 8/9 pt IBM Journal, printed by photolithography,
and bound in Great Britain at The Pitman Press, Bath

 British Library Cataloguing in Publication Data

```
Bloomfield, Barry Cambray
   An author index to selected British
   'little magazines', 1930-1939.
   ISBN 0-7201-0542-0
   1. Title
   016.052    A13
   Little magazines-Great Britain
   Periodicals-Indexes
```

For Valerie

who put up with it

Contents

In 1961 I began work on a study of the literary 'little magazines' published in Great Britain during the period 1930 to 1939. After a very short time it became apparent that a finding list would be needed for the many important contributions scattered throughout their pages, particularly since almost none of the titles was included in any of the standard indexes to periodicals. So I began to compile my own index and it is this which is presented here. The original study now has little chance of ever being completed but this may be a useful prolegomenon for another later scholar, and I hope it may stimulate others to compile similar indexes for literary magazines published in other decades of this century.

This is an author index to the magazines listed on p. xi, and it contains about 11,000 entries. Each entry gives first the author's name and then the title of his contribution. Where there is no title a brief title is supplied, *e.g.* Review, Poem, Play, and, in the case of reviews, this is usually followed in square brackets by the author and title of the work reviewed. Authors' names have been verified with other sources where possible and the most familiar form is normally used. For foreign names I have usually accepted the form of name given in the magazine itself and have not tried to edit this to conform with any systematic transliteration system; this means that Chinese, Russian and some other forms of name sometimes display inconsistencies. These details are then followed by the abbreviated title of the periodical, the volume and part number, the date of publication, the page reference, and a symbol which gives a general indication of the character of the contribution indexed, *e.g.* v = poetry; p = creative prose; i = illustration. At the end of each block of entries listing the contributions of a particular author will be found a list of the titles of the books he published during the period and the names of those persons who reviewed these books in the 'little magazines'. Occasionally it has

been possible to identify anonymous contributions; this has been done silently.

Most of the magazines have been fully indexed, including all minor contributions and book reviews. There are two exceptions: entries for *The ploughshare* only include those which had literary merit or interest, and not all the minor entries in *Comment* are indexed. (In general unsigned book reviews consisting of a paragraph or two have not been indexed unless they were of particular interest.) All the magazines indexed were published in the United Kingdom, with one exception, *Caravel*. This was included because it contains a considerable amount of poetry by young British writers. However I did consider and reject a number of magazines which are not indexed. Magazines were rejected because:

1) they were not what I understood by a 'little magazine';

2) they were already indexed in one of the general indexes to periodicals; or

3) they did not, in my opinion, include contributions of sufficient literary merit. (This applied to many school, college and literary 'do-it-yourself' type of magazines.)

I list below those magazines which were rejected for one or other of these reasons.

Albannach,
ed. by C. J. Russell and J. F. Hendry. 1938.
(An anthology.)
Apes and angles.
Vol. 1, no. 1—vol. 1, no. 4. Cambridge, 1935.
The beehive: an Eton magazine.
Lords, 1937.
Close-up
ed. by O. Blakeston. Vol. 1, no. 1—vol. 10, no. 4. Territet, 1927—1933. (A film magazine.)
For these few minutes,
ed. by E. Partridge. 1938. (An anthology).
Free expression.
No. 1—vol. 2, no. 9? London, 1939—1941?

Fritillary.
Vol. 1—37. Oxford, 1893—1931.
The gate.
Nos. 1—10. Windsor, 1930—1933.
The grasshopper: an Eton magazine.
No. 1. Lords, 1939.
Integration: a students' catholic review.
Vol. 1, no. 1—vol. 3, no. 3. Cambridge, 1939—1941.
Left book news.
Nos. 1—128. London, 1936—1947.
Lilliput.
No. 1—vol. 46, no. 7. London, 1937—1960.
Meteor.
Vol. 1—   . Rugby, 1867—
The new porcupine: a political journal.
Nos. 1—2. Cambridge, 1938.
The outlet: the literary live-wire,
ed. by A Petrogradov. Nos. 1—3. London, 1932.
Outlook.
Vol. 1, no. 1—vol. 1, no. 17. Dublin, 1931.
Outlook.
Vol. 1, no. 1—vol. 1, no. 10. Edinburgh, 1936—1937.
Parade: the British digest of good reading.
Vol. 1—4. London, 1937—1941.
Plebs.
Vol. 1—   Oxford, 1909—
The poet.
Vol. 1, no. 1—vol. 4, no. 3. Balerno, 1936—1939.
Poetry quarterly.
Vol. 1, no. 1—vol. 1, no. 6. London, [Fudge],
1933—1934.
Poetry studies.
Vol. 1, no. 1—vol. 6, no. [22?]. London,
1933—1938.
Poets in brief.
Nos. 1—6. Cambridge, 1932. (A series of pamphlets.)
The poppy.
No. 1. Cambridge, 1936.
Purpose.
Vol. 1, no. 1—vol. 12, no. 3/4. London, 1929—1940.
Rejection.
Vol. 1, no, 1—vol. 2, no. 11. London, 1932—1934.
Satire and burlesque: laughter with a sting.
Vol. 1, no. 1—vol. 1, no. 2. London, 1934.
Sixpenny.
No. 1. Eton, 1933.
The stork.
Vol. 1—5. London, 1930—1934. (The magazine of
Putnam, the publisher.)
The street singer.
No. 1. Eton, 1930.

This week.
Vol. 1, no. 1—vol. 1, no. 6. London, 1939.
The wayfarer.
Annual. Cambridge, 1934—1936.

In addition to this list of rejected periodicals there were unfortunately a few which proved impossible to trace in spite of all efforts. These I list with the details I have managed to find.

Awake!
Writers International, British section. 1930.
The dancing moment.
1931.
Fact and fiction: a magazine of short stories.
Nos. 1—6. London, 1934—1935.
Opus,
ed. by D. Val Baker. Nos. 1—14. 1939?—1943.
Poet's guild quarterly,
ed. by Ruth Elliott. Buckhurst Hill, 1931?
Static,
ed. by Richard Kersey. Nos. 1—2. 1931?

These may not have qualified for inclusion in this index but it would have been preferable to have examined copies. In addition it has not been possible to find any copies of numbers 6, 7 and 9 of volume 1 of the *Literary review,* all of which has otherwise been indexed. (Neither the national libraries in Great Britain nor the major libraries in North America appear to have copies of these elusive periodicals. I have advertised in newspapers and thrice written to the *Times Literary Supplement,* and in cases where the editor's name or one of his associates was known to me, have managed to track down the person in question, but no copies of the actual magazines have been forthcoming. However if in the future any reader of this introduction does locate any copies of these magazines I shall be grateful if he or she will take the trouble to write and let me know of its whereabouts.)

There are no subject entries in this index. This will be a handicap to many users, but in fact many of the entries have no readily definable subject, dealing as they do with modern literature, poetry, drama, or criticism in the most general sense. There is one exception to this in that the critical writing and film reviews which would have otherwise been scattered throughout the index have been grouped together under the head 'Film criticism'. As a rule films are reviewed under their titles and not by directors' names and it seemed therefore more sensible and convenient to bring such criticism together in one place.

I am most grateful to the following persons who have helped me in the course of compiling this index: Donovan Brown, Peter Davison, Kay Ekevall, John Johnson, Jack Lindsay, Edward Mendelson, Edgell Rickword, Julian Symons and Geoffrey Woledge. I am also grateful to the librarians and staffs of the following libraries: British Library Reference Division, Bodleian Library, University Library Cambridge, National Library of Wales, National Library of Scotland, British Library of Political and Economic Science, Croydon Public Reference Library, University of London Library, New York Public Library, Yale University Library, Harvard College Library, Poetry Collection at the Lockwood Memorial Library, State University of New York at Buffalo, and the University of Texas Library. I am also grateful to the School of Oriental and African Studies Library which released me on study leave for three months during the Summer of 1974 and enabled me to apply the finishing touches to this index and prepare it for publication.

January 1975   B.C. Bloomfield

List of magazines indexed

Abbreviations

Note.

*In the body of each entry the name of the author and the
title of each contribution is followed by the abbreviation
of the periodical title, the volume number (if any) in lower
case roman numerals, the part number in Arabic numerals,
the day and abbreviated month (or other date) of publication with the last two figures of the year number, the page
reference and lastly a lower case letter giving some idea of
the type of contribution indexed.*

A	April
Ag	August
Au	Autumn
b	bibliography
C	Christmas
c	critical article
D	December
d	drama
dr	theatre review
F	February
i	illustration
J	January
Je	June
Jy	July
M	March
m	music
My	May
N	November
Oc	October
p	creative prose
r	book review
S	September
Sp	Spring
Su	Summer
v	verse
W	Winter

A

A., K.
Review [*The problem parent,*
by A. S. Neill]
TC, iii 14 A32, 30 r

A., N.
Rondeau — after Villon.
LS, i 2 My34, 60 v

A., N. A.
Originality.
M, i 1 Je33, 32 v

A., S. H. V. and M., H.
Review [*Reading and discrimination,*
by D. Thompson].
TC, vi 35 Je34, 309—11 r

A., S. W.
C[roydon] R[ep] T[heatre] and
C[roydon] P[ublic] L[ibraries].
R, i 2 F34, 14 c

A. E. *pseud. see* Stephens,
James

Abbey, J. M.
The Baghdad ferry.
HR, 4 1931, 40 p

Abbott, Elsie
Slate quarry.
PP, 4 Oc38, 13—14 v

Abelard, Peter
In feste Sancti Joannis evangelistae,
tr. H. Waddell.
LQ, i 2 D36, [5—6] v

Abercrombie, Lascelles *and others*
Ralph Fox: a tribute.
LR, iii 1 F37, 2—4 c

Abercrombie, Patrick
Town and country planning
rev. by J. Dudding

Abercrombie, Ralph
Youth faces up to it
[*Young minds for old,* by L. Ralphs].
LR, ii 10 Jy36, 532 r

Aberpennar, Davies
Nawn; Trioled.
W, 11 W39, 301, 303 v
Review [*The map of love,*
by D. Thomas].
W, 11 W39, 306—8 r
Review [*Taliesin through Logres,*
by C. Williams]
W, 11 W39, 310 r

Ablett, F. Rushton
If I.
PQ, i 1 Sp39, 12—13 v

Achillopolo, C.
The Ashmolean.
NO, i 2 N33, 131 i

Ackland, Valentine
Communist poem, 1935.
LR, i 10 Jy35, 430 v
Country dealings.
LR, i 6 M35, 198—200 p
Country dealings II.
LR, i 8 My35, 311—14 p
Country dealings III.
LR, i 12 S35, 506—8 p
1937.
LR, iii 7 Ag37, 416 v
Spain [*Reporter in Spain,* by F. Pitcairn;
Spanish front, by C. Prieto;
*A preliminary official report on the
atrocities in Southern Spain,*
by the National Government at
Burgos (Franco)].
LR, ii 15 D36, 843 r
The Spanish struggle
[*Behind the Spanish barricades,*
by J. Langdon-Davies;
Spain in revolt,
by H. Gannes and T. Repard;
Spain to-day, by E. Conze].
LR, ii 16 J37, 914—15 r
Two pictures of the Spanish war
[*The war in Spain,* by R. Sender;

The Spanish cockpit, by F. Borkenau].
LR, iii 8 S37, 484—6 r
Winter.
LR, ii 6 M36, 250 v
Country conditions rev. by J. Dunman

Acland, Richard
Only one battle rev. by A. L. Morton

Acton, Harold *and* **Ch'en, Shih-Hsiang** *trs.*
Modern Chinese poetry
rev. by Ch'ien Chung-shu;
H. G. Porteus

Adamic, Louis
Cradle of Life rev. by S. Blumenfeld

Adams, Francis
Defeat?
ST, i 2 Ap33, 21 v

Adams, R. G.
Review [*Music ho!* by C. Lambert].
VP, i 2 Jy/S34, 53 r

Adams, Richard
Poem to E. R.
K, i 2 D39—J40, 64 v

Addison, William Wilkinson
And now.
JG, 39 W36, [13—14] v
The awakening.
JG, 33 Su35, [10] v
Circles.
JG, 70 Au39, [11—12] v
Cronies.
JG, 13 Su30, [18—19] v
Deny not vigour.
JG, 64 Sp38, [10] v
Easter.
JG, 24 Sp33, [12] v
The elms.
JG, 30 Au34, [22] v
Except the dream.
JG, 41 Su37, [22] v
Fences.
JG, 17 Su31, [23] v
First spring morning.
JG, 32 Sp35, [23] v

Addison, William Wilkinson (cont.)
The flower philosopher.
JG, 28 Sp34, [25] v
For strength.
JG, 15 W30, [26—27] v
Foreboding night.
JG, 37 Su36, [15] v
In a dry month.
JG, 71 W39, [14] v
Joseph.
JG, 38 Au36, [28] v
The keys of Eden.
JG, 14 Au30, [12] v
Knight-errantry.
JG, 25 Su33, [25] v
The maid.
JG, 29 Su34, [12] v
Masquerade.
JG, 63 W37, [16] v
Memory.
JG, 36 Sp36, [16—17] v
Mock the moon.
JG, 65 Su38, [27] v
October.
JG, 35 W35, [21] v
On hearing X— in his old age.
JG, 42 Au37, [11] v
On the beach.
JG, 66 Au38, [25] v
The questioner.
JG, 21 Su32, [23] v
Radiation.
JG, 68 Sp39, [16] v
The rain.
JG, 18 Au31, [20], v
Refraction.
JG, 69 Su39, [6] v
The river of stone.
JG, 20 Sp32, [18—19] v
The singing tree.
JG, 26 Au33, [7] v
Snowscape.
JG, 19 W31, [8] v
Storm.
JG, 23 W32, [10] v
Sunset.
JG, 67 W38, [31] v
The unknown God.
JG, 22 Au32, [7] v
Unmixed emotions.
JG, 16 Sp31, [24] v
A winter phantasy.
JG, 27 W33, [20—22] v
Youth and age.
JG, 40 Sp37, [12] v

Adlard, Mary
Sonnet.
DD, vii 26 S—Oc30, 409—10 v

Adler, Nathan
Out of work.
TC, vi 31 S—Oc33, 28 p

Adonis' garden.
T, 4 Je37, [5—7] v

An adventure,
by a five-year-old boy.
CPP, 2 Je36, 39 p

Aeschylus
Extract from the *Agamemnon*,
tr. by L. MacNeice.
GTP, 2 Ag36, [3] v
Extract from a translation of the
Agamemnon, by L. MacNeice.
GTP, 3 S36, 2—3 v
Final chorus, tr. by L. MacNeice.
GTP, 4 Oc36, 3 v
Agamemnon, tr. by L. MacNeice
rev. by D. Kahn; D. I. Dunnett

After lunch.
M, i 1 Je33, 46—47 p

'Against the peace of our lord
the King.'
LR, i 8 My35, 330 c

Agar, Eileen
The bird.
I, i 1 15Je31, 13 vi
Family trio.
I, i 2/3 15S31, 63 i
Oil painting.
I, i 4 15D31, 115 i
Religion and the artistic
imagination.
I, i 4 15D31, 102 c
Vivos voco.
I, i 2/3 15S31, 39 i

Agate, James
First nights rev. by J. Garrett

Agee, James
Dixie doodle.
W, 6/7 M39, [195—96] v
Permit me voyage
rev. by G. Grigson

Agius, Tancred Ambrose
The early English Benedictine
contribution to letters and poetry;
On hearing John McCormick sing.
CA, 11 1932, 335—51 cv
Epiphany at Lourdes.
CA, 2 S30, 25 v
In Bethlehem of Juda.
CA, 4 N30, 93 v
Melchisadec at Lourdes.
CA, 10 1931, 320 v
Skating.
CA, 3 Oc30, 45 v
The true nature of religious
poetry.
CA, 10 1931, 304—5 c

Ahmatova, Anna
Poem, tr. by S. Dolgorouky.
DD, xi 48 N—D34, 91 v
Poem, tr. by S. Dolgorouky.
DD, xi 44 M—A34, 19 v

Ahmed, Sheik
Dreaming.
SM, 3 1932, [loose insert] i
I met some soldiers.
SM, 4 *supp.* [1933?] i
Illustration.
SM, 5 *supp.* [1934] i

Aiken, Conrad Potter
Answers to an enquiry.
NV, 11 Oc34, 13 p
The four appearances.
T, 12/13 Oc38, 87—89 v
Prelude.
PR, 4 5M35, 1—2 v
Prelude.
T, 10 My38, 30 v
Three preludes.
EX, 6 Oc30, 33—36 v
King Coffin rev. by G. S. Fraser
Time in the rock
rev. by J. Symons; R. Todd

Ainley, Henry
Lines for a sun-dial in Wharfedale.
HR, 5 1932, 40 v

Ainslie, Douglas Grant Duff
Advice.
MS, ii 3 Oc31, 233 v

Aitken, J. G. R.
Letter.
NV, i 2 My39, 61—62 p

Ajax *pseud.*
Connolly and another jubilee.
LR, i 7 A35, 241—46 c
Poem.
LR, i 8 My35, 296 v
The revolutionist's handbook.
LR, i 1 Oc34, 41—44 c
Scenario of the film.
[*The private life of Henry VIII*,
by E. Betts].
LR, i 4 J35, 144 r
The writer's war.
LR, i 2 N34, 13—16 c
see also Donnelly, Charles

Ajax *pseud.* and Slater, Montagu
Enter from the left: a dialogue
on the theatre.
LR, i 5 F35, 173—76 c

Akers-Douglas, Eric
Tapestry.
F, 4 D30, 3—7 c

Tapestry.
F, 6 Je31, 189—96 c
Tapestry: the mediaeval point of
view.
F, 5 F31, 102—9 c

Alan, P.
After one year working in the
U.S.S.R.
ST, i 2 Ap33, 10—11 c

Alberti, Rafael
I, too, sing of America,
tr. by J. Cleugh.
NW, 3 Sp37, 203—5 v
Servants, tr. by A. L. Lloyd.
CPP, 7 N36, 125—26 v

Alden, Elizabeth F.
Afar.
JG, 33 Su35, [23] v
After the rain.
JG, 32 Sp35, [5] v
Bitter herbs.
JG, 65 Su38, [28] v
Blackthorn winter.
DD, ix 36 N—D32, 100 v
Calm.
JG, 36 Sp36, [31] v
The chalk pit.
JG, 21 Su32, [13—14] v
Dawn.
JG, 19 W31, [6] v
December sunset.
DD, ix 34 Jy—Ag32, 61 v
Dusk: Clissold Park.
DD, x 40 Jy—Ag33, 66 v
From the window.
JG, 29 Su34, [11] v
The green wave.
JG, 20 Sp32, [6] v
Home.
JG, 24 Sp33, [23] v
I question love.
JG, 35 W35, [24] v
Illness.
DD, ix 32 M—A32, 28 v
In March.
JG, 64 Sp38, [20] v
January colour.
JG, 40 Sp37, [11] v
Length of days.
JG, 66 Au38, [22] v
Like an Eastern scimitar.
DD, x 38 M—A33, 28 v
Moonlight.
JG, 67 W38, [32] v
The nursling.
JG, 27 W33, [10] v
On a modern work of art.
JG, 30 Au34, [14] v
The prisoner.
JG, 70 Au39. [21—22] v

Reality.
JG, 41 Su37, [7—8] v
The reminder.
JG, 69 Su39, [20] v
Sapphics; Unromantic love.
DD, viii 30 Au31, 108—9 v
The summer garden.
JG, 18 Au31, [10—11] v
Villanelle.
JG, 39 Au36, [22—23] v
Who by the shedding.
JG, 70 Au39, [28] v
Wind in the corn.
JG, 34 Au35, [15] v
Winter's end.
DD, viii 29 Su31, 60 v

Alden, Phyllis
Wood engraving.
F, 4 D30, 22 i

Aldington, Richard
Another book for suppression
[Songs, by W. Shakespeare].
EX, 6 Oc30, 20—22 c
Female thinking extravert.
PR, 3 19F35, 1—6 p
A dream in the Luxembourg
rev. by C. B. Spencer

Aldridge, James
Pictures.
EP, 1 Au35, 218 i

Aldridge, John see Brown, Lucie

Ali, Ahmed
In the train.
LR, iii 13 F38, 780—84 p
Our lane.
NW, 4 Au37, 77—88 p
Mr Shamsul Hasan.
LR, ii 12 S36, 634—37 p

Alington, Cyril Argentine
Athletic sports.
M, i l Je33, 41—2 c
The fool hath said
rev. by J. Chance

Allam, Edward
Stravinsky and neo-classicism.
VP, i 1 A—Je34, 20—23 c

Allan, J. M.
Flute concerto: a fragment.
JG, 66 Au38, [30] v
Wind at dawn.
JG, 41 Su37, [23—24) v

Allaun, Frank J.
Class-conscious angels.
ST, i 3 1933, 31—32 p

Allen, John
The socialist theatre.
LR, iii 7 Ag37, 417—22 c

Allen, Percy
Before sailing.
DD, xi 44 M—A34, 21 v
Song at parting.
DD, xi 47 S—Oc34, 72 v
To Josémée.
DD, xi 46 Jy—Ag34, 59 v

Allen, Walter Ernest
At Aunt Sarah's.
NW, 5 Sp38, 121—25 p
Football.
ND, 22 25N37, 32 p
Morning progress.
NS, i 5 Oc34, 380—85 p
You hit me.
NW, ns3 C39, 148—54 p

Aller, Frances
Consolation.
DD, ix 32 M—A32, 27 v
Mourning.
DD, ix 33 My-Je32, 42 v
Somerset: a conceit.
DD, xi, 45 My—Je34, 43 v
The thought.
DD, x 38 M—A33, 34 v

Allott, Kenneth
Against the clock.
T, 17 A39, 17—18 v
Abstract in Oxford.
PR, 15 1M36, 11—13 c
Any point on the circumference.
NV, 24 F37, 6—8 v
Auden in the theatre.
NV, 26/27 N37, 17—21 c
Barometer.
T, 10 My38, 35 v
The children.
NW, ns2 Sp39, 182 v
Christmas, 1938.
NV, i 2 My39, 34—35 v
Civilized commonsense
[Modern poetry, and Zoo,
by L. MacNeice].
NV, i 1 J39, 20—21 r
David Gascoyne
[Man's life is this meat].
PR, 16 6My36, 13—14 r
Declaration of independence.
PR, 17 27My36, 11—12 v
Der Kritiker Herbert Read
[Art now].
PR, 10 6N35, 7—10 r
Editorial.
PR, 17 27My36, 1—2 c
End of a year.
NV, 24 F37, 19 v

Allott, Kenneth (cont.)
Fable.
PR, 14 19F36, 8 v
Fête champêtre.
PR, 13 5F36, 6 v
Fête champêtre.
CPP, 2 Je36, 35—36 v
Hallow'een; Statement of fact.
NV, 16 Ag35, 10—11 v
Historical grimace.
NV, 23 C36, 15 v
1. Invocation. 2. Signs.
3. Lullaby. 4. Valediction.
NV, 19 F36, 4—7 v
Lament for a cricket eleven.
NV, 28 J38, 11—12 v
MacNeice, MacLeish and
Andrew Young
[Out of the picture; The fall of
the city; Nicodemus].
NV, 28 J38, 19—20 r
Men walk upright.
T, 11 Jy38, 60—63 v
Municipal myth I.
NV, 29 M38, 9 v
Not so hot
[The dog beneath the skin,
by W. H. Auden and C. Isherwood].
NV, 19 F36, 15 dr
A note on the poet.
PR, 12 4D35, 6—9 c
October poem.
PR, 19 20Oc36, 2—3 v
Offering.
NV, 21 Je36, 2—3 v
Play for puritans
[Trial of a judge, by S. Spender].
NV, 30 Su38, 20—21 dr
Poem.
NV, 17 Oc35, 6 v
Poem.
PR, 10 6N35, 14, 16 v
Poem.
PR, 11 27N35, 11—13 v
Poem.
NV, 22 S36, 4—6 v
A poem.
EP, 2 Su36, 62 v
Poem.
PR, 22 Je37, 8 v
Poem; Patch
NV, 25, My37, 11—12 v
Poem: for K.L.
PR, 16 6My36, 7 v
Poems.
PR, 18 17Je36, 15 v
Poets and the theatre audience.
T, 18 Je39, 40—42 c
Prize for good conduct;
Quicksilver.
NV, 20 A36, 6—8 v
Review [The winter house,
by J. N. Cameron].
PR, 11 27N35, 17 r

Review [The English novelists,
by D. Verschoyle].
PR, 17 27My36, 18 r
Review [Look, stranger!
by W. H. Auden].
PR, 20 17N36, 18, 20 r
Review [Surrealism (Faber,
1936)].
PR, 21 1M37, 20 r
Reviews [The natural need,
by J. Reeves; First poems,
by R. Heppenstall; Petron,
by H. S. Davies; First day,
by C. Dyment].
PR, 13 5F36, 17—18 r
Several things.
NV, 31/32 Au38, 4—7 c
The statue.
CPP, 4/5 Ag36, 91—92 v
Sunday excursion: for N. F.
and R. J.
T, 9 M38, 10 v
Three poems.
CPP, 3 Jy36, 50—52 v
A tract [On the frontier,
by W. H. Auden and C. Isherwood].
NV, i 1 J39, 24—25, r
Two Americans [The carnival,
by F. Prokosch; The world's body,
by J. C. Ransom].
T, 11 Jy38, 72—74 r
Two plays [The family reunion,
by T. S. Eliot; Danton's death,
by G. Büchner, tr. by S. Spender
and G. Rees].
NV, i 2 My39, 49—50 r
Two poems.
NW, 5 Sp38, 115—16 v
The underworld.
CPP, 8 D36, 151—52 p
Vicky and Victoria
[Victoria the Great (film)].
ND, 13 23S37, 30—31 r
Zero hour in Oxford.
ND, 13 23S37, 27—28 p
Poems rev. by B. Gutteridge;
J. Symons

Allott, Kenneth and Tait, Stephen
Out of the rhubarb tree
rev. by B. Watkin

Allwood, J. B.
Poem,
T, 14 D38, 127 v
Poem.
T, 15/16 F39, 158 v
Western.
T, 17 A39, 9 v

Alpha Group
Artists and the People's Front.
LR, ii 13 Oc36, 675—77 c

Alter, Victor
Comment réaliser le socialisme
rev. by W. N. Warbey

Alvensleben, Werner von
Automatische Kunst
[with translation].
LB, 13 15A39, 18— ?4c

Ambler, Benjamin George
Crowned; At parting.
DD, x 37 J—F33, 13 v
Heredity.
DD, x 42 N—D33, 101 v
Sunset on the marshes.
DD, ix 33 My—Je32, 47 v

Amory, P. J. Heathcoat-
see Heathcoat-Amory, P. J.

Amos, Margaret
Theory.
V, 6 Je30, 255 v

Anand, Mulk Raj
The barbers' trade union.
NW, 2 Au36, 8—15 p
Bombay mill.
LR, ii 8 My36, 374—77 p
A confession.
LR, iii 13 F38, 785—91 p
Duty.
NW, ns1 Au38, 208—12 p
Fruits of the earth.
NW, 3 Sp37, 243—47 p
The Indian scene [Kanthapura,
by R. Rao].
LR, iii 15 A38, 955—56 r
On the border.
LR, iii 7 Ag37, 388—96 p
Towards a new Indian literature.
LR, ii 12 S36, 613—23 c
The coolie rev. by G. West
Two leaves and a bud
rev. by A. Calder-Marshall
Untouchable
rev. by J. Sommerfield

Anders, Guenther
The corner, tr. by J. Cleugh.
NW, 2 Au36, 52—62 p
A question of nerves,
tr. by C. Ashleigh.
NW, ns3 C39, 260—65 p

Anderson, Forrest
Early poem.
CV, 4 1935, 6 v
Two poems.
CV, 1 Su34, 12—13 v
Two poems.
CV, 3 Su35, 16—17 v

Anderson, Ivor
By name.
DD, x 39 My—Je33, 51 v
A novel complaint.
DD, ix 35 S—Oc32, 82 v
Poppy song.
DD, ix 31 J—F32, 5 v

Anderson, John Redwood
A sunset.
JG, 31 W34, [4—5] v
At Karnac.
JG, 64 Sp38, [5—6] v
Ave atque vale.
JG, 71 W39, [7—8] v
Birth and death of lambs.
JG, 68 Sp39, [5—6]v
By Yarrow's banks.
JG, 42 Au37, [5—6] v
December night.
JG, 35 W35, [33—34] v
Estuaries.
JG, 32 Sp35, [6] v
The flower.
JG, 41 Su37, [6] v
Froddingham;
December afternoon.
JG, 33 Su35, [7] v
Hieroglyphics.
JG, 36 Sp36, [5—6] v
The martyrs.
JG, 66 Au38, [5] v
The plain.
JG, 40 Sp37, [5—7] v
Storm on the moors.
JG, 37 Su36, [6—7] v
Summer evening.
JG, 69 Su39, [5] v
Whom God hath joined.
JG, 67 W38, [6] v
Winter evening.
JG, 39 W36, [17—18] v

Anderson, Oliver
Love in our time
C, ii 36 29 Ag36, 67 v
Street scene in Springtime.
C, i 1 5 D35, 7 v

Anderson, Patrick
Mrs Middleton.
FB, iii 7 25N37, 34 v
My last duchess.
FB, iii 8 3M38, 59—60 p
The old school.
LD, ii 3 F38, 16 c
The Union.
LD, i 4 Je37, 15 c

Anderson, Sherwood
The corn planting.
P, 1 1938, 115—18, 120—22p
Trip to Kentucky.
TC, iii 16 Je32, 11—15 c

Anderton, Augustine Gregory
The English martyrs.
CA, 1 Ag30, 29—30 c

Andrews, R. F.
[*pseud.* Andrew F. Rothstein]
Leninism Trotskified
[*World revolution, 1917—1936*,
by C. L. R. James].
LR, iii 5 Je37, 291—98 r

Andrews, William Linton
I'm not bothered.
HR, 7 1934, 22—23 p

Angell, *Sir* Norman
Is mass suicide inevitable?
DV, 1 M32, 3—5 c
Let us all work together for peace.
PS, 18 Je—Jy38, 3—4 c
A progressive international policy.
TC, iv 20 Oc32, 29—30 c
World crisis: international
co-operation.
TC, v 27 My33, 175—78 c

Angus, Marion
The stranger.
MS, i 2 Su30, 6 v
A woman sings.
MS, iii 4 J33, 324 v
The turn of the day
rev. by A. Kennedy *pseud.*

Another man's child.
LR, i 10 Jy35, 385—90 d

Ansell, S. J.
Peur d'amour.
JG, 65 Su38, [16—17] v

Ansell, Sydney Thomas
Non paratus, Domine.
DD, xi 45 My—Je34, 48 v
Old is the world.
JG, 68 Sp39, [9—10] v

Anthony, Lionel
The death of the German
middle class.
TC, iv 23 J33, 3—5 c
The mood of the 'new' Germany.
TC, v 29 Jy33, 289—92 c
The petty bourgeois revolution.
TC, v 27 My33, 145—50 c

Ap Gwynn, Aneirin
No errata: no high spots
[*The development of Welsh poetry*,
by H. I. Bell].
W, 1 Su37, 28—29 r

Appel, Benjamin
Outside Yuma.
NS, i 2 A34, 146—52 p

Appleby, Mark
The bee.
CM, i 1 Sp33, 31—35 p
The plumed serpent.
CM, i 2 Su33, 74—79 c

Appleton, Edward Victor
The man who invented the
concertina.
HR, 5 1932, 43—44 c

Apricott, Albert Alfred
Music chronicle.
00, x 53 N30, 616—27 c
Music chronicle.
00, xi 55 Je31, 131—35 c
Music chronicle.
00, xi 54 M31, 49—53 c

Ap Talfan, Aneirin
Suburbia.
W, 10 Oc39, 275 v

Aragon, Louis
Paris Congress speech.
LR, i 11 Ag35, 473 c
Waltz, tr. by N. Cunard.
LR, i 1 Oc34, 3—5 v
The red front rev. by S. Spender
see also Kahn, Derek

Aranyi, J. d' *see* D'Aranyi, J.

Arascain is Mhairr, Ruaraidh
see Erskine of Marr, Ruaraidh

Archer, William George
Poems.
EP, 3 Sp37, 170—72 v
Poetry and belief.
EX, 5 F30, 29—34 c
Two poems; Uraon country.
CPP, 8 D36, 148—50 v
see also Dialogue for an Uraon
marriage; Uraon dance poem;
Uraon marriage sermon

Archer, William George *and*
Archer, Mildred
Santhal painting.
AX, 7 Au36, 27—28 c

Archimedes *pseud.*
Cambridge University
engineering department.
CL, ii 1 Au34, 19—28 c

Arconada, C. M.
Children of the Estremadura,
tr. by J. Cleugh.
NW, 3 Sp37, 235—42 p

Arkwright, Frank
The ABC of technocracy
rev. by H. Nussbaum

Arlen, Michael *pseud.*
The crooked coronet
rev. by E. Waugh

Arlett, Vera Isabel
The almond tree.
JG, 32 Sp35, [15] v
Ave.
JG, 42 Au37, [20] v
The ballad of the elfin knight.
JG, 19 W31, [18—20] v
Be not angry.
JG, 28 Sp34, [6—7] v
The dark country.
JG, 64 Sp38, [15] v
Dark stranger.
C, iii 54 2J37, 5 v
The day afterwards.
JG, 63 W37, [25] v
Day's end.
JG, 26 Au33, [18] v
The dead fairy.
JG, 18 Au31, [14—15] v
Dirge by anticipation.
JG, 34 Au35, [26—27] v
Epitaph.
JG, 22 Au32, [12] v
The evening fields.
JG, 29 Su34, [14] v
For one who did not say
goodbye.
JG, 17 Su31, [21] v
For the little house.
JG, 14 Au30, [13] v
Gold head.
JG, 30 Au34, [24—25] v
The hack writer.
C, iii 58 30J37, 37 v
The haunted house.
JG, 35 W35, [30] v
Hic jacet; The undying.
DD, viii 30 Au31, 110 v
The hour strikes.
JG, 33 Su35, [27] v
How long?
JG, 71 W39, [20] v
Icarus.
JG, 21 Su32, [26—27] v
If you were dead.
JG, 38, Au36, [5] v
The kingly hosts.
JG, 20 Sp32, [14—15] v
A late song.
JG, 39 W36, [23] v
The Lenten heart.
JG, 68 Sp39 [18—19] v
Mind and heart.
JG, 24 Sp33, [14] v
No room.
JG, 67 W38, [28—29] v
The other Elsinore.
JG, 37 Su36, [16] v
The poet asks for sleep.
JG, 25 Su33, [11] v

The princess who wanted
to dance.
JG, 66 Au38, [20—21] v
The queen who wore her crown
at breakfast-time.
JG, 67 W38, [35—36] v
The road to Assisi.
JG, 13 Su30, [9—10] v
Sonnet.
JG, 16 Sp31, [13] v
The starry silence.
JG, 41 Su37, [22] v
The still night.
JG, 69 Su39, [17] v
The thoughts.
JG, 15 W30, [16—17] v
The thrush who would not
say good-night.
JG, 70 Au39, [29] v
Time out of mind.
JG, 65 Su38, [22] v
The unfurnished room.
JG, 31 W34, [19] v
The unknown.
JG, 27 W33, [23] v
The way of the world.
JG, 23 W32, [22—23] v
West from Sussex.
JG, 36 Sp36, [24] v
The wind rider.
JG, 40 Sp37, [24—25] v

Armitage, Gilbert
Growing up.
NV, 2 M33, 10—11 v
The new Wyndham Lewis
[*One way song*].
NV, 7 F34, 12—17 r
A note on 'The wild body'.
T, 6/7 N37, [24—26] c
Review
[*Variations on a metaphysic
theme*, by W. Holmes].
NV, 4 Jy33, 19 r

Armstrong, J. R.
A charter for youth:
new education.
TC, vi 33 D—J33—34, 175—76 c
Education: the economic approach.
TC, iii 17 Jy32, 16—20 c
Education: the future.
TC, iii 18 Ag32, 1—6 c
Education: the naturalistic
approach.
TC, ii 12 F32, 4—7 c
Education: the realist approach.
1. The nursery school.
TC, iii 14 A32, 16—21 c
Education: the realist approach.
2. The elementary school.
TC, iii 15 My32, 21—25 c
Education:
the scientific approach.

TC, ii 10 D31, 14—18 c
This freedom.
TC, iv 23 J33, 17—21 c
Values in education.
TC, ii 9 N31, 14—16 c

Armstrong, Richard
Self-trimmer.
P, 6 1939, 38—45 p

Armstrong, Terence Ian Fytton
Full score rev. by A. Bristow
see also Gawsworth, John *pseud.*

Armstrong, William
Repertory in the North.
R, i 1 N33, 10 c

Arndt, Walter W.
Morganstern as Lucifer.
PR, 11 27N35, 9—10 c
To J. Y.
PR, 17 27My36, 7 v

Arndt, Walter W. *and* **Hodge**,
Alan *trs.*
Two poems by Hofmannsthal
and Rilke.
PR, 18 17Je36, 12—13 v

Arnell, Charles John
Afterwards.
DD, ix 33 My—Je32, 41 v
The colonel; She.
DD, vii 27 N—D30, 429—30 v
The Cornish Riviera Express
locomotive.
DD, viii 28 J—F31, 14 v
Defeat.
DD, x 39 My—Je33, 53 v
Escheated.
DD, ix, 34 Jy—Ag 32, 63 v
For a diary.
DD, x 40 Jy—Ag33, 64 v
For your birthday.
DD, vii 26 S—Oc30, 403 v
Helen.
JG, 13 Su30, [21—22] v
In memoriam: Edwin Faulkner.
JG, 39 W36, [7] v
January; February.
DD, viii 28 J—F31, 1 v
January.
DD, ix 31 J—F32, 3 v
July 1919; August.
DD, viii 29 Su31, 50 v
June.
DD, ix 36 N—D32, 102 v
The missal.
DD, x 38 M—A33, 33 v
November; December.
DD, vii 27 N—D30, 418 v
The poet.
DD, x 42 N—D33, 101 v

The poets and the supernatural.
DD, viii 29 Su31, 71—73 c
A roundelay.
DD, xi 46 Jy—Ag34, 67 v
The sea at rest.
DD, x 41 S—Oc33, 87 v
September; October.
DD, vii 26 S—Oc30, 365 v
September; October.
DD, viii 30 Au31, 87 v
The wanderer.
JG, 25 Su33, [23] v

Arnell, Doris
The glow-worm's wedding.
DD, vii 26 S—Oc30, 390 v

Arnold, Eric
Nietzsche and Mr Bevers.
TC, i 2 A31, 26—27 c

Arnold, Kathleen
Review
[*Experiments in educational
self-government*,
by A. L. G. Mackay;
English village schools,
by M. Wise].
TC, ii 9 N31, 29—30 r

Arnot, Robert Page
Is nobody going to stop
Mr Toynbee?
[*A study of history*, vols. 1—3,
by A. J. Toynbee].
LR, ii 7 A36, 342—46 r

Arnoux, Alexandre
from *Le Cabaret*, tr. by R. Parker.
EX, 6 Oc30, 7—12 p

Aron, Raymond *and* **Dandieu**, A.
*La décadence de la nation
française* rev. by J. Bard

Arp, Hans
The domestic stones,
tr. D. Gascoyne.
NV, 21 Je36, 7—8 v

Arrow, John
Young man's testament
rev. by G. West

Art et Liberté [Cairo Group]
From Egypt [manifesto].
LB, 13 A39, 15—17 p

Arthur, Charlotte
Hands.
BB, vii 2 M30, 33—40 p

Arundel, Alison,C.
Winter.
JG, 63 W37, [26—27] v

Asch, Sholem
The calf of paper
rev. by H. O. Whyte

Ashburner, Phoebe
Physics and chemistry.
OO, xi 55 Je31, 119 v

Ashby, Julian *pseud.*
Haulage engineer.
LR, ii 15 D36, 826—27 p

Ashleigh, Charles
A book born of struggle
[*Unemployed struggles*,
by W. Hannington].
LR, ii 16 J37, 912 r
Dos Passos and Conroy
[*The disinherited*, by J. Conroy;
In all countries, by J. Dos Passos].
LR, i 3 D34, 94—95 r
Here miners live!
[*Last cage down*, by H. Heslop].
LR, ii 4 J36, 191—92 r
It mustn't happen here
[*It can't happen here*,
by S. Lewis].
LR, ii 4 J36, 188—91, r
A job in a million — 3.
ND, 3 15Jy37, 14—16 p
A job in a million — 5.
ND, 5 29 Jy37, 13—15 p
The man who found out.
LR, i 3 D34, 80—82 p
No stifled children.
EY, 3 D35, 7 c
Reporting a reporter: Spivak
speaks to British Left writers.
LR, ii 6 M36, 241—45 c
see also Brecht, Bertholt;
Duermayer, H.; Ellis, Fred;
Petersen, J.; Seghers, A.;
Weiskopf, F. C.

Ashton, E. B.
[*pseud* of Ernst Basch]
The fascist rev. by R. Bishop

Astin, Marjorie
A last link with the Brontës
[Ellen Binns].
HR, 5 1932, 62 c

Auden, Wystan Hugh
Alfred.
NW, 2 Au36, 201—3 p
Ballad.
NV, 12 D34, 4—5 v
Birthday ode.
MS, ii 4 J32, 277—84 v
Blues.
NV, 25 My37, 4 v
A communist to others.
TC, iv 19 S32, 7—8 v

The dog beneath the skin:
opening chorus.
LR, i 8 My35, 289—90 v
Dover.
NV, 26/27 N37, 2—3 v
The dream; Foxtrot from a play.
NV, 20 A36, 12—13 v
The economic man.
NV, 21 Je36, 8 v
Eight poems.
NW, ns2 Sp39, 1—5 v
Enter with him these legends
love.
TC, v 30 Ag33, 357 v
Exiles.
NW, ns1 Au38, 4 v
Five poems,
NV, 5 Oc33, 14—17 v
From the film 'Coal-Face'.
NV, 30 Su38, 5 v
Honest doubt, by J. B.
NV, 21 Je36, 14—16 c
Interview.
CL, i 1 Su33, 5 v
James Honeyman.
PS, 20 N—D37, 10—11 v
Jehovah Housman and
Satan Housman
[*A. E. H.: a memoir*,
by L. Housman].
NV, 28 J38, 16—17 r
Look there, the sunk road winding.
TC, iv 24 F33, 16—17 v
The Malverns; Poem.
NO, i 2 N33, 148—52, 153 v
A modern use of masks.
GTP, 5 N36, 3—4 c
Poem.
TC, i 1 M31, 10—11 v
Poem.
DE, 1 New Year 32, 4 v
Poem.
NV, 4 Jy33, 8 v
Poem.
NV, 7 F34, 6—7 v
Poem.
R, i 3 A34, 5 v
Poem.
NO, ii 1 My34, 82—84 v
Poem.
NV, 9 Je34, 12 v
Poem.
R, i 6 Oc34, 8 v
Poem.
NW, 3 Sp37, 122—23 v
Poem.
NW, 4 Au37, 170—71 v
Poem.
NV, 26/27 N37, 31 v
Poetry and film.
J, 2 My37, 11—12 c
Psychology and criticism
[*In defence of Shelley*,
by H. Read].

Auden, Wystan Hugh (cont.)
NV, 20 A36, 22—24 r
Review
[*Culture and environment*,
by F. R. Leavis and D. Thompson;
How to teach reading,
by F. R. Leavis;
*How many children had Lady
Macbeth*, by L. C. Knights].
TC, v 27 My33, 188—90 r
Review
[*Illusion and reality*,
by C. Caudwell].
NV, 25 My37, 20—22 r
Selling the Group Theatre.
GTP, 1 Je36, [3] c
Song.
NV, 1 J33, 3—5 v
Song.
LS, ii 1 My34, 57 v
Speech from a play.
NV, 13 F35, 10—11 v
The sportsmen.
NV, 31/32 Au38, 2—4 p
Three poems.
NW, ns3 C39, 37—40 v
To a writer on his birthday.
NV, 17 Oc35, 7—9 v
To a young man on his
twenty-first birthday.
NO, i 1 My33, 73—74 v
Two ballads.
NW, 4 Au37, 161—69 v
Two poems.
TC, vi 32 N33, 71 v
The dance of death
rev. by G. Ewart; A. D. Hawkins;
F. Prince
Look, stranger!
rev. by K. Allott; H. G. Porteus;
S. Spender; D. A. Traversi
The orators rev. by G. Rees
The Oxford book of light verse
rev. by NV, i 1 J39, 26
Paid on both sides
rev. by W. Empson
Poems
rev. by A. D. Hawkins;
L. MacNeice
Spain rev. by S. Spender

Auden, Wystan Hugh *and*
Garrett, John
The poet's tongue
rev. by M. Slater;
NV, 16 Ag35, 20

Auden, Wystan Hugh *and*
Isherwood, C.
The ascent of F 6
rev. by D. I. Dunnett; B. Nixon;
H. G. Porteus; S. Spender;
J. Symons

8

The dog beneath the skin
rev. by K. Allott; W. Belcher;
J. Mair; G. S. Sayer; M. Slater;
LR, ii 6 M36, 273
Journey to a war
rev. by G. Grigson; R. Todd
On the frontier
rev. by K. Allott; J. G. MacLeod,
J. Symons; *Sir* J. Walker

Auden, Wystan Hugh *and*
MacNeice, Louis
Letters from Iceland
rev. by G. H. T.; E. Waugh

Auden, Wystan Hugh *and*
Worsley, T. C.
Education today and tomorrow
rev. by NV, i 2 My39, 52

Ault, Norman *ed.*
A treasury of unfamiliar lyrics
rev. by G. Taylor

Austin, Charles
Five poems.
TO, ii 8 N39, 6—8 v

Autran, Juliette
Letters from abroad; Paris.
BB, vii 2 M30, 106—9 c

Avery, L. L.
Lunch in a restaurant.
LR, i 6 M35, 210—12 p
The awakening of the sense of
sin.
TC, i 1 M31, 21—22 p

Axis [magazine]
rev. by A. Hodge

Ayala, Ramon Perez de *see*
Perez de Ayala, Ramon

Ayer, Alfred Jules
The case for behaviourism.
NO, i 2 N33 229—42 c

Ayerst, David George Ogilvie
Historical racket in play and
film.
R, i 4 My34, 7—8 c

B

B
Mr Sanders.
M, i 1 Je33, 6—14 p

B., C.
The red air force.
CL, ii 1 Au34, 29 v
Vienna 1934.
TU, 3 Je34, 4—6 c

B., G. G.
Review [*After strange gods*,
by T. S. Eliot].
TC, vi 35 Je34, 305—6 r

B., G. L.
Arraigned!
DD, viii 28 J-F31, 10 v

B., H. A.
Most of Rimbaud
[*Arthur Rimbaud*, by E. Starkie].
NV, 30 Su38, 25—26 r
Poem.
LD, i 4 Je37, 9 v
Wycombe.
LD, i 4 Je37, 22 v

B., H. S.
Review [*Stages of pursuit*,
by A. Miller].
LS, ii 1 My35, 47—49 r

B., J. M. G.
Cambridge.
LD, i 3 My37, 18 v

B., N.
An analysis of Hitlerism.
EQ, i 2 Ag34, 65—69 c

B., N. S.
April afternoon; À bas les pensées;
Nocturne.
TH, 2 10F39, 3—4 p

Babel, Isaak Emanuilovich
In the basement, tr. by G. Reavey.
CPP, 3 Jy 36, 63—69 p
With our father Makhno, tr. by
G. Reavey [only pub. in proof].
CPP, 8 D36, 143—44 p

Bach, Rudolf
The east wind, tr. by P. Selver.
SM, 5 1934, 121 v

Bacon, F. W.
A Fabian resurrection?
TC, v 29 Jy33, 293—97 c

Badock, Lanoy
Poem.
LS, i 1 F34, 46 v

Baerlein, Henry
The lake.
DD, ix 33 My—Je32, 40 v

Poems.
DD, ix 34 Jy—Ag32, 57 v
Poem.
DD, x 39, My—Je33, 48 v
see also Walden, Herwath

Baines, Henry Verdon
The violin.
DD, xi, 47 S—Oc34, 76 v

Baker, Agnes Monica
Invocation to Spring.
JG, 13 Su30, [16—17] v
Twilight song.
JG, 14 Au30, [23] v

Baker, George
The amazing adoption.
WW, i 3 Jy30, 60—95 p

Baker, H.
A letter from the country to a young
editor.
T, 12/13 Oc38, 94—95 v

Baker, Philip Noel
The private manufacture of armaments
rev. by L.W.

Baker, Phyllis
As the twig is bent; Girls' schools.
OB, i 1 M—A34, 23—24 c

Balchin, Nigel
The next song will be a dance.
ND, 3 15Jy37, 20—21 p
Trotsky or notsky.
ND, 8 19Ag37, 15 p

Baldwin, Faith
Literary shrine.
P, 6 1939, 179—95 p

Balfour, Patrick
British raj.
ND, 15 7Oc37, 14—15 p

Ball, Arthur
Boy and girl.
MS, iii 3 Oc32, 201 v

Ball, Evelyn
Two rondeaux.
DD, vii 26 S—Oc30, 411—12 v

Ball, Frederick Cyril
How F. C. Ball came to write poetry.
PP, 15 N39, 10—11 c
Irish dance.
PP, 8 F39, 4 v
Nursery rhyme.
PP, 11 My39, 20 v
Prayer for a rich industrialist.
PP, 6 D38, 12—13 v

To some former poets.
PP, 3 S38, 11—12 v

The ballad of Miss Colman.
CPP, 3, Jy36, 61—62 v

Ballou, J.
Spanish prelude rev. by S. Blumenfeld

Balme, D. M.
Epitaph.
CL, i 1 Su33, 2 v
Poem.
CM, i 2 Su33, 79 v
Balmont, Konstantin Dimitrievich
The voice of sunset, tr. by P. Selver.
SM, 4 1933, 109—10 v

Balsdon, John Percy Vyvian Dacre
Come follow.
P, 6 1939, 212—41 p
Panic abroad.
LD, i 2 M37, 27 v

Banks, Paul
The economic links of empire.
MS, iii 1 A32, 52—55 c

Bannister, Edith
Epitaph.
LD, i 4 Je37, 32 v
Poem.
PR, 2 12F35, 7 v
Poem.
PR, 1 1F35, 4 v
Review [*Eden end*, by J. B. Priestley].
PR, 2 12F35, 8 r

Barber, Norman
Clouds.
JG, 68 Sp39, [31] v

Barbusse, Henri
France at the crossroads,
tr. by A. D. Garman.
TC, iv 20 Oc32, 1—4 c
Paris Congress speech.
LR, i 11 Ag35, 470 c
Inferno rev. by G. West

Bard, Josef
An analysis of contemporary France
[*Décadence de la nation française*,
by R. Aron and A. Dandieu].
I, i 2/3 15S31, 76—77 r
Lucid intervals.
I, i 2/3 15S31, 88—89; I i 4 15D31,
125 p
Notes on religion and the artistic
movement.
I, i 4 15D31, 104—6 c
Notes on the sublime.
I, i 2/3 15S31, 54—61 c
Passages from 'Lucid intervals'.

I, i 1 15Je31, 15—18 v
The space of thought.
I, i 1 15Je31, 29—30 p
To the reader.
I, i 1 15Je31, 1—3 c

Barke, James
Lewis Grassic Gibbon.
LR, ii 5 F36, 220—25 c
Scotland's literary uncle.
[*Should auld acquaintance,*
by W. Power].
LR, iii 12 J38, 760—61 r
The Scottish national question.
LR, ii 14 N36, 739—44 c
Major operation rev. by J. Lindsay

Barker, George
Allegory of the adolescent and the adult.
NV, 28 J38, 6—7 v
Answers to an enquiry.
NV, 11 Oc34, 22 p
Biography of Orpheus-Apollo.
PL, i 1 F39, [17—18] v
Comment on Auden.
NV, 26/27 N37, 23 c
Coward's song.
NV, 2 M33, 2 v
The death of Yeats.
PL, i 2 A39, [1] v
Elegies I and II.
NV, i 1 J39, 3—6 v
Elegy no. 3.
PL, i 2 A39, [19—21] v
Elegy on tinned meat.
SV, 1 Su38, 27—28 v
Epistle to D. T.
NV, 25 My37, 2—3 v
Five stanzas on the five pointed star.
LR, iii 4 My37, 214 v
Four elegies.
NW, ns3 C39, 41—46 v
I am not wronged.
LR, i 6 M35, 225 v
Love poem.
TC, iv 23 J33, 13 v
Love poems.
TC, vi 35 Je34, 302 v
Lyric.
TC, v 30 Ag33, 351 v
The neo-Geordies.
SV, 7 C39, 2—3 v
A note on narrative poetry.
T, 18 Je39, 48—49 c
Ode to a dead aeronaut.
TC, iv 20 Oc32, 4 v
Poem on geography.
T, 11 Jy38, 57—60 v
Poem on people.
LR, ii 16 J37, 885 v
Poetry and contemporary inertia.
TC, iv 19 S32, 10—12 c
Resolution of dependence.
CPP, 9 Sp37, 42—43 v

Barker, George (cont.)
Review [*Known signatures,*
ed. by J. Gawsworth].
TC, iv 22 D32, 25—26 r
Review [*Poems*, by S. Spender]
TC, iv 24 F33, 28—30 r
Review [*William Blake*, by J. M. Murry].
TC, vi 32 N33, 115—16 r
The sleeping beauty.
T, 5 S37, [8—9] v
Sonnet.
TC, v 30 Ag33, 342 v
To Robert Owen.
W, 10 Oc39, 261 v
Tuition to recruits.
TC, iv 24 F33 17—18 v
Two poems.
EQ, i 1 My34, 22 v
X stanzas.
CPP, 4/5 Ag36, 92—94 v
Alanna autumnal rev. by A. D. Hawkins
Calamiterror
rev. by A. D. Hawkins; X *pseud.*
Poems rev. by N. K. Cecil; S. Spender;
V. M. Ward
Thirty preliminary poems
rev. by. A. D. Hawkins; S. Spender

Barker, Harley Granville- *see* Granville-
Barker, Harley

Barlow, Kenneth Elliott
Linament for Mr Sloan.
TC, v 30 Ag33, 371—74 c
Science and the M I T.
TC, i 3 My31, 23—25 c
Review [*The dictatorship of things*,
by G. Sainsbury]
TC, vi 31 S—Oc33, 60—61 r

Barlow, Philip
Saturday night function.
LD, ii 1 Oc37, 12—13 p

Barnard, Mary
Roots; Remarks on poetry and the
physical world; The trestle.
TO, i 4 Oc38, 6—7 v

Barnes, Djuna
Run, girls, run.
CV, 5 M36, [1—7] p
Transfiguration.
LB, 3 Je38, 2 v
Night wood rev. by D. Thomas

Barnes, T. R.
Yeats' new poems
[*New poems*, by W. B. Yeats].
TO, ii 5 J39, 25—26 r

Barnett, R. Durac
Four chalk drawings of road workers.
LR, iii 14 M38 860—61 i

Barraud, Enid Mary
A charter for youth: sex reform.
TC, vi 33 D—J33—34, 174—75 c
Censorship.
TC, i 4 Je31, 24 c
I sing the body electric.
TC, ii 11 J32, 13—15 c
The intermediate sex.
TC, i 5 Jy31, 13—16 c
Review [*Revelation*, by A. Birabeau;
Loveliest of friends, by G. S.
Donisthorpe].
TC, ii 7 S31, 24 r
Review [*Post mortem*, by N. Coward].
TC, i 5 Jy31, 24—25 r
Review [*Free love*, by A. Kollontai].
TC, iii 15 My32, 33 r
Reviews [*The master of the house*,
by R. Hall; *Sexual life in ancient Greece*,
by H. Licht].
TC, iii 14 A32, 31—32 r
Sanity in sex: the aims of the Sexology
group of the Prometheans.
TC, i 3 My31, 9—10 c

Barraud, John
Without a song.
JG, 19 W31, [7—8] v

Barricades on Bankside.
CL, i 4 Su34, 81—90 c

Barrie, *Sir* James Matthew
Left-handers.
M, i 1 Je33, 15 p

Barry, Alice Frances
October.
JG, 71 W39, [21] v
Precious stone.
JG, 69 Su39, [17] v

Barry, Gerald
Letter.
TC, ii 11 J32, 29—30 c
P E P.
TC, i 3 My31, 1—2 c

Barry, Leone
Two portraits.
S, 2 A/Jy 33, 12 v

Barter, John P.
The coming struggle for culture.
TC, vi 31 S—Oc33, 37—42 c

Bartholomew de Glanville
The mayden.
LQ, ii 1 My37, 16—17 p

Barton, A. W.
Seen from the train.
PQ, i 1 Sp39, 9 v

Barton, J. E.
Stout and oysters.
HR, 6 1933, 10—12 c

Barton, Philip
Old Derry down Derry
[*Edward Lear,* by A. Davidson].
B, 1 Su38, 18 r

Barton, Reyner
I killed my granny.
P, 6 1939, 62—72 p

Barwell, Peggy *and* **Morland**, Nigel
The reformer.
WW, i 3 Jy30, 59 v
Two poems.
WW, i 2 A30, 58—61 v

Basch, Ernst
see Ashton, E. B. *pseud.*

Basham, Arthur Ll.
The holy land.
C, i 19 11A36, 146 v
Passed over.
C, i 26 13Je36, 203—5 p
Rest.
DD, xi 43 J—F34, 14 v
Three classical Russian poems.
C, ii 34 15Ag36, 48 v
Turkey for Christmas.
C, i 2 14D35, 11, 16, 19 p
Two poems.
C, i 13 29F36, 100 v

Bastrup, Esther
A difficult hour.
LD, i 1 J37, 17—19 p

Bates, Herbert Ernest
A German incident.
PR, 5 17My35, 1—2 p
Review
[*Selected stories*, by H. Soderberg;
Selected stories, by A. France].
NS, ii 4 Ag35, 320 r
Sheep.
WW, i 1 J30, 2—8 p
Spring snow.
P, 1 1938, 107—14 p
Cut and come again rev. by G. West

Bates, Ralph
Companero Sagasta burns a church.
LR, ii 13 Oc36, 681—87 p
Comrade Vila.
NW, 2 Au36, 38—51 p
The launch.
NW, 1 Sp36, 1—8 p
The secret.
LR, i 7 A35, 247—54 p
Winifred Holtby.
LR, ii 2 N35, 49—50 c

Lean brown men rev. by A. L. Lloyd
The olive field rev. by R. Wright
Rainbow fish rev. by T. L. Hodgkin

Bateson, Frederick Noel Wilse
English poetry and the English language
rev. by G. Grigson

Baty, M. *adapter*
Crime et châtiment [play]
rev. by C. C. Doggett

Bawden, Edward
Design for a peace broadsheet.
LR, iii 4 My37, 229 i

Bax, Clifford
Leonardo da Vinci
rev. by H. G. Porteus

Baxter, Alice Mary
Northern landscape.
JG, 37 Su36, [25] v

Baxter, E. L.
Poem.
RM, 2 D34, 62 v

Beachcroft, Thomas Owen
England against Germany.
ND, 8 19 Ag37, 32 c
The god of music.
DD, xi 47, S–Oc34, 84 v
His fortieth birthday.
P, 6 1939, 7–24 p
We run better than we jump.
ND, 4 22 Jy37, 32 c
The man who started clean
rev. by E. Duthie; E. Waugh

Beales, Arthur Charles Frederick
The history of peace rev. by G. Trease

Beamand, W. J.
Funeral service over a dead monkey.
NS, i 2 A34, 153–60 p
Stay, traveller.
NS, ii 2 A35, 97–102 p

Beard, Paul
The present basis of the Literature group
[of the Prometheans].
TC, i 5 Jy31, 10–11 c

Beatty, Norah de C.
Reviews.
PQ, i 1 Sp39, 27–28 r

Beauchamp, John
Agriculture in Soviet Russia
rev. by J. R. Evans
British imperialism in India
rev. by T. H. Wintringham

Beaumont, Cyril William
Ballet commentary.
IP, i 1 6Ap39, 2–4 c

Beaumont, Germaine
La belle Suzanne, tr. by R. Cooke.
P, 4 1938, 31–35 p

Becher, Michael
The blind lion.
DD, xi 47 S–Oc34, 86 v

Beckett, Oliver
'xxxviii.
TH, 1 27J39, 2 v
Ecstaccatic, Wellorf.
TH, 2 10F39, 3–4 p
Souvenir d'ange perdue.
TH, 2 10F39, 1 v
Where travellers go.
TH, 3 24F39, 1 m
Wiesbaden pole; Consequential parody.
TH, 1 27J39, 3–4 p

Beckett, Samuel
Geer van Velde.
LB, 2 My38, 15 c
*Our exagminification round his
factification . . .*
rev. by H. Howarth

Beckner, Marie Daviess Warren
I shall keep faith.
PQ, i 2 Su39, 40 v

Bedborough, George
Arms and the clergy
rev. by T. H. Wintringham

Beecham, Audrey
Per fretum febris.
PL, i 1 F39, [10] v

Beecham, Helen Audrey
In the park; Song; Snows and forests;
Two poems.
SV, 2 Au38, 21–23 v
Poem.
PR, 18 17Je36, 6 v
Review
[*Poems*, by R. P. Hewett].
PR, 18 17Je36, 18–19 r

Beeching, Jack
Songs of the English rebel peasants and
serfs, 1381 A.D.
PP, 12 Je39, 7–9 c

Beecroft, F. S.
see Garrett, J.

Beerbohm, Max
Dr Brodrick.
F, 3 Oc30, 134 i

A plea for Thomas.
AC, i 1 C39, 5–7 p
Rodin's first steps in society.
F, 1 F30, 12 i

Beevers, John
Atameros.
T, 2 M37, [7–8] v
Beyond good and evil.
TC, i 1 M31, 16–18 c
Ezra as usual
[*Polite essays*, by E. Pound].
T, 2 M37, [18–19] r
I read Lewis.
T, 6/7 N37, [44] c
Yet again.
TC, i 3 My31, 25–26 c

Beith, Gilbert
Edward Carpenter rev. by J. R. Evans

Belcher, William
Theatre notes [*The dog beneath the skin*,
by W. H. Auden and C. Isherwood].
LT i 1 M36, 35–36 dr

Belfrage, Cedric
Promised Land rev. by A. West

Bell, Adrian Hanbury
The artists arrive.
ND, 1 1Jy37, 34–35 p
Down Constable's river.
ND, 5 29Jy37, 26–27 p
Hunter's moon.
ND, 15 7Oc37, 34–35 p
In the country.
ND, 25 16D37, 21 p
Regatta,
ND, 9 26Ag37, 24–25 p

Bell, Anthony W.
Trams.
HR, 5 1932, 60 c

Bell, Clive
An account of French painting
rev. by W. Martin

Bell, Eric Temple
Men of mathematics rev. by E. Waugh

Bell, Graham
Escape from escapism.
LR, iii 11 D37, 663–66 c

Bell, Harold Idris
The development of Welsh poetry
rev. by A. Ap Gwynn

Bell, Ian
Cambridge drama.
LD, ii 1 Oc37, 18 c

Bell, Ian R.
Mike.
FB, ii 4 25J37, 18 p

Bell, Julian
A brief view of poetic obscurity.
V, 6 Je30, 283—88 c
An epistle . . . to Richard Braithwaite.
V, 5 F30, 208—15 v
We did not fight rev. by E. Rickword

Bell, Oliver
Recreation.
PR, 1 1F35, 7 v
Underground.
PR, 6 31My35, 3 v

Bellairs, George
The curé's boots.
P, 2 1938, 200—8 p
The red flag.
P, 4 1938, 171—84 p

Bellington, R. E.
The moor; The magic carpet.
DD, ix 31 J—F32, 14 v

Belloc, Hilaire
Our Lord and our Lady *see* Fenby, Eric

Beloff, Max
Students seek peace.
LD, i 3 My37, 12—13 c

Belsey, John
September war.
PP, 15 N39, 7 v

Benda, Julien
Paris Congress speech.
LR i 11 Ag35, 473 c

Benet, Stephen Vincent
The devil and Daniel Webster.
P, 1 1938, 40—59 p
Johnny Pye and the fool-killer.
P, 2 1938, 13—40 p
The last of the legions.
P, 3 1938, 181—201 p
Letter from America.
NO, ii 3 N35, 232—41 p
Litany for dictatorships.
NO, ii 3 N35, 199—203 v
O'Hara's luck.
P, 4 1938, 111—32 p

Benet, William Rose
Harlem rev. by G. Knowland

Benham, Cyril
A job in a million—6.
ND, 6 5Ag37, 16—17 p

Benkard, Ernst
Undying faces rev. by I. Berlin

Benington, Wilson
The aqueduct, Maintenon.
JG, 28 Sp34, [10—11] v
The beggar: San Miniato.
JG, 30 Au34, [25—27] v
Earth is herself a star.
JG, 39 W36, [16] v
Exit.
JG, 24 Sp33, [8] v
From Petrarch.
JG, 69 Su39, [32] v
In a courtyard.
JG, 40 Sp37, [26] v
Knowledge.
JG, 70 Au39, [111] v
No news.
JG, 37 Su36, [26] v
Others who seem.
JG, 36 Sp36, [29] v
The phial.
JG, 27 W33, [15—18] v
The restless mind.
JG, 25 Su33, [16] v
Sonnet.
JG, 23 W32, [7] v
Stars.
JG, 67 W38, [27] v
Upland water.
JG, 32 Sp35, [25] v
Wisdom; Tide.
JG, 22 Au32, [22] v

Bennett, Arthur
On crossing the equator.
DD, viii 30 Au31, 107 v

Bennett, Joan
A bedside book
[*The pursuit of poetry*, ed. by
D. Flower].
SV, 6 Au39, 24—25 r

Bennett, John
Fascism in Britain.
TU, 1 1933, 36—40 c

Benney, Mark *pseud.*
Gusto misguided
[*Hallelujah, I'm a bum*, by L. Paul].
LR, iii 2 M37, 121 r
Low company rev. by D. Kahn

Benson, Theodora
Lion's mouth.
ND, 24 9D37, 11 p
Too little noise.
ND, 7 12Ag37, 18 c

Bentley, Albert
The demigod.
JG, 20 Sp32, [8—9] v

Bentley, Phyllis
Literature and society.
LR, i 12 S35, 488—91 c
Sleep in peace rev. by A. West

Bentley-Mott, E. *see* Zamiatine, E.

Berlin, Isaiah
Alexander Blok.
OO, xi 55 Je31, 73—76 c
Editorial.
OO x 53 N30, 561—65 c
Editorial.
OO, xi 54 M31, 1—2 c
Music chronicle.
OO, xii 57 F32, 61—65 c
Music chronicle.
OO, xii 58 My32, 133—38 c
Review [*Undying faces*, by E. Benkard].
OO, x 53 N30, 628—30 r
Review [*After the deluge*, by L. Woolf].
OO, xii 57 F32, 68—70 r
Some procrustations,
OO x 52 My30, 491—502 c
see also Blok, Alexander

Berlioz, Hector
The trojans [opera]
rev. by C.R.

Bernal, John Desmond
A note on poetry and politics.
CL, i 1 Su33, 10—15 c
Science and men
[*British scientists of the C19*,
by J. G. Crowther].
LR, ii 2 N35, 69—74 r
The scientist and the world today.
CL, i 2 W33, 36—45 c

Bernanos, George
The diary of a country priest
rev. by E. Waugh

Berry, Francis
Autumn pastoral.
PR, 8 19Je35, 16 v
The book of the prophet.
PR, 11 27N35, 7—8 v
Cremation.
PR, 14 19F36, 7 v
Eliot's *Sweeney agonistes*.
PR, 5 17My35, 8—9, 10—14 c
Mr Eliot and *Ash Wednesday*.
PR, 10 6N35, 2—5 c
The mulberry bush.
PR, 12 4D35, 2—4 c
Proem.
PR, 9 23Oc35, 10 v
Review [*Principles of Shakespearian
production*,
by G. W. Knight].
PR, 16 6My36, 14—15 r
A ride in a sports car.

C, i 10 8F36, 79 v
Sorrow under the sun.
PR, 8 19Je35, 7 v

Berryman, John
The trial.
T, 12/13 Oc38, 99 v

Bertram, Anthony
The king sees red
rev. by A. L. Morton
Men adrift rev. by J. Stewart

Best, Michael
The new Moscow
[*Moscow in the making*,
by *Sir E. D. Simon et al*].
LR, iii 6 Jy37, 346–51 r

Betjeman, John
Diary of Percy Progress, parts I–V.
ND, 3 15Jy37, 8–9; 6 5Ag37, 8,10;
9 26Ag37, 8–9; 21 18N37, 13–14;
25 16D37, 11–12 p
In Holy Trinity, Sloane Street: MCMVII.
Y, i 1 M39, 23 v
Oxford?
PR, 15 11M36, 1–4 c
Review [*Death while swimming*,
by O. Blakeston].
S, 2 A/Jy 33, 14–15 r
The Wykehamist at home.
NO, ii 1 My34, 57 v
Continual dew rev. by E. Waugh

Betts, Ernest
The private life of Henry VIII
[film script] rev. by Ajax *pseud.*

Betts, Phyllis Yvonne
Meditation in the belly of a whale.
ND, 10 2S37, 21 p
Our continental correspondent.
ND, 16 14Oc37, 22–23 p
The snob's guide to good form.
ND, 17 21Oc37, 17–19 p
Uncle Cavendish.
ND, 18 28Oc37, 12–13 p

Beveridge, Andrew C.
Accident in the mine.
LR, iii 1 F37, 42 i

Bezymenski, Aleksandr Il'ich
Tragedy night [pt2, cantos 14 & 15]
tr. by A. Brown.
LR, ii, 5 F36, 217–19 v

Bewley, Neville
Fables.
CM, i 4 Sp34, 161–62 p

Bhat, K. S.
ABC: an absurdity of Hoxton life.

SM, 4 1933, 16–36 d
Mother.
SM, 1 Je31, 5–9 p
Prasena.
SM, 3 1932, 7–11 p
Shakuni. SM, 5 1934, 1–10 p
That's why.
SM, 2 S31, 76–87 p
see also Gowardhandas

Bhattacharya, Bhabani
India: reform or revolution?
DV, 3 My32, 69–73 c

Biddulph, Geoffrey
The golden calf.
DE, 1 New Year 32, 4 p

Biggs, J. R.
Woodcut.
P, 1 1938, 119 i

Bill *pseud.*
From 'The passionate pilgrim'.
PP, 15 N39, 16 v

Bincroft, James G.
Devon.
DD, ix 31 J–F32, 6 v
In summer-time.
DD, ix 35 S–Oc32, 74 v

Binder, Pearl
André Gide.
LR, i 11 Ag35, 449 i
Beethoven–Toscanini.
LR, iii 11 D37, 674–76 c
Big business.
LR, iii 3 A37, 142 i
Chalking squad.
LR, i 8 My35, 331 i
From 'Odd jobs'.
LR, i 4 J35, 133 i
Happy New Year.
LR, iii 12 J38, 711 i
Love lane, Shadwell.
LR, i 1 Oc34, 23 i
Ludmilla's birthday.
LR, ii 12 S36, 642–45 p
Miner.
LR, i 11 Ag35, 434 i
Moscow boulevard.
LR, iii 10 N37, 614 i
Paris, June 1936.
LR, ii 10 Jy36, 503 i
Pont du Carroussel.
NW, 2 Au36, 173–78 p
Unemployed.
SM, 3 1932, front. i
Misha and Masha rev. by R. Fox
Odd jobs rev. by A. L. Morton

Binns, Lionel O. H.
Childhood,

JG, 31 W34, [23] v
A world's awakening.
JG, 30 Au34, [28] v

Binyon, Laurence
Miyajima.
HR, 4 1931, 44 v
Purgatorio, canto XXVII.
TO, i 3 Jy38, 4–6 v

Birabeau, André
Revelation rev. by E. M. Barraud

Birch, Dennis
Cry for the Cotswolds.
JG, 64 Sp38, [18–19] v
Les tricotenses [sic].
JG, 67 W38, [14] v

Birch, Lionel
To all that.
EX, 5 F30, 27–28 v

Bird, Cyril Kenneth
see Fougasse *pseud.*

Birtles, Dora
Sicilian sun.
P, 6 1939, 158–78 p

Bishop, Donald
Invocation.
C, i 16 21M36, 127 v

Bishop, John Peale
The statue of shadow; Colloquy with
a king-crab.
T, 12/13 Oc38, 92–93 v

Bishop, Reginald
Fascism in theory and practice
[*The fascist: his state and his mind*,
E. B. Ashton;
The triumph of Barabbas, by G. Giglio].
LR, iii 8 S37, 488–91 r
Light on chaos
[*World politics, 1918–1936*,
by R. P. Dutt].
LR, ii 11 Ag36, 583 r
Mr Brockway
[*Workers' front*, by A. F. Brockway].
LR, iii 15 A38, 952–53 r
U.S.S.R. [*Soviet communism*,
by S. & B. Webb; *U.S.S.R. handbook*;
The Soviet state, by B. W. Maxwell;
The Soviet Union and world problems,
ed. by S. N. Ha.per;
Britain and the Soviets].
LR ii 8 My36, 395–98 r

Black, G.
Horst Mendel-German?
TC, vi 36 S34, 331–40 p

Black, M.
Cynic or sceptic.
EX, 5 F30, 42—45 c

Black, Misha
An equity for artists?
LR, ii 7 A36, 330—35 c
Review [*Low and Terry*,
by D. Low and H. Thoroughgood].
VP, i 2 Jy/S34, 53—54 r

Blackie, John Ernest Haldane
The old sentimentalism.
F, 2 Je30, 124—28 c

Blackmur, Richard Palmer
On excited knees; World aback.
T, 12/13 Oc38, 96 v

Blackstone, Bernard
Poem.
CM, ii 1 Su35, 243 v
Stretto.
CM, i 4 Sp34, 175 v

Blagoyeva, Stella D.
Dimitrov
rev. by T. H. Wintringham

Blaikie, Edward
The present day.
TU, 1 1933, 52—53, v
Visit to Lennard.
NO, i 2 N33, 161—68 p

Blake, A. E.
Can we agree on this?
TC, i 5 Jy31, 1—4 c
Statescraft as science: the aims of the
political and economic section of the
Prometheans.
TC, i 1 M31, 12—13 c

Blake, E. C.
Alfred in heaven.
C, ii 38 12S36, 78 p
The masterpiece.
C, ii 52 19D36, 203 p
Mist promise,
C, iii 58 30J37, 37 v

Blake, William
Illustrations . . . for Thornton's Virgil
rev. by NV, 29 M38, 23

Blaker, Richard
Medal without bar rev. by F. H.

Blakeston, Oswell
The beauty.
LT, i 8 Oc36, 6—8 p
Aren't we all?

SM, 3 1932, 12—22 p
At the fair.
SM, 4 *supp.* 1933, i
Black mist.
PR, 13 5F36, 11 v
Cinema notes.
CV, 4 1935, 19—20 c
Cinemart.
CV, 5 M36 [21] v
Coconut bulls-eye.
PR, 22 Je37, 18—19 p
Detectives in wonderland.
TC, vi 35 Je34, 301 v
Diaposon,
CV, 3 Su35, 15 p
Drawings by Brodzky.
J, 1 J36, 25 r
Economics for social workers, economics
for architects, economics for doctors.
W, 11 W39, 304 p
The greater truths [Charles Williams].
LT, i 5 Jy36, 20—22 c
Movies and the critics.
DE, 1 New year32, 1 c
Note on published scenarios.
LT, i 8 Oc36, 16 c
Number one; Number five; Maestro;
Lunar eclipse; Fountain fanfare.
S, 2 A/Jy 33, 24—25 v
The party.
SM, 2 S31, 69—75 p
A psychological novel
[*Mezzomorto*, by V. Crockett].
LT, i 1 M36, 16 r
Refugee.
FB, iv 10 N38, 13—15 p
Review [*Creative art in England*,
by W. Johnstone].
LT, i 10 D36, 30—31 r
Reviews
[*This, my brother*, by J. Rood;
Diary of a Soviet marriage, P. Romanov].
LT, i 11 J37, 39, 41 r
The specimen.
LT, i 3 My36, 46—49 p
Standard currency.
FB, v 1 F39, 12—14 p
Three fragments.
S, 2 A/Jy33, 13 p
Three poems.
NO, ii 1 My34, 31 v
Tree of refuge.
LT, i 3 My36, 53 v
Two fables.
J, 1 J36, 10—12 p
Two poems.
NO, ii 2 J35, 171 v
'Up and away and nowhere to stop'.
PR, 9 23Oc35, 2 v
Witch way.
S, 1 J33, 12 p
Death while swimming
rev. by J. Betjeman
see also Burford, Roger

Blakeway, Michael G.
Full circle,
PQ, i 1 Sp39, 6 v

Blatchford, Robert
Skoal!
HR, 6 1933, 57 p

Bliss, Douglas Percy
Highland gathering.
MS, vi 1 A35, 17 i
Woodcut.
P, 1 1938, 144 i

Bliss, Geoffrey
Free-will.
CA, 2 S30, 24 v

Bloch, Jean Richard
Literary creation and human society.
LR, i 11 Ag35, 464—68 c

Bloch, Miriam Regina
Song.
DD, ix 32 M—A32, 23 v
Time.
DD, ix 35 S—Oc32, 76 v

Blok, Alexander
The collapse of humanism, tr. by
I. Berlin.
00, xi 55 Je31, 89—112 c
The downfall of humanism, tr. by R. Gill
EQ, i 3 N34, 133—42 c

Blomfield, Joan
Simplicity the best policy.
LD, i 3 My37, 11—12 p

Bluen, Herbert
Baudelaire.
JG, 70 Au39, [24—25] v
The place I love.
JG, 66 Au38, [5—6] v
The orchard.
JG, 69 Su39, [6] v
A prayer.
JG, 40 Sp37, [25] v
The speed fiend.
JG, 67 W38, [36] v
Squirrels.
JG, 42 Au37, [26] v
Trees.
JG, 39 W36, [13] v
Trees in autumn.
JG, 65 Su38, [15] v

Blum, Etta
Four poems.
CV, 2 D34, 14—16 v
Four poems.
CV, 3 Su35, 12—14 v

Blumenfeld, Josephine
Dip, Lizzie, dip
rev. by L. A. Pavey

Blumenfeld, Simon
Crossing the border.
LR, i 4 J35, 101—4 p
Four novels
[*Rose Forbes,* by G. Buchanan;
Star-begotten, by H. G. Wells;
A bridge to divide them, by G. Rees;
Rex v. Rhodes, by B. Hamilton].
LR, iii 6 Jy37, 369—71 r
The miracle.
LR, ii 9 Je36, 454—58 p
Jews march.
LR, i 7 A35, 259—64 p
Mischief maker.
LR, i 3 D34, 52—58 p
Prize novelists and others
[*End of Cornwall,* by R. Preston;
Jordanstown, by J. Johnson;
Spanish prelude, by J. Ballou;
Cradle of life, by L. Adamic;
King Wren, by H. Mann;
Star-maker, by O. Stapledon].
LR, iii 7 Ag37, 434—37 r
Writers international.
LR, i 3 D34, 79—80 c
Jew boy rev. by A. Williams-Ellis
Phineas Kahn
rev. by. A. Calder-Marshall

Blunden, Edmund
Anti-basilisk.
LD, i 1 M37, 16 v
Apparitions in summer.
00, xii 58 My32, 100 v
By the Belgian frontier.
K, i 2 D39—J40, 41 v
An institution and a moral
[*Oxford poetry, 1931*].
00, xi 56 N31, 190—98 r
The lost battalion.
LS, i 1 F34, 18 v
Old remedies.
WW, i 3 Jy30, 5 v
Railway note.
LD, ii 3 F38, 15 v
Sixpence for the river.
PR, 1 1F35, 1—2 v
Near and far rev. by S. Spender
Poems, 1914—1930
rev. by R. H. Goodman

Blunt, Alfred Walter Frank
God's orchestra.
HR, 6 1933, 13 v

Blunt, Anthony
Cubism.
V, 6 Je30, 256—64 c
Dalon and his workers' monument.
LR, ii 13 Oc36, 693—98 c

Gauguin [*The life of Paul Gauguin,*
by R. Burnett].
LR, iii 1 F37, 58—59 r
The Italian exhibition.
V, 5 F30, 227—36 c
Lord Hastings at the Lefevre Gallieres.
LR, ii 16 J37, 898 c
Rationalist art and anti-rationalist art.
LR, ii 10 Jy36, iv—vi c
The 'realism' quarrel.
LR, iii 3 A37, 169—71 c

Boag, John
The abominable snowman.
ND, 10 2S37, 16 p

Boatfield, Graham
Life cycle.
PP, 10 Ap39, 19 v

Bodington, S.
The cycle; Words idle words.
F, 1 F30, 36—37 v
Poem.
F, 4 D30, 24 v

Boland, Michael
Sunset?
LR, ii 6 M36, 259 i

Boldero, Martin *pseud.*
see Grigson, Geoffrey

Bolgar, Boyan *pseud.*
Parisian mosaic,
tr. by M. H. M [ouilpied].
LS, i 3 N34, 57—62 p

Bolton, Teresa Hicks-
see Hicks-Bolton, Teresa

Bond, Freda C.
Death and the townswoman.
BB, vii 2 M30, 64 v

Bond, Ralph
A bit of gristle for the starving dog.
LR, iii 14 M38, 845—49 c

Booth, G. K.
A conceit.
PR, 11 27N35, 2—3 p
Scene from novel.
PR, 8 19Je35, 1—3, 5 p

Booth, Meyrick
Review [*Youth and sex,*
by M. Booth; *Adolescent girlhood,*
by M. Chadwick].
TC, iv 19 S32, 28 r

Borcio, Salvatore di
The degenerates.
F, 1 F30, 40—44 p

Borde, Andrew
Nos vagabunduli: two friars, tr. by
A. Field.
SM, 2 S31, 68 v

Borgese, Giuseppe Antonio
Goliath rev. by. F. E. Jones

Borkenau, Franz
Spanish cockpit rev. by V. Ackland

Borley, Colby
A woman's life.
DD, xi 48 N—D34, 94 v

Borrill, Louis
Land without hope.
LR, iii 9 Oc37, 550—52 p
Little people of the people.
LR, iii 15 A38, 919—22 c

Bossewell, John
The catte.
LQ, ii 1 My37, 18—19 p

Boswell, James
And to the glory everlasting.
LR, i 5 F35, 170 i
Another skiing accident.
LR, ii 4 J36, 160 i
Blackmail set-up.
LR, iii 16 My38, 985 i
Can't afford two bob.
LR, ii 5 F36, 202 i
Confession of faith.
CL, ii 1 Oc35, 9 i
Design for dying.
LR, iii 15 A38, 924—25 i
Drawing.
LR, iii 16 My38, 990 i
The Duke's speech.
LR, i 10 Jy35, 405 i
Empire builder.
LR, iii 13 F38, 779 i
The full life.
LR, iii 3 A37, 151 i
The good old tunes.
LR, ii 11 Ag36, 548 i
Hands off Abyssinia.
LR, ii 1 Oc35, 36 i
Hatton Garden luncheon.
LR, i 2 N34, 20 i
'He has made for us a pathway . . .'
LR, i 8 My35, 321 i
His Majesty's servants.
LR, i 6 M35, 226 i
I'm the last of the Texas rangers.
LR, i 10 Jy35, 420 i
Jubilee.
LR, i 9 Je35, 349 i
The lonely heart.
LR, i 3 D34, 57 i
'My first is a fair flower'.
LR, i 6 M35, 236 i

Boswell, James (cont.)
'The old flags reel and the old drums rattle'.
LR, i 2 N34, 9 i
Path to glory.
LR, iii 2 M37, 103 i
The press.
LR, i 5 F35, 172 i
Six-figure income.
LR, iii 5 Je37, 260 i
Surrealist exhibition London 1936.
LR, ii 10 Jy36, 509 i
To go with the others.
LR, ii 1 Oc35, 23 i
Two drawings.
LR, iii 6 Jy37, 341 i
We knew we could trust you.
LR, ii 6 M36, 251 i
You gotta have blue blood.
LR, i 1 Oc34, 9 i

Boswell, James *and others*
Bank Holiday sketch book.
LR, ii 11 Ag36, 568–69 i

Botterill, Denis
Changing gear.
VP, i 1 A/Je34, 15–17 c
Cheapjack with valuables
[*ABC of reading*, by E. Pound].
VP, i 2 Jy/S34, 60 r
The dead laureate.
JG, 13 Su30, [12] v
For Mary.
JG, 68 Sp39, [31] v
Memorial inscription.
JG, 69 Su39, [13] v
Morning.
HR, 7 1934, 35 v
Nostalgic for Spengler.
HR, 7 1934, 66 v
Solvation [sic].
VP, i 2 Jy/S34, 33–35 p
Think of her – autumn.
HR, 4 1931, 70 v
Time and a technician
[*Variations on a time theme,* by E. Muir]
VP, i 2 Jy/S34, 52 r
Tour in the park.
SV, 1 Su38, 19 v
Two sonnets from 'A pilgrimage'.
JG, 15 W30, [18–19] v
Prelude to a pilgrimage.
JG, 14 Au30, [7] v
Three by two.
JG, 14 Au30, [18] v

Bottome, Phyllis
The mortal storm rev. by E. Duthie

Bottomley, Gordon
Review [*To circumjack cencrastus,*
by H. MacDiarmid].
MS, i 4 J31, 60–64 r

[W. B. Yeats] His legacy to the theatre.
AW, Su39, 11–14 c

Bottrall, Francis James Ronald
Epitaph for a riveter,
NV, 1 J33, 11 v
Two poems.
TO, ii 6 Ap39, 3 v
Festivals of fire rev. by G. Grigson
The turning path rev. by R. March

Boughton, Rutland
Capitalist arts in decay.
VP, i 2 Jy/S34, 41–42 c

Boulter, Winifred
The day before yesterday.
ND, 20 11N37, 22 c
High hat notes from Paris.
ND, 15 7Oc37, 26–27 c
More fashions from Paris.
ND, 12 16S37, 23 c
The Paris fashion shows.
ND, 10 2S37, 24 c
Paris fashions.
ND, 25 16D37, 24 c

Bourdillon, H.
This disreputable universe.
LS, ii 1 My35, 26–31 v

Bourne, P. J.
Andante in a country churchyard.
PE, 4 N36, 118–22 p
Old wineskins for new bottles.
PE, 2 S36, 40–42 c
Thoughts after Notting Hill.
PE, 1 Ag36, 4–9 c
The whore and the madonna.
PE, 3 Oc36, 67–68 p

Boutens, Petrus Cornelis
The Christ-child,
tr. by H. J. C. Grierson.
MS v 1/2 Je34, 51–54 v

Bowen, David
The film and some of its relations
to the novel.
FB, ii 4 25J37, 7–8 c

Bowen, Elizabeth
At the theatre.
ND, 16 14Oc37, 37–38; ND, 17
21Oc37, 37–38; ND, 18 28Oc37,
29–30; ND, 19 4N37, 29–30; ND,
20 11N37, 29–30; ND, 21 18N37,
37–38; ND, 22 25N37, 30; ND, 23
2D37, 29–30; ND, 24 9D37, 30;
ND, 25 16D37, 29–30; ND, 26 23D37,
29–30 dr
Comus [and] *Revudeville.*
ND, 5 29Jy37, 29 dr
Hamlet [and] *Women of property.*

ND, 3 15Jy37, 29 dr
Letter from Ireland.
ND, 18 28Oc37, 20–21 p
No sleep for the wicked.
ND, 2 8Jy37, 29 dr
St. Moritz.
ND, 4 22Jy37, 29 dr
Salzburg in the distance.
ND, 11 9S37, 22–23 p
The theatre.
ND, 6 5Ag37, 30 dr
Victoria regina [by L. Housman].
ND, 1 1Jy37, 37 dr

Bower, Fred
Autobiography rev. by T. Mann

Bower-Shore, Clifford
The bus.
C, i 4 28D35, 27 p

Bowers, Penelope
Exile.
RM, 2 D34, 61 v

Bowley, Richard T.
Value for a pound.
LR, i 7 A35, 264 v

Bowra, Cecil Maurice
George Moore.
NO, i 1 My33, 43–51 c
Stefan George.
NO, i 3 F34, 316–31 c
The triumph of symbolism.
OO, xii 57 F32, 1–25 c

Boyd, A. *see* Neruda, P.

Boyd, A. C.
Death of a poet.
P, 4 1938, 36 v

Boyd, Alix
Pan.
DD, xi 43 J–F34, 4 v
Susan.
DD, x 42 N–D33, 102 v

Boyle, Kay
Big fiddle.
FB, v 1 F39, 5–7 p
The crows.
K, i 2 D39–J40, 44 p
January the eighth.
CV, 5 M36, [9] p
Mrs Carrigan's daughter.
K, i 1 17N39, 9–10 p
Second generation.
SV, 6 Au39, 3–4 p
The sky is woven of the four directions
of the wind.
S, 2 A/Jy33, 3–7 p

16

The taxi ride.
SV, 2 Au38, 16—21 p
Two short stories.
CV, 4 1935, 16—17 p
World tour.
SV, 4[A] Sp39, 2—3 v
Death of a man rev. by A. L. Morton
The first lover rev. by D. Gillespie
Monday night rev. by G. S. Fraser

Boyle, Stuart
Mr Baldwin's version of the year's
problem picture.
LR, ii 7 A36, 313 i

Bozhovitch, G.
The lair, tr. by N. B. Jopson.
EQ, i 2 Ag34, 121—26 p

Bradbook, H. L.
The development of Yeats's poetry.
CM, ii 1 Su35, 201—6 c

Bradbury, Gilbert
The mansion.
ST, 1 2 A33, 23—24 p

Braddock, Joseph
Peace.
DD, xi 45 My—Je34, 44 v
The sirens.
DD, xi 46 Jy—Ag34, 53—54 v
Song's coronet.
DD, xi 48 N—D34, 89 v

Bradford, Florence M.
Quietude.
PQ, i 2 Su39, 39 v

Bradshaw, Kenneth
Lost leader.
LR, i 10 Jy35, 416—18 p
Monday morning in a machine shop.
LR, i 6 M35, 201—3 p
Special area.
LR, i 12 S35, 509—21 p

Bradshaw, Laurence
Thoughts on religion and art.
I, i 4 15D31, 103 c
Wood engraving.
I, i 4 15D31, 109 i
Wood engraving.
I, i 2/3 15S31, 87 i
Wood engraving.
I, i 2/3 15S31, 53 i
Wood engraving.
I, i 1 15Je31, 9 i

Bradshaw, Norman
Aucassin.
K, i 1 17N39, 8 v
A bed-time story.
FB, v 1 F39, 10—12 p

Common epitaph.
FB, v 1 F39, 4 v
Defence of ivory.
PR, 22 Je37, 17—18 v
Not thus we die.
B, 1 Su38, 8—9 v

Brady, Robert Alexander
*The spirit and structure of German
fascism*
rev. by A. Henderson

Bramstedt, Ernst Kohn-
see Kohn-Bramstedt, Ernst

Bramwell, James
Poem.
LS, i 3 N34, 56 v
Beyond the sunrise rev. by G. Grigson

Branch, E. D. L.
Epigrams.
DD, viii 29 Su31, 79 v
Epitaph.
DD, ix 33 My—Je32, 44 v
The heritage.
DD, xi 46 Jy—Ag34, 60 v
Interval; Sonnet; Summer wind.
DD, ix 36 N—D32, 89, 103 v
The lover; Valediction.
DD, vii, 27 N—D30, 422 v
Lumen luminum.
DD, vii 26 S—Oc30, 401 v
Mercutio; Morning.
DD, viii 30 Au31, 89 v
Sonnet.
DD, vii 26 S—Oc30, 400 v
Sonnet.
DD, ix 32 M—A32, 20 v
Sonnet.
DD, x 37 J—F33, 5 v
Sonnet; Unknown.
DD, x 40 Jy—Ag33, 59 v
Sonnet; Brunswick square 6 a.m.
DD, viii 28 J—F31, 27 v
Two sonnets; The tramp.
DD, xi 44 M—A34, 24, 27 v
Winter.
DD, ix 31 J—F32, 3 v

Branch, Edith
Spy [*The labour spy racket*,
by L. Huberman] !
LR, iii 14 M38, 878—80 r

Brand, A. P.
Poem.
PP, 13/14 Jy—Ag39, 10 v

Brand, Patrick
Miss Povey's constant reader.
SM, 3 1932, 23—38 p

Branson, Clive
The German prisoner and the nightingale
in San Pedro; The Asturian miners.
PP, 11 My39, 6—7 v
San Pedro.
NW, ns2 Sp39, 53 v

Breakespeare, Nicholas
The foreign policy of the Vatican.
AR, i 2 Jy37, 98—105 c

Brearley, Hilda
Adagio.
JG, 19 W31, [9] v
Grief.
JG, 31 W34, [21] v
How sleep the brave?
JG, 35 W35, [10] v
In the vicarage garden.
JG, 15 W30, [15] v
Infelix.
JG, 32 Sp35, [4] v
Lines.
JG, 24 Sp33, [16] v
Midsummer.
JG, 14 Au30, [14] v
On the pennines.
HR, 4 1931, 39 v
Trees.
JG, 41 Su37, [13] v
Winter gone.
HR, 4 1931, 21 v

Brecht, Bertholt
Concerning the label emigrant,
tr. by S. Spender.
NW, 5 Sp38, 42 v
The German drama: pre-Hitler.
LR, ii 10 Jy36, 504—8 c
The informer, tr. by C. Ashleigh.
NW, ns2 Sp39, 113—20 d
A penny for the poor rev. by J. Lindsay

Bredan, M.
Rue de Seine.
JG, 64 Sp38, [16—17] v

Breen, Francis
The shadows.
NS, ii 4 Ag35, 278—85 p

Brémond, André
Art and inspiration.
NV, 14 A35, 5—12 c

Brendon, Ismay
Unsullied.
DD, viii 30 Au31, 108 v

Brennan, Alan
Herrings.
C, ii 50 5D36, 187 v

Brennan, Charles
Sicut folium raptum de vento.
CA, 3 Oc30, 39 v

Brennan, Eileen
Reformed.
C, iii 58 30J37, 35 p

Brennan, H. *see* Seyfoollina, L.

Brereton, Cloudesley
The atoms in high fever.
DD, ix 36 N—D32, 94 v
Foreboding.
DD, ix 34 Jy—Ag32, 51 v
Silences.
DD, xi 44 M—A34, 29 v
Somnia vera.
DD, x 40 Jy—Ag33, 65 v

Breton, André
Four poems, tr. by D. Devlin.
CPP, 4/5 Ag36, 82—85 v
Poem, tr. by G. S. Fraser.
K, i 2 D39—J40, 53 v
Some passages from The lighthouse
of the bride,
tr. by H. Jennings.
LB, 4/5 Jy38, 17—19 p
Two poems,
tr. by D. Gascoyne and R. Todd.
CPP, 2 Je36, 25—27 v
Wolfgang Paalen [plus partial tr.].
LB, 10 F39, 13—17 c
Yves Tanguy.
LB, 4/5 Jy38, 32 c

Breton, André *and* **Eluard,** Paul
The pre-natal life of man,
tr. by J. Jacquot.
CPP, 2 Je36, 37—38 p

Breton, André *and* **Rivera,** Diego
Pour un art révolutionnaire indépendant
[plus tr.].
LB, 6 Oc38, 25, 29—31; 7 D38, 29—32 p

Breton, Louis Le *see* Le Breton, Louis

Brett, Bernard
Women wanted.
NS, i 4 Ag34, 282—84 p

Brewer, J. L.
The doctor.
NS, i 5 Oc34, 364 p

Brezina, Otokar
Aims, tr. by P. Selver.
SM, 2 S31, 62—67 p
The wine of the strong.
EQ, i 1 My34, 50—52 v

Bridges, Robert
Letter.
CA, 2 S30, 22 c
see also Naylor, B.

Bridgman, Olive R.
At the Western cataract, Victoria Falls.
DD, xi 45 My—Je34, 45 v

Bridie, James [*pseud.* O. H. Mavor]
Mrs Waterbury's millennium.
MS, v 1/2 Je34, 68—80 d
St. Eloi and the bear.
MS, iv 1 A33, 12—17 d
Storm in a teacup rev. by R. Wright

Bridson, Douglas Geoffrey
Ten to midnight.
TC, v 26 Ap33, 97 v

Brierley, Walter
Summer noon.
NS, i 5 Oc34, 348—52 p

Brieux, Eugène
Maternité rev. by J. Garrett

Briffault, Robert
A civilization of lies.
TC, iv 24 F33, 1—4 c
Sin and sex rev. by
TC, iii 18 Ag32, 28—29

Briggs, Bertha Traill
Spring.
DD, xi 44 M—A34, 32 v
Winter.
DD, x 41 S—Oc33, 88 v

Briggs, W. F.
Bradford.
HR, 4 1931, 8 i

Bristow, Alec
The dead don't work.
TC, v 29 Jy33, 284—88 p
Eightpence halfpenny.
TC, vi 35 Je34, 275—85 p
Joy and the critics.
TC, i 2 A31, 27—28 c
Review [*Full score,*
sel. by T. I. Fytton Armstrong].
TC, v 26 A33, 124—25 r
Review [*Five for silver,*
by M. Whitaker].
TC, iv 22 D32, 28—29 r
Review [*Fugue,* by O. Moore].
TC, iii 16 Je32, 26—27 r

Bristowe, Sybil
Christmas: his birthday.
DD, x 42 N—D32, 97—98 v
Love's alchemy.

DD, ix 32 M—A32, 30 v
Poem.
DD, x 38 M—A33, 32 v
To the creator of all things.
DD, ix 35 S—Oc32, 80 v

Britain and the Soviets
rev. by R. Bishop

Britain without capitalists
rev. by C. Clark

British Union quarterly
rev. by R. March

Britten, Geoffrey W.
Love in Paddington.
C, iii 58 30J37, 37—38 v

Britting, Georg
Journey to France, tr. by J. M. Smith.
MS, v 4 J35, 290—95 p
The lovers and the old woman,
tr. by R. H. Hull.
EQ, i 4 F35, 259—63 p

Britton, Lionel
Comment on the basis of the Sexology gr
TC, iv 21 N32, 22—23 c
Literature and the young pen.
DV, 1 M32, 22—24 c
Politics for the higher animals.
TC, i 3 My31, 7—9 c
Spacetime inn rev. by G. West

Broadley, Thomas W.
Chellow Dean.
JG, 36 Sp36, [17] v

Broadway idyll.
NS, i 4 Ag34, 290—93 p

Broch, Hermann
A passing cloud, tr. by W. Muir.
MS, iv 4 J34, 304—12 p
The proposal.
MS, iii 2 Ag32, 98—103 p

Brock, Louis
Onwards and upwards with the arts.
R, i 3 A32, 14 p

Brockway, Archibald Fenner
Comment on the report
[of the Political and Economic group
of the Promethean society].
TC, ii 10 D31, 8—9 c
Disarmament by example.
TC, i 1 M31, 3—5 c
Mahatma Gandhi.
TC, ii 8 Oc31, 5—7 c
World crisis: workers' unity.
TC, v 27 My33, 179—82 c
Hungry England rev. by W. N. Warbey

Will Roosevelt succeed?
rev. by W. N. Warbey
Workers front rev. by R. Bishop

Brockway, Frederick
Checkmate.
LB, 6 Oc38, 19 c
Chirico's lover.
LB, 6 Oc38, 12 v
Magritte.
LB, 2 My38, 23 c
Three pictures by Paul Delvaux.
LB, 3 Je38, 8 c
see also De Chirico, G.

Brodlie, George
Last tryst.
VS, i 4 M/My39, 20 v

Brodzky, Horace
Pen drawing.
J, 2 My36, 7 i
Pen drawing.
J, 1 J36, 13 i
Drawings rev. by O. Blakeston

Brogan, Colm
The Irish in Scotland.
NA, i 1 Au39, 23—29 c

Broneivski, Vwadiswav
Two poems, tr. by J. N. and L. L.
NW, 3 Sp37, 68—71 v

Bronowski, Jacob
Crisis.
DE, 1 New year 32, 1 p
D. H. Lawrence.
EX, 7 Sp31, 5—13 c
Fifth army.
EX, 5 F30, 11—12 v
Fragments.
EX, 6 Oc30, 47—49 v
Poems.
EX, 7 Sp31, 33—36 v
Postscript.
EX, 5 F30, 34—35 c
Two poems.
NW, ns1 Au38, 134—36 v

Brook, Barnaby
The chance.
HR, 4 1931, 65—67 p

Brooke, Peter
A close shave.
ND, 25 16Oc37, 16—17 p

Brooks, Bill
Way to live.
PP, 15 N39, 4 v

Brooks, Cleanth
Birth of Aphrodite; November landscape.
OO, xi 54 M31, 35—36 v

Brophy, John
West end.
WW, i 1 J30, 9—60 p

Brown, A. G. K.
The tyranny of the Olympic Games.
LD, i 3 My37, 22—23 p

Brown, Albert
The ancient solicitor.
PP, 4 Oc38, 6 v
The phenomenon.
PP, 2 Ag38, 4 v

Brown, Alec
Criticism and propaganda
[*Soviet Russian literature,* by G. Struve].
LR, ii 3 D35, 141—43 r
It needn't happen here
[*In the second year,* by S. Jameson].
LR, ii 6 M36, 280—81 r
The miners' struggle
[*The miners' two bob,*
ed. by W. H. Williams;
Stay-down miner, by M. Slater].
LR, ii 5 F36, 226—27 r
Starvation or commonsense.
LR, ii 7 A36, 315—20 c
Three poems.
NW, ns1 Au38, 193—94 v
Where crime is different
[*Soviet Russia fights crime,*
by L. von Koerber].
LR, i 5 F35, 191—92 r
White girl
[*Adventures of the white girl in her
search for knowledge,*
by M. Hyman].
LR, i 5 F35, 192 r
Writers international.
LR, i 3 D34, 76—77 c
Breakfast in bed rev. by T. L. Hodgkin
Daughters of Albion rev. by J. Lehmann
The fate of the middle classes
rev. by R. Wright
The lovely girl rev. by J. Lindsay
see also Bezymenski, A.; Mirsky, D. S.;
Pasternak, B.; Tikhonov, N.

Brown, Alfred
Three essays.
WW, i 3 Jy30, 20—31 p

Brown, Alfred John
Bradford.
HR, 6 1933, 54 v
Old Raggalds inn; November apples.
HR, 5 1932, 25, 32 v
These fields.
HR, 6 1933, 9 v

Toyland.
HR, 5 1932, 51—52 p

Brown, Arthur
The German anti-war Congress.
RM, 2 D34, 36 c

Brown, Bob
The bloody beer battle.
NW, 3 Sp37, 88—93 p

Brown, Donovan
Eights week: Lancashire and Oxford.
TU, i 3 Je34, [1], 3 i
The hunger march.
TU, i 2 34, 37—40 c
The Nuffield scholarship.
TU, i 3 Je34, 44—46 c
The visiting lecturer; Editorial.
TU, i 2 1934, 2, 3—5 i, c

Brown, Ethan Allan
Clive.
OO, x 53 N30, 609—15 p
Forenoon.
OO xi 55 Je31, 120— 30 p
'Ike'.
OO, x 52 My30, 522—30 p
Long week-end.
OO, x 51 F30, 403—13 p
Sunday siesta.
OO, xi 54 M31, 30—34 p
William Blent.
OO, xii 57 F32, 27—29 p

Brown, Francis Charles Claydon Yeats-
see Yeats-Brown, F. C. C.

Brown, H.
Elegy on the death of Yeats; Gretchen
and the grave people.
T, 17 A39, 12—13 v

Brown, Ivor
The inn-keeper.
HR, 7 1934, 17—18 c
James Bridie.
R, i 5 Je34, 6—7 c

Brown, Lucie *and* **Aldridge,** John
The memory of Basil Taylor.
EP, 3 Sp37, 191—92 c

Brown, N. S.
Question.
TH, 1 27J39, 2 v

Browne, Alistair
Freud and materialism.
LR, ii 9 Je36, 431—36 c

Browne, Felicia
Sketches.
LR, ii 13 Oc36, 688 i

Browne, Wynyard
Lord Timon.
CM, i 1 Sp33, 16—21 p
Song lyric; A letter to a reverend doctor.
CL, i 1 Su33, 8—9 v
Two poems.
CM, i 2 Su33, 62—65 v

Brownrigg, Philip
A job in a million-11.
ND, 11 9S37, 18—19 p

Brownson, J. E.
Agnes Merry.
SM, 2 S31, 51—61 p

Broyle, M.
The perfect stranger.
C, 1 1 7D35, 8 *passim* p

Bruce, Constance Marian
Early morning in April, 1939.
JG, 69 Su39, [7] v
Floating bazaar.
JG, 38 Au36, [7] v
Hermione.
JG, 70 Au39, [26] v
Quest.
JG, 34 Au35, [31] v
York.
JG, 36 Sp36, [8] v

Bruce, George
Jute spinner.
VS, i 3 D38—F39, 8 v
To the Nelson School singers.
MS, vi 4 J36, 307 v
To a child crying.
MS, vi 2 Jy35, 142 v

Bruguiere, Francis
Professionally speaking.
S, 2 A—Jy33, 16—17 p

Bryan, John
Foam; Retrospect.
CM, i 2 Su33, 61 v
Return ticket.
CM, i 3 Au33, 125—29 p
Spring in Kensington gardens.
CM, i 3 Au33, 124 v

Bryant, Michael
The flight from socialism.
TC, ii 8 Oc31, 20—21 c
The rights of man.
TC, i 6 Ag31, 13—14 c

Bryher [*pseud.* Annie Winifred Ellerman]
Nautilus; Always the islands; October.
S, 2 A—Jy33, 8—10 v
Prescience.
CV, 5 M36, [19] v

Brzeska, Henri Gaudier- *see*
Gaudier-Brzeska, Henri

Buchan
The shadow.
LR, iii 12 J38, 732—33 i
What! Not murdered the Spanish
workers yet?
LR, ii 12 S36, 603 i

Buchan, John
Other gods.
M, i 1 Je33, 21—24 p

Buchan, William
The open window.
DD, xi 45 My—Je34, 36 v

Buchanan, George
Two new documentary plays
[*Waiting for Lefty*, by C. Odets;
Stay down miner, by M. Slater].
GTP, 1 Je36, [4] dr
Rose Forbes rev. by S. Blumenfeld

Buck, Pearl Sydenstricker
The exile rev. by R. Wright
A house divided rev. by S. Wang

Buckland, Robert
The length of a street.
P, 5 1939, 9—23 p

Buckley, Diana
The falling wave.
LS, i 1 F34, 16—17 p

Buckmaster, Celia
Friday; Poem.
T, 17 A39, 14 v
Story.
SV, 4 Su39, 2—3 p
Voyage without end.
W, 11 W39, 298—99 p

Bucknell, A. F.
In praise of Kalidasa.
BB, vii 2 M30, 78—81 c

Budgen, Frank
James Joyce and the making of Ulysses
rev. by A. Hope

Buechner, George
Danton's death,
tr. by S. Spender and G. Rees
rev. by K. Allott; N. Heseltine

Buisson, Marguerite
Druid's altar, Bingley.
HR, 5 1932, 29 v
Genius.
JG, 19 W31, [7] v
Hay fever.

JG, 63 W37, |31—32| v
Primavera.
JG, 24 Sp33, [21—22] v
Sonnet.
JG, 23 W32, [14] v
Thoughts at night.
JG, 18 Au31, [10] v

Bukharin, Nikolai Ivanovich *and others*
Marxism and modern thought
rev. by A. West

Bullough, Geoffrey
Assuagement.
MS, iii 3 Oc32, 215 v
Poem.
MS, iv 2 Jy33, 125 v
Sonnet.
MS, iv 4 J34, 315 v
The trend of modern poetry
rev. by G. Grigson

Bunin, Ivan
The grammar of love
rev. by A. Calder-Marshall

Bunuel, Luis
A giraffe, tr. by D. Gascoyne.
CPP, 2 Je36, 41—43 p

Bunyard, Edward A.
Table talk.
ND, 17 21Oc37, 34 c
Table talk.
ND, 21 18N37, 26 c

Burdekin, Katherine
A story.
EP, 2 Su36, 139—44 p
Burdett, Osbert
Prose.
M, i 1 Je33, 56—57 p

Burford, Roger
Damn big guns.
S, 1 J33, 14 p
Large genie.
S, 2 A—Jy33, 29 p
On Richard Thoma
[*The promised land; Green chaos*].
S, 2 A—Jy33, 20—21 r
Snakes and ladders.
J, 1 J36, 14 v
Valley poem.
SV, 2 Au38, 31 v

Burford, Roger *and* **Blakeston,** Oswell
Hounds of time.
LT, i 11 J37, 4—15 p
The poet as specialist.
NO, i 3 F34, 348—52 c

Burgos. National government
*A preliminary official report on the
atrocities in Southern Spain*
rev. by V. Ackland

Burke, Michael
The Irish theatre.
NA, i 1 Au39, 70—77 c

Burke, Patrick
¡Adios, España!
FB, iii 7 25N37, 39—40 p
San Fermin.
FB, iii 8 3M38, 43—45 p
Spike.
FB, iv 10 N38, 16—17 p
Those were the days.
FB, iii 9 6Je38, 65—66 p

Burke, Patrick *and* **Waller,** John
Yah! Yah! Merrie New Year!
FB, iv 10 N38, 19—20 p

Burn, Max
On dictatorship.
LT, i 3 My36, 64—65 c
On literature.
LT, i 4 Je36, 7—11, 15 c

Burnett, Harvey
Review
[*Walter Sickert,* by V. Woolf].
LS, i 3 N34, 28—29 r

Burnett, Whit
The maker of signs
rev. by A. Calder-Marshall

Burnett, Whit *and* **Foley,** Martha *eds.*
Story in America, 1933—34
rev. by A. Calder-Marshall

Burney, Edward
Civilisation and tolerance.
TC, iii 15 My32, 16—20 c
Civilisation and tolerance, 2.
TC, iii 16 Je32, 16—19 c

Burns, Emile
The revolutionary way out.
TC, iii 15 My32, 1—3 c
*Capitalism, communism and the
transition*
rev. by W. N. Warbey

Burns, Robert
Letters, ed. by J. de L. Ferguson
rev. by C. Carswell

Burns, Tom
Street corner.
NW, ns1 Au38, 68—76 p
Two stories.
NW, 4 Au37, 102—11 p

Burra, Edward John
The dance.
F, 4 D30, 35 i
Delicatessen.
F, 4 D30, 41 i

Burra, Peter James Salkeld
The Agamemnon.
GTP, 5 N36, 2 dr
Baroque and gothic sentimentalism.
F, 3 Oc30, 159—82 c
Las meninas.
F, 6 Je31, 187 v
The prayer of John Mandeville.
F, 5 F31, 113—19 v
The season.
F, 2 Je30, 88—89 v

Burrows, R. A.
Abominable snowmen.
FB, iii 9 6Je38, 75—77 p

Burstein, Sonia Rosa
Aphasia; To Cassandra; Rock-rose.
SM, 1 Je31, 10—11 v
Four outraged sonnets.
SM, 4 1933, 37—38 v
The iconoclast.
SM, 3 1932, 39—40 v
Prayer of the undefeated; Bewilderment.
SM, 5 1934, 11—12 v

Burton, Audrey
The shadow of the mine.
P, 3 1938, 109—16 p

Burton, Douglas
Review
[*The colonial policy of British
imperialism,* by R. Fox].
TC, vi 35 Je34, 312 r

Burton, Henry
The quarry in the wood; The lily in the
wood.
DD, ix 31 J—F32, 11 v

Bush, Alan Dudley
Music and the working class struggle.
LR, ii 12 S36, 646—51 c

Bush, Alan Dudley *and* **Swingler,**
Randall *eds.*
The workers' song book rev. by J. Lipton

Busvine, Katharine K.
The ballad of the bastard bustard.
ND, 9 26Ag37, 18 v
Death in the afternoon.
ND, 20 11N37, 16 v
Loop bank.
ND, 22 25N37, 18 v
Luxury flat.
ND, 24 9D37, 12—14 p

The man from Kalamazoo.
ND, 14 30S37, 13—15 p

Butler, Samuel
Further extracts from the notebooks
rev. by Jaques *pseud.*

Butt, L. A.
Stay down miner [by M. Slater].
LR, ii 9 Je36, 475 dr

Butts, Mary
On an American wonder child who
translated Homer at eight years old.
S, 1 J33, 9—10 v
Picus Martius; Thinking of saints and
Petronius Arbiter; Douarnenez; Heart
break house.
SM, 3 1932, 41—48 v
Last stories rev. by R. Davies
Traps for unbelievers
rev. by G. Pendle

Byrde, Richard
Impressions: Chesterton as a poet.
C, ii 29 11Jy36, 2 c

Byrne, Lionel Stanley Rice
C. A. Alington.
M, i 1 Je33, 33—38 c

C

C.
All but blind.
M, i 1 Je33, 53—55 p

C., A. *see* Neruda, P.

Caceres, Esther de
Cantos del Espiritu Santo.
TO, i 3 Jy38, 7 v

Caird, J. B.
Review
[*Pride and passion: Robert Burns,
1759—1796,* by D. Ferguson].
NA, i 1 Au39, 82—86 r

Cairncross, Andrew Scott
The problem of Hamlet
rev. by H. Howarth

Calder-Marshall, Arthur
Editorial.
OO, x 51 F30, 397—402 c
Full fathom five.
LD, i 4 Je37, 6—7 p
New novels

Calder-Marshall, Arthur (cont.)
[*Two leaves and a bud*,
by M. R. Anand; *Phineas Kahn*,
by S. Blumenfeld;
Adam of a new world,
by J. Lindsay;
Here to-day,
by P. Hansford Johnson;
The winding road unfolds,
by T. S. Hope].
LR, iii 4 My37, 238–41 r
Obituary: Clere Trevor James
Herbert Parsons, 1908–1931.
OO, xi 55 Je31, 138–40 c
Pickle my bones.
NS, ii 6 D36, 419–25 p
Propaganda and aesthetics
[*The land of plenty*,
by R. Cantwell;
Shadow over Spennylam,
by F. W. Lister;
No pockets in a shroud,
by H. McCoy;
Night outlasts the whippoorwill,
by S. North].
LR, iii 5 Je37, 300–302 r
Review
[*The daring young man on the
flying trapeze*, by W. Saroyan;
Story in America, 1933–34,
ed. by W. Burnett and M. Foley;
The maker of signs,
by W. Burnett].
NS, ii 3 Je35, 237–38 r
Review
[*The grammar of love*,
by I. Bunin].
NS, ii 3 Je35, 240 r
Review
[*Proletarian literature in the U.S.:
an anthology*].
NS, ii 8 A36, 637–38 r
Review
[*Progress of stories*,
by L. Riding].
NS, ii 8 A36, 638–39 r
Romains and Dos Passos.
LR, ii 16 J37, 874–81 c
Roosevelt and labour.
LR, iii 15 A38, 901–4 c
The sense of sin; Poems.
OO, x 51 F30, 414–18, 420 p, v
The swan.
NS, i 1 F34, 24–26 p
The wild Morisco.
OO, x 52 My30, 503–13 c
The changing scene
rev. by J. L. Grant; E. Waugh
A date with a duchess
rev. by E. Waugh
Kneel to the rising sun
rev. by G. West
Pie in the sky
rev. by J. Lindsay

22

Callan, Norman
Teaching poetry.
T, 18 Je39, 54–58 c

Calvert, James
Asides from filming:
Catalonia 1937.
LR, iii 14 M38, 857–59 c
L'autre grande illusion.
LR, iii 14 M38, 853–54 c

Calvert, Raymond
Sing in silence.
NS, ii 1 F35, 22–26 p

Cameron, John Norman
Advertising.
EP, 3 Sp37, 255–58 c
Answers to an enquiry.
NV, 11 Oc34, 15 p
Four poems,
NV, 4 Jy33, 6–8 v
Homiletic studies: on generosity.
EP, 3 Sp37, 63–65 p
Poems.
EP, 3 Sp37, 138–39 v
Nostalgia for death;
Forgive me sire.
NV, 16 Ag35, 8–9 v
Three poems.
NV, 5 Oc33, 13–14 v
Three poems.
NV, 20, A36, 14 v
Two poems.
NV, 7 F34, 9–10, v
Two poems.
NV, 9 Je34, 2–3 v
Two poems.
NV, 12 D34, 3–4 v
The unfinished race.
NV, 6 D33, 5 v
The winter house
rev. by K. Allott; G. Grigson
see also Rimbaud, A.

Cameron, Mary *pseud.*
Merrily I go to hell
rev. by A. D. Hawkins

Cameron-Douglas, Jean
Warlocks.
FB, iii 7 25N37, 27–28 p

Cammaerts, Emile
Guido Gezelle.
CA, 7 Je31, 218–23 c

Campbell, David A. S.
Murrumbidgee matins.
FB, iii 7 25N37, 24 v
from Outback.
PP, 6 D38, 10 v

Campbell, Dominica M.

The pagoda of our lady of
dreams.
CA, 3 Oc30, 60–62 p

Campbell, Don
Moonlight in an abbey.
DD, viii 29 Su31, 56 v

Campbell, Ignatius Roy Dunnachie
Andalusian corn;
The people's army.
RR, 8 J39, [6] v
Answers to an enquiry.
NV, 11 Oc34, 14 p
The singer.
RR, 9 A39, [20] v
Adamastor rev. by S. Spender
Flowering rifle
rev. by
NV, i 2 My39, 52; R. Todd
The Georgiad
rev. by H. G. Porteus;
J. H. Whyte

Campbell, J. L.
The sword of light [by D. Ryan].
NA, i 1 Au39, 86–88 r

Campbell, J. R.
Trotsky's 'Explanations'
[*The case of Leon Trotsky*].
LR, iii 11 D37, 685–88 r

Campbell, M.
Duke street rev. by G. West

Campbell, R. M.
Hospital in Melbourne.
NO, i 3 F34, 332–33 v

Canayenne, Jean
Death by misadventure.
TO, i 1 J38, 23–24 p

Candlin, Clara M.
From the Chinese.
DD, xi 47 S–Oc34, 81 v

Cankar, Isidor
Art and the age.
EQ, i 3 N34, 194–96 c

Cantwell, Robert
The land of plenty
rev. by A. Calder-Marshall

Capocci, Valentina *see*
Deledda, G.

Capon, Eric
Dream of childhood
[*The challenge of childhood*,
by J. Wicksteed].
LR, ii 12 S36, 663 r

Card, Maurice
John Jenkins.
TO, ii 5 J39, 7–9 c

Carlton, Grace
Joy and sympathy.
DD, x 38 M–A33, 33 v
Moods.
DD, ix 35 S–Oc32, 81 v

Carlyle, Thomas
It happened before: 1831.
LR, iii 4 My37, 200 p

Carnevali, Emanuel
Excerpt from autobiography.
K, i 1 17N39, 16–17 p
Mother.
SV, 3 W38, 39–40 p

Carpenter, Maurice
Dove.
J, 1 J36, 14 v
Sleep turning.
PL, i 2 A39, [9–11] v
We ask for life.
LR, iii 1 F37, 30 v
A Welsh girl.
LR, iii 6 Jy37, 340 v

Carpenter, Miles
Ballad of a volunteer;
Ballad of a new life.
PP, 8 F39, 6, 12–13 v
England's conscience.
PP, 6 D38, 3–4 v
Extract from a Ballad of
three bob.
PP, 11 My39, 16–17 v
Four pilgrims.
PP, 10 A39, 8 v
The key.
PP, 15 N39, 6 v
Parley voo.
PP, 3 S38, 18–19 v
The three crows.
PP, 1 Jy38, 13–14 v
Youth and poetry.
PP, 10 A39, 3–4 c

Carr, Edward Hallett
Karl Marx
rev. by F. Lafitte; H. L. Perkoff

Carr, Richard Comyns
Mythology and hygiene.
F, 2 Je30, 114–20 c
Running around in circles.
F, 4 D30, 35–39 c

Carré, E. F.
You have forgotten; Rest in peace.
DD, x 40 Jy–Ag33, 70 v

Carrick, Leonard
Cinema.
IP, i 1 6A39, 7–8 c

Carrington, Hugh
Te Kaikoura, High Chief
and magician.
RR, 9 A39, [18–20] p

Carswell, Catherine
Apocalypse and D. H. Lawrence.
MS, ii 2 Jy31, 111–17 c
Encyclopedia Scotica.
LR, ii 14 N36, 765–67 c
England, D. H. Lawrence
and Russia.
I, i 2/3 15S31, 46–50 c
Envoy.
PR, 3 19F35, 6 v
The mother.
MS, ii 1 A31, 20 v
Review
[*The letters of Robert Burns*,
ed. by J. de L. Ferguson].
MS, ii 4 J32, 349–51 r
The savage pilgrimage
rev. by J. P. Hogan

Carswell, Donald
Henry Mackenzie.
MS, ii 2 Jy31, 136–40 c
The Scottish universities and
some other considerations.
MS, i 4 J31, 54–57 c
Why Scott is neglected.
MS, iii 2 Ag32, 111–13 c

Carswell, Donald *and*
Carswell, Catherine
The Scots week-end
rev. by R. Todd

Carter, Barbara Barclay *tr.*
The voyage of Ulysses.
CA, 1 Ag30, 13 v
Old nurse rev. by M. Evans
see also Dante Alighieri

Carter, Daphne
Sunday night.
JG, 66 Au38, [36] v

Carter, Frederick
A drawing.
SM, 2 S31, 50 i

Carter, Frederick Albert
Aat i-walkin'.
JG, 17 Su31, [24–25] v
Abyssinia.
JG, 39 W36, [4] v
After t'sewin' meetin'.
HR, 4 1931, 17–21 d
Changed allegiance.

JG, 16 Sp31, [10] v
Elegy on Lesbia's linnet.
JG, 14 Au30, [22] v
Ideal and real.
JG, 18 Au31, [22–23] v
Marche funebre.
JG, 13 Su30, [24] v
The postman.
JG, 23 W32, [24] v
A tenor voice.
JG, 20 Sp32, [27] v
To a poet.
JG, 15 W30, [29] v
To a poet-friend.
JG, 25 Su33, [9] v
To an Irish singer.
JG, 34 Au35, [32] v

Carter, H. A.
Another day.
NS, ii 2 A35, 143–47 p
Saturday night.
NW, ns2 Sp39, 156–62 p

Carter, Rose A.
Approaching blindness.
DD, x 42 N–D33, 103 v
The brook.
DD, xi 47 S–Oc34, 82 v

Carus, Dorothy
The brothers.
P, 5 1939, 59–82 p
Brown flood.
P, 6 1939, 25–36 p

Case, R. W. H.
Baht 'at.
HR, 6 1933, 55–56 p
Easter.
JG, 14 Au30, [29] v

Case against the sexual impulse.
LR, ii 3 D35, 119–21 c

Case of Leon Trotsky
rev. by J. R. Campbell

Casson, Hugh
Cambridge clocks don't strike.
ND, 22 25N37, 29 c
The demolition of Oxford.
ND, 3 15Jy37, 27–28 c
Design for sea-faring.
ND, 17 21Oc37, 32–33 c
Good building and bad theatre.
ND, 11 9S37, 27 c
Roadhouse Tudor.
ND, 8 19Ag37, 26–27 c

Casson, Stanley
Paul Nash.
OO, xi 56 N31, 209–11 c

Casson, Stanley (cont.)
Recent architectural additions
at Oxford.
NO, ii 2 J35, 126—36 c

Cassou, Jean
Letter to cousin Mary,
tr. by R. Lehmann.
NW, 2 Au36, 204—9 p
Paris congress speech.
LR, i 11 Ag35, 475 c

Castle, C. B.
Industrial Easter.
LD, ii 1 Oc37, 23 p

Castle, Phyllis
Wood engraving.
F, 1 F30, 55 i
Wood engraving.
F, 2 Je30, 97 i

Castle, Robert
Bal masqué.
B, 2 W38, 6 v
Girl Eva; Analysis of a love.
FB, v 1 F39, 2—4 p, v
Girl into hare.
LD, ii 2 D37, 22—24 p

Cathie, Cameron
Close of day.
C, ii 50 5D36, 186—87 p
Nothing matters.
C, i 19 11A36, 149—50 p

Catlin, George Edward Gordon
Manifesto: the book of the
Federation of Progressive
Societies and individuals.
TC, vi 36 S34, 374—76 r

Caudwell, Christopher *pseud.*
Three poems.
NV, i 1 J39, 14—16 v
To Aldous Huxley.
LR, iii 11 D37, 657—61 c
Illusion and reality
rev. by W. H. Auden;
D. I. Dunnett; D. Garman;
G. M. Turnell
Studies in a dying culture
rev. by A. Darbyshire

Causton, Bernard
How and why *Dope?*
00, xii 57 F32, 66—67 c
Manifesto.
DE, 1 New year 1932, 2—4 c

Cavalcanti, Alberto
French scissors.
TO, ii 5 J39, 31—32 c

Introducing E. L. T. Mesens.
LB, 1 A38, 19 c

Cave, Angela
Love-in-the-moon.
DD, vii 27 N—D30, 454 v

Cecil, David
National Portrait Gallery.
F, 2 Je30, 82—87 p

Cecil, N. K.
Head noises
[*Poems*, by G. Barker].
LR, i 9 Je35, 383 r
Socialism and psychotherapy.
LR, ii 5 F36, 208—12 c
What Marx can teach Freud
[*The new road to progress*,
by S. D. Schmalhausen].
LR, ii 3 D35, 138—40 r

Cecil, Robert
School and religion.
OB, i 3 W34, 18—21 c

Celine, Louis Ferdinand
Bagatelles pour un masseuse
rev. by G. M. Turnell

Cendrars, Blaise
The new head, tr. by C. G.
CV, 1 Su34, 10—11 p

Cernuda, Luis
Federico Garcia Lorca.
LR, iii 16 My38, 976—81 c

Chadwick, G. W. St. J.
Green poet.
FB, ii 5 5M37, 36—37 p

Chadwick, Mary
Adolescent girlhood
rev. by
TC, iv 19 S32, 28

Chadwick, Tom
Derby day.
P, 6 1939, 144—45, i
Village in Cumberland.
P, 5 1939, 178 i
Wayside laundry.
P, 5 1939, 58 i

Chait-parab song,
tr. by W. V. Grigson.
NV, 22 S36, 13—15 v

Chamberlain, Brenda
The harvesters.
WR, ii 3 Oc39, 148 i

Chamberlain, Brenda *and*

Petts, R. John
From other hills.
WR, ii 4 N39, 197—205 p, i

Chamberlain, Peter
Fanciful.
NS, ii 1 F35, 60—64 p
Sing holiday
rev. by E. Waugh
What the sweet hell
rev. by E. J. O'Brien

Champion, Alan
Clarinet serenade.
FB, iii 6 21Oc37, 19 v

Champness, H. M.
Giurgiu.
CM, i 4 Sp34, 173—74 p

Chamson, André
Metamorphoses of the snow,
tr. by J. Rodker.
NW, ns1 Au38, 138—46 p
My enemy, tr. by J. Rodker.
NW, 1 Sp36, 73—86 p
Paris Congress speech.
LR, i 11 Ag35, 470 c
The power of words.
NW, 4 Au37, 7—17 p
Tabusse, tr. by J. Rodker.
NW, 5 Sp38, 84—102 p
Tabusse and the powers.
NW, ns2 Sp39, 83—94 p
The white beastie,
tr. by J. Rodker.
NW, 2 Au36, 218—26 p

Chance, Janet
Comment on the basis of the
Sexology group.
TC, iv 21 N32, 21—22 c
Fools, this way
[*The fool hath said,*
by C. A. Alington].
TC, v 29 Jy33, 310—13 r
A modern sex charter:
speech at High Leigh conference.
TC, iv 20 Oc32, 30—31 c
Review
[*Yours unfaithfully,*
by M. Malleson].
TC, v 27 My33, 192—93 r

Chapman, Edward
Jess Oakroyd.
HR, 5 1932, 24 c

Chapman, Guy *ed.*
Vain glory rev. by E. Waugh

Chapman, N. E. W.
Book of Life.
FB, iii 6 21Oc37, 15—16 p

Motive.
FB, iii 7 25N37, 26 p

Chapman, Penistan
Two stories.
NS, ii 7 F36, 488—96 p

Chapman, Robert William
Where 1937?
FB, ii 4 25J37 15—16 c

Chappelow, Eric Barry Wilfred
Autumnal.
JG, 22 Au32, [21] v
Beauty will come again.
JG, 28 Sp34, [16] v
Carol.
JG, 15 W30, [21—22] v
Clarion.
DD, vii 27 N—D30, 455 v
The dead knight.
JG, 66 Au38, [18] v
Dedicatory to an author.
JG, 18 Au31, [25] v
Dei carmen naturalis.
JG, 42 Au37, [32—33] v
Farewell awhile.
JG, 27 W33, [18] v
Fons spei.
JG, 63 W37, [19] v
Harvesters' hymn to Demeter.
DD, vii 27 N—D30, 452—54 v
In a green shade.
JG, 67 W38, [32—33] v
Invocation to song.
JG, 29 Su34, [24—25] v
Joy and the year.
DD, ix 31 J—F32, 12 v
The knight.
JG, 35 W35, [23—24] v
Lo, if all the joy.
JG, 16 Sp31, [14] v
Musagetes.
JG, 17 Su31, [8] v
Myself when young.
JG, 33 Su35, [21—23] v
O sweet new-comer.
JG, 64 Sp38, [28—29] v
Parnassus.
JG, 26 Au33, [19] v
The phoenix.
JG, 69 Su39, [18—19] v
Praeterita.
JG, 41 Su37, [18] v
Quid prodest?
JG, 71 W39, [15] v
The rose bower.
JG, 30 Au34, [16—17] v
St. Katherine's, Exeter.
JG, 37 Su36, [19] v
Sea idyll.
JG, 38 Au36, [6] v
The ship of dreams.
JG, 25 Su33, [23—25] v

Sir Hugh in Barbary.
JG, 21 Su32, [24—26] v
Song; Spring.
DD, ix 32 M—A32, 26, 30 v
Spring's aubade.
JG, 32 Sp35, [20—21] v
Spring's returning.
JG, 24 Sp33, [18—19] v
Summer.
DD, ix 34 Jy—Ag32, 56 v
Summons to song.
JG, 40 Sp37, [23] v
Sunt lacrymae rerum.
JG, 39 W36, [7] v
Threnody: in memoriam patris.
JG, 65 Su38, [22, 25—26] v
Timor mortis conturbat me.
DD, vii 26 S—Oc30, 409 v
To any statesman of the old
school.
DD, ix 35 S—Oc32, 77 v
Up Widcombe way; Bath.
JG, 34 Au35, [20—21] v
When Helen sailed.
JG, 20 Sp32, [16] v
Winter.
JG, 23 W32, [6] v

Char, René
The raving messengers of
frantic poetry,
tr. by D. Gascoyne.
CPP, 2 Je36, 31 v

Charlton, Joan
Hearth.
P, 4 1938, 169 v

Charlton, Lionel Evelyn Oswald
Militarising a nation
[*The nation at war*,
by E. Ludendorff].
LR, ii 13 Oc36, 723 r
Mutiny
[*Mutiny*, by T. H. Wintringham].
LR, ii 15 D36, 848 r

Charman, G. H.
Poem; Sonnet.
T, 17 A39, 3—4 v

Charques, Richard Denis
*Contemporary literature and
social revolution*
rev. by D. MacLean; A. C. Sewter.
Soviet education
rev. by M. Roberts

Chatterjee, Sarat Chandra
The drought, tr. by S. Sinha.
LR, ii 12 S36, 628—34 p

Chave, Owen
Malleus hymnorum.
LT, i 10 D36, 16—21 p

Chavée, Achille
L'instruction obligatoire.
LB, 10 F39, 18—19 v

Chavette, Eugène
Guillotined by persuasion,
tr. by C. Duff.
TC, vi 34 M34, 240—45 d

Chen, Jack
Modern Chinese pictorial art.
LR, iii 10 N37, 603—5 c

Ch'en, Shih-Hsiang *see* Acton, H.

Cherry, Graham
Lyric.
JG, 71 W39, [12—13] v
Matched.
JG, 69 Su39, [15] v

Chesterton, Frances
The cradle of the winds.
CA, 8 1931, 248—49 v

Chesterton, Gilbert Keith
A note on Father Brown.
HR, 7 1934, 32 c
A note on the vulgar tongue.
CA, 4 N30, 89—91 c

Chia Wu *see* Chou Wen

Ch'ien Chung-shu
Review
[*Modern Chinese poetry*,
tr. by H. Acton and Ch'en,
Shih-Hsiang].
PR, 15 1M36, 21—22 r

Chien Yuan-chang
Poem.
TO, i 3 Jy38, 22 v

Childe, Wilfred Rowland
The angel of Loidis.
JG, 13 Su30, [14—15] v
Aryana.
JG, 70 Au39, [5] v
Assumption.
JG, 38 Au36, [5] v
The beggar's prayer.
JG, 32 Sp35, [8] v
The candle of Spring.
JG, 36 Sp36, [6] v
Chanson gothique.
JG, 26 Au33, [22—23] v
The child with the white
convolvulus.
JG, 42 Au37, [14] v

Childe, Wilfred Rowland (cont.)
The children in the snow.
JG, 28 Sp34, [12—13] v
Chrysocrystallinos.
JG, 67 W38, [26] v
Cosmic muse.
JG, 16 Sp31, [19—20] v
Czech legend.
JG, 17 Su31, [12] v
Dawn in Avalon.
JG, 69 Su39, [14—15] v
Delight in fountains.
DD, ix 33 My—Je32, 34 v
The face of the spouse.
CA, 11 1932, 352 v
Friedrich von Orlande.
JG, 37 Su36, [28] v
The friend.
DD, xi 48 N—D34, 101 v
The goldfinches.
DD, ix 34 Jy—Ag32, 53 v
The gothic rose.
CA, 8 1931, 233 v
Haworth in May.
JG, 33 Su35, [13] v
Herb robert.
JG, 40 Sp37, [8, 11] v
The heritage of April.
JG, 64 Sp38, [8] v
Die hummel Blume.
CA, 2 S30, 28 v
Images of sunset.
DD, ix 36 N—D32, 91 v
In the Bismarck garten.
JG, 31 W34, [11] v
Isis.
JG, 63 W37, [7] v
Landscape in faëry.
DD, ix 31 J—F32, 4 v
The legend of Yann Salacin.
CA, 5 M31, 123—24 v
The little kingdom.
JG, 35 W35, [5—6] v
Little Prince Errivalle.
JG, 18 Au31, [13] v
The little trees on Woodhouse
moor.
JG, 34 Au35, [27] v
Mountain spring.
JG, 20 Sp32, [20] v
The nesting robins,
JG, 24 Sp33, [19] v
The new poet laureate as
theologian
[The trial of Jesus,
by J. Masefield].
CA, 2 S30, 26—27 r
Noon in the orchard.
JG, 25 Su33, [13] v
A note on the poetry of
Walter de la Mare.
CA, 4 N30, 92—93 c
Notes on modern poetry;
In the valley of the Neckar.

CA, 3 Oc30, 41—44 c, v
Pelerinage,
JG, 15 W30, [24—25] v
Peregrinus.
CA, 9 1931, 284 v
The philosophy of Coventry
Patmore's poetry.
CA, 7 Je31, 201—4 c
The plainsong of the flowers.
JG, 65 Su38, [6—7] v
The poetry of John Masefield.
CA, 9 1931, 281—82 c
The poetry of Lascelles
Abercrombie.
CA, 5 M31, 120—22 c
Prayer to the Madonna of the
poor.
JG, 23 W32, [5] v
Rain.
JG, 41 Su37, [14] v
Sea garden.
HR, 4 1931, 31 v
Siesta.
JG, 14 Au30, [19] v
Snow country legend.
JG, 71 W39, [11] v
Song of the virgins concerning
the god of doves.
DD, vii 30 Au31, 84 v
The south country.
JG, 30 Au34, [10—11] v
Stella Matutina.
JG, 21 Su32, [7—8] v
Strasburg.
JG, 22 Au32, [19—20] v
Sunday in the Black Forest.
CA, 1 Ag30, 21 v
The thorn.
JG, 29 Su34, [6—7] v
Timble; Dichter in Wald.
HR, 7 1934, 36, 64 v
The tree that was not cut down.
JG, 39 W36, [27—29] p
West Riding.
HR, 6 1933, 41 v
Wharfedale.
JG, 66 Au38, [17] v
The window of winter morning.
JG, 68 Sp39, [14] v
Winter morning.
JG, 19 W31, [5] v

Childs, Marquis William
Sweden: the middle way
rev. by D. Hubback

Chilman, Eric
A picture by Watteau.
DD, vii 27 N—D30, 430—31 v

Chirico, Giorgio de see
De Chirico, Giorgio

Chisholm, Hugh
Ode.
NV, i 1 J39, 8—12 v
Poem.
NV, 28 J38, 7 v
While in April.
LD, ii 2 D37, 22 v

Chou Wen
The three of them,
tr. by Chia Wu and N. Wales.
NW, 5 Sp38, 174—81 p

Christian, Christopher
Reproach.
V, 5 F30, 251 v

Christian, John
Shakespeare — imagery and the
poet's mind: Hamlet in particular.
LT, i 3 My36, 12, 14—16, 58 c

Christopher, Barbara
Joy.
DD, ix 35 S—Oc32, 80 v
Twenty-one.
DD, vii 26 S—Oc30, 389 v
Summer's requiem.
DD, x 40 Jy—Ag33, 72 v

Chubb, Ralph
Morning — the shepherd boy's
song.
I, i 1 15Je31, 10 v, i
The mystic tree.
I, i 2/3 15S31, 45 v, i
Poetry.
I, i 2/3 15S31, 68—71 c
The visionary: invocation.
I, i 1 15Je31, 32 v

Church, Richard
The need; Assurance.
T, 3 A37, [4—5] v
Twelve noon
rev. by G. Knowland

Citrine, Walter
I search for truth in Russia
rev. by G. Graham

Clare, John
Sketches in the life
rev. by R. H. Goodman

Clare, Peter
Panorama.
PE, 3 Oc 36, 74—77 p
Spenglerian mood.
PE, 2 S36, 38—40 p

Clark, Colin
Britain under socialism

[*Britain without capitalists*].
LR, ii 15 D36, 841—42 r

Clark, E. J. Anthony
Epitaph.
FB, iii 9 6Je38, 73 v
Image.
FB, iii 7 25N37, 28 v
In and out.
FB, iii 9 6Je38, 80 p
Lebensfreude; Roman mass.
FB, iii 7 25N37, 40 v
The need for elephants.
FB, iii 7 25N37, 30 p
Quarrel.
FB, iii 9 6Je38, 66 v

Clark, Edward
Alan Bush's new concerto
broadcast.
LR, iii 15 A38, 933—34 c

Clark, Frederick Le Gros
The new literature for children
[*Palaces on Monday*,
by M. Fischer;
Turning night into day,
by M. Ilin].
LR, iii 10 N37, 632—33 r
Poverty, health and war
[*Poverty and public health*,
by G. C. M. M'Gonigle and
J. Kirby].
LR, ii 11 Ag36, 581—83 r
Science and the people.
LR, ii 13 Oc36, 678—79 c
Between two men
rev. by J. Sommerfield

Clark, Kenneth
Shall we return to nature.
NO, i 1 My33, 19—23 c

Clark, Laurence
Mountains in Argolis; Hysteria;
Persephone in Hell.
CM, i 4 Sp34, 171—72 v
Prelude.
PL, i 1 F39, [9] v
Rain at night; Song; The wave;
October snow.
SM, i 3 Au33, 134—35 v

Clark, Leonard
Love poem.
PQ, i 1 Sp39, 15 v

Clarke, Austin
Poet and artist.
AW, Su39, 8—9 c

Clarke, D.
Hunger.
NW, ns2 Sp39, 145—55 p

Clarke, Egerton
The gardener.
CA, 4 N30, 94 v
The hill of trees.
CA, 1 Ag30, 4 v
Lauds.
CA, 8 1931, 252—53 v
The London street.
CA, 2 S30, 27 v
Sonnet for Adrienne.
CA, 3 Oc30, 41 v
They.
CA, 12 1932, 378 v

Clarke, Mollie
Three stories.
NS, ii 3 Je35, 214—20 p

Clarke, Roger
The adolescence of the bourgeoisie.
TC, iv 22 D32, 4—6 c
Communism and the churches.
TC, iv 20 Oc32, 6—8 c
The peril of politics.
TC, vi 31 S—Oc33, 43—46 c
Recognition.
TC, ii 12 F32, 7—9 c
Sermon.
TC, ii 7 S31, 10 v

Clarke, Victor
Canal.
P, 4 1938 60 i
Tree and plough.
P, 6 1939, 90 i

Clavering, Basil
New York — an impression.
LT, i 8 Oc36, 14—16 p

Cleage, David G.
The wife who loved her husband.
FB, iii 8 3M38, 62—63 p

Clephane, Irene
Towards sex freedom
rev. by P. Polson

Cleugh, John *see* Alberti, R.;
Anders, G.; Arconada, C. M.;
Huppert, H.; Kantorowicz, A.;
Leonhard, R.; Petersen, J.;
Uhse, B.

Clonmore, William Cecil James
Philip John Paul Howard *Lord
Pope Pius XI and world
peace* rev. by E. Waugh

Cloud, Yvonne
Criticising the left.
NV, i 1 J39, 29—30 c
Two styles
[*Dead star's light*,

by E. Connor; *Champion*,
by J. Hilton].
LR, iii 16 My38, 1016—17 r

Clout, Colin *pseud*.
Credo.
CL, i 4 Su34, ii v

Cluer, Elisabeth
Bolero.
P, 3 1938 144—79 p

Clyder, Peter
The new German university.
TU, 4 F35, 19—24 c

Clynes, John Robert
Memoirs
rev. by M. Muggeridge

Coates, J. B.
About it and about.
TC, iv 20 Oc32, 17—19 c

Coates, William Paton *and*
Coates, Zelda Kahan
*Armed intervention in Russia,
1918—1922* rev. by D. Garman
The second five-year plan
rev. by CL, ii 1 Au34, 30

Cob *pseud*.
Verse.
LR, i 8 My35, 296 v

Coburn, Oliver
Moscow and Berlin.
K, i 1 17N39, 23 v

Cochrane, Francis
Colonel Popinjay.
ND, 4 22Jy37, 20 v

Cockburn, J. M.
Maisters and men.
MS, v 3 Oc34, 141—149 p

Cockin, M. H. Battle
Dolour,
FB, i 4 4F36, 10 v
Poem.
FB, iii 6 21Oc37, 19 v

Cocteau, Jean
Monte Carlo lady,
tr. by C. Fitzgibbon.
Y, i 1 M39, 8—10 v

Coghill, Nevill
Homage to pioneers.
R, i 3 A34, 6—7 c
Logical meditations on the
boat race.

Coghill, Nevill (cont.)
LD, i 3 My37, 15—16 v
The masque of Satan.
LD, i 4 Je37, 12—13, 15 v
Observations on Mass-
Observation.
LD, ii 3 F38, 7—8 v
The star system.
R, i 2 F34, 6 c
The tapster's tale.
LD, i 2 M37, 9—13 v
What I think about Oxford.
LD, i 2 J37, 2—3 v

Cohen-Portheim, Paul
The spirit of London
rev. by A. L. Morton

Cohn, Gerald
Hunger and terror.
ST, i 2 A33, 13—14 p

Cohn, Norman
Poem.
RM, 1 Je34, 16 v

Coke, Percival Hale
Finis.
JG, 41 Su37, [29] v
Illusion.
JG, 37 Su36, [29] v
Song.
JG, 40 Sp37, [16] v
The temples of Atlantis.
JG, 33 Su35, [5—6] v
To — — —.
JG, 39 W36, [15] v
The way home.
JG, 35 W35, [14] v
We heard Pan piping.
JG, 34 Au35, [8] v

Cohnen, Ilse
Gustave Mahler.
LT, i 11 J37, 46—47 c

Cole, George Douglas Howard
A critique of British communism.
TU, 1 1933, 7—11 c
An exhibition of 'left' history.
LR, iii 7 Ag37, 408—14 c
Economic tracts for the times
rev. by H. Nussbaum
*The intelligent man's guide
through world chaos*
rev. by H. Nussbaum
The people's front
rev. by H. Fyfe
What Marx really meant
rev. by W. N. Warbey

Cole, George Douglas Howard
and **Cole**, Margaret

The condition of Britain
rev. by J. K[emp]

Cole, Herbert
Illustration.
SM, 5 [1934] supp. i
Salome.
SM, 4 [1933?] supp. i

Cole, Hugh
Review
[*1919*, by J. Dos Passos].
TC, iii 18 Ag32, 23—24 r

Cole, L.
Contentment.
JG, 68 Sp39, [23] v
Freedom.
JG, 67 W38, [12—13] v
Here or there.
JG, 70 Au39, [30] v
March.
JG, 69 Su39, [19] v
The owl.
JG, 66 Au38, [12] v

Cole, Margaret *see* **Cole**, G-D. H.

Coleman, Emily Holmes- *see*
Holmes-Coleman, Emily

Coleridge, Samuel Taylor
Coleridge on imagination,
ed. by I. A. Richards
rev. by H. House
The political thought . . .
sel. by R. J. White
rev. by G. Grigson

Coles, S. F. A.
Dawn at Carthage.
I, i 4 15D31, 108 v
Van Gogh in the Borinage.
I, i 2/3 15S31, 78—81 p

Collard, Lorna Keeling
The cross.
JG, 15 W30, [8—9] v
In memoriam.
JG, 21 Su32, [20—21] v
January music.
JG, 17 Su31, [26] v
Peace.
JG, 22 Au32, [18] v
Two triolets.
JG, 14 Au30, [14—15] v
White ladies.
JG, 13 Su30, [19] v

Collier, John
The frog prince.
Y, i 2 My39, 52—59 p
Possibly a banana.
CPP, 8 D36, 154—57 p

Collins, H. P.
Arnold Bennett.
TC, i 3 My31, 22—23 c

Collis, Robert
Review
[*Ulster and the British Empire,
1939*, by H. Harrison].
NA, i 1 Au39, 86—88 r

Colquhoun, Ithell
The double-village.
LB, 7 D38, 23 p
The moths.
LB, 10 F39, 11 p
What do I need to paint
a picture?
The volcano; The echoing bruise.
LB, 17 15 Je39, 13, 15—18 p

Coltham, Stephen
Parable of a poet.
C, ii 44 24Oc36, 132 p

Common, Jack
Seven shifts rev. by J. Lipton

Confucius *see* Pound, E. L.
Ta hiao

Conner, Rearden
I am death
rev. by A. L. Morton

Connolly, Cyril
The house of Arquelus.
ND, 7 12Ag37, 8—9; 10 2 S37,
8, 10—11; 26 23D37, 12—15 p

Connor, Elizabeth
[*pseud.* Una Troy]
Dead star's light rev. by Y. Cloud

Conquest, R.
The agents.
T, 14 D38, 125 v
Sonnet.
T, 10 My38, 41 v

Conroy, Jack
The disinherited
rev. by C. Ashleigh

Constanduros, Mabel
A foreword to
'The poison flower'.
R, i 2 F34, 11 c

Conybeare, Anthony
Evening fen mist;
In the highlands.
CM, i 4 Sp34, 168 v

28

Conze, Edward
The scientific method of thinking
rev. by T. A. Jackson
Spain today rev. by V. Ackland

Cook, Eric
Dickens the radical
[*Charles Dickens*
by T. A. Jackson].
LR, iii 5 Je37, 304—6 r

Cooke, Alistair
New York letter.
ND, 12 16S37, 18—19;
16 14Oc37, 24—25;
20 11N37, 17—18 p

Cooke, Charles
Triple jump.
NS, i 2 A34, 105—14 p
Water rat.
NS, i 5 Oc34, 394—404 p

Cooke, Dorian
Experience.
T, 15/16 F39, 156—57 v
Gethsemane poem.
PL, i 2 A39, [26] v
Heathen hill.
PL, i 1 F39, [29—30] v
The mask of inferno.
SV, 4 Su39, 8—11 p
My little monster.
SV, 2 Au38, 28 v
Poem.
SV, 6 Au39, 23 v
Poem.
VS, i 3 D38—F39, 9 v
Poems.
SV, 3 W38, 31—32 v
Poems.
SV, 4 Su39, 4—5 v
The priest and the server.
SV, 3 W38, 3—4 p

Cooke, Ralph *tr. see*
Beaumont, Germaine; Lafage,
Leon

Coombe, Frances
Avalon.
DD, x 42 N—D33, 98—99 v
The greenwood.
DD, x 39 My—Je33 55 v
Poem.
DD, x 38 M—A33, 30 v

Coombes, Bert Lewis
Better off.
LR, iii 14 M38, 869—72 p
The flame.
NW, 3 Sp37, 131—34 p
Machine man.

NW, 5 Sp38, 193—195 p
Miner.
LR, ii 15 D36, 828—29 p
Twenty tons of coal.
NW, ns3 C39, 159—74 p

Coombes, Leslie
Who dares to be free?
PP, 15 N39, 5 v

Cooper, H.
Scene from 'In memoriam'.
LR, ii 3 D35, 97—104 d

Cooper, Lettice Ulpha
Overture to birthday.
HR, 6 1933, 51—53 p

Cooper, Martin du Pré
The future of music.
NO, i 2 N33, 221—27 c
Rimsky-Korsakoff.
OO, xi 56 N31, 200—208;
xii 57 F32, 30—41 c
'That strain again'.
OO, x 52 My30, 531—36 c

Cooper, T. Alstead
After dinner.
C, ii 31 25Jy36, 22—23 p
The chimney,
C, ii 36 29Ag36, 63 p
Cottage and chickens.
C, i 24 16My36, 187 p
Lament.
C, iii 55 9J37, 12 v
The man and the pit.
C, ii 46 7N36, 152 p
Rivers.
DD, xi 48 N—D34, 103 v

Coppard, Alfred Edgar
Elegy.
HR, 6 1933 35 v
Poem.
J, 1 J36, 8 v
Polly Oliver rev. by L. A. Pavey

Corbett, Brian
Poem 60.
C, iii 57 23J37, 30—31 v

Corbett, Mary K.
Editorial.
LS, i 2 My34, 3—4 c
Perish the Jew!
LS, i 2 My34, 62—68 c

Corbett, Mary K. *and*
Morrison, B.
Manifesto.
LS, i 1 F34, 65—68 p

Corby, Herbert W.

All-in.
T, 3 A37, [5] v
Arabesque for Beryl.
C, i 17 28M36, 132 p
Poem.
T, 5 S37, [14] v

Corey, G. H.
A way toward revolution
[*Thirty pieces,* by S. Salt].
CV, 5 M36, [24—26] r

Corey, Lewis
Planning in the U.S.A.
TC, vi 31 S—Oc33, 16—22;
vi 32 N33, 102—9 c

Corfield, Helen
Beautiful thoughts.
DD, xi 48 N—D34, 102 v
Easter anew.
DD, ix 33 My—Je33, 47 v
Poem.
DD, x 41 S—Oc33, 80 v
Silver rain.
DD, x 42 N—D42, 106 v

Corke, Barry
The condemned man;
PQ, i 1 Sp39 21—22 v

Cormack, George
Holiday.
JG, 65 Su38, [20—21] v

Cornford, John
Full moon at Tierz:
before the storming of Huesca.
LR, iii 2 M37, 69—70 v
Left?
CL, i 2 W33, 25—29 c
A letter from Aragon.
LR, ii 14 N36, 771 v
The struggle for power in
western Europe.
CL, i 3 Sp34, 49—58 c
Three poems.
NW, 4 Au37, 36—39 v
John Cornford, 1913—1937.
LR, iii 2 M37, 67—68 c

Coska *pseud.*
The castle.
JG, 66 Au38, [16] v
Desperate interview.
JG, 67 W38, [24—25] v

Cosmo *pseud.*
Not spoiling the child.
OB, i 3 Je35, 21—23 c
The Old School: a review
[ed. by G. Greene].
OB, i 3 W34, 45—46 r

Cotterill, Norah
The artistic temperament.
HR, 4 1931 29—30 c
Excursion.
HR, 7 1934, 60—62 p
The roamer.
HR, 5 1932, 53—56 p
Rose of love.
JG, 37 Su36, [23—25] v

Couch, *Sir* Arthur Quiller-
see Quiller-Couch, *Sir* Arthur

Courtauld, Minton
Buttercups;
Letter from England.
CM, i 1 Sp33, 7—9 v
Theodolite.
CL, ii 1 Au34, 29 v
Two poems.
CM, i 3 Au33, 130 v

Covell, Clarice M.
The dream searcher.
JG, 22 Au32, [24—25] v
An interior.
JG, 27 W33, [24—25] v
Undertones.
JG, 18 Au31, [11] v

Coward, Noel
The Quinta Bates.
M, i 1 Je33, 48—49 v
Post mortem
rev. by E. M. Barraud

Cowley, W.
Jesus, Cambridge.
JG, 40 Sp37, [15] v

Cox, Anthony *see* Madge, John

Coxe, Anthony
A job in a million-8.
ND, 8 19Ag37, 16, 18p
Light reading for specialists.
ND, 4 22Jy37, 14—16 p
Navy week.
ND, 6 5Ag37, 28 c

Coxhead, Elizabeth
Charles Chaplin 1936;
Things to avoid
[*Modern times; Things to come*].
LR, ii 6 M36, 274—5 r
Films bear left.
LR, iii 14 M38, 850—51 c
Films speaking English.
NW, ns3 C39, 29—34 c
For work or war?
LR, iii 1 F37, 49 c
Industrial front
[*Men and jobs*].
LR, ii 8 My38, 414 r

The nutrition film
[*Nutrition*].
LR, ii 14 N36, 777 r
Touches reality
[*Today we live*].
LR, iii 8 S37, 506 r
Towards a new Soviet film
[*We from Kronstadt*].
LR, iii 3 A37, 188—89 r
Trials of an empire builder
[*Rhodes of Africa*].
LR, ii 7 A36, 349 r

Cozzens, James Gould
The animal's fair.
P, 2 1938, 121—45 p
Child's play.
P, 1 1938 123—43 p
Son and heir.
P, 5 1939, 155—76 p

Craig, Alec
Adult sex education.
TC, v 28 Je33, 246—48 c
Letter.
TC, ii 11 J32, 28—29 c
Letter.
TC, iii 16 Je32, 25 c
Materialism and revolution.
TC, iv 23 J33, 24—25 c
Poem.
NV, 6 D33, 5—6 v
Review
[*English justice*,
by Solicitor *pseud.*].
TC, iv 22 D32, 26 r
Sexual axiology.
TC, vi 31 S—Oc33, 50—52 c;
vii 32 N33, 109
Soviet law on marriage.
TC, iv 24 F33, 9—11 c
Tactics for reformers.
TC, v 30 Ag33, 375—76 c
Weight the scales.
TC, vi 32 N33, 111 c

Craig, Edward Gordon
A plea for two theatres.
LQ, ii 1 My37, 1—14 c

Craig, J. O.
When Irish eyes are smiling.
FB, iii 6 21Oc37, 13 p

Craig, Maurice James
Elegy on a dying attitude.
FB, v 2 My39, 30 v
King David; W. B. Yeats;
Cloud and rain at Kilbroney.
TH, 1 27J39, 4 p, v
Poem in the worst taste;
Epistle to a friend.
TH, 2 10F39, 2, 4 v
The quiet waters;

Explosion at New forge factory.
TH, 3 24F39, 3—4 p

Craven, Cecily
Prison
[*Walls have mouths*,
by W. F. R. Macartney].
LR, ii 13 Oc36, 712 r

Crawshay-Williams, Eliot
God on the war.
WR, ii 2 S39, 66—76 p

Creighton, Basil
Ariadne.
HR, 7 1934, 58—59 p

Crémieux, Benjamin
The new generation and the
world revolution,
tr. by J. H. Whyte.
MS, vi 1 A35, 54—59 c
On the Scots.
MS, v 3 Oc34, 150—53 c
Inquiètude et reconstruction
rev. by G. Pendle

Creswell, Walter Darcy
The poet's progress
rev. by C. B. Spencer

Crichton, Ronald
An opera by Bernard van Dieren.
FB, i 1 4F36, 19—20 c

Cripps, Arthur Shearly
An Essex road-song.
CA, 2 S30, 28 v
On a mother's centenary
remembrance.
CA, 9 1931, 282—83 v
Stella gentium.
CA, 11 1932, 351 v

Cripps, John *and* Heathcoat-
Amory, P. J.
Fascism and communism at
Oxford.
NO, i 2 N33, 169—85 c

Croce, Benedetto
The defence of poetry
rev. by H. Read

Crockett, Rutherford
A Yorkshire dale village.
HR, 5 1932, 25—29 p

Crockett, Vivian
Mezzomorto
rev. by O. Blakeston

Cronin, Archibald Joseph
The citadel rev. by T. L. Hodgkin

Cronyn, George William
The fool of Venus
rev. by H. de Mouilpied

Crosby, Caresse
Sweet leaves.
DD, viii 30 Au31, 92 v

Cross, Charles
The smoked herring,
tr. by A. L. Lloyd.
CPP, 2 Je36, 33 v

Cross, Elizabeth *ed.*
Letters from an N. C. O. . . .
in Palestine.
LR, iii 3 A37, 152—155 p

Cross, John
Kitty Janson.
LR, ii 15 D36, 820—23 p

Cross, M.
Preparation; Night.
PP, 8 F39, 19 v

Crossman, Richard Howard
Stafford
D. H. Lawrence:
the new internationalism.
F, 5 F31, 67—78 c
The dewpond;
Return from abroad.
F, 4 D30, 41 v
Hitler,
NO, ii 2 J35, 97—112 c
The Labour party and war.
NO, ii 2 My34, 85—94 c
Nekyia by the factory.
F, 2 Je30, 98—99 v
Poem.
F, 4 D30, 7 v
The return.
F, 1 F30, 62 v
Tristan und Isolde;
The sight-seer; Poem.
F, 6 Je31, 183—85 v
The turn of the year.
F, 4 D30, 22—24 v
Two epigrams.
F, 1 F30, 56 v

Crow, John
England in deep water.
ND, 5 29Jy37, 32 p
Ignoring the ball.
ND, 3 15Jy37, 32 c
'The kind that England likes . . .'
ND, 8 19Ag37, 31 c
A night with the eskimos.
ND, 20 11N37, 32 c
A punch from an iron foundry.
ND, 10 2S37, 31 c

Sex and cinders.
ND, 13 23S37, 32 c

Crowe, Marygold Cecilia
The bridge.
JG, 36 Sp36, [21] v
Chestnut tree.
JG, 14 Au30, [21] v
The closed door.
JG, 66 Au38, [15] v
Dove to nightingale.
JG, 63 W37, [25] v
Duality.
JG, 20 Sp32, [11] v
Elfin isle.
JG, 17 Su31, [13] v
Elixir.
JG, 29 Su34, [17] v
Golden eyes.
JG, 34 Au35, [30—31] v
Hannah's thoughts.
JG, 38 Au36, [23] v
Harlequin won?
JG, 25 Su33, [12] v
Heaven remembered.
JG, 64 Sp38, [27] v
A letter to Hans Anderson
[sic] in Heaven.
JG, 35 W35, [13—14] v
A little litany.
JG, 15 W30, [5—6] v
A love song.
JG, 16 Sp31, [12—13] v
My cherry tree in Autumn.
JG, 23 W32, [4] v
Paradise regained.
JG, 24 Sp33, [25—26] v
Revelation.
JG, 18 Au31 [12] v
Robin and willow tree.
JG, 40 Sp37, [12] v
Slumber song of O-Sute.
JG, 13 Su30, [26] v
Some gardens.
JG, 27 W33, [13] v
Straw.
JG, 41 Su37 [33—35] v
The summit.
JG, 19 W31, [6] v
Suspense.
JG, 26 Au33, [29] v
Twilight.
JG, 37 Su36, [12] v
The veil.
JG, 21 Su32, [17—18] v
Where stars grow.
JG, 30 Au34, [5] v
A white day.
JG, 22 Au32, [17] v

Crowther, James Gerald
Is Einstein necessary?
[*The world as I see it,*
by A. Einstein].

LR, i 9 Je35, 378—81 r
*British scientists of the
nineteenth century*
rev. by J. D. Bernal
Soviet science
rev. by T. H. Wintringham

Crozier, Mary
Autumn singing.
F, 5 F31, 82—84 v
Hilary.
F, 6 Je31, 172—74 v

Cruickshank, Alfred M.
Trinidad-1939.
PP, 15 N39, 14 v

Crump, William Bunting
An old Yorkshire cartographer
[John Warburton].
HR, 5 1932, 57—58 c

Cruse, Amy
The Victorians and their books
rev. by A. Foss

Cullen, John
Paris, 1930.
EX, 7 Sp31, 14—16 v
Poem.
V, 6 Je30, 282 v
Poems.
EP, 1 Au35, 130—33 v
see also Riding, Laura

Cullin, David
The encounter.
OO, x 51 F30, 431—38 p

Cullis, Michael F.
Alcaeus: three scholia.
TO, i 3 Jy38, 8 v

Culshaw, Thomas
Dear eyes.
CA 3 Oc30, 47 v
Winter twilight.
CA, 2 S30, 29 v

Cumine, Geoffrey
Ballade; Ballade of Hoodoo
Howdahs.
PP, 8 F39, 9—10 v
Interruption.
PP, 10 A39, 11 v

Cummings, Arthur John
Greetings on May day.
LR, iii 16 My38, 960 c
The radicals of today.
LR, ii 15 D36, 804—6 c

Cummings, Edward Estlin
Answers to an enquiry.

Cummings, Edward Estlin (cont.)
NV, 11 Oc34, 10—11 p
Poem.
CPP, 1 My36, 4—5 v
Poem.
CPP, 3 Jy36, 50 v
Poem.
CPP, 4/5 Ag36, 86—87 v
Three poems.
TO, i 1 J38, 2—3 v

Cunard, Nancy
Africa answers back
[by A. K. Nyabongo]
LR, ii 9 Je36, 469—70 r
Black consul
[by A. Vinogradov].
LR, i 7 A35, 287—288 r
March the third.
CV, 5 M36, [11] p
Rape.
TC, vi 35 Je34, 272—74 v
Three negro poets.
LR, iii 9 Oc37, 529—36 c
see also Aragon, L.; Neruda, P.;
Roumain, J.

Cunninghame, A. T.
The anti-humanism of
T. E. Hulme.
MS, iii 4 J33, 326—32 c
D. H. Lawrence's last poems:
an excursus.
MS, iv 2 Jy33, 126—32 c
A dialogue
MS, iii 1 A32, 41—50 c
The humanism of André Gide.
MS, iii 3 Oc32, 209—15 c
The pale cast of thought:
some notes on experimentation
in modern verse.
MS, ii 4 J32, 312—14 c
On hearing James Joyce.
MS, ii 3 Oc31, 207—15 c
Recent English poets
[*New signatures* and
New country, ed. by M. Roberts].
EQ, i 1 My34, 53 r
Scott in 1932.
MS, iii 2 Ag32, 114—18 c
Scottish nationalism and
imperialism.
MS, ii 2 Jy31, 123—27 c
The Scottish 'nineties'.
MS, iv 3 Oc33, 192—95 c
Sir J. M. Barrie, 1st Bt.,
O.M., LL.D., D.Litt.
MS, iv 1 A33, 40—46 c
The Spenglerian melodrama.
MS, iii 2 Ag32, 133—40 c

Cunninghame-Graham,
Robert Bontine
Mirages rev. by E. J. O'Brien

Currey, Ralph Nixon
Fifth of November.
ND, 19 4N37, 2 v
Song in the Hebrides.
P, 4 1938, 153 v

The Cutty wren.
NV, 17 Oc35, 14—15 v

Cyon, Francois Lafitte-
see Lafitte-Cyon, François

Cyon, Paul
Review
[*An outline for boys and girls and
their parents,*
ed. by N. Mitchison].
TC, iv 20 Oc32, 25 r

D

D
The child's rosary.
JG, 13 Su30, [25—26] v

D., D. J.
The solider.
LR, i 9 Je35, 370—73 p
Strike action.
LR, ii 1 Oc35, 29—32 p

D., F.
The morning start.
LR, i 6 M35, 203—7 p
A reminiscence.
LR, ii 2 N35, 91—92 p

D., H. [*i.e.* Hilda Doolittle]
Magician.
S, 1 J33, 2—6 v
Prose chorus.
CV, 5 M36, [13—14] p

D., H. H.
Country view.
LR, i 7 A35, 257—58 p
Milk-o!
LR, ii 8 My36, 390—91 c
Our vicar.
LR, i 9 Je35, 374 p
Threshing day — and it rained.
LR, i 6 M35, 209—10 p
Tom Jenkins.
ST, i 1 F33, 19—21 p

D., J.
'Converted'.
ST, i 2 A33, 22 v
Review [*They that take the sword,*
by D. Jerrold].
FB, i 1 4F36, 23—24 r

D., L. C.
Literature and the world situation.
TU, 2 1934, 21—34 c
Oxford philosophy.
TU, 3 Je34, 23—27 c

D., P. M.
Review [*The last civilian,*
by E. Glaeser].
FB, i 1 4F36, 23 r

D., R. L.
Architecture to-day.
VP, i 1 A—Je34, 24—27 c

Daiches, David
Review [*A hope for poetry,*
by C. Day Lewis; *Poetic experience,*
by T. Gilby].
NO, ii 2 J35, 187—95 r
The 'universal' element in Donne and
others.
NO, ii 2 J35, 154—67 c
Literature and society
rev. by E. Rickword

Daiken, Leslie Herbert
Backward to liberalism
[*Salud!* by P. O'Donnell].
LR, iii 5 Je37, 308—9 r
Californian poppies.
C, iii 56 16J37, 21 v

Dakin, John R.
Doubt.
JG, 18 Au31, [21] v
Evening: slow movement.
JG, 32 Sp35, [20] v
History.
JG, 37 Su36, [10] v
The last rose.
JG, 19 W31, [21] v
Lyra graecia.
JG, 20 Sp32, [10] v
Mean in memoriam.
JG, 22 Au32, [13] v
Moonset.
JG, 27 W33, [6] v
Night piece.
JG, 34 Au35, [18—19] v
Nocturne.
JG, 21 Su32, [19] v
Paris and Helen.
JG, 30 Au34, [12] v
Proem to Spring.
JG, 36 Sp36, [10] v
Prologue.
JG, 25 Su33, [4] v
Reality.
JG, 23 W32, [13] v
Return.
JG, 38 Au36, [31] v
Shadow light.

JG, 29 Su34, [7] v
Sleeping beauty.
JG, 28 Sp34, [26] v
Sonnet.
JG, 17 Su31, [7] v
Sonnet.
JG, 16 Sp31, [17] v
Surrender.
JG, 26 Au33, [20—21] v
Young love.
JG, 24 Sp33, [25] v

Dali, Salvador
The art of Picasso, tr. by D. Gascoyne.
CPP, 4/5 Ag36, 80—82 v
Cradled pamphlet, tr. by A. L. Lloyd.
CPP, 2 Je36, 29 v

Dalkeith, L. H.
Good-bye twilight rev. by J. Lindsay

Dall, Ian
Elegy.
DD, x 42 N—D33, 94 v
The place of meeting.
DD, xi 43 J—F33, 1—2 v
The raid.
DD, ix 32 M—A32, 24—25 v
Tomnahurich.
DD, x 38 M—A33, 20 v

Danby, John Francis
What thunder said.
CM, ii 1 Su35, 246—53 c

Dandieu, Arnaud *see* Aron, Raymond

Dane, Clemence
Fate cries out rev. by L. A. Pavey

Dangerfield, George
The strange death of liberal England
rev. by S. Graves

Daniel *pseud.*
In the lion's den: Victor Gollancz.
ND, 13 23S37, 16—18 c
In the lion's den, 2: Sir Thomas Inskip.
ND, 14 30S37, 16—18 c
In the lion's den, 3: Colonel de Basil.
ND, 15 7Oc37, 18—20 c
In the lion's den, 4: Ambassador new
style [Ribbentrop].
ND, 16 14Oc37, 18—20 c
In the lion's den, 5: Architect laureate
[Lutyens].
ND, 18 28Oc37, 16—18 c
In the lion's den, 6: H. A. Gwynne.
ND, 20 11N37, 13—14 c
In the lion's den, 7: St. Nicolas.
ND, 21 18N37, 17—19 c
In the lion's den, 8: Lord Halifax.
ND, 22 25N37, 15—16 p

Daniel-Rops, Henry
[*pseud.* J. C. H. Petiot]
Ce qui meurt et ce qui naît
rev. by G. M. Turnell

Dante Alighieri
Winter ode, tr. by B. B. Carter.
CA, 2 S30, 14—15 v

Danvers-Walker, Aubrey Charles
Heaven and Charing Cross
rev. by L. Durrell

D'Aranyi, Jelly
Some thoughts on violin playing.
F, 2 Je30, 107—11 c

Darbyshire, Alec Edward
From a sequence.
PR, 20 17N36, 17 v
From bourgeoisdom to reality
[*Studies in a dying culture*, by
C. Caudwell].
B, 3 Sp39, 17—19 r
Harrow.
B, 2 W38, 11 v
Poem.
PR, 22 Je37, 8—9 v
Pome [sic].
PR, 21 1M37, 14 v
Review [*The disappearing castle*,
by C. Madge].
PR, 22 Je37, 19—20 r
Their repose.
FB, iv 10 N38, 12 v
What hell and redemption!
FB, v 2 My39, 22—24 c

D'Arcy, Martin Cyril
Art and beauty
[*Art and scholasticism*, by J. Maritain].
OO, x 53 N30, 566—77 r
Review [*Oxford poetry, 1930*].
OO, xi 54 M31, 58—59 r

Daubney, Robert Henry
Poem.
PR, 2 12F35, 5 v

Davenport, John
Ballad for a week-end.
EX, 6 Oc30, 24—26 v
Mr Bovey's triumph.
NS, ii 4 Ag35, 312—15 p
Laughter.
EX, 5 F30, 36—37 v
Pride.
V, 5 F30, 218—21 p

David, G. *see* Silone, I.

Davidson, Alan
Where do I come in?
TC, i 2 A31, 28 c

Davidson, Angus
Edward Lear rev. by P. Barton

Davidson, Harold
In my garret.
LR, i 6 M35, 220 v

Davidson, J. Morrison
It happened before: 1890.
LR, iii 4 My37, 201 p

Davidson, Lionel
The principle of the thing.
NW, ns3 C39, 198—201 p

Davidson, Robert
Three poems.
TO, i 2 A38, 3—4 v

Davies, Charles
Pikelets and a penny.
WR, ii 3 Oc39, 159—64 p

Davies, Elwyn
June the first.
W, 3 Au37, 83 v
Young man going away.
W, 3 Au37, 107—10 p

Davies, Gwilym
Beyond our frontiers.
WR, i 1 F39, 38—41 c
Beyond our frontiers.
WR, ii 1 Ag39, 45 c

Davies, Hugh Sykes
Cosmogony.
V, 6 Je30, 280—81 v
Eclogue.
EX, 6 Oc30, 3—6 v
Eclogue II.
EX, 7 Sp31, 57—59 v
Homer and Vico.
NV, 8 A34, 12—18 c
The League of Nations.
EX, 5 F30, 6—10 c
Myth.
EX, 5 F30, 20—21 v
The ornate style.
EX, 7 Sp31, 17—24 c
Poem.
LB, 2 My38, 7 v
Poem.
CPP, 7 N36, 129 v
Sympathies with surrealism.
NV, 20 A36, 15—21 c
Petron rev. by K. Allott; D. Gascoyne
see also Read, Herbert

Davies, Idris
Black tips; Collier boy.
PP, 7 J39, 4—5 v
Dai.
LR, ii 1 16 J37, 866 v

Davies, Idris (cont.)
Dame of the empire.
C, ii 52 19D36, 205—6 v
The day is come; Steel.
PP, 11 My39, 3 v
Dowlais.
PP, 8 F39, 5 v
Gwalia deserta.
C, ii 39 19S36, 92 p
Interlude; Sonnet; Reminiscence.
W, 1 Su37, 17—18 v
Irish railway station.
C, ii 43 17Oc36, 127 v
Irish railway station; Near Rhymney;
Dai's empire.
W, 4 M38, 152—53 v
Land of my mothers.
C, iii 57 23J37, 27 p
Land of my mothers.
W, 4 M38, 141—44 p
Love poem.
PL, i 2 A39, [3] v
Mineowner.
LR, ii 1 Oc35, 33 v
Mining valley; The poet.
WR, ii 3 Oc39, 140 v
Morning comes again.
W, 10 Oc39, 271 v
Shadows and cakes.
W, 3 Au37, 115—16 p
Simplicity, difficulty, obscurity,
experience.
NV, i 1 J39, 30—31 p
Souvenirs from Erin.
W, 2 Ag37, 56—60 p
William Morris.
W, 3 Au37, 83 v
Written on Rhymney hill (August 1938).
PP, 10 A39, 6 v
Gwalia deserta rev. by G. Grigson;
D. S. Savage

Davies, John David Griffiths
The atonement.
HR, 4 1931, 34—35 p

Davies, John L. Langdon-
see Langdon-Davies, John L.

Davies, Noelle
Moonrise in the hills
JG, 18 Au31, [7—8] v
St. Bernard's fountain,
Clairvaux.
JG, 19 W31, [10—11] v
September gold.
JG, 20 Sp32, [22—23] v

Davies, Rhys
Absinthe.
J, 1 J36, 4—8 p
Deplorable story.
W, 3 Au37, 90—98 p
Evelyn and Ivor.

WW, i 2 A30, 42—57 p
Leda; Atthis; Key;
Lost kingdom.
SM, 2 S31, 48 v
A note on Mary Butts
[*Last stories*].
W, 6/7 M39, 207 r
Phaedra.
W, 8/9 Ag39, 219—24 d
Seine; Louvre.
S, 2 A/Jy33, 18—19 v
Jubilee blues
rev. by L. Roberts
My Wales
rev. by E. Evans; L. Jones
The red hills rev. by G. West
A time to laugh
rev. by G. Jones

Davies, William Henry
Flirting; The faithful one.
PR, 2 12F35, 1—2 v
Two poems.
WR, i 1 F39, 16 v
*The loneliest mountain and
other poems* rev. by G. Jones

Davies, William Robertson
Dramatic suicide.
LD, ii 2 D37, 7, 9 dr

Davis, H.
Come words our tools.
CL, i 3 Sp34, ii v
see also Kemp, H. V.

Davis, H. *and* Kemp, H. V.
The rise and fall of bourgeois
poetry, part 1.
CL, i 3 Sp34, 68—77 c

Davison, John
The dance.
FB, i 2 3M36, 38—39 p

Dawson, William Harbutt
Germany under the treaty
rev. by G. West

Dawson-Scott, A. C.
Dreams; And you?
DD, ix 36 N—D32, 90 v
Poem.
DD, x 39 My—Je33, 45 v
Where is thy sting?
DD, x 38 M—A33, 20 v

Day, Bertram
Supper at Emmaus.
PQ, i 2 Su39, 44 v

Day Lewis, Cecil
Addresses to death.
NW, 5 Sp38, 1—4 v

Bombers,
LR, iii 3 A37, 156 v
Comment on Auden.
NV, 26/27 N37, 26—27 c
The conflict.
NV, 4 Jy33, 5 v
English writers and a people's
front.
LR, ii 13 Oc36, 671—74 c
An expensive education.
LR, iii 1 F37, 43—45 c
Extract from
'A hope for poetry'.
TU, i 2 1934, 6—16 c
The face of the land.
LR, iii 7 Ag37, 423—26 c
First anniversary.
F, 2 Je30, 80 v
Gerard Manley Hopkins
[*The note-books and papers* . . .
ed. by H. House].
LR, iii 3 A37, 172—75 r
Goingson in Gloucestershire.
LR, iii 5 Je37, 273—75 c
In me two worlds.
NO, i 2 N33, 187—88 v
Johnny Head-in-air.
TC, vi 34 M34, 212—15 v
Labour and fascism:
the writer's task.
LR, ii 14 N36, 731—33 c
Lines from work in progress.
LS, ii 1 My35, 25 v
Newsreel.
LR, iii 13 F38, 794 v
Poem from a sequence.
F, 6 Je31, 196 v
Poetry to-day
[*Oxford book of modern verse*,
ed. by W. B. Yeats;
The year's poetry, 1936,
ed. by J. Lehmann and
D. K. Roberts].
LR, ii 16 J37, 899—901 r
Review
[*Dialectical materialism and
communism*, by L. Rudas].
TC, vi 35 Je34, 313 r
Revolutionaries and poetry.
LR, i 10 Jy35, 397—402 c
The road these times must take.
LR, i 1 N34, 34 v
Surrealists get the bird.
NV, 19 F36, 20—21 c
Sword and pen.
LR, ii 15 D36, 794—96 c
Tinker.
NW, 3 Sp37, 178—84 p
Two poems from
'The magic mountain'.
NV, 1 J33, 6—8 v
Writers' international.
LR, i 4 J35, 128—29 c
Collected poems, 1929—1933

rev. by NV, 15 Je35, 18;
M. Slater
The friendly tree
rev. by A. L. Morton
From feathers to iron
rev. by W. B. Green;
TC, iii 14 A32, 29
A hope for poetry
rev. by D. Daiches; A. Hope
The magnetic mountain
rev. by G. Grigson; A. L. Morton;
G. Rees
The mind in chains
rev. by M. Slater; E. Waugh
Noah and the waters
rev. by NV, 21 Je36, 17;
E. Rickword
Overtures to death
rev. by R. Fuller;
NV, i 2 My39, 52
Revolution in writing
rev. by D. Garman
Starting point
rev. by T. L. Hodgkin
A time to dance
rev. by NV, 15 Je35, 18
see also Sykes, J. A.

Deane, Lorna Kay
Blue dawn.
DD, x 42 N—D33, 100 v
Poem.
DD, x 41 S—Oc33, 85 v
The silent song.
DD, xi 44 M—A34, 21 v

Death in the marsh.
LR, ii 5 F36, 203—7 p

De Chirico, Giorgio
Le mystère et la création
[with tr. by F. Brockway].
LB, 6 Oc38, 14 c

De Fontmell, E. V. *pseud.*
The binding.
WW, i 4 Oc30, 78—91 p
The man with the twisted neck.
WW, i 1 J30, 61—71 p

D'Egville, Alan H.
The chic have a word for it.
ND, 10 2S37, 20 p

Dehmel, Richard
Two poems, tr. by P. Selver.
SM, 4 1933, 108 v

DeJong, David Cornell
Two poems.
CV, 3 Su35, 10—11 v

Delahaye, J. V.
The people's front.
LR, ii 13 Oc36, 668—69 c

De La Mare, Walter
'Here lies . . .'; The dead jay.
PL, i 1 F39, [5—6] v
The shocker shocked.
ND, 10 2S37, 14 v
The fleeting and other poems
rev. by S. Spender
Memory
rev. by G. Grigson; J. Short

Deledda, Grazia
The child who was hidden,
tr. by V. Capocci.
BB, vii 2 M30, 49—59 p

Demant, Vigo August
Christian polity
rev. by D. J. B. Hawkins

Demarest, Donald
Homage to Stevie Smith.
TH, 3 24F39, 4 v
Katabasis.
TH, 1 27J39, 2 v

Dembleby, John Malham- *see*
Malham-Dembleby, John

De Mouilpied, Helen *see*
Mouilpied, Helen de

Dempsey, Bernard W.
The American scene.
AR, i 4 J38, 331—36 c

Denney, Reuel
The children.
T, 12/13 Oc38, 104 v

Dent, Guy
Andalusian rhapsody.
P, 2 1938, 41—54 p
Vision.
NS, i 4 Ag34, 276—81 p

Derleth, August W,
Frost in October.
NS, ii 3 Je35, 209—13 p
Stuff of dream.
NS, ii 5 Oc35, 380—85 p

Derrick, Thomas
Celtic twilight.
R, i 6 Oc34, 2 i

Derry, K. M.
Sea-scape.
DD, xi 48 N—D34, 90 v

Derwent, George Harcourt
Johnstone *3rd Lord*
The crossroads.
LB, 11 M39, 6—7 p

Dessaignes, G. R. *see*
Ribemont-Dessaignes, G.

Devlin, Christopher
Hopkins and Duns Scotus.
NV, 14 A35, 12—17 c

Devlin, Denis *see* Breton, A.

Dewsbury, Ronald
Ants and shafts;
Married life and older gods.
LT, i 5 Jy36, 44—48 p, v
The hairdresser;
Culture 'class'.
S, 2 A—Jy33, 22 p
London scenario.
LT, i 11 J37, 22 v

Dialogue for an Uraon marriage,
tr. by W. G. Archer.
CPP, 10 Au37, 31—32 p

Di Borcio, S. *see* Borcio, S. di

Dickens, Anthony
Review [*Songs and poems,*
by G. Ewart].
PL, i 1 F39, [32] r

Dieste, Rafael
The spectacle of wonders,
tr. by A. L. Lloyd.
NW, 4 Au37, 232—44 d

Dilettante *pseud.*
Letters from abroad: Berlin.
BB, vii 2 M30, 102—6 c

Dimitrov, George
Dimitrov to writers.
LR, i 9 Je35, 343—46 c

Dinnis, Enid
To one dwelling incluse.
CA, 2 S30, 25 v

Dirge; If you wait.
LT, i 1 M36, 6—7 v

Dixon, Maurice
The moon on the wine.
NS, ii 8 A36, 601—7 p

Djavakhishvili, M.
The cup, tr. by S. Garry.
NW, 4 Au37, 199—228 p

Dobb, Maurice
Letter.
TC, iii 16 Je32, 24 c
Marxism and the crisis.
TC, iii 16 Je32, 1—5 c
Social credit:
a reply to Mr Drummond.
CL, i 4 Su34, 107—8 c

Dobell, Eva
Sing a song o' sixpence.
DD, x 39 My—Je33, 50 v

Dobrée, Bonamy
There is no need to despair.
HR, 7 1934, 7—8 c
Modern prose style
rev. by G. Findlater
see also Manwaring, George Ernest

Dobrée, Valentine
To blush unseen
rev. by G. West

Dodd, Martha
Death in Tiflis.
P, 6 1939, 196—211 p

Döblin, Alfred
Men without mercy
rev. by C. Madge

Doggett, C. C.
Drama review
[*Crime et châtiment*,
adapted by M. Baty;
Genesis II, by A. Menon;
Squaring the circle,
by V. Kataev;
The rock, by T. S. Eliot;
Masses and men,
by E. Toller;
The blind goddess;
by E. Toller.
They shall not die,
by J. Wexley].
VP, i 2 Jy—S34, 46—49 dr
Sailors of Cattaro [by F. Wolf].
VP, i 1 A—Je34, 28 dr

Dolgorouky, *Princess* Sophie *tr.*
see Ahmatova, Anna

Dollar, A. T.
Silent shore.
DD, xi 46 Jy—Ag34, 61 v

Dolphin, May I. E.
The bay: Departure.
DD, viii 29 Su31, 75 v
Conisborough castle.
JG, 28 Sp34, [27—28] v
Courtesy.
JG, 38 Au36, [30—31] v

Departure.
JG, 17 Su31, [9] v
Easterly mist.
JG, 65 Su38, [27—28] v
The felling.
JG, 67 W38, [11] v
The forge.
JG, 40 Sp37, [31—32] v
From Bethlehem.
JG, 71 W39, [25] v
The garden club.
JG, 26 Au33, [11—12] v
Intercession.
JG, 13 Su30, [7—8] v
Iron works.
JG, 36 Sp36, [8—10] v
The moor in winter.
JG, 31 W34, [21] v
Sirens.
JG, 69 Su39, [22—23] v
The slum.
JG, 25 Su33, [17—18] v
Somewhere in Italy.
JG, 64 Sp38, [17] v
Sunset at Fez.
JG, 29 Su34, [21—22] v
There was a great silence.
JG, 21 Su32, [22—23] v
When the wind of night is high.
PQ, i 1 Sp39, 17 v

Donaldson, Jack
Good and hot.
ND, 16 14Oc37, 32 r
From Stravinsky to swing.
ND, 4 22Jy37, 26 r
The gramophone.
ND, 21 18N37, 34, 36 r
Hand-picked [records]
for Christmas.
ND, 25 16D37, 27 r
Music notes.
ND, 5 29Jy37, 28 c
Some unfinished music.
ND, 8 19Ag37, 27—28 c
Taboo.
ND, 11 9S37, 28 r
Top hats and tiaras.
ND, 1 1Jy37, 30 c

Donington, Robert *and*
Donington, Barbara
The citizen faces war
rev. by T. Lincoln

Donisthorpe, Gladys Sheila
Loveliest of friends
rev. by E. M. Barraud

Donnelly, Charles
Irish history
[*On another man's wounds*,
by E. O'Malley; *Unique dictator*,
by D. Ryan].

LR, ii 16 J37, 919 r
Portrait of a revolution.
LR, ii 1 Oc35, 1—2 c

Donnelly, Charles *and*
Ajax *pseud.*
Connolly and Casement.
LR, ii 7 A36, 289—95 c

Donnelly, Ignatius
Literature speaks out.
NV, 15 Je35, 21—22 c

Dooley, Pat
Selling books in Ireland.
LR, ii 9 Je36, 450—53 c

Doone, Rupert
On the production of
'Agamemnon'.
GTP, 4 Oc36, 2—3 dr
Symphonic ballets.
GTP, 2 Ag36, [1] c
Valeska Gert, dancer.
GTP, 1 Je36, [2] c
What about the theatre?
NV, 18 D35, 9—10 c
see also MacNeice, Louis

Dope [periodical]
rev. by B. Causton

Doren, Mark Van *see*
Van Doren, Mark

Dos Passos, John
The big money
rev. by J. Lindsay
In all countries
rev. by C. Ashleigh
1919 rev. by H. Cole

Dostoevsky, Fyodor
Baal: impressions of London,
tr. by R. Gill.
EQ, i 2 Ag34, 77—87 p

Doughty, Charles
*Selected passages from
'The dawn in Britain'*,
ed. by B. Fairley
rev. by NV, 17 Oc35, 21;
J. R. Morley

Douglas, *Lord* Alfred
'English benedictines':
a personal statement;
Oscar Wilde in relation to
the Catholic church.
CA, 11 1932, 328—34 c
Oscar Wilde — catholic and poet.
CA, 5 M31, 124—25 c
Speech.
CA, 12 1932, 380—81 p

Douglas, Clifford Hugh
Delusions in regard to money
and their effect.
MS, i 1 Sp30, 20—24 c

Douglas, E. Akers- see
Akers-Douglas, E.

Douglas, Ena
Dance; Metropolis.
C, ii 37 5S36, 72 v
Nocturne.
RR, 3 My37, [16] v
Poem.
RR, 4 S37, [19] v
Poem.
RR, 1 Oc36, 18 v
To a poet.
J, 1 J36, 24 v

Douglas, Jean Cameron- see
Cameron-Douglas, Jean

Douglas, Keith Castellain
Caravan.
PR, 22 Je37, 11 v
Dejection.
NV, 29 M38, 8 v
Haydn — clock symphony.
K, i 2 D39—J40, 43 v
Kristin.
B, 2 W38, 12 v
Poem.
B, 3 Sp39, 6 v
Poem from a sequence.
B, 2 W38, 2 v
Sonnet.
B, 3 Sp39, 8 v
Spring sailor; Poor Mary.
FB, v 2 My39, 24 v

Dover, Cedric
Literary opportunity in America.
LR, iii 16 My38, 982—84 c
Half caste rev. by R. Jardine

Dow, Alexander Warren-
see Warren-Dow, Alexander

Dowding, Walter
Gwri, the star and the Gorsedd.
WR, ii 1 Ag39, 6—11 p

Dower, Kenneth Cecil Gandar-
see Gandar-Dower, Kenneth
Cecil

Downing, J. W.
The talkie dances
[The Congress dances].
DV, 1 M32, 19—20 r

Downs, Barbara and
Watkin, Bruce
See how they laughed.

LD, ii 1 D37, 13, 15—16 p

Dratler, Jay J.
Manhattan side street
rev. by A. L. Morton

Dreiser, Theodore
Individualism and the jungle.
TC, iv 19 S32, 4—6 c

Drew, Summers
The lady of the blue pavilion;
Two songs for a lady in the
romantic manner.
F, 6 Je31, 162—63 v
On the margin of Andre Gide
F, 1 F30, 57—61 c
Two poems.
F, 5 F31, 90 v

Drinkwater, John
Foreword.
R, 1 i N33, 1 p
Three American vignettes.
WW, i 2 A30, 3—6 v

Dru, Alexander tr.
see Kierkegaard, Søren Aabye

Drummond, John
The cantos of Ezra Pound
[A draft of XXX cantos,
by Ezra Pound].
CM, i 1 Sp33, 36—46 r
The critics work in progress.
CM, i 4 Sp34, 176—79 c
Culture [Scrutiny].
CL, i 2 W33, 46—48 r
1 CL, i 1 Su33, 6—7 v
The mind of Mr W. H. Auden.
TO, i 3 Jy38, 23—26 c
Reply.
TO, ii 5 J39, 17—19 c
Social credit.
CL, i 2 W33, 32—36 c

Drury, Oliver F.
The encroaching sea.
JG, 23 W32, [22] v

Dryden, Peter
For gathered flowers are dead,
Yasmin.
FB, iii 6 21Oc37, 11—12 p

Ducasse, Isidor Lucien
comte de Lautréamont, pseud.
Les chants de Maldoror,
tr. by J. Ridley and F. Scarfe.
CPP, 6 Oc36, 106—13 p
From the Songs of Maldoror,
tr. by J. Ridley and F. Scarfe.
CPP, 9 Sp37, 7—17 p

Dudding, John
Review
[Town and country planning,
by P. Abercrombie].
TC, v 27 My33, 192 r

Duermayer, H.
The death of Karl Fokker,
tr. by C. Ashleigh.
NW, ns2 Sp39, 61—63 p

Dueshery, Julian Percy Thornton-
see Thornton-Duesbery, Julian
Percy

Dufau-Labeyrie, Francis
La chanteuse.
W, 3 Au37, 85 v

Duff, Charles
Streamlined meals.
ND, 1 1Jy37, 28 c
James Joyce and the plain reader
rev. by S. Gilbert
see also Chavette, E.

Duff, Grant
Croce and modern Italy.
MS, iii 1 A32, 31—38 c

Duff, Reginald
The need for a negative
renaissance.
TC, iv 24 F33, 7—9 c
Ready-made misfit.
TC, vi 32 N33, 91—99 p

Duffy, Hans
But why Abelard?
ND, 4 22Jy37, 8—9 p

Duhamel, Georges
America the menace
rev. by J. R. Evans
Salavin rev. by J. Lindsay

Dulac, Edmond
Without the twilight.
[W. B. Yeats].
AW, Su39, 14—16 c
Words and music.
TO, ii 5 J39, 5—6 c

Dunbar-Marshall, Francis
The visitors.
PQ, i 1 Sp39, 10 v

Duncan, Chamley
The train to Caisterhead.
NS, ii 2 A35, 81—90 p

Duncan, Ronald
Architecture.
TO, ii 5 J39, 10 c

Duncan, Ronald (cont.)
Blast and about and about
[*Scrutiny* and *Criterion*].
TO, i 1 J38, 26—27 c
Commentary.
TO, i 3 Jy38, 1—3 c
Continuation of scene III;
scene IV.
TO, ii 5 J39, 11—14; ii 6 A39,
20—32 d
Crabbe: a note.
TO, i 2 A38, 22—24 c
Editorial.
TO, ii 8 N39, 1—2;
TO, ii 7 Ag39, 1—6;
TO, ii 6 A39, 1—2;
TO, ii 5 J39, 1—4 c
Oratory and censorship.
TO, ii 7 Ag39, 10—13 c
Pimp, skunk, and profiteer;
Ora pro nobis.
To, ii 8 N39, 10—32 d
Scene one.
TO, i 1 J38, 10—17 d
Scene two: part one [and]
continuation.
TO, i 2 A38, 5—11; i 3
Jy38, 11—15 d
Words and music. Scene III.
TO, i 4 Oc38, 10—15 c, d
Yeats.
TO, ii 7 Ag39, 19—21 c

Dunlop, John
Chalk deposits.
LD, i 3 My37, 10 v

Dunlop, Ronald Ossory
Art and propaganda.
J, 2 My36, 26 c

Dunman, Jack
The agricultural labourer speaks
[*Country conditions*,
by V. Ackland].
LR, ii 16 J37, 918 r

Dunn, Joe
Action by a ship's committee.
ST, i 3 1933, 13—16 p

Dunnett, Denzil, J.
Catullus of Verona.
PR, 18 17Je36, 2—5 c
Editorial.
PR, 20 17N36, 1—2 c
Editorial.
PR, 21 1M37, 1—2 c
Editorial.
PR, 22 Je37, 1—2 c
Editorial.
PR, 19 20Oc36, 1 c
Fancy is blind.
FB, iii 7 25N37, 33 v

Hospital morning.
PR, 12 4D35, 9 v
The leaf-sweepers.
PR, 20 17N36, 16 v
A Marxist look at literature
[*Illusion and reality*,
by C. Caudwell].
PR, 23 N37, 6—7 r
The persecutor speaks.
FB, iv 10 N38, 12 v
Review
[*The ascent of F6*,
by W. H. Auden and C. Isherwood].
PR, 19 20Oc36, 14—15 r
Review [*Anabasis*,
by St. John Perse;
The Alcestis of Euripides].
PR, 21 1M37, 19—20 r
Rilke and after.
PR, 14 19F36, 2—5 c
Spotlights on Aeschylus
[*The Agamemnon*].
PR, 20 17N36, 3—9 r
Their conscience
[*T. E. Hulme*, by M. Roberts;
Poems, by F. T. Prince].
B, 2 W38, 7—9 r
When in disgrace.
PR, 23 N37, 8—9 v

Dunsany, Edward John Moreton
Drax Plunkett *Lord*
In a Yorkshire valley.
HR, 7 1934, 20 v

Duplessis
Drawing.
J, 2 My36, 17 i

Durrell, Gerald
An African dialogue.
SV, 4 Su39, 2 v

Durrell, Lawrence
Asylum in the snow.
SV, 3 W38, 43—54 p
Carol in Corfu.
SV, 3 W38, 2 v
Ego.
SV, 1 Su38, 22—25 p
The ego's own egg;
The hanged man;
Father Nicholas his death;
The poet, I; A small scripture;
Adam.
SV, 4A Sp39, 4—9 v
Epitaph; Island fugue.
PL, i 1 F39, [22—24] v
A letter from the land of the gods.
RR, 8 J39, [7] p
Theatre
[*Heaven and Charing Cross*,
by A. Danvers-Walker;
Family reunion, by T. S. Eliot].

IP, i 1 6A39, 17—19 dr
Theatre [*Family reunion*,
by T. S. Eliot].
PL, i 2 A39, [30] dr
Zero.
SV, 6 Au39, 8—18 p
The black book
rev. by P. O'Connor
Pied piper of lovers
rev. by J. Mair

Durtain, Luc
Paris Congress speech.
LR, i 11 Ag35, 473 c

Duthie, Eric
Three more novels
[*The man who started clean*,
by T. O. Beachcroft;
The mortal storm,
by P. Bottome;
Cockroaches and diamonds,
by J. Goss].
LR, iii 11 D37, 694—96 r

Dutt, Rajani Palme
Fascism and social revolution
rev. by W. N. Warbey
World politics, 1918—1936
rev. by R. Bishop

Dutton, Patricia
Meteor.
JG, 18 Au31, [25—26] v
Mists.
JG, 24 Sp33, [8—9] v
Moon-sight.
JG, 16 Sp31, [25—26] v
The sleeper.
JG, 20 Sp32, [15] v

D'Wit, Vivian
Rejection.
PQ, i 2 Su39, 45 v

Dwyer, Peter
Etruscan smile.
FB, i 1 4F36, 6—7 p

Dyer, Grant A.
Wimbledon backhand.
ND, 2 8Jy37, 32 c

Dyke, Watson
Aunt Rose Ellen.
HR, 7 1934, 34—35 p

Dyment, Clifford
Burial at sea.
DD, ix 36 N—D32, 101 v
Charing Cross.
K, i 1 17N39, 29 v
The departure.
NW, 3 Sp37, 185—92 p

The eyes; A daughter of music;
Summer; Movements in Spring.
PL, i 2 A39 [4—6] v
Labour exchange.
NW, ns2 Sp39, 181 v
The lady.
PL, i 1 F39, [6] v
Memorials.
B, 3 Sp39, 3 v
One night of love.
B, 1 Su38, 4 v
Tears, idle tears
[*The autumn world*,
by D. S. Savage].
PL, i 2 A39, [28] r
Younger generation.
B, 1 Su38, 12—13 v
First day
rev. by K. Allott; J. R. Morley
Straight or curly
rev. by G. Grigson

Dyson, *Sir* Frank
Local men of science.
HR, 6 1933, 14—15 c

Dyson, William
Hollywood.
R, i 4 My34, 2 i

E

E., A. W.
Stevedore
[by P. Peters and G. Sklar].
LR, i 9 Je35, 346 r

E., E. D.
The decachord.
DD, viii 30 Au31, 90—91 v

E., M. F.
Poetry for sixpence
[*The century's poetry*,
ed. by D. K. Roberts].
NV, i 1 J39, 26 r

Earp, Thomas Wade
The Leicester Galleries
exhibition.
T, 6/7 N37, [15—17] c

East, Raymond
B. B. C.
LR, i 12 S35, 522—23 c

Easton, John
Snapdragon.
WW, i 4 Oc30, 12—24 p

Easton, Malcolm
A job in a million-9.
ND, 9 26Ag37, 14, 16, 18 p
Kensington interior.
OO, x 51 F30, 438 v
Wind and roses.
OO, x 52 My30, 530 v

Eaton, L. C.
Sport in an American school.
FB, i 2 3M36, 44—45 c

Eberhart, Richard
Necessity.
EX, 5 F30, 4—5 v
Poem.
EX, 7 Sp31, 16 v
Quern.
EX, 6 Oc30, 39 v
Rumination.
SV, 4 Su39, 32 v
Reading the spirit
rev. by R. Todd

Eddison, Robert
A child's guide to repertory.
R, i 4 My34, 9—10 c

Eddy, George Sherwood
Challenge of Russia
rev. by J. R. Evans

Eddy, Mary Olive
Little Sanderling.
PQ, i 3 Su39, 43 v

Ede, Harold Stanley
Modern art.
AX, 1 J35, 21—23 c

Edgelow, Marguerite
Day in the forest.
JG, 70 Au39, [25] v
Figment of a dream.
JG, 71 W39, [31] v
Outcast.
JG, 69 Su39, [21] v

Edmunds, Edna
England.
FB, iii 6 21Oc37, 7 v

Edwards, Arthur Trystan
Some reflections on the new
Bodleian.
LD, i 1 J37, 8—9 c

Edwards, Beryl
A windy hill near Rye.
P, 2 1938, 56 i
Wood engraving.
P, 2 1938, 150 i

Edwards, Harold Llewellyn

Ravenscourt
The allusionist school of poetry.
W, 2 Ag37, 41—45 c
Five poems.
W, 6/7 M39, 197—98 v
From knees up, muvver Brown.
W, 5 Su38, 173—74 v
Interiority
[*French introspectives*,
by P. M. Jones].
W, 5 Su38, 182—83 r
Lugano, August 1937; One life.
W, 4 M38, 151 v

Edwards, Lionel
Erato descendant.
TH, 2 10F39, 2 v

Edwards, Noll
Going up.
NS, ii 3 Je35, 195—97 p

Egerton, Mary Louisa
God's troubadour
[Jacopone da Todi].
CA, 5 M31, 115—20 c

Ehrenburg, Ilya
Paris Congress speech.
LR, i 11 Ag35, 475 c
Spain reveals Italy's tragedy.
LR, iii 4 My37, 196—98 c

Eight Uraon marriage poems.
NV, 22 S36, 10—11 v

Einstein, Albert
The world as I see it
rev. by J. G. Crowther

Eland, Cyril E.
The playhouse
[*Dr Knock*, by J. Romains].
PR, 3 19F35, 14 dr

Elder, Raibeart
Ashes without sackcloth.
P, 4 1938, 185—207 p

Eldridge, Mildred E.
Llechryddan.
WR, ii 2 S39, 76 i

Eldridge, Noel
The Nth crusade.
K, i 1 17N39, 13—14 c

Elgee, Frank
A song of Vega.
JG, 63 W37, [36] v

Elgee, Harriet Wragg
Coltsfoot.
JG, 63 W37, [12] v

Elgee, Harriet Wragg (cont.)
Dea mater.
JG, 18 Au31, [26–27] v
February prayer.
JG, 32 Sp35, [32] v
Golden crocus.
JG, 41 Su37, [29] v
If we would sing.
JG, 15 W30, [9] v
The love of God.
JG, 28 Sp34, [20] v
O lovely mortal.
JG, 69 Su39, [31] v
Offering.
JG, 64 Sp38, [23] v
A question.
JG, 23 W32, [6–7] v
Witches and broomsticks.
HR, 7 1934, 52–53 c

Elias, Sid
The iniquity of the means test.
TC, iii 14 A32, 21–24 c

Eliot, Thomas Stearns
Audiences, producers, plays,
poets.
NV, 18 D35, 3–4 c
Five points on dramatic writing.
TO, i 3 Jy38, 101 c
The lion and the fox
[by P. W. Lewis].
T, 6/7 N37, [6–9] ; 8 J38,
[24] r
Religious drama and the
church.
R, i 6 Oc34, 4–5 c
After strange gods
rev. by G. G. B.
Ash Wednesday
rev. by W. Stewart
Collected poems, 1909–1935
rev. by A. Hodge
The family reunion
rev. by K. Allott; A. Darbyshire;
L. Durrell; J. G. MacLeod
Murder in the cathedral
rev. by J. Mair; V. M. Ward
The rock
rev. by C. C. Doggett; T. Good;
C. Madge
Selected essays
rev. by H. House
Sweeney agonistes
rev. by F. Berry; H. G. Porteus;
G. Rees
Thoughts after Lambeth
rev. by D. Jay
*The use of poetry and the use
of criticism* rev. by H. House

Ellerman, Annie Winifred
see Bryher *pseud.*

40

Elliott, John
The new gods.
B, 2 W38, 18 v

Ellis, Ainslie
Better this way.
W, 10 Oc39, 278 v
Projection.
LB, 12 15M39, 17 v
Field for research.
LB, 8/9 J39, 48 v

Ellis, Amabel Williams-
see Williams-Ellis, Amabel

Ellis, Clough Williams-
see Williams-Ellis, Clough

Ellis, Fred
From a note-book.
LR, i 7 A35, 283 i

Ellis, Fred *and*
Ashleigh, Charles
Fred Ellis in London.
LR, ii 12 S36, 608–12 p

Ellis, Henry Havelock
Comment on the basis of the
Sexology group.
TC, iv 21 N32, 20–21 c
J. William Lloyd.
TC, i 2 A31, 5–7 c
The problem of race regeneration.
I: The improvement of the
environment.
TC, i 6 Ag31, 1–5 c
The problem of race
regeneration, II–V.
TC, ii 7 S31, 1–3;
TC, ii 8 Oc31, 1–5;
TC, ii 9 N31, 1–4;
TC, ii 10 D31, 1–5 c
The problem of sterilisation.
TC, vi 35 Je34, 262–64 c
War and the fighting instinct.
PS, 5 N–D34, 3, 9 c
More essays of love and virtue
rev. by J. R. Evans; H. House
*Views and reviews: first series,
1884–1919*
rev. by J. R. Evans
*Views and reviews: second
series, 1920–1932*
rev. by H. J. Massingham

Ellis-Fermor, Una
The Jacobean drama
rev. by F. D. Klingender;
J. R. Morley

Elliston, George
Bright April.
PQ, i 2 Su39, 40 v

Ellit, Jack
Sound says good-bye to
music; sound film.
DE, 2 Su32, 3 c

Elton, Arthur
The gods move house.
LB, 4/5 Jy38, 2, 9–12 c
Realist films today.
LR, ii 9 Je36, 426–30 c

Elton, Oliver
The English muse
rev. by G. Grigson

Eluard, Paul
At present, tr. by D. Gascoyne.
NV, 21 Je36, 9 v
From *Les yeux fertiles,*
tr. by H. Howarth.
LD, i 2 M37, 22 v
Humphrey Jennings.
LB, 11 M39, 17 v
Joan Miro, tr. by G. Reavey.
LB, 2 My38, 4 v
Man Ray
[plus tr. by Man Ray].
LB, 10 F39, 8–10 v
Max Ernst, tr. by G. Reavey.
LB, 7 D38, 5, 7 v
Nine poems,
tr. by J. Jacquot, R. Todd,
D. Gascoyne, G. Reavey,
A. L. Lloyd.
CPP, 2 Je36, 18–22 v
One for all,
tr. by D. Gascoyne.
NV, 7 F34, 11–12 v
Poem, tr. by G. Reavey.
CPP, 8 D36, 151 v
René Magritte, tr. by M. Ray.
LB, 1 A38, 15 v
Statement, tr. by D. Gascoyne.
CPP, 2 Je36, 18 p
Two alike, tr. by R. Todd.
MS, vi 3 Oc35, 242–43 v
La victoire de Guernica
[plus tr. by G. Reavey and
R. Penrose].
LB, 6 Oc38, 7–8 v
Yves Tanguy.
LB, 4/5 Jy38, 36 v
Facile rev. by D. Gascoyne
La rose publique
rev. by D. Gascoyne
Thorns of thunder
rev. by A. Hodge
see also Breton, A.; Phare, E. E.

Elvin, René
Music in London.
LT, i 1 M36, 37–38 c
Olympian spring.
LT, i 5 Jy36, 8–16 p

A sceptical introduction to
the Surrealist exhibition.
LT, i 5 Jy36, 39 c

Elvin, Verrier *see*
Hivale, Shamrao

Emminger, F. W.
Egotist.
PQ, i 2 Su39, 36 v

Empson, William
Bacchus.
NV, 2 M33, 8—9 v
Correspondence.
OO, xi 54 M31, 54—57 c
Courage means running.
CPP, 1 My36, 6 v
Just a smack at Auden.
CPP, 10 Au37, 24—26 v
Learning Chinese.
ND, 8 19Ag37, 19 p
Letter from China.
ND, 22 25N37, 20—21 p
Note on local flora.
EX, 5 F30, 26 v
A note on W. H. Auden's
'Paid on both sides'.
EX, 7 Sp31, 60—61 c
Notice this gate.
ND, 1 1Jy37, 24 p
'O Miselle passer'.
OO, x 52 My30, 470—78 c
Poem; Description of a view.
EX, 6 Oc30, 12—13 v
Poem about a ball in the
nineteenth century.
EX, 7 Sp31, 59 v
Sleeping out in the cloister.
V, 6 Je30, 265 v
Travel note.
NV, 16 Ag35, 9 v
Travel note.
ND, 6 5Ag37, 29 p
Two o'clock.
EX, 6 Oc30, 32 v
Poems rev. by L. MacNeice
Some versions of pastoral
rev. by J. B. Harvey; J. Mair;
NV 18 D35 17
see also Hatakeyama, C.

Emsworthy, George
Quatrain.
DD, xi 44 M—A34, 20 v

Engels, Friedrich
Anti-Duhring
rev. by T. H. Wintringham
see also Marx, Karl

Engle, Paul
Belleau Wood.
NO, ii 3 N35, 242—49 v

New York.
PR, 2 12F35, 7 v
Signature of spring.
NO, ii 2 J35, 137—38 v
Two extracts.
LS, ii 1 My35, 43—45 v
American song
rev. by G. Grigson

English, Ernest *pseud.*
Ain't science wonderful.
LR, i 7 A35, 267—69 c
America has a word for it.
LR, i 8 My35, 290 c
Security.
LR, i 4 J35, 116—17 v

Engstrand, Stuart
The tomato field
rev. by J. Lindsay

The enquiring mind.
LS, i 2 My34, 26—27 c

Epilogue [periodical] no. 2
rev. by H. Howarth

Ericsen, James
The moon and the wheels.
C, ii 33 8Ag36, 39 p
Tenebrae.
C, ii 39 19S36, 93 v

Erni, Hans
The Lucerne exhibition.
AX, 2 A35, 27—28 c

Erskine, Anne
En route.
DD, xi 46 Jy—Ag34, 66 v

Erskine of Marr, Ruaraidh
Comradh-sgalain.
MS, i 4 J31, 50—53 p
Smuain no dha mu Chomradh-
Sgalain.
MS, i 2 Su30, 38—40 c
The Stewart Kings of England.
MS, ii 1 A31, 21—25;
MS, ii 2Jy31, 163—67;
MS, ii 3 Oc31, 234—36;
MS, iii 1 A32, 58—59 c
Unrealities.
MS, i 1 Sp30, 29—33 c

Escott, Harry
The dandelion.
JG, 42 Au37, [18] v
Defiance.
JG, 64 Sp38, [21] v
Guernsey daffodils.
JG, 68 Sp39, [28] v
Intimacy.
JG, 69 Su39, [24] v

It cannot die.
JG, 70 Au39, [14] v
Light or shade.
JG, 71 W39, [17] v
The realist's dilemma.
JG, 63 W37, [29] v

Escott, Rudolf
The dray horse.
JG, 67 W38, [8—9] v
These women.
JG, 70 Au39, [35] v

Essenin, Sergei
Poems, tr. by R. M. Hewitt.
EQ, i 1 My34, 35 v

Essex, Edwin
The poetry of Michael Field.
CA, 8 1931, 234—45 c

Etheridge, Ken
Abstract; Mask; Spring fragment.
W, 1 Su37, 14—16 v
Annunciation.
W, 4 M38, 138—39 v
Carnations.
C, iii 58 30J37, 36 v
Carnations.
WR, ii 3 Oc39, 142 v
Colour box.
C, i 21 25A36, 167 v
Country walk; Credo;
Young starlings; Flowering
cosmos.
W, 2 Ag37, 65—68 v
Night by the sea.
C, ii 35 22Ag36, 59—60 v
An old collier.
C, ii 41 3Oc36, 110—11 v
Primaries.
C, i 25 23My36, 199 v
Reactions.
C, i 6 11J36, 48 v
Swan-song in the sun
[*Song of the sun*, by E. Rhys].
W, 2 Ag37, 76—77 r
Will birds.
C, ii 40 26S36, 100—101 p

Etherington, Maurice
As you like it: a play for poseurs.
R, i 4 My34, 14 c

Ettrick *pseud.*
The ideal laureate.
DD, vii 27 N—D30, 444—46 c
The wagging of the dog by its
tail.
DD, viii 30 Au31, 96—98 v
A wise maxim.
DD, viii 30 Au31, 98 v

Eureka *pseud.*
Kisch in Australia.
LR, i 10 Jy35, 403—6 c

Euripides
Alcestis, tr. by D. Fitts and
R. Fitzgerald rev. by D. I. Dunnett
Ion, tr. by H. D.
rev. by J. Symons

Evans, Artro
The American.
BB, vii 2 M30, 88—92 p

Evans, Caradoc
Your sin will find you out.
W, 8/9 Ag39, 214—219 p

Evans, David
Poems I and II.
W, 5 Su38, 178—79 v
Sona dialect.
W, 8/9 Ag39, 240 v
Three poems.
W, 6/7 M39, 204—5 v

Evans, George Ewart
Answer to questionnaire.
W, 8/9 Ag39, 225—26 c
At the seaside.
W, 6/7 M39, 203—4 v
He saith among the trumpets,
ha! ha!
W, 5 Su38, 167—70 p
Pause for conversation.
W, 2 Ag37, 46—52 p
Poem.
W, 10 Oc39, 276 v
The valleys [*My Wales,*
by R. Davies;
Unfinished journey,
by J. Jones;
A bridge to divide them,
by G. Rees;
Times like these,
by J. G. Jones.
Cwmardy, by L. Jones].
W, 3 Au37, 128—30 r

Evans, Joan
Nature in design
rev. by A. G. Sewter

Evans, Mair
Tradition and the Faber stories.
W, 4 M38, 150 v

Evans, Jon Randell
The black month.
TC, ii 12 F32, 1—3 c
Editorial.
TC, vi 33 D—J33—34, 129—32,
148 c
Editorial: the function of

progressive societies.
TC, vi 32 N33, 66—67 c
Editorial:
towards a brave new world.
TC, vi 36 S34, 321—26 c
The punishment and the crime.
TC, i 5 My31, 18—21 c
Review [*Edward Carpenter,*
ed. by G. Beith].
TC, i 5 Jy31, 25 r
Review [*The Sacco-Vanzetti case,*
by O. K. Fraenkel].
TC, ii 10 D31, 29 r
Review
[*Germany—Fascist or Soviet,*
by H. R. Knickerbocker;
European dictatorships,
by C. Sforza;
Ten years of tyranny in Italy,
by P. Nenni].
TC, iii 15 My32, 28 r
Review
[*Memoirs of Prince von Bulow,*
vol 3].
TC, iii 17 Jy32, 28—29 r
Review
[*Tomorrow will be different,*
by D. George].
TC, iii 17 Jy32, 29—30 r
Review
[*Challenge of Russia,*
by S. Eddy;
*The new Russia; Agriculture in
Soviet Russia,* by J. Beauchamp;
Seven years in Soviet Russia,
by P. Scheffer].
TC, ii 9 N31, 25—27 r
Review [*Moscow has a plan,*
by M. Ilin;
Among the nudists,
by F. and M. Merrill;
Modern Germanies,
by C. Hamilton].
TC, ii 7 S31, 22—23 r
Review
[*More essays of love and virtue,*
by H. H. Ellis;
America the menace,
by G. Duhamel;
The scientific outlook,
by B. Russell].
TC, ii 8 Oc31, 26—28 r
Review
[*Views and reviews: first series,*
by H. H. Ellis;
Stalin, by Essad-Bey].
TC, iii 15 My32, 32 r
Watson, Holmes and Moriarty.
TC, i 3 My31, 18—22 c
What does the public want?
TC, iv 19 S32, 1—4 c

Evans, Margiad
Review [*Welsh border country,*

by P. T. Jones *et al.*]
W, 10 Oc39, 285—86 r
Country dance [*Deep waters,*
by R. E. Mitchell; *Old nurse,*
by B. B. Carter; *The blue bed,*
by G. Jones].
W, 2 Ag37, 71—73 r

Evans, Mfanwy
Abstract art: collecting the
fragments.
NO, ii 3 N35, 258—63 c
Beginning with Picasso.
AX, 2 A35, 3 c
Dead or alive.
AX, 1 J35, 3—4 c
Helion today: a personal
comment.
AX, 3 N35, 4, 8—9 c
Order, order!
AX, 6 Su36, 4—8 c
Paul Nash, 1937.
AX, 8 W37, 12—13 c

Everall, Robert
Ancient glass.
CA, 9 1931, 277 v

Evergreen [periodical]
rev. by A. T. Cunningham

Every, George
Civilisation contracts.
B, 3 Sp39, 6—7 v
Xmas poem.
B, 3 Sp39, 5 v

Ewart, Gavin
Ambivalence.
PL, i 1 F39, [19] v
Answers to an enquiry.
NV, 11 Oc34, 18 p
Audenesque [*The dance of death,*
by W. H. Auden].
NV, 7 F34, 21—22 r
Audenesque for an initiation.
NV, 6 D33, 12—13 v
Cage me a Harrisson.
T, 11 Jy38, 65—66 v
Dollfuss day, 1935.
CPP, 3 Jy36, 54 v
The English wife.
CPP, 1 My36, 3—4 v
Home.
Y, i 1 M39, 18 v
Inner circle.
NS, i 3 Je34, 234—35 p
John Betjeman's Brighton.
Y, i 2 My39, 76—77 v
The life of the young.
TU, 4 F35, 29—32 v
The old ladies.
FB, i 2 3M36, 45 v
March, April, May.

NV, 4 Jy33, 10 v
Miss Twye.
NV, 30 Su38, 11 v
No flowers by request; Poem.
NV, 5 Oc33, 12—13 v
Note.
C, 6/7 N37, [43] c
The old school.
OB, i 2 Je—Jy34, 12—13 v
'On the author's photograph';
Phallus in wonderland.
NV, 3 My33, 4—11 v
Poem.
NV, 9 Je34, 13 v
Poem.
CL, ii 1 Au34, 14—15 v
Poem.
RM, 2 D34, 56—57 v
Poem.
FB, ii 4 25J37, 20 v
Poem.
, 8 J38, [7] v
Poem before sleep.
CM, ii 1 Su35, 222—23 v
Poem on reality.
OB, i 1 M—A34, 34 v
Poems.
OB, i 4 Je35, 41 v
Public school.
OB, i 3 W34, 16 v
Review
The year's poetry, 1936,
ed. D. K. Roberts and
J. Lehmannl.
C, 3 A37, [20] r
St. Paul.
NV, 4 Jy33, 4 v
Scrutiny of 'Scrutiny', 1.
TC, vii 31 S—Oc33, 54—55 c
Sentimental blues.
FB, i 3 9My36, 61 v
Shakespeare's dream.
LD, ii 1 Oc37, 7 v
Three poems.
CPP, 4/5 Ag36, 87—88 v
Verse from an opera —
The village dragon'.
CPP, 10 Au37, 43—49 v
A young man's lament; Song.
, 2 M37, [9—10] v
Poems and songs
rev. by A. Dickins; R. Fuller
see also Södergran, E.

wart, Gavin and Symons, Julian
Two views of a play
Trial of a judge,
by S. Spender].
, 10 My38, 52—54 c

wen, Alfred Harry
The renaissance of virtue.
, i 8 D34, 7—8 c

Television and the repertory
theatre.
R, i 5 Je34, 12—13 c

The examiner [periodical]
rev. by M. Scott

Eyles, Vivyan
Beloved earth.
OO, xi 56 N31, 172—81 p
The stranger within their gates.
OO, xii 58 My32, 89—99 p
The stranger within their gates.
TC, v 27 My33, 62—69 p
Worship.
OO, xii 57 F32, 44—48 p

Eyre, Lorimer
Wedding down in Georgia.
P, 4 1938, 71—86 p

F

F., A. W.
Review [*Peace on earth*,
by the Left Theatre].
TU, 4 F35, 52—54 dr

Fabian Nursery Propaganda
Group
Armaments bulletin.
TC, iii 17 Jy32, 31—32 c
Bulletin.
TC, iii 15 My32, 36;
TC, iii 16 Je32, 31—32;
TC, iii 18 Ag32, 31—32;
TC, iv 19 S32, 31—32;
TC, iv 22 D32, 30—32;
TC, iv 23 J33, 31—32 c

Fact [periodical] no. 3
rev. by D. Garman

Fae *pseud.*
Cottenham.
FB, i 1 4F36, 22 p

Fairburn, Arthur Rex Dugard
From 'Poems of the dark and
the light'.
I, i 2/3 15S31, 72—75 v
Mr T. S. Eliot and the church.
EQ, i 3 N34, 186—93 c
Winter's night.
I, i 4 15D31, 108 v

Faithfull, Theodore, J.
An ideal sex education.
TC, vi 32 N33, 78—82 c

Falconer, George
Improvisation.
DD, xi 47 S—Oc34, 77 v

Farewell,
M, i 1 Je33, 60 v

Farey, Michael
Art at the universities.
FB, ii 4 25J37, 10—11 c

Farleigh, John
World revival in timber.
LR, ii 5 F36, 213 i

Farr, Ruth E.
Pride.
NS, i 6 D34, 461—68 p

Farrell, Brian Anthony
Student self-government.
NO, i 3 F34, 261—65 c

Farrell, James Thomas
Fellow countrymen
rev. by D. Gillespie
A note on literary criticism
rev. by J. Lindsay
Studs Lonigan
rev. by R. Wright

Fascist quarterly [periodical]
rev. by T. Lincoln

Faulkner, Edwin
Art.
JG, 36 Sp36, [14] v
Dartmoor: a sonnet.
DD, vii 26 S—Oc30, 388 v
The mystery.
JG, 31 W34, [14] v
The mystic in the desert.
DD, viii 29 Su31, 66v
Nocturne; Song.
DD, viii 28 J—F31, 9—10 v
Pan's pipings.
DD, vii 27 N—D30, 447 v
The paradox.
JG, 34 Au35, [28] v
The philosopher and the outcast.
DD, ix 31 J—F32, 10 v
The poetry of Sir William Watson.
DD, vii 26 S—Oc30, 376—80 c
The position of Keats.
DD, vii 27 N—D30, 434—39 c
Reviews and notices.
DD, vii 26 S—Oc30, 416—17;
vii 27 N—D30, 461—63 r
The song-thrush at sundown.
JG, 28 Sp34, [28—29] v
Spinoza.
JG, 24 Sp33, [7] v
The world of Herrick.
DD, viii 28 J—F31, 15—21 c

Faulkner, William
Light in August
rev. by H. G. Porteus
Soldier's pay, etc.
rev. by G. A. Highet

Fausset, Hugh I'Anson
A modern prelude
rev. by J. P. Hogan

Favorsky, V. A.
Lenin.
LR, iii 10 N37, 587 i

Fearing, Kenneth
Take a letter;
C stands for civilisation.
T, 12/13 Oc38, 100—101 v

Fearon, George
Repertory and Coventry.
R, i 7 N34, 12 c

Fedden, Robin
[*i.e.* Henry Romilly]
The mutual weapon;
Resurrection; Winter sleep.
V, 6 Je30, 267—69 v
Now with his love.
V, 5 F30, 216—17 v

Federation of Progressive
Societies
High Leigh Conference report.
TC, iv 20 Oc32, 26—32 c

Feibleman, James Kern
The lecture on science.
TC, v 28 Je33, 218 v
Plato in the swamps.
LT, i 10 D36, 22 v

Fellowes, Enid Hamilton-
see Hamilton-Fellowes, Enid

Fen, Elizaveta
Escape.
NS, i 4 Ag34, 294—314 p
Monte estremo.
NS, ii 4 Ag35, 258—73 p

Fenby, Charles
Dog fish.
NS, ii 1 F35, 13—21 p

Fenby, Eric
Our lord and our lady
[words by H. Belloc].
HR, 7 1934, 33 m

Fenellosa, Ernest
Chinese written character
rev. by A. Hodge

Fenwick
Winter sports hints for novices.
ND, 24 9D37, 23—24 p

Fergus, David H.
You'll think I'm daft.
LR, iii 10 N37, 610—12 p

Ferguson, Delancey
*Pride and passion: Robert Burns,
1759—1796*
rev. by J. B. Caird

Fergusson, Russell
The mad and the moneyed.
ND, 6 5Ag37, 31c

Fermor, Una Ellis- *see*
Ellis-Fermor, Una

Fernandez, E.
The sappers, tr. by H. Simpson.
NW, ns2 Sp39, 31—33 p

Ferrie, William
Introduction to broadcasting.
VP, i 1 A—Je34, 2—3 c

Feuchtwanger, Leon
Paris Congress speech.
LR, i 11 Ag35, 469 c

Ffrench-Salkeld, Cecil
Pervigilium veneris.
C, i 28 27Je36, 223—24 v

Fielding, Michael
Birth control:
the sociological factor.
TC, i 4 Je31, 4—6 c

Field, Arthur *tr. see*
Borde, Andrew

Field, Ben
The market.
NW, 3 Sp37, 225—34 p

Field, Jonathan *see*
Wang, Shelley

Fiennes, David
Carrots and thistles.
FB, ii 5 5M37, 37—39 c

Films reviewed:
China strikes back
rev. by F. Jackson
The Congress dances
rev. by J. W. Downing
Housing problems
rev. by B. Nixon
Land without bread

rev. by F. Jackson
Men and jobs
rev. by E. Coxhead
Modern times
rev. by E. Coxhead
New Babylon rev. by P. P.
Night mail rev. by B. Nixon
Nutrition rev. by E. Coxhead
Peace of Britain
rev. by F. Jackson
Rhodes of Africa
rev. by E. Coxhead
Things to come
rev. by E. Coxhead
Today we live
rev. by E. Coxhead
We from Kronstadt
rev. by E. Coxhead
Note: Criticism of separate films
and films generally can be found
under the following authors:
K. Allott; O. Blakeston;
L. Carrick; A. Cavalcanti;
E. Coxhead; J. Gaudin;
V. Glenville; W. Goldman;
G. Greene; R. Herring;
H. Howarth; J. L. Irvine;
F. Jackson; H. Kabir; Kino;
L. Lye; B. Nixon; G. F. Noxon;
R. Papineau; W. A. Reynolds;
W. Roberts; P. Rotha; Scotland;
M. Seton; V. Small;
R. Spottiswoode; J. Todd;
G. M. Turnell; B. Viertel;
N. Wilson; B. Wright.

Findlater, Gavin
Beauty and the beast.
MS, vi 2 Jy35, 143—46 c
On twentieth-century prose.
[*Modern prose style,*
by B. Dobrée].
MS, v 4 J35, 260 r

Finnemore, Hilda
A bonfire; The grass of the field.
DD, xi 45 My—Je34, 50 v

Firefly, Rufus T. *pseud.*
On literary rackets.
PP, 9 M39, 10—12 c

The first British artists' congress.
LR, iii 5 Je37, 289 c

A first-class luxury
[*English poetical autographs,*
ed. by D. Flower and
A. N. L. Munby].
NV, 31/32 Au38, 21 r

Firth, Raymond William
Art and life in New Guinea
rev. by R. Todd

Fischer, Ernst
The path of the Austrian left
opposition to communism.
TU, 4 F35, 7—15 c

Fischer, Marjorie
Palaces on Monday
rev. by F. Le Gros Clark

Fisher, Arista
The talk of the town.
NS, ii 3 Je35, 221—31 p

Fisher, Charles
Poem.
W, 1 Su37, 24 v
Poem.
W, 10 Oc39, 273 v
Where dragons dance.
W, 4 M38, 144—46 p

Fisher, F. J.
see Williams-Ellis, Amabel

Fisher, John
Marxist musuem in Berlin.
LR, ii 2 M36, 247—49 c

Fisher, R. C.
The Paris exhibition.
LR, iii 8 S37, 478—82 c

Fisher, S.
Poem.
DD, x 38 M—A33, 27 v

Fisher, Vardis
We are betrayed
rev. by G. West

Fitch, H. C.
Sonatina in red and gold.
DD, xi 46 Jy—Ag34, 62—63 v

Fitton, James
Art in industry.
LR, i 7 A35, 253 i
The Bishop of London's balance
sheet.
LR, i 6 M35, 219 i
Chambermaid.
LR, ii 3 D35, 113 i
Champion of the free.
LR, ii 9 Je36, 419 i
Esprit de corps.
LR, i 3 D34, 92 i
Footing the Sedition Bill.
LR, ii 7 A36, 304 i
For charity.
LR, i 5 F35, 163 i
The girl who took the
wrong turning.
CL, ii 1 Oc35, 21 i
Illustration.

LR, ii 1 Oc35, 31 i
The lion lies down with the
lamb.
LR, ii 14 N36, 734 i
Making an honest woman
of her.
LR, ii 5 F36, 193 i
A new use for perambulators.
LR, i 2 N34, 25 i
The people's friend Black Beauty.
LR, i 2 N34, 34 i
Recruits wanted.
LR, iii 10 N37, 609 i
The rival firms.
LR, i 3 D34, 50 i
Sir T. U. Cit.
LR, ii 11 Ag36, 543 i
Sunday oracle
LR, iii 1 F37, 7 i
Twelve good men and true.
LR, i 9 Je35, 363 i
We've got a housing plan.
LR, ii 8 My36, 358 i
Who killed Cock Robin?
LR, ii 2 N35, 67 i
With my body I thee worship.
LR, i 10 Jy35, 395 i

Fitton, James *and others*
A calendar for 1936
rev. by A. L. Lloyd

Fitts, Dudley *see*
Taggard, Genevieve

Fitzgerald, Brian Vesey- *see*
Vesey-Fitzgerald, Brian

Fitzgerald, W.
Wild life is beautiful on a platter.
T, 12/13 Oc38, 105 v

Fitzgibbon, Dillon Constantine
Editorial.
Y, i 1 M39, 3—4 c
Editorial.
Y, i 2 My39, 51—52 c
Luncheon party.
LD, i 1 J37, 17 p
Ronald Firbank:
an appreciation.
PR, 23 N37, 2—3 c
The stroke of genius.
LD, i 2 M37, 17—18 p
see also Cocteau, J.

Fitzhugh, Terence
Madrid.
PP, 15 N39, 6 v

Flavus *pseud.*
Prospects for the Boat race.
FB, i 2 3M36, 43 c

Fleming, Peter
At the theatre.
ND, 15 7Oc37, 37 dr
The theatre.
ND, 7 12Ag37, 29 dr
The theatre.
ND, 10 2S37, 29 dr
The theatre.
ND, 12 16S37, 29 dr
One's company
rev. by T. Lincoln

Fletcher, John Gould
Christianity and the modern
artist.
I, i 4 15D31, 101 c
In Tintern valley.
I, i 1 15Je31, 12 v
The man beneath the mountain.
I, i 2/3 15S31, 62 v
Pablo Picasso.
I, i 2/3 15S31, 36—37 c
Poetry and the modern
consciousness.
I, i 4 15D31, 117—24 c
Three fables.
I, i 1 15Je31, 22—24 p

Fletcher, Joseph Smith
Close of play.
HR, 6 1933, 21—28 p

Fleur-de-Lys *pseud.*
The pencil.
LR, i 2 N34, 37—38 p

Fleure, Herbert John
The Welsh people.
W, 10 Oc39, 265—69 c

Flight, Claude
Surrealism.
IP, i 1 6A39, 9—11 c

Flodden field.
T, 4 Je37, [10—11] v

Flower, Desmond John
Newman *ed.*
The pursuit of poetry
rev. by J. Bennett
see also Morand, Paul

Flower, Desmond John
Newman *and* Munby, A. N. L.
English poetical autographs
rev. by NV, 31/32 Au38, 21;
A. J. A. Symons

Flower, Margaret *and*
Flower, Desmond John Newman
*Cassell's anthology of English
poetry* rev. by G. Taylor

Flower, Robin Ernest William
Monkey music, I [and] II.
R, i 4 My34, 10, 14 v

Flugel, John Carl
Comment on the basis of the
Sexology group.
TC, iv 21 N32, 20 c
Sex and dress.
TC, ii 13 M32, 13—18 c

Fodor, Marcel William
South of Hitler
rev. by F. E. Jones

Fogazzaro, Antonio
The last will,
tr. by E. Richardson,
EQ, i 3 N34, 153—58 p

Foggie, Neil
Norwegian conversation.
VS, i 3 D38—F39, 10 v

Foley, Martha *ed. see*
Burnett, Whit

Follick, Mont
Facing facts rev. by H. Fyfe.

Fontmell, E. V. de
see De Fontmell, E. V. *pseud.*

Foot, Michael Mackintosh
and others
Young Oxford and war
rev. by G. West

Footman, David
Half way east
rev. by L. A. Pavey

Forbes, Rosemary
The island.
DD, viii 29 Su31, 58 v

Ford, Charles Henri
From 'Confessions of a freak'.
SV, 4A Sp39, 10—12 p
Poem for Paul Eluard.
LB, 7 D38, 16 v
Poems and prose.
CV, 4 1935, 10—13 v
Sonnets.
CV, 3 Su35, 3—7 v
The garden of disorder
rev. by J. Symons; H. Treece;
P. Tyler

Ford, Gertrude
For a March birthday.
DD, vii 27 N—D30, 432—33 v

Ford, Walter
Hymn to the diversity of
creation.
C, i 14 7M36, 112 v
Note on a newspaper
conversation.
PP, 10 A39, 18 v
Obscurity in verse and bees
in bonnets.
PP, 6 D38, 14—15 c
Poetry and who cares anyway?
PP, 8 F39, 13—15 c
Song of the war.
PP, 15 N39, 3 v
Song to be rendered by a
mass choir of capitalists for the
edification of workers ignorant
of economic laws.
PP, 5 N38, 14 v

Forrist, R. S.
Homage to Kafka.
PE, 3 Oc36, 99—101 c
Lady Mary Wortley Montagu
and [P.] Wyndham Lewis
[*Letters* of Lady Mary
Wortley Montagu;
Filibusters in Barbary,
by P. Wyndham Lewis].
PE, 2 S36, 61—63 r
Luigi Pirandello.
PE, 1 Ag36, 31 c
While the play lasts.
PE, 4 N36, 138—40 p

Forster, Edward Morgan
The last parade.
NW, 4 Au37, 1—5 p
Goldsworthy Lowes Dickinson
rev. by A. L. Morton

Fortescue, Tim
Interval.
LD, i 2 M37, 7, 9 p

Foss, Arthur
Review
[*The Victorians and their books*,
by A. Cruse].
LD, i 1 J37, 11 r

Foss, Hubert James
Composition in England.
LD, i 4 Je37, 16—18 c

Foster, Phoebe
The tree.
DD, xi 43 J—F34, 15 v

Foster, William *pseud.*
see Lodge, Oliver William Foster

Foster-Melliar, R. A.
En passant.

JG, 25 Su33, [7] v
Lines from 'Evensong',
JG, 28 Sp34, [7] v
Love's limousine.
JG, 24 Sp33, [5] v
Springtide, 1918 and 1938.
JG, 68 Sp39, [20—22] v
To the lady of 'Upalong'.
JG, 63 W37, [5] v

Fougasse *pseud.* of C. K. Bird.
Cartoon.
R, i 8 D34, 2 i

Fox, Douglas C.
Warkalemada kolingi yaoburrda
[aborigine].
TO, ii 7 Ag39, 6—10 c
see also Frobenius, Leo

Fox, Ralph
Abyssinian methods.
LR, ii 2 N35, 81—82 c
Conversation with a lama.
NW, 2 Au36, 179—88 p
Cultured
[*A journal of these days*,
by A. J. Nock].
LR, i 6 M35, 240 r
Henri Barbusse.
CL, ii 1 Oc35, 2—6 c
How men live.
LR, i 5 F35, 161—65 c
Kingdom Coming.
LR, i 8 My35, 292—95 c
Lawrence the twentieth
century hero.
LR, i 10 Jy35, 391—96 c
The open conspirator
[*An experiment in autobiography*,
by H. G. Wells].
LR, i 3 D34, 87—91 r
A picture of socialist life
[*Misha and Masha*,
by P. Binder].
LR, ii 16 J37, 913 r
A wasted life.
NW, 1 Sp36, 118—31 p
*The colonial policy of British
imperialism* rev. by D. Burton
The novel and the people
rev. by J. Lindsay; G. M. Turnell
This was their youth
rev. by T. L. Hodgkin

Fox, Swane
Art.
IP, i 1 6A39, 19—21 c

Foxall, Edgar
Democracy throws up a prophet.
NV, 2 M33, 12 v
Mr. Vulcan thus.
TC, v 28 Je33, 226 v

46

A note on working class
solidarity.
NV, 5 Oc33, 5 v
On years passing.
CV, 5 M36, [16] v
Poem.
CPP, 4/5 Ag36, 88—89 v
Poem.
CPP, 8 D36, 157 v
Poem.
CPP, 10 Au37, 26 v
Two poems.
TC, vi 35 Je34, 290 v

Foyle, Christina
Fashions in books.
K, i 2 D39—J40, 41—43 c

Fraenkel, Osmond K.
The Sacco-Vanzetti case
rev. by J. R. Evans

Fragment.
T, 4 Je37, [8] v

France, Anatole
Selected stories
rev. by H. E. Bates

France-Hayhurst, B.
The hedonists's prayer.
DD, ix 32 M—A32, 31 v
Love has come to stay.
DD, xi 48 N—D34, 104 v

Francelli, Mario
Eclogue.
Y, i 1 N39, 27 v
The family reunion,
by T. S. Eliot.
Y, i 2 My39, 91—96 c

Francesco da Milano
La canzone de Li Uccelli.
TO, i 1 J38, 19—20 m

Francis, Catherine Mills-
see Mills-Francis, Catherine

Francis, Evelyn
In the big firm.
LR, ii 1 Oc35, 34—37 p

Frank, Hannah
Illustration,
signed Al Araaf.
SM, 5supp. [1934], i
Job.
SM, 4supp. [1933?], i

Frank, Leonhard
Three of the three million
rev. by R. Wright

Frank, Waldo
Fascism.
TC, vi 32 N33, 87 c
Paris Congress speech.
LR, i 11 Ag35, 471 c
Where I stand.
TC, vi 33 D33—J34, 133—38 c

Frankfort, Henri
New works by Barbara Hepworth.
AX, 3 Jy35, 14 c

Frankland, Mabel
Barkston Ash.
JG, 70 Au39, [18—19] v
An hour.
JG, 68 Sp39, [18] v

Franklin, Sidney
The school and the corps.
OB, i 3 W34, 30—31 c

Fraser, Claude Lovat
Cover.
HR, 4 1931, cover i

Fraser, George Sutherland
Approaches to reality
[*The carnival,* by F. Prokosch;
The earth compels,
by L. MacNeice].
SV, 2 Au38, 32—37 r
Fragments from Paris.
K, i 2 D39—J40, 60—64 p
An incident of the campaign.
SV, 1 Su38, 11—18 p
Lean street.
SV, 6 Au39, 22 v
A moral tale
[*King Coffin,* by C. Aiken].
SV, 7 C39, 22—24 r
St. Andrews.
FB, iv 10 N38, 7 v
Spender's tragic statement
[*Trial of a judge*].
SV, 1 Su38, 33—36 r
To Ianthe.
C, ii 46 7N36, 155 v
Voices from America.
[*The trouble with tigers,*
by W. Saroyan;
Monday night, by K. Boyle].
SV, 4 Su39, 34—39 r
see also Breton, A.

Fraser, Gordon
Death of a spy.
K, i 1 17N39, 21—23 p

Fraser, Norrie
Ourselves alone.
VS, i 2 S—N38, 23—24 c

Fraser, Olave
The Vikings.
CM, ii 1 Su35, 221 v

Freedgood, Morton
Good nigger.
NW, 2 Au36, 92—95 p
Last of his tribe.
NW, 4 Au37, 178—84 p

Freeman, Joy
Nothing more.
NS, i 3 Je34, 209—10 p

Freeman, Richard Gavin
The Achilles heel of
communist theory?
TU, 1 1933, 12—27 c
Bolshevism and social
democracy.
TU, 2 1934, 49—60 c

Freixa, Rudolf
At the high village.
JG, 30 Au34, [21—22] v
Beautiful was our house.
JG, 26 Au33, [11] v
Books.
JG, 67 W38, [18—19] v
The fish.
JG, 23 W32, [21] v
The garden.
JG, 41 Su37, [23] v
I who dread death.
JG, 38 Au36, [20] v
It is not enough.
JG, 42 Au37, [24] v
Last day.
JG, 39 W36, [5—6] v
Northward
JG, 65 Su38, [14] v
One day my body.
JG, 21 Su32, [6] v
On the cliff edge.
JG, 28 Sp34, [26] v
Sonnet.
JG, 25 Su33, [6] v
Sonnet on the love sonnet.
JG, 24 Sp33, [6—7] v
Summer lightning.
JG, 29 Su34, [8] v
Time.
JG, 22 Au32, [16] v

Fremlin, Celia
The gods training college.
LD, i 3 My37, 18—19 p
The time railway.
LS, ii 1 My35, 5—8 p

Friel, George
Her brother died.
NS, ii 7 F36, 481—87 p
Home!

Friel, George (cont.)
MS, vi 4 J36, 339—45 p
You can see it for yourself.
NS, ii 1 F35, 65—69 p

Frobenius, Leo *and*
Fox, Douglas C.
African genius
rev. by D. Thompson

From a Soviet writer's
notebook: on the state farm.
VP, i 2 Jy—S34, 37—38 p

Frost, Margaret
from Summer nightfall.
PR, 11 27N35, 11 v

Fry, Edwin Maxwell
The spirit of the new
architecture.
EQ, i 1 My34, 60—62 c

Fuji, Takeshi
Two poems.
TO, i 1 J38, 6 v

Fuller, Jean V. O.
Many are called.
C, i 7 18J36, 55—56 p

Fuller, Ronald
The jest.
DD, vii 26 S—Oc30, 408 v

Fuller, Roy B.
The audience and politics.
T, 18 Je39, 50—52 c
August,
SV, 4A Sp39, 19 v
Ballad of the last heir; Poems
1 to 6.
T, 9 M38, 2—9 v
New Year; Poem.
NV, 19 F36, 13 v
Poem.
NV, 12 D34, 10 v
Poem.
PR, 19 20Oc36, 9 v
Poem.
CPP, 6 Oc36, 117 v
Poem.
CPP, 7 N36, 129—30 v
Poem.
T, 5 S37, [11] v
Poem.
NW, 5 Sp38, 233—35 v
Poem.
NW, 3 Sp37, 85—87 v
Poem.
T, 14 D38, 125 v

Poem; Death.
T, 17 A39, 2—3 v
Poem; Poem.
T, 8 J38, [5—6] v
Poem; Poem.
T, 2 M37, [11—12] v
Poems by editors
[*Confusions about X,*
by J. Symons;
Several observations,
by G. Grigson].
T, 17 A39, 24—26 r
Review
[*Poems,* by R. Warner].
T, 4 Je37, [21—22] r
Review
[*New writing,* no. 5].
T, 11 Jy38, 74 r
Review
[*Post-Victorian poetry,*
by H. Palmer].
T, 11 Jy38, 75 r
Review
[*Overtures to death,*
by C. Day Lewis].
T, 14 D38, 140 r
Review
[*Poems and songs,*
by G. Ewart].
T, 15/16 F39, 170—71 r
Thriller.
CPP, 9 Sp37, 44 v
To murder someone.
T, 15/16 F39, 157 v

Furmanov, Dmitri Andreyevich
Chapayev
rev. by T. H. Wintringham

Furnell, Grace
Working like a fiend.
PP, 11 My39, 18 v

Fyfe, Henry Hamilton
Comment on the Promethean
Society report.
TC, iii 18 Ag32, 13 c
A most urgent need.
LR, ii 13 Oc36, 669 c
The people's front
[by G. D. H. Cole].
LR, iii 7 Ag37, 431—32 r
The press and mass hysteria.
LR, i 5 F35, 169—72 c
The press and the people's
front.
LR, ii 15 D36, 807—10 c
Two Daniels come to
judgment
[*Inside Europe,* by J. Gunther;
Facing facts, by M. Follick].
LR, ii 2 M36, 282—83 r

G

G., G.
On human nature.
FB, i 2 3M36, 45 v

G., H.
German proletarian literature.
PP. 13/14 Jy—Ag39, 14—19 c

G., L.
Red front; Red harvest;
To the murdered children of Shanghai.
ST, i 1 F33, 5, 13, 16 v
A song for Deptford and Battersea.
ST, i 2 A33, 7 v

G., R. *see* Freeman, Richard Gavin

G., V.
Hands.
OO, xi 55 Je31, 113—18 p

Gabriel
From scenes like these auld Scotia's
grandeur springs.
LR, ii 14 N36, 745 i

Gall, Ivan
Daybreak, tr. by P. Selver.
SM, 4 1933, 112 v

Gallagher, William
My life on the Clyde
rev. by T. A. Jackson

Galletley, Leonard
The argument.
JG, 19 W31, [27—28] v
Aspen.
JG, 30 Au34, [13] v
Autumn evening.
JG, 67 W38, [7] v
The carrier's cart.
JG, 26 Au33, [12] v
Council for the heart.
JG, 33 Su35, [14] v
Diverse.
JG, 25 Su33, [21] v
Doomed cherry trees.
JG, 29 Su34, [9] v
Duet.
JG, 24 Sp33, [11] v
Glamour.
JG, 23 W32, [14—15] v
A green evening.
JG, 37 Su36, [20] v
In a garden.
JG, 15 W30, [22—23] v
In a spring glade.
JG, 20 Sp32, [5—6] v
Inishtor.

DD, vii 27 N—D30, 433 v
Leaving the old house.
JG, 34 Au35, [17] v
Lines.
JG, 27 W33, [12] v
Morning fog.
DD, vii 26 S—Oc30, 402—3 v
The other voice.
JG, 13 Su30, [29—31] v
The raven croaks.
JG, 32 Sp35, [16] v
Rhododendrons reflected.
JG, 38 Au36, [9] v
September night.
JG, 22 Au32, [23] v
Sleep.
DD, ix 36 N—D32, 102 v
Soul to body.
JG, 70 Au39, [32] v
Squirrels.
JG, 21 Su32, [21] v
Stolen fruit.
JG, 28 Sp34, [19] v
Swans and herons.
DD, viii 28 J—F31, 8 v
Than speech more eloquent.
JG, 65 Su38, [11] v
This quiet lane.
JG, 36 Sp36, [30] v
Time the exactor.
DD, ix 34 Jy—Ag32, 64 v
To Keats.
JG, 66 Au38, [9—10] v
To sleep.
JG, 40 Sp37, [26] v
The wayward river.
JG, 18 Au31, [9] v
What the sea sang.
JG, 17 Su31, [6—7] v
A wild night.
JG, 68 Sp39, [10] v
Would our foolish hearts remember.
JG, 35 W35, [16] v

Gallop, Rodney
Saints and ploughs in Mexico.
NW, ns2 Sp39, 214—19 p

Galloway, Alex
In the factory.
PP, 13/14 Jy—Ag39, 13 v
The labourers.
VS, i 4 M—My39, 16 v
On leaving school.
PP, 10 A39, 4 v

Galsworthy, John
Foreword.
HR, 4 1931, [5] c
War and peace.
TC, i 6 Ag31, 15—16 c
Forsytes, Pendyces and others
rev. by L. A. Pavey

Galves, Manuel
Les chemins de la mort
rev. by G. Pendle

Galwey, Geoffrey Valentine
Boanerges.
P, 2 1938, 167—78 p

Gandar-Dower, K. C.
Flashlight photograph.
ND, 11 9S37, 14—16 p

Gandhi, Mohandas Karamchand
Religion and art.
I, i 4 15D31, 99 c

Gannes, Harry *and* **Repard,** Theodore
Spain in revolt rev. by V. Ackland

Garcia Lorca, Federico
Absent soul.
CPP, 7 N36, 124—25 v
Body present.
CPP, 7 N36, 123—24 v
The dawn, tr. by A. L. Lloyd.
NW, 4 Au37, 177 v
The faithless wife, tr. by A. L. Lloyd.
LR, iii 2 M37, 73—74 v
Lament for Ignacio Sanchez Mejias,
tr. by A. L. Lloyd.
CPP, 7 N36, 122—23 v
The martyrdom of St. Eulalia,
tr. by A. L. Lloyd.
EQ, i 3 N34, 183—85 v
Song, tr. by A. L. Loyd.
CPP, 7 N36, 125 v
Song, tr. by S. Richardson.
NW, ns1 Au38, 109 v
Poems, tr. by S. Spender and J. L. Gili
rev. by N. Heseltine; H. Treece

Gardiner, Charles Wrey
Eyes in the dark.
PQ, i 1 Sp39, 10 v
Reviews.
PQ, i 1 Sp39, 23—27 r

Gardner, Diana
Engravings.
PL, i 1 F39, [15], 20, 27 i

Gardner, John
The amateur, the professional and the
composer.
LD, i 1 J37, 14—15 c
The failure of modern music.
LD, i 2 M37, 24—25 c
Kurt Weill and the sophisticated attempt
at popular music.
Y, i 1 N39, 28—31 c
Opera and the amateur.
LD, ii 1 Oc37, 19—20 c

Gardner, Ralph
International brigade.
PP, 7 J39, 10 v
Refugee.
PP, 10 A39, 10 v

Garioch, Robert *pseud.*
Idyll on Sontra.
TO, i 2 A38, 19—21 p
Review [*Autumn journal,*
by L. MacNeice; *Albannach,*
ed. by G. J. Russell and J. F. Hendry].
NA, i 1 Au39, 91—96 r
Review [*The kingis quair,*
ed. by W. Mackay Mackenzie].
NA, i 1 Au39, 102—4 r
Three lonely passengers.
NA, i 1 Au39, 66—68 p

Garman, Douglas
Armed intervention
[*Armed intervention in Russia,
1919—1922,*
by W. R. and Z. K. Coates].
LR, i 8 My35, 335—36 r
Good enough for *Punch?*
[*Peace with honour,* by A. A. Milne].
LR, ii 2 N35, 93—95 r
Ibsen's early development.
LR, iii 4 My37, 215—23 c
A jubilee medal.
LR, i 8 My35, 295—96 v
Look landward, angel!
[*Self-subsistence for the unemployed,*
by J. W. Scott.]
LR, i 11 Ag35, 476—78 r
Montagu Slater's *Easter.*
LR, ii 4 J36, 180 dr
Not I, but the wind [by F. Lawrence].
LR, i 7 A35, 286—87 r
Six on revolutionary art
[*Revolution in writing,* by C. Day Lewis;
Five on revolutionary art,
by H. Read and others].
LR, ii 4 J36, 181—83 r
Tennyson and his age.
LR, ii 11 Ag36, 570—79 c
Testament of a revolutionary
[*Illusion and reality,* by C. Caudwell].
LR, iii 6 Jy37, 352—54 r
What? . . The devil?
LR, i 1 Oc34, 34—36 c
Writers' international.
LR, i 5 F35, 180—82 c
Writing in revolt [*Fact,* no. 3].
LR, iii 8 S37, 498—99 r
Post mortem on politicians
rev. by G. West
see also Barbusse, H.

Garnett, Margaret
A reply to 'All we like sheep'.
LD, i 4 Je37, 27, 29 c

Garrett, George
Apostate.
LR, ii 6 M36, 260—66 p
The first hunger march.
NW, 3 Sp37, 72—84 p
Fishmeal.
NW, 2 Au36, 71—91 p
The overcoat.
LR, i 8 My35, 315—23 p
The parish.
LR, iii 9 Oc37, 542—48 p
The redcap.
CL, ii 1 Oc35, 7—14 p

Garrett, John
Broadway scene.
R, i 3 A34, 12 dr
Editorial.
R, i 1 N33, 3; R, i 2 F34, 3; R, i 3 A34,
3; R, i 4 My34, 3; R, i 5 Je34, 3; R, i 6
Oc34, 3; R, i 7 N34, 3; R, i 8 D34, 3 c
More wine than water.
R, i 6 Oc34, 16 dr
Narcissism or criticism
[*First nights,* by J. Agate].
R, i 8 D34, 12 r
Purposeful plays and derivative dogmas
[*Maternité,* by E. Brieux;
Sunshine house, by H. C. Voller].
R, i 1 N33, 18—19 dr
see also Auden, Wystan Hugh

Garrett, John *and* **Beecroft,** F. S. *eds.*
Whole issue.
T, 4 Je37

Garry, Stephen *pseud.*
see Djavakhishvili, M.; Gladkov, F.;
Kldiashvili, S.; Tchikvadze, P.; Tikhonov,
N.; Zoschenko, M.

Garthwaite, A. W.
Spain — April 1939.
K, i 2 D39—J40, 55—56 p

Garvin, Katherine
The schoolroom carol.
DD, xi 43 J—F34, 11—12 v

Gascoyne, David Emery
And the seventh dream is the dream
of Isis.
NV, 5 Oc33, 9—12 v
Answers to an enquiry.
NV, 11 Oc34, 11—13 p
Comment on Auden.
NV, 26/27 N37, 24—25 c
Competition.
CPP, 1 My36, 5 v
The conspirators.
NW, ns3 C39, 60—64 v
The end is near the beginning.
NV, 16 Ag35, 5 v
Five poems.

NV, 15 Je35, 4—6 v
Fragments from The symptomatic
world.
CPP, 6 Oc36, 113—15; 7 N36, 134—35 v
The great day.
J, 1 J36, 15—17 p
Henry Miller.
C, ii 39, 19S36, 87—88 c
I. The last hour. II. De profundis.
III. Lachrymae. IV. Ex nihilo.
PL, i 2 A39, [14—15] v
The light of the lion's mane.
CPP, 8 D36, 160—62 p
Morning dissertation; Poem.
NV, 6 D33, 11—12 v
Mozart 'Sursum corda'.
SV, 4 Su39, 33 v
Pieta.
SV, 6 Au39, 21 v
On spontaneity [*Petron,*
by H. S. Davies; *Facile,*
by P. Eluard].
NV, 18 D35, 19 r
Phenomena.
CPP, 7 N36, 135 p
Poem.
EQ, i 4 F35, 222 v
Poetry: reality.
LT, i 3 My36, 6—8 c
The public rose [*La rose publique,*
by P. Eluard].
NV, 13 F35, 18 r
Snow in Europe.
NW, ns2 Sp39, 175 v
A sudden squall.
J, 2 My36, 4 v
The symptomatic world: fragment.
J, 1 J36, 17 v
'The truth is blind . . .'
NV, 18 D35, 14—15 v
Two poems.
PR, 16 6My36, 1—2 v
Two poems.
CPP, 2 Je36, 34—35 v
Two poems; Sonnet.
NV, 12 D34, 5—6 v
Hölderlin's madness rev. by F. Scarfe
Man's life is this meat
rev. by K. Allott; J. B. Harvey
A short survey of surrealism
rev. by Hastings *pseud.*; C. Madge;
R. Penrose
see also Arp, H.; Breton, A.; Bunuel, L.;
Char, R.; Dali, S.; Eluard, P.; Giacometti,
A.; Henry, M.; Hugnet, G.; Peret, B.;
Prassinos, G.; Ribemont-Dessaignes, G.;
Rimbaud, A.; Rosey, G.; Unik, P.

Gaskell, Hugh Selwyn
Who are you diggin' for, sexton-man?
DD, vii 27 N—D30, 443 v

The gate [periodical]
rev. by OB, i 1 M—A34, 2, 5

Gates, Sidney Barrington
Bateman's.
NS, ii 1 F35, 35—39 p

Gaudier-Brzeska, Henri
Four charcoal drawings.
TO, ii 6 A39, 4—7 i
Stylo drawing.
J, 1 J36, 21 i

Gaudin, Jack
Escalators.
CL, i 1 Su33, 2 v
A note on cinema.
CL, i 2 W33, 29—32 c
Shame!
CL, i 3 Sp34, 78—80 c

Gaved, Joan A.
Flora.
JG, 33 Su35, [6] v
Rondel.
JG, 34 Au35, [21] v

Gawsworth, John [*pseud.*
T. I. F. Armstrong]
Aetolia.
CV, 5 M36, [21] v
Books [*Tumbling in the bay,*
by O. St. J. Gogarty;
The sheltering tree, by N. Syrett].
IP, i 1 6A39, 4—6 r
Dentdale.
JG, Su39, [14] v
The meteors.
JG, 69 Su39, [14] v
Of comfort.
JG, 71 W39, [14] v
Private view.
SM, 2 S31, 47 v
Song; Dictator.
PL, i 1 F39, [7—8] v
Apes, japes and Hitlerism
rev. by TC, iii 18 Ag32, 25
Known signatures rev by Barker, G.
Snowballs, by O. Scrannel
rev. by A. D. Hawkins

Gay, Maisie
Why I prefer a pub.
R, i 2 F34, 10 p

Gee, Kenneth W.
The sculptor.
DD, ix 33 My—Je32, 45 v
Three women at the well; Pan.
DD, viii 28 J—F31, 5—7 v

Gelder, Stuart *see* Lawrence, Lettice Ada

Gell, P.
Preparing for revolution.
CL, i 2 W33, 24 v

Gellert, Hugo
Illustration to 'Capital'.
LR, i 11 Ag35, 455 i

Genge, G. Radcliffe
Nozze di Monica.
HR, 4 1931, 64 v

Genoss *pseud.*
Signing-on.
LR, i 1 Oc34, 46 p

George, Daniel *pseud.*
Tomorrow will be different
rev. by J. R. Evans

Geraint, George
Red coal.
LR, iii 1 F37, 35—41 p

Gerhardi, William
Memoirs of a polyglot
rev. by A. D. Hawkins

Gerome, P.
Paris Congress speech.
LR, i 11 Ag35, 469 c

Gershenzon, Mikhail Osipovich
On human values, tr. by R. Gill.
EQ, i 1 My34, 12—17 c

Giacometti, Alberto
Poem in seven spaces, tr. by D. Gascoyne.
NV, 6 D33, 8 v

Gibb, James
Fidelio at Sadler's Wells.
LR, iii 11 D37, 677 c

Gibberd, Kathleen
At sea.
NS, ii 2 A35, 103—12 p
The poor ladies.
NS, ii 5 Oc35, 359—67 p

Gibbon, Lewis Grassic
Writers' international.
LR, i 5 F35, 179—80 c
Grey granite rev. by J. Lehmann

Gibbons, Mrs R.
A chinese vase.
P, 2 1938, 95—107 p

Gibbons, Stella
Sisters.
P, 3 1938, 17—47 p

Gibbs-Smith, Charles Harvard
Review [*Blessington d'Orsay,*
by M. Sadleir].
HR, 7 1934, 69 r

Gibson, G. E.
Ben.
LR, i 10 Jy35, 414—15 p

Gibson, Lydia
Glamour.
LR, ii 16 J37, 861 i

Gibson, Noel
Absit invidia.
PP, 12 Je39, 15 v

Gibson, Susan
Dawn's forerunner.
DD, viii 29 Su31, 78 v
The retreat.
DD, vii 26 S—Oc30, 381 v

Gibson, Wilfrid Wilson
Becalmed.
JG, 41 Su37, [5] v
Clean through the crystal wave.
JG, 37 Su36, [5] v
The haul.
JG, 34 Au35, [5] v
The leafless tree.
HR, 4 1931, 17 v
Sea swallow.
HR, 7 1934, 51 v
The symbol.
JG, 71 W39, [5] v

Gibson, Will
Growing.
NS, ii 5 Oc35, 368—79 p

Gide, André
The individual.
LR, i 11 Ag35, 447—52 c
Back from the U.S.S.R.
rev. by P. Sloan
see also Tureck, L.

Gielgud, Val Henry
Outrage in Manchukuo
rev. by A. Powell

Gifford, Nina
Bavarian café.
P, 6 1939, 37 i
College courtyard.
P, 3 1938, 202 i

Gilbert, Stuart
A footnote to *Work in progress.*
EX, 7 Sp31, 30—33 c
Paris letter.
ND, 5 29Jy37, 20—21; ND, 17 21Oc37,
24—25; ND, 24 9D37, 20, 22 p
Review [*James Joyce and the plain*

reader, by C. Duff] .
TC, iii 15 My32, 27—28 r
Sauce for the goose.
TC, i 3 My31, 2—3 c

Gilby, Thomas
Poetic experience
rev. by D. Daiches

Gill, Eric
Art pure and mixed.
LR, ii 9 Je36, 420—23 c
Artist and craftsman.
LR, ii 2 N35, 79—80 c
Greetings on May day.
LR, iii 16 My38, 962 c
On art and propaganda.
LR, i 9 Je35, 341—42 c
Sculpture and the living model.
OO, xii 58 My32, 101—20 c
Slavery and freedom.
LQ, i 1 N36, [7—10] p
Beauty looks after itself
rev. by A. C. Sewter
Unemployment rev. by A. C. Sewter

Gill, Richard *tr.*
see Blok, A.; Dostoevsky, F.; Gershenzon,
M. O.

Gillespie, David
Short stories [*The first lover,*
by K. Boyle; *A purse of coppers,*
by S. O'Faolain; *Short stories
of Liam O'Flaherty; Fellow countrymen,*
by J. T. Farrell; *Best short stories of 1937,*
ed. by E. J. O'Brien].
LR, iii 13 F38, 821—25 r

Gillett, Tony
From prison.
CL, i 4 Su34, 100—1 v

Gillies, W. G.
The work of W. G. Gillies.
NA, i 1 Au39, 30—35 i

Gillson, T.
Poem.
P, 3 1938, 143 v

Gilson, Etienne
Christendom and the French tradition,
tr. by D. J. B. Hawkins.
AR, i 4 J38, 262—81 c

Giono, Jean
The bread-baking, tr. by J. Rodker.
NW, ns2 Sp39, 220—26 p
The corn dies, tr. by J. Rodker.
NW, 3 Sp37, 209—24 p
Jofroi de la Maussan, tr. by J. H. Whyte.
MS, iv 3 Oc33, 197—206 p

51

Gitlin, Murray
The hump.
NS, i 5 Oc34, 371–79 p

Gladkov, Fedor Vasilevich
Shock tempo, tr. by S. Garry.
NW, 5 Sp38, 182–86 p

Glaeser, Ernst
The last civilian
rev. by P. M. D.

Glanfield, Edward
Vision for a retrograde.
LD, i 1 J37, 3 p

Glendinning, Alex
Notes on a tradition.
NV, 2 M33, 14 v

Glenville, Victor
Film production: a survey of new films
and books.
LR, ii 13 Oc36, 708–10 c

Gloag, John
The Antique Dealers Fair.
ND, 15 7Oc37, 28 c

Glover, C. Gordon
Homiletic studies: enthusiasm.
EP, 2 Su36, 84–89 c

Glover, Edward George
The psychology of pacifism.
TC, vi 34 M34, 226–35 c
The dangers of being human
rev. by L. J. Isserlis

Godiwala, Hiralal
Sonnet – the song of labour.
RM, 1 Je34, 30 v

Godwin, E. A.
Film diary.
IP, i 1 6A39, 8–9 c

Goff, Margaret Locherbie-
see Locherbie-Goff, Margaret

Gogarty, Oliver St John
Yeats.
AW, Su39, 19–20 c
Tumbling in the hay
rev. by J. Gawsworth

Gold, Michael
Hell's Kitchen.
TC, v 28 Je33, 227–39 p
Kino of a factory town.
TC, iii 17 Jy32, 6–13 p
Paris Congress speech.
LR, i 11 Ag35, 469 c

Goldie, Fay King
Mine boy.
NW, ns3 C39, 155–58 p

Goldman, Bosworth
Calms in Torbay.
ND, 1 1Jy37, 40 c
The carefree English.
ND, 9 26Ag37, 32 c
Yachting.
ND, 11 9S37, 32 c

Goldman, William
Down at Mendel's.
NW, 4 Au37, 112–27 p
Literature and the East End.
NW, ns1 Au38, 77–86 c
The Marx brothers too.
LR, ii 15 D36, 830–31 c
Night follows day.
LR, iii 2 M37, 104–6 p
A night out.
LR, ii 10 Jy36, 510–13 p
A star in life.
NW, 2 Au36, 146–59 p
A youthful idyll.
NW, ns3 C39, 92–110 p

Goldring, Douglas
Pacifists in peace and war
rev. by G. West

Goldschmidt, A. M. E.
'Alice in Wonderland' psycho-analysed.
NO, i 1 My33, 68–72 c

Goldschmidt, Anthony
Monetary Utopias [*Tomorrow's money;
Political and economic writings*,
by C. V. Orage;
Property and improperty,
by J. A. Hobson].
LR, iii 6 Jy37, 374–75 r

Goldschmidt, Karl
Advertising: national characteristics.
EP, 3 Sp37, 230–39 c

Goldsmith, Margaret
Seven women against the world
rev. by P. Polson

Gongora y Argote, Luis de
Epithalamium from 'Las soledades',
tr. by E. M. Wilson.
EX, 7 Sp31, 47–49 v

Gonzalez Tunon, Raul
Long live the revolution,
tr. by A. L. Lloyd.
NW, 3 Sp37, 51 v

Good, J. L.
God made the country?
K, i 2 D39–J40, 56 v

Good, Thomas
Mr T. S. Eliot and orthodoxy [*The rock*]
NO, ii 3 N35, 267–71 r

Goodden, Wyndham
Allegory.
F, 2 Je30, 122–23 v
Centre-piece of screen-setting for
'The humours of the court'.
F, 1 F30, 1 i
Church bells; Sonnet.
F, 1 F30, 20–21 v
Fragment.
F, 6 Je31, 171 v
Sonnet; Contrast.
F, 4 D30, 40 v

Goodman, C.
Salud.
PP, 9 M39, 14–15 v
Throwbacks or contrast.
PP, 9 M39, 13–14 v

Goodman, Richard H.
Address.
CL, i 4 Su34, 90–93 v
Dead; His songs; Portrait of an aristocrat.
OO, xi 54 M31, 28–29 v
'Die duistre zon'.
OO, xi 55 Je31, 67–72 c
Elegy.
CL, i 2 W33, 23 v
First canto of a work in progress.
CL, i 3 Sp34, 60–67 v
For Ernst Thaelmann.
LR, i 4 J35, 123–24 v
Four poems.
OO, xi 55 Je31, 86–88 v
I see you standing.
OO, xii 57 F32, 26 v
I think of the day.
OO, xii 57 F32, 49 v
The lovers; Absence.
OO, xii 58 My32, 121–22 v
The manifesto.
OO, xii 58 My32, 88 v
A mother of China.
LR, iii 14 M38, 837–40 p
The new Napoleons.
LR, iii 13 F38, 773–78 c
Poem.
OO, x 52 My30, 502 v
Poem.
TC, vi 31 S–Oc33, 46 v
Prelude to a work in progress.
OO, x 51 F30, 419–20 v
Putai.
LR, iii 15 A38, 914–18 p
Red star over China [by E. Snow].
LR, iii 11 D37, 682–85 r

Réflexion sur la psychologie contem-
poraine.
OO, x 51 F30, 448 v
Review [*The armed muse,*
by H. E. Palmer; *The ecliptic,*
by J. G. MacLeod].
OO, x 53 N30, 638—39 r
Review [*Poems, 1914—1930,*
by E. Blunden].
OO, xi 54 M31, 61—64 r
Review
[*Sketches in the life of John Clare,*
by himself].
OO, xi 55 Je31, 141—43 r
Self's agents; End.
OO, x 53 N30, 608 v
Speech.
TC, iv 24 F33, 18—19 v
The squadrons.
TC, iv 21 N32, 15 v
These lives the sun breathed.
TC, vi 33 D33—J34, 160 v
Three poems.
OO, xi 56 N31, 161—62 v
To an unknown face.
OO, x 53 N30, 597 v

Goodwin, Geraint
Ap Towyn.
WR, ii 4 N39, 185—92 p

Gordon, Ian A.
The old miners.
MS, iv 2 Jy33, 117 v

Gordon, Steve
Boxing prospects.
FB, i 2 3M36, 44 c
The Cambridge boxing prospects.
FB, ii 5 5M37, 39—40 c

Gordon Walker, Patrick C.
The Balliol players.
R, i 5 Je34, 10—11 c
What is wrong with the History school
at Oxford.
NO, ii 1 My34, 49—56 c

Gorer, Geoffrey
Hot Striptease rev. by J. L. Grant

Gorer, Richard
Pavane and galliard.
CM, i 1 Sp33, 27—30 p
Programme notes for contemporary
composers.
CM, i 2 Su33, 71—73 c
Towards the light.
CM, i 3 Au33, 93—99 p

Gorky, Maxim
Challenge to intellectuals.
TC, iv 22 D32, 6—8 c
'The intellectual is imprisoned'.

ST, i 3 1933, 10—11 c
London.
LR, ii 12 S36, 604—7 p
Mother, as dramatised by B. Nixon
rev. by R. Wright

Gorky, Maxim *and others, eds.*
History of the civil war in the U.S.S.R.
rev. by R. Jardine
Problems of Soviet literature
rev. by C. Madge

Goss, John
Cockroaches and diamonds
rev. by E. Duthie

Gould, C.
François Mauriac.
F, 6 Je31, 208—12 c

Gould, Gerald *and others*
The year's poetry, [1935]
rev. by J. Lipton; J. Mair

Gow, Ronald
'Reasonable supervision thereof'.
R, i 5 Je34, 4 c

Gowardhandas
Monsoon, tr. by K. S. Bhat.
SM, 2 S31, 47 v

Grace, Josepha
The crippled girl.
PQ, i 1 Sp39, 19 v

Graham, Alethea
L'homme moyen sensuel.
V, 6 Je30, 279 v

Graham, Cuthbert
Teuchat storm.
MS, v 3 Oc34, 149 v
Wyndham Lewis and the 'fanatical Celt'.
MS, vi 3 Oc35, 210—15 c

Graham, Gore
Does the chimney still smoke?
LR, ii 13 Oc36, 705—7 p
Mr Plover and the U.S.S.R.
ST, i 1 F33, 6—10 p
Pigeon Bill.
NW, 1 Sp36, 147—58 p
Prometheus and the Bolsheviks
[by J. Lehmann].
LR, iii 8 S37, 495—96 r
Two travellers
[*Moscow admits a critic,*
by B. Pares;
I search for truth in Russia,
by W. Citrine[.
LR, ii 11 Ag36, 589—91 r
Uncle Jack's great coat.
ST, i 1 F33, 22—25 p

Graham, Robert Bontine Cunninghame-
see Cunninghame-Graham, R. B.

Graham, Virginia
Happy holiday hints.
ND, 2 8Jy37, 8—9 p
Heather mixture.
ND, 7 12Ag37, 16, 18 c

Grahame, Kenneth
Stability.
HR, 7 1934, 9—10 p

Granducci, Josephine B.
At dawning.
PQ, i 2 Su39, 41 v

Grandville, Jean Gerard
Un autre monde
rev. by L. Le Breton

Granger, Frank
The fiend in our universities.
EQ, i 4 F35, 266—72 c

Grant, James L.
The English and American scene
[*The changing scene,*
by A. Calder-Marshall;
Hot striptease, by G. Gorer].
LR, iii 9 Oc37, 560—61 r
Little wood nymph.
LT, i 11 J37, 17—20 p
Gipsy of Bloomsbury.
LT, i 10 D36, 5—9 p

Granville-Barker, Harley *and*
Granville-Barker, Helen
Introduction to the Quinteros.
R, i 4 My34, 12 c

Graves, H. E.
Soldier, soldier,
NS, ii 8 A36, 570—73 p

Graves, Philip R.
The old man's song, from the Welsh of
Llywarththen.
WR, ii 2 S39, 78—79 v

Graves, Robert von Ranke
Advertising: book advertising.
EP, 3 Sp37, 239—40 c
Answers to an enquiry.
NV, 11 Oc34, 5—6 c
Coleridge and Wordsworth;
Keats and Shelley.
EP, 1 Au35, 157—74 c
Homiletic studies: stealing.
EP, 2 Su36, 65—75 c
A letter.
LR, ii 3 D35, 128—29 c
Marginal themes: Lucretius

Graves, Robert von ranke (cont.)
[De rerum natura] and Jeans
[Eos].
EP, 2 Su36, 208—20 c
Neo-Georgian eternity [E. M. Forster].
EP, 2 Su36, 231—42 c
Note on the pastoral.
EP, 1 Au36, 200—207 c
Official and unofficial literature.
EP, 2 Su36, 57—61 c
A poem-sequence.
EP, 1 Au35, 87—92 v
Poems.
EP, 2 Su36, 145—47 v
Poems.
EP, 3 Sp37, 164—69 v
Collected poems
rev. by G. Grigson; J. Symons
see also Riding, Laura; Riding, Laura
and others

Graves, Sally [*i.e.* Elizabeth Mildred]
Dido.
PR, 1 1F35, 5 v
Editorial.
LS, i 3 N34, 3—4 c
Followers of Marie.
PR, 2 12F35, 5—6 v
Metamorphosis; Cleopatra.
LS, ii 1 My35, 46 v
Poems.
EP, 3 Sp37, 151 v
Relations between Turkey and the
Entente powers, 1919—1922.
LS, i 2 My34, 28—44 c
The religion of a minority
[*The rise of European liberalism*,
by H. J. Laski;
The strange death of liberal England,
by G. Dangerfield].
LR, ii 13 Oc36, 715—16 r
Review [*Rosy-fingered dawn*,
by R. M. Hodgson].
LS, i 3 N34, 70—72 r
South Leigh; Alice at Margate.
LS, i 1 F34, 48—49 v

Gray, John
Let us pray rev. by R. Wright

Gray, Nicolette
Abstract art.
NO, ii 3 N35, 250—57 c

Grayle, Gerda
Joy and the year.
DD, viii 30 Au31, 93 v
Mary Magdalen.
DD, ix 32 M—A32, 21—22 v
To larches in winter.
DD, viii 28 J—F31, 35 v

The great silkie of sale sherry.
T, 4 Je37, [3] v

Greeks and Romans.
M, i 1 Je33, 17—20 p

Green, B. J.
Strike.
LR, ii 1 Oc35, 24—29 p

Green, Basil
Clear, blue sky.
LR, ii 11 Ag36, 561—64 p

Green, Frederick Laurence
The gallery shuts at ten.
NW, ns3 C39, 111—16 p

Green, George Frederick
A love story.
NW, ns2 Sp39, 64—74 p
One boy's town.
NW, 5 Sp38, 103—9 p
The recruit.
NW, 3 Sp37, 146—53 p
A skilled hand.
NS, ii 3 Je35, 175—94 p

Green, Henry
Party going
rev. by G. B. Scurfield

Green, R.
On education: economy cuts.
TC, v 25 M33, 30—33 c

Green, W. B.
Quorsus haec?
F, 5 F31, 121—33; 6 Je31, 137—58 p
Review [*From feathers to iron*,
by C. Day Lewis].
OO, xi 56 N31, 228—30 r
Three poems.
F, 5 F31, 79—81 v
Three poems.
F, 6 Je31, 186—87 v

Greene, G. J.
The July reapers.
CM, i 1 Sp33, 15 v

Greene, Graham
Cinema.
ND, 21 18N37, 38—39; ND, 22 25N37,
31; ND, 23 2D37, 31; ND, 25 16D37,
30—31 r
Comment on Auden.
NV, 26/27 N37, 29—30 c
Film lunch.
ND, 12 16S37, 14, 16 c
The films.
ND, 16 14Oc37, 39; ND, 17 21Oc37, 39;
ND, 18 28Oc37, 31; ND, 19 4N37, 31;
ND, 24 9D37, 31; ND, 26 23D37, 31 r
A flicker from the flames.
ND, 11 9S37, 30 r

Horror for adults.
ND, 2 8Jy37, 30 r
Knight without armour and *Metropole*.
ND, 14 30S37, 38—39 r
Lenin and lavender.
ND, 1 1Jy37, 38 r
More song than dance.
ND, 10 25S37, 30 r
The nudest book of the week
[*Eve in the sunlight*,
by B. Park and Y. Gregory]
ND, 15 7Oc37, 33 r
On the West Coast.
ND, 5 29Jy37, 30—31 r
Pawn's move and knight's move.
ND, 8 19Ag37, 30 r
The road back and *Gangway*.
ND, 15 7Oc37, 38—39 r
Tribute to Harpo.
ND, 7 12Ag37, 30—31 r
Two English pictures.
ND, 12 16S37, 30 r
What man has made of man.
ND, 3 15Jy37, 30 r
What's left is celluloid.
ND, 9 26Ag37, 30 r
Without beard or bed.
ND, 4 22Jy37, 30 r
The old school rev. by Cosmo *pseud.*

Greenstreet, Iris
Poem.
LT, i 11 J37, 16 v

Greenwood, Mabel
Dresden china.
DD, vii 26 S—Oc30, 386 v

Greenwood, Walter
His worship the mayor
rev. by A. L. Lloyd

Gregory, Horace
Dempsey, Dempsey.
CPP, 7 N36, 126—27 v
Poetry in America.
NV, 4 Jy33, 11—16 c

Gregory, Leonora
The lost kid.
NS, i 6 D34, 437—38 p

Gregory, Padraic
After death.
CA, 8 1931, 251 v
A martyred poet [J. M. Plunkett].
CA, 4 N30, 70—76 c

Gregory, Yvonne *see* Park, Bertram

Gregson, H.
Plenty more at the gate.
LR, ii 5 F36, 215—16 p

Gresser, Ann
Factory library.
LR, i 5 F35, 177—78 c

Grey, Elaine
Revenge . . . and larches.
C, iii 54 2J37, 4 v

Grey, Ruth Victoria
Chagrin.
K, i 1 17N39, 15—16 p

Gribble, Bill
To a weary comrade; Comrade of ours.
PP, 12 Je39, 4—6 v

Grierson, Herbert John Clifford
Robert Henryson..
MS, iv 4 J34, 294—303 c
see also Boutens, P. C.

Grieve, Christopher Murray
The Caledonian antisyzgy and the
Gaelic idea.
MS, ii 2 Jy31, 141—54;
4 J32, 333—37 v, c
Clan Albainn and other matters.
MS, i 2 Su30, 7—10 c
First love.
EQ, i 1 My34, 59 v
The last great Burns discovery.
MS, iv 4 J34, 316—19 p
Neil Munro.
MS, i 4 J31, 20—24 c
Scottish national development, civic
publicity and other matters.
MS, ii 1 A31, 32—44 c
A study of T. S. Eliot
[*T. S. Eliot: a study,*
by T. M'Greevy].
MS, ii 1 A31, 82—85 r
Two poets [*Brief words,*
by W. Soutar; *Horizons of death,*
by N. MacLeod].
MS, vi 2 Jy35, 169—71 r
see also MacDiarmid, H. *pseud.*

Griffith, Hubert
Nine years of drama.
BB, vii 2 M30, 42—48 c
Some thoughts on comedy.
R, i 8 D34, 11, 16 c
Seeing Soviet Russia rev. by F. R.

Griffith, Jack
Sacked.
WR, i 1 F39, 27—32 p
Something to be thankful for.
NS, i 5 Oc34, 335—39 p

Griffith, Llewelyn Wyn
If there be time.
W, 2 Ag37, 70 v
Madam Rumour; February night.

W, 1 Su37, 19—20 v
The sea between.
WR, ii 2 S39, 80—83 p
The Welsh influence [on Hopkins].
NV, 14 A35, 27—29 c

Griffith, Llewelyn Wyn *and*
Heseltine, Nigel
Comments on 'In parenthesis'.
W, 4 M38, 157 r

Griffiths, Elsa Stamford
Early morning on the headland.
JG, 70 Au39, [16] v
A memory.
JG, 63 W37, [8] v
The old house.
JG, 40 Sp37, [20—21] v

Grigson, Geoffrey Edward Harvey
About life.
NV, 22 S36, 6 v
And forgetful of Europe; Ucello on the
heath; Mediterranean.
NV, 30 Su38, 6—8 v
And next Mr Graves [*Collected poems,*
by R. Graves].
NV, i 1 J39, 21—22 r
Anthology-making
[*The Faber book of modern verse,*
ed. by M. Roberts; *The progress
of poetry,*
ed. by I. Parsons].
NV, 20 A36, 26—27 r
Around Cadbury castle.
NV, 28 J38, 10 v
Auden as a monster.
NV, 26/27 N37, 13—17 c
Baby mustn't touch
[*The walls of glass,* by A. S. J.
Tessimond;
Discrete series, by G. Oppen].
NV, 9 Je34, 20—22 r
Before a fall.
NV, 19 F36, 12 v
Black and red
[*Blasting and bombardiering,*
by P. W. Lewis].
NV, 28 J38, 21 r
1. Blood and bran.
2. Hopkins and Hopkinese.
NV, 14 A35, 21—26 c
Books lately published.
NV, 23 C36, 25—26, r
But between flower and flower.
NV, 3 My33, 13 v
Cacus, aventinae timor atque infamia
silvae.
NV, 19 F36, 19—20 c
Comment on England.
AX, 1 J35, 8, 10 c
'Criterion' and 'London mercury'.
NV, i 2 My39, 62—63 c
The danger of taste.

NV, 4 Jy35, 1—2 c
Day Lewis joins up.
NV, 25 My37, 23—24 c
Dream.
NV, 5 Oc33, 8 v
Education in the twenties
[*Lions and shadows,* by C. Isherwood].
NV, 29 M38, 18—19 r
Elements of verse
[*The winter house,* by J. N. Cameron;
Songs of the forest,
by S. Hivale and V. Elwin].
NV, 19 F36, 16—18 r
An enquiry.
NV, 11 Oc34, 2—3 p
A fact, boys.
PR, 18 17Je36, 14 v
Faith or feeling? [*New country,*
ed. by M. Roberts;
The magnetic mountain, by C. Day Lewis].
NV, 2 M33, 15—17 r
A fanatic heart [*The winding stair,*
by W. B. Yeats].
NV, 6 D33, 24—26 r
First of all, Miss Laura Riding
[*Collected poems,* by L. Riding;
Poems, by F. T. Prince;
Stony ground, by E. Tucker;
Gwalia deserta, by I. Davies].
NV, 31/32 Au38, 24—26 r
Flip-flap-flop, or a wet whiting
[*Post-Victorian poetry,*
by H. Palmer].
NV, 30 Su38, 26 r
From 'The Listener'
[*Poems of tomorrow,*
ed. by J. A. Smith].
NV, 15 Je35, 20 r
Henry Moore and ourselves.
AX, 3 Jy35, 9—10 c
Housman for ourselves
[*More poems,* by A. E. Housman].
NV, 23 C36, 22—24 r
Impertinent translations
[*Sonnets to Orpheus,* by R. M. Rilke,
tr. by J. B. Leishman].
NV, 23 C36, 16—19 r
In Munich, city of art.
NV, 25 My37, 10 v
Invade, invade.
NV, 3 My33, 20 v
John Crowe Ransom.
NV, 16 Ag35, 12—17 c
Language and verse
[*English poetry and the English language,*
by F. W. Bateson].
NV, 13 F35, 20—21 r
A little pig's tale
[*Straight or curly,* by C. Dyment].
NV, 24 F37, 20—21 r
Living by the sea.
NV, 12 D34, 7 v
Logos.
NV, 4 Jy33, 10 v

Grigson, Geoffrey Edward Harvey (cont.)
Lonely, but not lonely enough.
NV, 31/32 Au38, 16–17 c
Lucastration
[*The criticism of poetry*,
by F. L. Lucas].
NV, 5 Oc33, 17 r
Meeting by the Gjulika meadow.
NV, 25 My37, 14–15 v
The methodism of Ezra Pound
[*A draft of XXX cantos*, by E. Pound].
NV, 5 Oc33, 17–22 r
Mr Spender's book of criticism
[*The destructive element*,
by S. Spender].
NV, 15 Je35, 15–18 r
Mud in their blood [*American song*,
by P. Engle; *Permit me voyage*, by
J. Agee; *Ten introductions*,
by G. Taggard and D. Fitts].
NV 13 F35, 19–20 r
New books.
NV, 21 Je36, 19–20 r
New books on poetry – and
Miss Sitwell
[*Descent from Parnassus*,
by D. Powell;
The trend of modern poetry,
by G. Bullough;
Aspects of modern poetry,
by E. Sitwell].
NV, 12 D34, 13–17 c
New poems by MacNeice and Prokosch
[*The earth compels* and
I cross the Minch,
by L. MacNeice; *The carnival*,
by F. Prokosch; *Memory*,
by W. de la Mare; *Poems*,
by C. H. Peacock].
NV, 30 Su38, 17–19 r
New Verse goes Trotskyite?
NV, 23 C36, 24 c
News; Books published lately.
NV, 24 F37, 21–24 c
No life.
NV, 13 F35, 13–14 v
A note on this number.
NV, 31/32 Au38, 2 c
Poem.
NV, 23 C36, 14–15 v
Poem; Again and again; About now.
NV, 21 Je36, 6–7 v
A poem of Mexico
[*Conquistador*, by A. MacLeish].
NV, 4 Jy33, 17–18 r
Poetry, objects and belief
[*Poetry and anarchism*, by H. Read;
Poetry and crisis, by G. M. Turnell;
The political thought of S. T. Coleridge,
by R. J. White].
NV, 31/32 Au38, 22–24 r
Poets and the theatre.
NV, 18 D35, 2–3 c
Politics: a request.

NV, 2 M33, 1–2 p
A queer country.
NV, 21 Je36, 13–14 p
A queer country.
PR, 18 17Je36, 6–7 v
The reason for this.
NV, 26/27 N37, 1 c
Regional order.
NV, 1 J33, 8 v
Remarks.
NV, 28 J38, 14–15; NV, 29 M38,
13–16 c
Remarks on painting and Mr Auden.
NV, i 1 J39, 17–19 c
Review [*The English muse*,
by O. Elton; *Modern English poetry*,
by R. L. Megroz].
NV, 2 M33, 17 r
Review [*First poems*,
by R. Heppenstall].
NV, 18 D35, 20 r
Review
[*The Oxford book of modern verse*,
ed. by W. B. Yeats].
NV, 23 C36, 21 r
Rex Warner [*Poems*].
NV, 28 J38, 22 r
Robert Graves [*Poems, 1930–1933*].
NV, 3 My33, 23–24 r
Rum tum tum on a broken drum
[*Flowering rifle*, by R. Campbell;
Goodbye to Berlin, by C. Isherwood;
Poems for Spain,
ed. by S. Spender and J. Lehmann;
School for barbarians, by E. Mann;
Education today and tomorrow,
by W. H. Auden and T. C. Worsley;
New writing, n.s.1.;
Overtures to death,
by C. Day Lewis].
NV, i 2 My39, 52–56 r
Science and Mass-Observations: poets
and poor Tom.
NV, 29 M38, 16–18 c
The solid sea.
NV, 7 F34, 10 v
The stuffed goldfinch
[*Ideas of order*, by W. Stevens;
Second hymn to Lenin,
by H. MacDiarmid].
NV, 19 F36, 18–19 r
Third year.
NV, 12 D34, 2 p
This number.
NV, 14 A35, 2 p
Three poems.
NV, 20 A36, 8–9 v
Thy chase had a beast in view
[*A vision*, by W. B. Yeats;
The herne's egg, by W. B. Yeats;
Essays 1931 to 1936, by W. B. Yeats;
The living torch, by A. E. *pseud.*]
NV, 29 M38, 20–22 r
Twenty seven sonnets

[*Journey to a war*,
by W. H. Auden and C. Isherwood].
NV, i 2 My39, 47–49 r
Two first books [*Difficult morning*,
by R. Swingler; *Spring encounter*,
by J. Pudney].
NV, 7 F34, 20 r
Two poets
[*Collected poems, 1921–1931*,
by W. C. Williams; *Festivals of fire*,
by R. Bottrall].
NV, 8 A34, 18–19 r
Two warnings [*Four walls*,
by L. Whistler; *Beyond the sunrise*,
by J. Bramwell].
NV, 10 Ag34, 15–17 r
Villon or Flecker
[*Poems*, by A. MacLeish].
NV, 17 Oc35, 19–20 r
Why.
NV, 1 J33, 1–2 c
Why not die?
NV, 21 Je36, 21–22 c
New verse: an anthology
rev. by J. Symons
Several observations
rev. by R. Fuller; H. G. Porteus
see also Roberts, Denys Kilham

Grigson, Geoffrey Edward Harvey *and*
Piper, John
England's climate.
AX, 7 Au36, 5–9 c

Grigson, Wilfred Vernon
see A Leja . . .; Chait-parab song

Grogan, A. S.
Heinrich Heine.
LR, iii 3 A37, 159–63 c

Grohmann, Will
Klee at Berne.
AX, 2, A35, 12–13 c

Groom, Elizabeth
Angel frustrating storm.
I, i 2/3 15S31, 34 i
The regatta.
I, i 2/3 15S31, 83 i

Grosch, Alfred
Smudger.
C, i 12 22F36, 92, 96 p

Grossman, Vassily Sememovich
In the town of Berdichev.
NW, 2 Au36, 131–45 p

Grove, D.
By sedan chair to power.
LR, i 12 S35, 503–5 c

Guedalla, Philip
Argentine tango rev. by G. Pendle

Guehenno, Jean
Paris Congress speech.
LR, i 11 Ag35, 474 c

Guest, Carmel Haden
Give us conflict
rev. by T. L. Hodgkin

Guilloux, Louis
A man and a woman, tr. by J. Rodker.
NW, ns1 Au38, 165—72 p
A present for the deputy,
tr. by J. Rodker.
NW, 3 Sp37, 27—39 p
When I was one and twenty oh!,
tr. by J. Rodker.
NW, 2 Au36, 160—72 p

Gullen, Roger *pseud. and*
Roberts, Buckley
Where's that bomb?
rev. by D. Kahn

Gunn, Neil Miller
The wild.
MS, i 2 Su30, 17—19 p
Scotland a nation.
LR, ii 14 N36, 735—38 c
The serpent.
MS, i 1 Sp30, 36 v
Tragedy into dream.
MS, ii 1 A31, 64—65 p

Gunther, John
Inside Europe rev. by H. Fyfe

Gurner, Ronald
'Henry'.
R, i 5 Je34, 11 c

Guthrie, James
The different art of hand painting.
MS, i 1 Sp30, 34—36 c
Edward Thomas.
WR, ii 1 Ag39, 23—31 c

Gutteridge, Bernard H.
Funereal; Creed, Song.
T, 2 M37, [3—4] v
Home revisited.
NV, i 1 J39, 7 v
Kenneth Allott: realism and modishness
[*Poems*].
NV, i 1 J39, 23—24 r
Man into a churchyard.
NV, 16 Ag35, 10 v
The mirror.
CPP, 4/5 Ag36, 85—86 v
Now like a landscape; Spanish earth.
NW, ns3 C39, 58—59 v
Poem.

CPP, 7 N36, 127—28 v
Poem.
CPP, 10 Au37, 29—31 v
Poem.
NV, 30 Su38, 4—5 v
Poem.
NV, 28 J38, 8—9 v
Sermon from the hills.
NV, 19 F36, 10 v
Sonnet in spring.
NV, 17 Oc35, 17 v
Temper.
CPP, 8 D36, 150 v
Wishes.
NV, 17 Oc35, 3 v

Guyon, René
Sex and life ethics
rev. by A. Craig

Gwerinwr
From the heart of Wales.
WR, i 1 F39, 42—43 c

Gwrandawr
The common listener.
WR, i 1 F39, 44—45 c

Gwynne-Jones, Alan
A pastoral scene.
HR, 4 1931, front. i

Gyseghem, André van
see Van Gyseghem, André

H

H., D.
To a ham-sandwich;
Valse triste.
M, i 1 Je33, 47, 57 v

H., E. G.
Lady Macbeth and the
O.U.D.S.
LD, i 2 M37, 15—16 dr

H., J. S.
1937 exhibition.
LR, iii 4 My37, 230—31 c

H., F.
The bookshelf
[*Her privates we*,
by Private 19022;
All our yesterdays,
by H. M. Tomlinson;
A room of one's own,
by V. Woolf;

Studies in literature: third series,
by Sir A. Quiller-Couch;
Medal without bar,
by R. Blaker].
BB, vii 2 M30, 93—100 r

H., P.
Boulogne, 1917.
DD, ix 31 J—F32, 9 v

H., P. *tr. see also*
Miličič, Sibe

Hacker, Ronald F.
There will now be an interval.
PQ, i 2 Su39, 37 v

Hadden, Munday
Linocut portrait.
RR, 5 J38, [1] i

Hadfield, Alan
An I were perfect in love lore.
JG, 63 W37, [28] v
Earth and spirit.
JG, 70 Au39, [17] v
Foal's fin.
JG, 68 Sp39, [30] v
For Audrey, or any fine lassie.
JG, 40 Sp37, [19—20] v
For day spring and the quiet
dewfall.
JG, 64 Sp38, [31] v
For Joan.
JG, 41 Su37 [36] v
Forest flame.
JG, 38 Au36, [32] v
Kettlesing.
JG, 67 W38, [10—11] v
Knaresborough:
Manor House well.
JG, 42 Au37, [25] v
The marquetry of timber town.
JG, 39 W36, [10] v
Starlight, the river and she.
JG, 69 Su39, [32] v

Hadfield, John
A quiet afternoon.
WW, i 3 Jy30, 13—19 p

Hadfield, Raymond
Repertory and its object.
R, i 7 N34, 7C

Haig, Alison
Comment on Christmas.
ND, 23 2D37, 22;
ND 25 16D37, 22 c
Comment on clothes.
ND, 1 1Jy37, 26, 28;
ND, 2 8Jy37, 22;
ND, 3 15Jy37 22;
ND, 4 22Jy37, 22;

Haig, Alison (cont.)
ND, 5 29Jy37, 22;
ND, 6 5Ag37, 22;
ND, 8 19Ag37, 20;
ND, 9 26Ag37, 22, 24;
ND, 15 7Oc37, 24;
ND, 16 14Oc37, 26, 28;
ND, 17 21Oc37, 26;
ND, 19 4N37, 22;
ND, 26 23D37, 22 c
Comment on decor.
ND, 12 16S37, 22;
ND, 14 30S37, 24;
ND, 20 11N37, 20 c
Comment on fashions.
ND, 7 12Ag37, 24;
ND, 10 2S37, 22;
ND, 11 9S37, 24;
ND, 13 23S37, 22;
ND, 18 28Oc37, 22;
ND, 24 9D37, 24, 26;
ND, 22 25N37, 22 c
Comment on presents.
ND, 21 18N37, 24, 26 c
Rag girls merry-go-round.
ND, 15 7Oc37, 16—17 c

Haines, Robin
In memory.
NV, i 2 My39, 40—41 v

Haire, Norman
Comment on the basis of the
Sexology group.
TC, iv 21 N32, 21 c
A sane sex life.
TC, iii 15 My32, 11—14 c

Haldane, Charlotte
Passionaria.
LR, iii 15 A38, 926 v

Haldane, John Burden Sanderson
Greetings on May day.
LR, iii 16 My38, 961 c

Hale, Philippa
Boulogne, 1917.
DD, vii 26 S—Oc30, 408 v
see also H., P.

Hale, Robin
Poems.
EP, 3 Sp37, 161—63 v

Halfpenny, Eric
Music.
IP, i 1 6A39, 11—13 c

Hall, Anmer
Fifty years ago.
R, i 8 D34, 10, 12 c

Hall, James A.
After an action in Spain.
JG, 39 W36, [31] v
To my dog.
DD, xi 43 J—F34, 14 v

Hall, John Clive
Dead men.
B, 2 W38, 19 v
For an explorer dead in the
Arctic.
K, i 1 17N39, 5 v
For D. H. singing.
FB, v 1 F39, 7 v
If to-day I had come to a
dead end.
SV, 1 Su38, 25 v
Poem at a window; Curtains.
B, 3 Sp39, 10—11 v
'Poetry' a new magazine
[*Poetry London*].
FB, v 2 My39, 40 r
Remember wind kills.
B, 3 Sp39, 8 v
The singers.
B, 2 W38, 5 v
Song,
K, i 2 D39—J40, 64 v
A time to build up
[*London mercury*].
FB, v 2 My39, 21—22 r

Hall, Marguerite Radclyffe
The master of the house
rev. by E. M. Barraud

Hall, Norman
The last hero;
The whispering gallery;
Particular face.
T, 1 J37, [6—7] v
Perrault revisiting.
T, 10 My38, 42—43 v
Poem: Palm Sunday.
T, 3 A37 [10] v

Halle, Fannina W.
Women in Soviet literature
rev. by K. Radek

Halliday, Wilfred Joseph
To Dorothy Una Ratcliffe.
JG, 41 Su37, [11—13] v

Halpern, Wolf Abiram
The dialectic of Germany,
OO, xi 56 N31, 182—89 c

Halsey, Freda
Pre-reformation poetry.
CA, 8 1931, 230—33 c

Halward, Leslie
Arch Anderson.

NW, 4 Au37, 128—41 p
Belcher's hod.
NS, ii 2 A35, 123—28 p
Boss.
NW, 2 Au36, 33—37 p
The doll.
NS, i 2 A34, 141—45 p
The money's all right.
LR, ii 16 J37, 862—66 p
The mother.
NS, ii 7 F36, 553—55 p
No use blaming him.
NW, ns2 Sp39, 75—82 p
Old sweat.
LR, iii 7 Ag37, 397—99 p
Old-timer.
NS, ii 4 Ag35, 288—93 p
Our Fred.
P, 4 1938, 134—43 p
Let me tell you
rev. by J. Lipton
To tea on Sunday
rev. by R. Wright

Hambledon, Phyllis
The music master and the
chaperone.
HR, 5 1932, 45—47 p

Hambledon, Ronald
For P. W.
TO, ii 7 Ag39, 18 v

Hamer, Robert
Good Friday.
NV, 8 A34, 9—10 v
Letter to a Pharisee.
CL, i 1 Su33, 3—4 v
Omnis animal; Poem.
CM, i 2 Su33, 55 v
Poem; Sonnet; Poem.
NV, 13 F35, 12—13 v
Three poems.
CM, i 1 Sp33, 12—13 v
Torch song.
NV, 9 Je34, 10 v

Hamilton, Bruce
Rex. v Rhodes
rev. by S. Blumenfeld

Hamilton, Cicely Mary
Modern France
rev. by G. West
Modern Germanies
rev. by J. R. Evans

Hamilton, Margaret
Dirge at seventeen.
P, 5 1939, 83—84 v

Hamilton-Fellowes, Enid
A ballade of golf.
DD, viii 28 J—F31, 21 v

Hampshire, Stuart N.
Thomas Mann and André Gide
[*Stories of three decades*,
by T. Mann].
LR, iii 1 F37, 60–61 r

Hampson, John
The curious little boy.
NS, i 5 Oc34, 353–56 p
Good food.
NW, 1 Sp36, 58–60 p
Good luck.
NW, ns3 C39, 175–78 p
Transition.
NS, ii 7 F36, 556–57 p

Hankin, Edith
A start.
NS, ii 3 Je35, 232–36 p

Hanley, James
Black gold.
W, 2 Ag37, 38–40 p
Day's end.
NW, 3 Sp37, 166–77 p
The dead.
LR, iii 7 Ag37, 384–87 p
The dreamer.
J, 2 My36, 2–3 p
The furys.
LR, i 2 N34, 3–12 p
Living water.
P, 1 1938, 75–83 p
The moneylender.
LR, ii 8 My36, 363–69 p
Powys and company
[*Welsh ambassadors*,
by L. Marlowe].
LR, ii 6 M36, 279 r
Rubbish.
SM, 1 Je31, 12–35 p
'Schooldays' competition
report.
LR, ii 7 A36, 305–6 c
The secret journey.
LR, i 8 My35, 297–306 p
Seven men.
NW, 5 Sp38, 210–32 p
Aria and finale
rev. by G. West
Boy rev. by G. West
Ebb and flood rev. by G. West
Grey children
rev. by T. L. Hodgkin
The secret journey
rev. by G. West

Hanley, Timothy
Glory goes before.
WR, ii 2 S39, 95 i

Hann, Geoffrey
Autumn; Dreamer.
CM, ii 1 Su35, 222 v

Hann, George
The Dauphin.
RR, 3 My37, [5] i
The Maharajah of Patiala;
Alma Venus.
RR, 6 Jy38, [6, 17] i
Negro girl.
RR, 1 Oc36, [9] i
Offrande;
H.R.H. The Duchess of
Gloucester.
RR, 7 Oc38, [12, 15] i
Reproduction of an oil
painting.
RR, 10 Je39, [14] i

Hannen, Nicholas
The National Theatre.
Y, i 2 My39, 82–84 c

Hannington, Walter
*The problem of the distressed
areas* rev. by S. Swingler
Unemployed struggles
rev. by C. Ashleigh

Hanrott, E. G.
The O.U.D.S. Richard II.
FB, i 2 3M36, 36–38 dr
see also H., E. G.

Hanschell, Deryck
Approach to music.
AR, i 1 A37, 52–58;
AR i 2 Jy37, 127–37 c
Review
[*Apology for dancing*,
by R. Heppenstall].
AR, i 1 A37, 66–67 r
Soviet music.
AR, i 3 Oc37, 234–36 c

Hanschell, Helen
History and the class war.
AR, i 3 Oc37, 187–94 c

Hansen, Christian
Our continental correspondent.
ND, 12 16S37, 20–21 p

Hansen, Harry *ed.*
*O. Henry memorial and prize
stories* rev. by G. West

Hansom, Rose Marie
Death of a poet.
TO, i 1 J38, 31 v
The kitten and the cathedral.
TO, i 2 A38, 21 v
Poem.
TO, i 3 Jy38, 26 v

Hanson, A. H.
Musical technique in

disintegration.
LS, i 2 My34, 15–25 c
Prison:
impressions of three days.
TU, i 2 1934, 17–20 p

Hanson, Jack
Young worker.
LR, i 10 Jy35, 412–13 p

Hardy, Evelyn
The innkeeper's wife.
NS, ii 3 Je35, 198–208 p

Hardy, J.
*The first American
revolution.*
rev. by A. L. Morton

Hardy, Marcella
Carao: a bird legend of
Paraguay.
HR, 4 1931, 68–69 p

Hare, M. L.
Sonnet; Go south then.
F, 6 Je31, 197 v

Hargrave, John
Comment on the Promethean
Society report.
TC, iii 18 Ag32, 14–15 c

Harker, Ronald E.
The barrow.
JG, 21 Su32, [8] v
City edition.
JG, 22 Au32, [10–11] v
Then let her pass.
JG, 26 Au33, [25] v

Harper, Samuel Northrup *ed.*
*The Soviet Union and world
problems* rev. by R. Bishop

Harris, Frank David
Rescue.
PQ, ii 2 Su39, 42 v

Harris, Grace Conner
B flat minor.
PQ, i 2 Su39, 43 v

Harris, Kenneth
Kingdom come.
K, i 1 17N39, 32 v

Harrison, Henry
*Ulster and the British Empire,
1939* rev. by R. Collis

Harrison, W. Arnold
A broadside.
TC, vi 32 N33, 110–11 c

Harrison, W. Scott
The Royal Scottish Academy
1930.
MS, i 2 Su30, 41—44 c

Harrisson, Thomas Harnett
Industrial spring.
NW, ns2 Sp39, 201—13 p
Mass opposition and
Tom Harrisson.
LD, ii 3 F38, 7—15 c
Whistle while you work.
NW, ns1 Au38, 47—67 p

Harry, T. R.
The peace that is no peace.
PP, 15 N39, 16 v

Hart, Henry *ed.*
American writers congress
rev. by C. Madge

Harte, Charles
Blackleg.
NW, 1 Sp36, 49—54 p

Hartkopf, Roy E.
The echo.
PP, 11 My39, 17 v
Lines on first seeing the
photographs of twelve A.R.P.
dictators in the press.
PP, 13/14 Jy—Ag39, 8 v
The sportsman
(the glorious twelfth).
PP, 5 N38, 15 v
The story of William Conway
Pearson.
PP, 7 J39, 11—13 p
We the people.
PP, 9 M39, 16 v

Hartley, Ruth Edith
Church bells.
C, ii 29 11Jy36, 3 p

Hartman, Jo
Carthage.
JG, 15 W30 [17] v
Choice.
JG, 30 Au34, [29] v
Egyptian cycle.
JG, 20 Sp32, [24—25] v
Epic of an artist.
JG, 18 Au31, [27—28] v
The first man.
JG, 33 Su35, [19—21] v
Ghetto violinist.
JG, 39 W36, [30] v
Mongol mistress.
JG, 14 Au30, [11] v
On nearing Jerusalem.
JG, 13 Su30, [29] v
San Francisco.

JG, 68 Sp39, [33] v
Song of Orpheus.
JG, 26 Au33, [27] v

Hartnoll, Phyllis
Theory and practice
[*The city keep*, by R. Malam].
OO, xi 55 Je31, 154—56 r

Hartshorne, Edward Yarnall *jr.*
*The German universities and
National Socialism*
rev. by A. Henderson

Harvey, Frederick William
A few reflections on modern
verse.
CA, 10 1931, 316—19 c
Four poems.
CA, 7 Je31, 213—14 v
Hen and chickens.
CA, 3 Oc30, 48—49 v
Hills; Three poems.
CA, 2 S30, 5, 15—16 v
The idiot.
CA, 1 Ag30, 17 v
The storm is done.
CA, 11 1932, 352 v
Two poems.
CA, 4 N30, 88 v

Harvey, J. Brian
The communist approach to
D. H. Lawrence.
PR, 18 17Je36, 16—18 c
Communist poem, 1935.
PR, 11 27N35, 3—4 v
The drama of the refugee
[*Professor Mamlock*; *Floridsdorf*,
by F. Wolf; *Other plays*;
Not for children, by E. Rice].
LR, ii 3 D35, 135—36 dr
An extract from 'The artist'.
PR, 15 1M36, 5—7 p
Four poets
[*Man's life is this meat*,
by D. Gascoyne;
Poems, by M. Roberts;
Poems, by J. Lipton;
Poems, by R. P. Hewett].
LR, ii 10 Jy36, 530—31 r
Meeting in a valley.
NW, 4 Au37, 142—49 p
Proletarian or pastoral
[*Some versions of pastoral*,
by W. Empson]?
LR, ii 5 F36, 230—32 r
Separation.
PR, 19 20Oc36, 12—13 v
Statement.
PR, 16 6My36, 4—6 v

Harwood, Alice
De profundis,

JG, 40 Sp37, [24] v
Fleet street.
JG, 71 W39 [20] v
Old portraits.
JG, 69 Su39, [22] v
Presences.
JG, 67 W38, [5] v
Selfless moment.
JG, 63 W37, [8—9] v
Statues of London.
JG, 39 W36, [14] v
To a book out of print.
JG, 66 Au38, [10] v
The undefined.
JG, 68 Sp39, [13—14] v
War and peace.
JG, 42 Au37, [16—17] v
Wood magic.
JG, 64 Sp38, [28] v

Hassall, Christopher
The controversy.
F, 4 D30, 8 v
Devil's dyke
rev. by H. B. Mallalieu

Hastings
The christening.
LR, i 6 M35, 205 i

Hastings *pseud.*
The surrealists
[*A short survey of surrealism*,
by D. Gascoyne].
LR, ii 4 J36, 186—87 r

Hastings, Douglas Macdonald
The last duel.
ND, 23 2D37, 19—21 p

Hatakeyama, C.
Echo, tr. by W. Empson.
CPP, 7 N36, 130 v

Hauser, Heinrich
Once your enemy
rev. by E. Rickword

Havers, Kathleen R.
Little ole Spain.
PP, 2 Ag38, 19—20 v

Hawkins, Alec Desmond
After the ball.
LT, i 3 My36, 9—11 p
'All the results'!
TC, i 5 Jy31, 12 v
Elegy for the old.
T, 8 J38, [13—14] v
Happy ending.
LT, i 1 M36, 8—13 p
Lacrimae Christi.
TC, i 2 A31, 24 v

The man who died
[by D. H. Lawrence].
TC, ii 9 N31, 17—20 r
Notes for a sermon.
TC, iv 22 D32, 13—16 c
Poetry and broadcasting.
T, 18 Je39, 35—39 c
Review
[*The waves*, by V. Woolf].
TC, ii 11 J32, 27 r
Review
[*Interpreting the universe*,
by J. MacMurray].
TC, v 28 Je33, 252—53 r
Review
[*Merrily I go to hell*,
by M. Cameron].
TC, iv 21 N32, 28 r
Review [*Much sky*,
by G. Pendle].
TC, v 25 M33, 48—50 r
Review
[*The benefits of assassination*,
by M. M.].
TC, iv 21 N32, 30—31 r
Review [*New poems*,
by D. H. Lawrence;
The letters of D. H. Lawrence,
ed. by A. Huxley].
TC, iv 23 J33, 25—28 r
Review [*Wyndham Lewis*,
by H. G. Porteus].
TC, iv 23 J33, 29—31 r
Review
[*Thirty preliminary poems*,
by G. Barker;
Alanna autumnal,
by G. Barker].
TC, vi 32 N33, 116—18 r
Review [*Determinations*,
by F. R. Leavis].
TC, vi 36 S34, 381 r
Review [*The dance of death*,
by W. H. Auden;
Poems, by W. H. Auden;
Spring encounter, by J. Pudney;
Difficult morning,
by R. Swingler;
The widow, by A. Jackson;
Arabesque, by H. Morland].
TC, vi 33 D33—J34, 183—86 r
Review [*Sense and poetry*,
by J. Sparrow;
Critique of poetry, by
by M. Roberts].
TC, vi 35 Je34, 311—12 r
Review
[*Memoirs of a polyglot*,
by W. Gerhardi].
TC, ii 10 D31, 27—29 r
Review
[*A cure for unemployment*,
by L. O'Flaherty;
Snowballs, by O. Scrannel;

The neutrality of God,
by C. H. Norman].
TC, ii 12 F32, 29 r
Review [*Calamiterror*,
by G. Barker;
Sebastian, by R. Heppenstall].
T, 4 Je37, [17—21] r
Why rage the ungodly?
TC, i 5 Jy31, 22—23 c
Young Lorenzo
[*The early life of D. H. Lawrence*,
by A. Lawrence and G. S. Gelder].
TC, iii 14 A32, 27—28 r
Hawk among the sparrows
rev. by J. Symons

Hawkins, Denis John Bernard
Creators of the modern world:
1. René Descartes.
AR, i 2 Jy37, 80—94 c
Dialectical materialism.
AR, i 3 Oc37, 167—75 c
Militarism and pacificism.
AR, i 1 A37, 19—25 c
Review [*The modern mind*,
by M. Roberts].
AR, i 3 Oc37, 243—45 r
Review [*Recent philosophy*,
by J. Laird; *Christian polity*,
by V. A. Demant].
AR, i 1 A37, 59—61 r
see also Gilson, Etienne

Hawthorne, James
Caveat emptor
[*Catalonia infelix*,
by E. A. Peers].
LR, iii 12 J38, 747—50 r
Soldier's hearth.
LR, iii 6 Jy37, 320—23 p

Hay, George Campbell
Gaelic and literary form.
VS, ii 1 Je—Ag39, 14—18 c
Seven poems.
VS, i 4 M—My39, 13—16 v

Hay, J. M.
Writer's international.
LR, i 6 M35, 221—22 c

Hayes, Richard
[W. B. Yeats] his nationalism.
AW, Su39, 10—11 c

Hayhurst, B. France-
see France-Hayhurst, B.

Hayhurst, B. Tanner
If you were here.
DD, viii 30, Au31, 116 v

Hayter, Stanley William
News of Arp.
DE, 2 Su32, 2 c

Hayward, John
Choosing a [radio] set.
ND, 9 26Ag37, 28 c
The clean book of the week
[*My best story for boys*].
ND, 15 7Oc37, 32—33 r
Dog days for listeners.
ND, 2 8Jy37, 28 c
Entente cordiale.
ND, 25 16D37, 13—14 c
Music on the air.
ND, 6 5Ag37, 26 c
Radio: a commentary.
ND, 14 30S37, 35;
ND, 19 4N37, 27;
ND, 26 23Oc37, 28 c
Xmas cheer.
ND, 21 18N37, 12 v

Heard, Gerald
This surprising world
rev. by G. West
The ascent of humanity,
rev. by D. R. Morrison

Hearle, Lysbeth
At Easter.
JG, 25 Su33, [20—21] v
Cloud mirage.
JG, 29 Su34, [25] v
Dream.
JG, 16 Sp31, [27] v
Migration.
JG, 32 Sp35, [29—30] v
Spring's perpetuity.
JG, 20 Sp32, [13] v
Two songs.
JG, 17 Su31, [25] v
Zero hour.
JG, 64 Sp38, [14—15] v

Heath, Frederick
A soldier's confession.
BB, vii 2 M30, 10—17 p

Heathcoat-Amory, P. J.
see Cripps, John

Heaton, Elizabeth
Summer doggerel.
NV, 3 My33, 15 v

Heaven, William A.
Brief biography.
P, 3 1938, 206—43 p

Hecker, Julius Friedrich
Where east meets west.
TC, vi 31 S—Oc33, 8—15 c
Communism and religion.

Hecker, Julius Friedrich (cont.)
rev. by W. N. Warbey
Moscow dialogues
rev. by W. N. Warbey

Hedges, Doris
Tanya's son.
NS, ii 1 F35, 1—7 p

Heinemann, Margot
Three poems.
NW, 4 Au37, 59—61 v

Helfen, O. Maenchen-
see Maenchen-Helfen, O.

Hellings, Peter
Display.
W, 10 Oc39, 272 v

Hélion, Jean
From reduction to growth.
AX, 2 A35, 19—24 c
Poussin, Seurat and double
rhythm.
AX, 6 Su36, 9—17 c

Hemingway, Ernest
To have and to have not
rev. by E. Waugh

Hems, Jack
Poetry of revolution.
ST, i 3 1933, 24—25 c

Henderson, Alexander
Fascism begins at home
[*The spirit and structure of
German fascism,* by R. A. Brady].
LR, iii 10 N37, 622—24 r
Girl in Nazi Germany
[*After midnight,* by I. Keun].
LR, iii 15 A38, 943—44 r
Student and swastika
[*The German universities and
National Socialism,*
by E. Y. Hartshorne, jr].
LR, iii 7 Ag37, 442—43 r
What the Nazis have done for
culture.
LR, iii 6 Jy37, 325—32 c
Writers and revolution in
Germany [*Our street,*
by J. Petersen;
*Autocracy and the middle
classes in Germany,*
by E. Kohn-Bramstedt].
LR, iii 13 F38, 825—28 r

Henderson, Alexander John
Blonde Venus.
DD, x 41 S—Oc33, 83 v
In hospital.
DV, 3 My32, 94—96 p

A murder story.
DV, 1 M32, 24—30 p
The revolt for order
[*The work, wealth and
happiness of mankind,*
by H. G. Wells].
DV, 2 A32, 50—52 r
A sleepless night.
DD, x 38 M—A33, 28 v
Traveller's song.
DD, xi 48 N—D34, 100 v

Henderson, Arthur
Labour's way to peace
rev. by T. H. Wintringham

Henderson, Florence L.
The little lanes of Devonshire.
JG, 14 Au30, [10—11] v
Lords of the air.
DD, vii 27 N—D30, 420 v
Second childhood.
JG, 28 Sp34, [15—16] v

Henderson, Philip
Indian writers
[*New Indian literature,*
no. 1; *When one is in it,*
by I. Singh].
LR, ii 8 My36, 410—11 r
Sudden rain.
TC, iv 21 N32, 15 v
Literature
rev. by T. E. Macaulay;
E. Rickword
The novel today rev. by J. Lindsay

Henderson, W.
Victorian street ballads
rev. by NV, 29 M38, 22

Hendry, James Findley
Clann Fhionnlaidh.
W, 11 W39, 302 v
Europe: 1939.
SV, 7 C39, 25 v
From
'A life of General Chunkledom'.
W, 11 W39, 294—95 p
From 'An ode to a cotton-town'.
PL, i 1 F39, [30] v
From 'The eye in the triangle'.
SV, 3 W38, 8—11 p
Hell-flax town.
RR, 6 Jy38, [8] v
Journey from Yorkshire to
Scotland.
VS, i 1 Je—Ag38, 21 v
Lady Macbeth of Mzensk.
LR, ii 2 M36, 272—73 c
Left behind; All-in sonnet;
Miners' dynamite.
W, 5 Su38, 170—72 v
Picasso: for Guernica;

Word as weapon, 1.
SV, 4A Sp39, 18 v
The price of profits:
[*No mean city,*
by A. McArthur and H. K. Long].
LR, ii 5 F36, 232—33 r
Scottish miners.
VS, i 2 S—N38, 22 v
Song of the subway.
DD, xi 46 Jy—Ag34, 68 v
Transition sonnet;
Portrait of David.
VS, i 3 D38—F39, 8—9 v
Your life — you're welcome.
SV, 2 Au38, 10—14 p
see also Russell, C. J.

Henein, Georges,
A contre-cloison.
LB, 17 15Je39, 20—21 p

Henghes
My sculptures bear strange names.
LB, 13 15A39, 9—10 p

Henri, Ernst
Hitler over Europe
rev. by N. Hopkins; G. West

Henry, Maurice
The bronze, piano,
tr. by D. Gascoyne.
CPP, 2 Je36, 32 v

Henry, Philip
Professionals in the rough.
ND, 7 12 Ag37, 32 c

Henshaw, Margaret
Forty years of America
[*Forty years,* by T. Laer].
LR, iii 10 N37, 633—34 r

Henslow, Miles
A job in a million-7.
ND, 7 12Ag37, 19—20 p

Heppenstall, Rayner
And the fire music; Mnemonic.
PL, i 1 F39, [19—20] v
Celebrating Joan of Arc.
ST, 1 3 1933, 29—30, 32 p
Episode.
CV, 5 M36, [18] v
Fanfare.
ST, i 2 A33, 17 v
Habitations.
B, 3 Sp39, 9 v
Homage to Léon Bloy.
B, 3 Sp39, 4—5 v
An homiletical raspberry.
TC, vi 31 S—Oc33, 53—54 c
My contemporaries; More
contemporaries; Prayer for the

abrogation of law; For daily
protection during a prosperous
month.
SV, 4A Sp39, 49—50 v
Programme notes.
TC, v 29 Jy33, 298—304 c
The resurrection of the body.
SV, 7 C39, 16—18 p
Risorgimento.
NV, 3 My33, 19 v
Sirius.
TC, vi 32, N33, 99 v
Socialism:
polite and histrionic.
TC, vi 33 D33—J34, 161—69 c
Three poems.
PR, 6 31My35, 8—9 v
An apology for dancing
rev. by D. Hanschell
First poems
rev. by K. Allott; G. Grigson
Sebastian rev. by A. D. Hawkins

Heriz-Smith, Peter
I killed a monster.
LD, ii 1 Oc37, 21—22 p

Hermes, Gertrude
Adam and Eve.
P, 2 1938, 94 i
The serpent at the nest.
I, i 2/3 15S31, 51 i
Wood engraving.
I, i 1 15Je31, 32 i

Hernandez, Miguel
Hear this voice,
tr. by I. and S. Spender.
NW, 5 Sp38, 56—58 v

Herrera Petere, Jose
Against the cold in the
mountains,
tr. by A. L. Lloyd.
NW, 3 Sp37, 49—50 v

Herring, Robert
Broadens the mind if;
Song, of a kind.
W, 4 M38, 154—55 v
French films in front.
NW, ns1 Au38, 173—83 c
No nice girl's song.
W, 5 Su38, 175 v
Steel.
S, 1 J33, 13 v
Two poems.
CV, 5 M36, [22—23] v
Where I come from.
W, 6/7 M39, 199—200 p

Heseltine, Nigel
Canu y byd mawr.

RR, 9 A39, [11—12] v
The drunk.
SV, 1 Su38, 29—31 p
Dylan Thomas [*25 poems*].
W, 2 Ag37, 74—75 r
Fragmentary remains of a poem
by Taliesin.
RR, 6 Jy38, [11] v
From Mr Spender's translation
bureau. [*Poems,*
by F. Garcia Lorca;
Danton's death, by G. Buechner].
W, 10 Oc39, 287—89 r
Lament.
RR, 2 F37, [8] v
The lay reader.
W, 8/9 Ag39, 227—31 p
Poems.
W, 1 Su37, 10—13 v
Review [*At swim-two-birds,*
by F. O'Brien].
W, 11 W39, 308—9 r
Solid cry.
W, 10 Oc39, 276—77 v
To a girl marrying a man with
a wooden leg.
W, 11 W39, 303 v
see also Griffith, Llewelyn Wyn

Heslop, Harold
Last cage down
rev. by C. Ashleigh

Hesse, Herman
The cyclone, tr. by A. Kennedy.
MS, ii 4 J32, 285—99 p

Hewett, Hope
Walking through Merioneth
rev. by D. S. Savage

Hewett, Peter [*i.e.* Ronald Peter]
Poem.
PR, 16 6My36, 2 v
Poem for autumn.
PR, 19 20Oc36, 10 v
Time spent, I. Adolescens;
Confessio limpidis.
RM, 1 Je34, 25—29 p, v
Two poems.
LR, ii 9 Je36, 437—37 v
Two poems.
NW, ns2 Sp39, 176—79 v
Poems
rev. by H. A. Beecham;
J. B. Harvey

Hewett, T. H.
Reading love-poetry.
JG, 17 Su31, [26] v

Hewitt, John
Prelude to consternation.
TC, v 28 Je33, 256 v

Tiphead.
TC, v 25 M33, 24 v

Hewitt, R. M. *tr. see*
Essenin, Sergei

Heynemann, Mabel Blundell
Frizinghall and Frizingley Hall.
HR, 4 1931, 25—26 c

Heywood, Terence
Evening in Bottnafjord, Sweden.
JG, 70 Au39, [31] v
On leaving school: to a master.
JG, 71 W39, [15] v
Rose in December.
JG, 68 Sp39, [32] v
Triangle in an orchestra.
JG, 69 Su39, [29] v

Hibbitt, Edward A.
The Brittlesnaps
rev. by J. Lindsay

Hicks-Bolton, Teresa
Sonnet to our lady before the
cross.
CA, 4 N30, 88 v

Hidden, Norman F.
Eldern.
RM, 2 D34, 58—59 p
The English honours school.
PR, 7 12Je35, 6—8 c
Psychode.
RM, 1 Je34, 6—8 p

Higashi, Jyun
Passion; Winter.
TO, i 1 J38, 8 v

Higgins, Frederick Robert
A ballad to Oliver Gogarty.
NA, i 1 Au39, 16—18 v
As Irish poet [W. B. Yeats].
AW, Su39, 6—8 c

Highet, Gilbert Arthur
Acts of faith.
F, 5 F31, 91—98 d
The apple.
F, 2 Je30, 100—106 d
Asclepiads.
F, 6 Je31, 161 v
City children.
F, 4 D30, 42 v
Here come the soldiers.
F, 1 F30, 46—53 v
La lutte de Maroc.
OO, xii 57 F32, 25 v
Nautch; Isolation.
F, 1 F30, 64—65 v
On Lord Mosenheimer's mansion.
F, 1 F30, 56 v

Highet, Gilbert Arthur (cont.)
Regardait la sillage.
OO, xii 57 F32, 60 v
The revolution of the word.
NO, i 3 F34, 288—304 c
Title to follow.
F, 6 Je31, 164—69 c
Urban eclogue.
F, 6 Je31, 188 v
William Faulkner
[*Soldier's pay*;
The sound and the fury].
NO, i 3 F34, 355—56 r

Hildebrand, Dietrich von
In defence of purity
rev. by H. House

Hiler, Hilaire
Some personal affirmations
regarding painting;
Four paintings.
TO, i 2 A38, 18 p, i

Hill, Eleanor Deane
A dance.
DD, viii 29 Su31, 53—55 v

Hill, Karin
At evening.
NS, i 3 Je34, 184—86 p

Hills, Coleridge
Eleven visions of Rachel.
CM, i 2 Su33, 58—59 v
From 'The dragonfly'.
CM, i 3 Au33, 106—7 p

Hilton, Jack
Elsie.
LR, iii 4 My37, 207—13 p
Slack-stopping men.
LR, ii 9 Je36, 439—47 p
Champion
rev. by Y. Cloud.

Hilton, John
Flip-flap.
OO, xi 54 M31, 4—7 p
Poem.
OO, xi 54 M31, 16—17 v

Hinde, Dennis
The glacier.
C, i 13 29F36, 99—100 p

Hinder, Ruth M.
Shadows.
PQ, i 1 Sp39, 16 v

Hindus, Maurice
Under Moscow skies
rev. by H. O. Whyte

Hitchens, Ivon
Pen drawing.
J, 2 My36, 27 i

Hivale, Shamrao *and*
Elvin, Verrier
Songs of the forest
rev. by G. Grigson

Hlaváček, Karel
Prelude to a volume of poems,
tr. by P. Selver.
SM, 4 1933, 111 v

Hobhouse, Christopher
The theatre.
ND, 8 19Ag37, 29;
ND, 9 26Ag37, 29 dr

Hobson, John Atkinson
Property and improperty
rev. by A. Goldschmidt

Hobson, Rodney
A-hunting you can go — but
leave me out of it.
ND, 23 2D37, 14 v
Babe in the Hollywood.
ND, 11 9S37, 12 v
Pass the recruit, please.
ND, 5 29Jy37, 18 p
Some little known facts about
my love-life.
ND, 1 1Jy37, 10 p

Hodge, Alan
A suivre les brises de fil fin.
PR, 4 5M35, 15 v
Change of landscape.
PR, 22 Je37, 9—10 v
Coup d'état.
PR, 17 27My36, 14 v
Dylan Thomas [*18 poems*]
PR, 16 6My36, 11—12 r
E. E. Cummings.
PR, 21 1M37, 8—9 c
Editorial.
PR, 18 17Je36, 1 c
Edward Thomas.
PR, 15 1M36, 17—18, 20 c
Epilogue; Catalogue.
PR, 14 19F36, 9 v
For one who wept on his
birthday.
PR, 6 31My35, 15 v
From the French of
Guillaume Apollinaire.
PR, 12 4D35, 13 v
Gardens.
PR, 21 1M37, 3—4 v
Homiletic studies: on courage.
EP, 3 Sp37, 66—74 p

Knock, knock; Who.
PR, 19 20Oc36, 11, 13 v
A note on American poetry.
PR, 20 17N36, 10—13 c
A note on 'Axis',
PR, 3 19F35, 15 r
Poem.
PR, 7 12Je35, 16 v
Poem.
PR, 3 19F35, 16 v
Poems.
EP, 2 Su36, 190—92 v
Poems.
EP, 3 Sp37, 152—57 v
Putsch.
PR, 17 27My36, 3 v
A rejoinder to Mr Pound.
PR, 7 12Je35, 9, 11—12 c
Review
[*A draft of cantos XXXI—XLI*,
by E. Pound].
PR, 5 17My35, 15 r
Review [*Selected poems*,
by M. Moore].
PR, 6 31My35, 13—15 r
Review
[*Chinese written characters*,
by E. Fenollosa; *Ta hiao*,
by Confucius].
PR, 16 6My36, 13 r
Review [*Reactionary essays*,
by A. Tate; *New writing*, no. 1;
Collected poems, 1909—1935,
by T. S. Eliot].
PR, 17 27My36, 17—19, 20 r
Review [*Thorns of thunder*,
by P. Eluard].
PR, 18 17Je36, 20 r
Review [*Inhale and exhale*,
by W. Saroyan;
Convalescent conversations,
by M. Vara; *Mutiny*,
by T. H. Wintringham].
PR, 20 17N36, 22, 24 r
Review [*Polite essays*,
by E. Pound].
PR, 21 1M37, 18 r
Song.
FB, i 2 3M36, 42 v
Song.
PR, 10 6N35, 10—11 v
A visit to little boy blue.
PR, 16 6My36, 6 v
see also Arndt, Walter W;
Riding, Laura *and others*;
Suckling, Norman.

Hodge, Alan *and* **Riding,** Laura
Philosophy and poetry.
EP, 2 Su36, 148—160 c

Hodge, Alan *and* **Sayer,** George
Composition.
PR, 13 5F36, 7 v

Hodge, Rupert
Although you laugh.
NV, i 2 My39, 38 v

Hodgkin, Edward
Englishman and Indian
[*Their ways divide,*
by D. Kincaid].
LR, ii 12 S36, 659 r

Hodgkin, T. L.
The individual and the group
[*They that reap,*
by G. Lopez y Fuentes;
I live under a black sun,
by E. Sitwell;
Starting point, by C. Day Lewis].
LR, iii 10 N37, 627—29 r
New novels [*Rainbow fish,*
by R. Bates; *The citadel,*
by A. J. Cronin].
LR, iii 8 S37, 502—4 r
Novels and social change
[*This was their youth,*
by R. Fox;
Grey children, by J. Hanley;
Breakfast in bed, by A. Brown;
The moon is making,
by S. Jameson].
LR, iii 11 D37, 690—92 r
Review [*Song on your bugles,*
by E. Knight].
LR, iii 3 A37, 180 r
Review [*No escape,*
by R. Swingler;
Give us conflict, by C. H. Guest].
LR, iii 2 M37, 109—10 r

Hodgson, John
The great god waste.
TC, ii 8 Oc31, 11—16;
TC, ii 9 N31, 5—10;
TC, ii 10 D31, 19—22;
TC, ii 11 J32, 10—13;
TC, ii 12 F32, 19—23;
TC, ii 13 M32, 21—25 c

Hodgson, Rose Marie
Editorial.
LS, i 1 F34, 3—4 c
Little girl at school.
LS, i 2 My34, 45—48 p
Rosy-fingered dawn
rev. by S. Graves

Hodson, James Lansdale
Red night rev. by R. Wright

Hofer, Andreas *pseud.*
The workers' fight in Austria.
LR, iii 15 A38, 904—9 c

Hogan, J. P.
Barrier.

TC, vi 33 D33—J34, 154—60 p
An old man's tale.
NS, i 1 F34, 49—51 p
Review
[*The problem of Arnold Bennett,*
by G. West; *H. G. Wells,*
by G. West].
TC, iv 21 N32, 29—30 r
Review [*A modern prelude,*
by H. I'Anson Fausset].
TC, vi 32 N33, 113—15 r
Review [*The savage pilgrimage,*
by C. Carswell;
Reminiscences of D. H. Lawrence,
by J. M. Murry].
TC, v 25 M33, 53—54 r
Review
[*The name and nature of poetry,*
by A. E. Housman].
TC, v 29 Jy33, 317—18 r
Supper.
TC, iv 23 J33, 14—17 p
A winter's tale.
NS, i 4 Ag34, 315—24 p

Hogarth, Basil
The new movement in
Scottish music.
MS, ii 1 A31, 57—64 c

Hogben, Lancelot
Message.
VS, i 2 S—N38, 1 c

Hohler, E. C.
E tenebris.
M, i 1 Je33, 58—59 p

Holden, Inez
Conversation tragedy.
LT, i 11 J37, 31—35 p

Holding, Eileen
London shows.
AX, 2 A35, 29—30;
AX 3 Jy35, 27;
AX 5 Sp36, 27—28 c

Hole, Christina
The tree.
P, 6 1939, 91—101 p

Hole, Philippa
Mourning.
DD, x 42 N—D33, 95 v
On Halidon.
DD, xi 44 M—A34, 19 v
Review
[*To circumjack cencrastus,*
by H. MacDiarmid].
DD, viii 30 Au31, 130—31 r
Review
[*The Lyceum book of verse,*
ed. by M. Stanley-Wrench].

DD, viii 30 Au31, 131—32 r
Sleep.
DD, xi 43 J—F34, 13 v
Triolet.
DD, vii 26 S—Oc30, 413—14 v

Hole, W. G.
Air-faring.
DD, xi 44 M—A34, 18 v
Country lore.
DD, xi 48 N—D34, 91 v
The lonely thrush.
DD, ix 36 N—D32, 88 v
The oak and the woodcutters.
DD, x 40 Jy—Ag33, 60—61 v
The splendid procession.
DD, x 37 J—F33, 4 v
Sunday's song.
DD, xi 43 J—F34, 1 v
When all is done.
DD, xi 45 My—Je34, 46 v

Holland, Cecilia
The aurora.
PQ, i 1 Sp39, 6 v

Holland, H. E.
Icarus.
DD, ix 35 S—Oc32, 79 v

Holland, H. G.
Shadows.
DD, x 40 Jy—Ag33, 71 v
Tell-tale.
DD, x 38 M—A33, 36 v
Willows.
DD, x 42 N—D33, 106 v
Winter.
DD, xi 46 Jy—Ag34, 66 v

Holland, James
Age cannot wither.
LR, i 7 A35, 266 i
The B.C.C. exposed.
LR, iii 1 F37, 29 i
A contemporary destiny.
LR, ii 2 N35, 71 i
Drawing.
LR, iii 11 D37, 668 i
Drawing.
LR, iii 7 Ag37, 405 i
Giovanezza.
LR, i 10 Jy35, 389 i
Happy days.
LR, ii 6 M36, 246 i
Happy New Year.
LR, ii 4 J36, 155 i
Hullo, big boy.
LR, iii 8 S37, 483 i
Incitement to disaffection.
LR, i 4 J35, 115 i
Malnutrition.
LR, i 9 Je35, 355 i
Memories of Cowes.

Holland, James (cont.)
LR, i 3 D34, 62 i
O what a mighty brain.
LR, iii 9 Oc37, 552 i
Our heritage the sea.
LR, i 8 My35, 313 i
Paris sketchbook.
LR, iii 7 Ag37, 415 i
The pattern of government
a cabinet portrait.
LR, ii 7 A36, 321 i
R.S.V.P.
LR, iii 3 A37, 132 i
Resurrection.
LR, ii 10 Jy36, 517 i
The sailor's return.
LR, i 6 M35, 193 i
Security of the middle classes.
LR, ii 3 D35, 127 i
Sunday afternoon,
Salisbury plain.
LR, iii 9 Oc37, 549 i
The tumult and the shouting dies.
LR, i 8 My35, 305 i
The unwilling hangmen.
LR, ii 5 F36, 197 i
What! No maypole?
LR, ii 8 My36, 362 i
With a ladder and some glasses.
LR, i 5 F35, 153 i
Won't somebody start a fire?
LR, iii 2 M37, 87 i
You can't make 'em mad with a
rag like that.
LR, ii 13 Oc36, 677 i

Hollinshead, Ann
Christmas.
RR, 9 A39, [16] v

Hollis, Christopher
As the world goes round.
ND, 12 16S37, 8–9;
ND, 13 23S37, 10–11;
ND, 14 30S37, 11–14;
ND, 15 7Oc37, 11–12;
ND, 16 14Oc37, 11–12;
ND, 17 21Oc37, 11–12;
ND, 18 28Oc37, 9–10;
ND, 19 4N37, 9–10;
ND, 20 11N37, 9;
ND, 21 18N37, 11–12;
ND, 22 25N37, 9–10;
ND, 23 2D37, 9–10 c
Ballad.
CA, 1 Ag30, 28 v
Ballad of our lady of Manresa.
CA, 4 N30, 76 v

Holme, Christopher
England on the spot.
DE, 2 Su32, 2 p

Holmes, Cecil

Poem.
LD, ii 1 Oc37, 20 v

Holmes, Roger
Constancy.
DD, ix 31 J–F32, 13 v

Holmes, Winifred
Mirage.
C, i 8 25J36, 63 v
Variations on a time theme
rev. by G. Armitage

Holmes-Coleman, Emily
Samson to Delilah.
EQ, i 3 N34, 169–71 v
The tree.
S, 2 A–Jy33, 11 v

Holorenshaw, Henry
A John-Baptist and nine minor
prophets
[*Life of Jesus,* by C. Noel;
Towards the Christian revolution].
LR, iii 9 Oc37, 553–56 r

Holst, Gustav
A unison hymn.
HR, 5 1932, 23 m

Holt, Oliver
Wood engraving.
F, 2 Je30, 92 i

Holt, William
From writing history to making it.
LR, i 1 Oc34, 45–46 p

Holtby, Winifred
The casualty list.
HR, 5 1932, 37–39 p
Lipstick for school marms.
LS, i 3 N34, 5–8 c
The maternal instinct.
PS, 5 N–D34, 4–5 p
Such a wonderful evening.
PS, 1 J34, 4–5 p
What we read and why we read it.
LR, i 4 J35, 111–14 c
South riding rev. by R. Wright
Women rev. by N. Mitchison

Hone, Roger
Now is the testing time.
PP, 8 F39, 7 V

Hood, Cordula M.
The desert night.
PQ, i 2 Su39, 42 v

Hood, Stuart,
Du rote fahn'.
MS, vi 4 J36, 338 v

Hook, Sidney
Hegel to Marx.
TC, v 25 M33, 2–13 c
Hegel to Marx [II].
TC, v 26 A33, 102–12 c

Hooke, Nina Warner
Arabesque.
P, 5 1939, 44–57 p

Hooley, Teresa
Pavlova enters heaven.
CA, 8 1931, 250 v
Prelude à l'après-midi d'un faune.
CA, 9 1931, 275 v

Hoops, Reinald
Dort, wo alles endet.
MS, ii 1 A31, 31 v

Hope
Edwardian undergraduates.
FB, i 1 4F36, 11 i

Hope, Alison
Review [*Four walls,*
by L. Whistler].
LS, i 3 N34, 73–76 r
Review
[*James Joyce and the making
of Ulysses,* by F. Budgen].
LS, i 1 F34, 62–63 r
Review [*Vienna,* by S. Spender;
A hope for poetry,
by C. Day Lewis].
PR, 1 1F35, 9, 11–12 r
World without end.
LS, i 3 N34, 80 v

Hope, Thomas Suthren
The winding road unfolds
rev. by A. Calder-Marshall

Hopkins, Gerard Manley
Books, articles, etc. on Hopkins.
NV, 14 A35, 30 c
Further letters
rev. by NV, 30 Su38, 22–23
The notebooks and papers
rev. by C. Day Lewis

Hopkins, Kenneth
His lampoon.
RR, 11 S39, [15] v

Hopkins, N.
Review [*Hitler over Europe,*
by E. Henri].
VP, i 2 Jy–S34, 56–57 r

Hopkins, Pryns
Education's need of civilization.
TC, i 2 A31, 13–15 c

Hopkinson, David
Poem.
NO, ii 2 J35, 140—41 v

Hopkinson, George G.
Curtain.
HR, 4 1931, 72 c
Editorial.
HR, 5 1932, 71—72;
HR, 6 1933, 58;
HR, 7 1934, 68 c
Sir Henry Whitehead, Kt., J. P.
HR, 4 1931, 33 c

Hopkinson, Henry Thomas
Acting — or not?
R, i 6 Oc34, 6—7 c
I have been drowned.
NW, 3 Sp37, 135—45 p
No happy returns.
NW, ns1 Au38, 36—43 p
Over the bridge.
P, 1 1938, 145—75 p
University rugger.
ND, 23 2D37, 32 c

Hopkinson, T. H.
Best for the boys.
ND, 14 30S37, 40 c
Ice hockey.
ND, 17 21Oc37, 40 p

Horacio, German
Drawings and note by
N. Dawson.
LR, iii 11 D37, 644—45 i

Horn, Frederick A.
By Cezanne.
HR, 7 1934, 21 v
Cover.
HR, 5 1932, cover;
HR, 6 1933, cover;
HR, 7, 1934, cover i
Transcendency.
HR, 7 1934, 59 v

Horner, Arthur L.
The arts, science and literature
as allies of the working class.
LR, ii 13 Oc36, 670 c

Hornsby, Nancy
Acting retrospect.
R, i 1 N33, 11 c

Hort, G. M.
Super-cinema.
LT, i 10 D36, 22 v

Horton, B. B.
Jewels.
DD, xi 45 My—Je34, 47 v

Houghton, Claude
Chaos is come again
rev. by G. West

House, Humphry
An essay in morals.
OO, x 51 F30, 453—57 c
Mr Eliot as a critic
[*Selected essays*].
NO, i 1 My33, 95—105 r
A note on Hopkins's religious
life.
NV, 14 A35, 3—5 c
Richards on Coleridge
[*Coleridge on imagination*,
by I. A. Richards].
NV, 13 F35, 15—18 r
The use of poetry
[*The use of peotry and the use
of criticism*, by T. S. Eliot].
NV, 7 F34, 17—20 r
Virgins.
OO, x 52 My30, 481—88 c
The virtue of purity
[*In defence of purity*,
by D. von Hildebrand;
More essays of love and virtue,
by H. H. Ellis].
OO, xi 56 N31, 163—71 c

Housman, A. W.
The ballad of Anne Hathaway.
JG, 67 W38, [20] v
The bee market.
JG, 36 Su36, [9] v
La berceuse.
JG, 22 Au32, [7] v
Bougival.
JG, 13 Su30, [11—12] v
By the waters of Babylon.
JG, 27 W33, [14] v
The cat.
JG, 36 Sp36, [36] v
Church parade.
JG, 28 Su34, [17—18] v
Cumner Hall, 1560.
JG, 66 Au38, [18—19] v
Dixmude.
JG, 17 Su31, [17] v
A fete at St. Denis.
JG, 15 W30, [12—14] v
Hallgerda.
DD, viii 29 Su31, 67—68 v
Hampstead.
JG, 30 Au34, [20] v
The harp of Brian Boru.
JG, 19 W31, [16—17] v
The heaven of Tycho Brahe.
JG, 14 Au30, [5—6] v
Homer.
JG, 38 Au36, [16] v
It was a lover and his lass.
JG, 40 Sp37, [36] v
A king soliloquises.

JG, 26 Au33, [6—7] v
Lou mort vieu.
JG, 42 Au37, [29—31] p
Mrs Beeton.
JG, 36 Sp36, [15] v
Old friends.
JG, 64 Sp38, [35—36] v
'The other country'.
JG, 16 Sp31, [12] v
Paradise lost.
JG, 41 Su37, [18—19] v
A Paris sketch.
JG, 35 W35, [18—19] v
Prima donna.
JG, 34 Au35, [21] v
Redivivus.
JG, 20 Sp32, [7] v
A review in the Tuileries gardens.
JG, 21 Su32, [5—6] v
Rosemary.
JG, 64 Sp38, [27] v
The secret.
JG, 65 Su38, [12—13] v
Sister Mary Monica.
JG, 23 W32, [12] v
Souvent femme varie,
fou qui se fie en elle.
JG, 33 Su35, [16] v
Superstition.
JG, 65 Su38, [31] v
Thersites.
JG, 29 Su34, [16] v
To Hans Christian Andersen.
JG, 39 W36, [8—9] v
Two men.
JG, 42 Au37, [21] v
Villanelle.
JG, 18 Au31, [24] v
Youth.
JG, 40 Sp37, [18] v

Housman, Alfred Edward
More poems rev. by G. Grigson
The name and nature of poetry
rev. by J. P. Hogan

Housman, Laurence
Honour.
K, i 2 D39—J40, 37—38 c
A.E.H.: a memoir
rev. by W. H. Auden
Victoria regina rev. by E. Bowen

Houston, Gertrude Graig *see*
Rose, William

How Nazis think.
NO, i 1 My33, 10—18 c

Howard, Edgar
The fair.
WR, ii 2 S39, 101—6 p
Peat.
P, 2 1938, 151—66 p

Howard, Jesse
News poem.
TO, ii 5 J39, 16 v

Howard, Lionel
New forces in Germany.
TC, v 30 Ag33, 343—46 c
Standing water.
TC, vi 32 N33, 88—90 c

Howarth, Herbert
A chapter of autobiography.
FB, v 2 My39, 31—33 p
Clifford Odets: three plays.
PR, 18 17Je36, 8—11 r
The cult of absurdity.
LD, ii 1 Oc37, 15—16 c
Deannarchist.
B, 1 Su38, 5—7 c
Dream and law [*The trial*,
by F. Kafka].
PR, 23 N37, 10—13 r
Eluard and personal poetry.
PR, 21 1M37, 4—6 c
Field for an epic.
PR, 14 19F36, 10, 11 c
Five points for
Virginia Woolf.
PR, 13 5F36, 8—9 c
French films and Duvivier.
LD, ii 3 F38, 19, 21 c
God in her own image.
LD, ii 2 D37, 11—12 c
Hippolytus.
FB, iii 9 6Je38, 69—70 c
Mass Observation and the
higher criticism.
FB, v 1 F39, 15—16 c
Mediterranean ode.
B, 2 W38, 3—4 v
The norm as hero.
PR, 16 6My36, 8—11 c
A note on the dénouement
of F6.
PR, 20 17N36, 20—21 c
On the sands.
PR, 23 N37, 1 v
Perpetuum mobile.
K, i 1 17N39, 10 v
Poem.
PR, 20 17N36, 2 v
Pope's labyrinth.
FB, iv 10 N38, 5—7 c
Protest for Mr Empson.
FB, i 3 9My36, 54—55 c
Pursuing the study of Lawrence.
PR, 19 20Oc36, 4—9 c
Recent events in the world of
poetry.
B, 3 Sp39, 12—13 c
Review [*25 poems*,
by D. Thomas].
PR, 19 20Oc36, 16 r
Review [*Epilogue*, no. 2;

*Our exagminification round
his factification* . . .
ed. by S. Beckett;
The problem of Hamlet,
by A. S. Cairncross].
PR, 20 17N36, 22—24 r
Seascape.
PR, 22 Je37, 17 v
She will know what I mean.
PR, 21 1M37, 2 v
Sonnet.
PR, 16 6My36, 11 v
see also Eluard, P.

Howarth, Herbert *and*
Thomson, Hector
Queen Anne dead —
King George crowned.
LD, i 4 Je37, 21 p

Howarth, Leslie
Gorebloodsby's ghost.
FB, ii 4 25J37, 9—10 p

Howell, Phyllis
Autumn night.
DD, viii 29 Su31, 66 v
Mercury; Songs unsung.
DD, viii 28 J—F31, 23 v
The silver horseman.
DD, viii 30 Au31, 102 v

Howes, Frank
Art, philosophy and criticism.
F, 2 Je30, 69—74 c
Bourgeois music:
a counter attack.
FB, i 3 9My36, 51—52 c

Hsu I-fen
Thinking of a girl friend,
tr. by Z. L. Yih and C. Doyle.
JG, 70 Au39, [4] v

Hubback, Diana
Sweden's economy
[*Sweden, the middle way*,
by M. W. Childs].
LR, ii 15 D36, 850 r

Hubbard, Hilda
The gorse.
DD, xi 48 N—D34, 102 v
A marvel.
DD, xi 46 Jy—Ag34, 67 v
The permanent way.
DD, x 42 N—D33, 101 v

Hubbard, Irene M.
H'apet'h; The virgin mother.
DD, x 41 S—Oc33, 84 v
Our beginning, our end, and our
ultimate substance; The desolate
mother.

DD, x 38 M—A33, 22, 26 v
The quest.
DD, xi 46 Jy—Ag34, 65 v

Huberman, Leo
The labour spy racket.
rev. by E. Branch
Man's worldly goods
rev. by J. Kemp

Hudson, Lockhart
Novitiate.
DD, x 39 My—Je33, 52 v
To ———.
DD, x 42 N—D33, 94 v

Hughes, Donald
Lear and the critics.
R, i 6 Oc34, 5 v

Hughes, Irene
Cafés in Cairo.
BB, vii 2 M30, 8—9 p

Hughes, Kathleen M.
Chanson d'automne.
PQ, i 1 Sp39, 7 v

Hughes, Langston
Jacques Romains.
LR, i 5 F35, 150 c

Hughes, Mary
Stella maris.
CA, 4 N30, 93 v

Hughes, Pennethorne
For Dr Arnold.
TC, iv 22 D32, 9 v
Three a.m.
I, i 2/3 15S31, 67 v
Three poems.
I, i 2/3 15S31, 86 v

Hughes, Trevor
Cobbler's wane.
C, ii 30 18Jy36, 16—17 p
In the valley.
C, i 11 15F36, 83, 88 p

Hughes, Thomas Rowland
Wheels.
WR, ii 1 Ag39, 13—14 v

Hughes-Stanton, Blair
Mother and child.
LD, i 4 Je37, 2 i
Wood engraving.
I, i 2/3 15S31, 67 i
Wood engraving.
I, i 1 15Je31, 11 i

Hugnet, Georges
Poem, tr. by D. Gascoyne.

CPP, 2 Je36, 29—30 v
Oeillades ciselées en branche
rev. by J. Scutenaire

Hugnet, Georges *and*
Seligmann, Kurt
Une écriture lisible
rev. by J. Scutenaire

Hugo, Victor
Les génies.
LQ, i 1 N36, [17—20] p

Hull, R. M.
The jacket.
LD, ii 1 Oc37, 3 v

Hull, Robert Hoare
Constant Lambert.
OO, x 51 F30, 449—52 c
see also Britting, Georg

Hume, Peter
American transport.
FB, ii 4 25J37, 17 c

Humphries, Emyr
[*also spelt* Humphreys]
The curate.
W, 10 Oc39, 270 v
1536—1936; A young man
considers his prospects.
W, 6/7 M39, 202—3 v
Sympathy; Unloading hay.
W, 8/9 Ag39, 226, 231 v

Hunt, Hugh
Interview.
R, i 6 Oc34, 11 c

Hunt, Sidney
Mad red angel.
I, i 1 15Je31, 25 p
Narrative.
I, i 2/3 15S31, 82 p
Night life of Yendis Nuth;
Sunstare optopoem.
S, 1 J33, 7—8 p, v
Wood engraving.
I, i 2/3 15S31, 71 i
Wood engraving.
I, i 1 15Je31, 30 i

Hunter, Mary
It shall be deathless.
JG, 65 Su38, [20] v
Long days.
JG, 27 W33, [7—8] v
Vision.
JG, 20 Sp32, [26—27] v

Hunter, Robert
Beethoven's death mask.
FB, iv 10 N38, 2 v

Huppert, Hugo
Voyage to Odessa,
tr. by J. Cleugh.
NW, 3 Sp37, 95—103 p

Hurd, Robert Alexander
Edinburgh today:
the enemies of the future.
MS, ii 1 A31, 53—56 c

Hutchings, Reginald
Four poems.
J, 1 J36, 26 v
Portrait in dust.
J, 1 J36, 9 p

Hutchinson, Hilton
Maurice Ravel.
LD, ii 3 F38, 18—19 c

Hutchinson, Ray Coryton
The last page.
BB, vii 2 M30, 65—77 p

Hutchinson, Lester
Conspiracy at Meerut
rev. by M. Slater

Hutchinson, Ward
Homiletic studies: laziness.
EP, 2 Su36, 76—83 c
A poem.
EP, 2 Su36, 161 v
Poems.
EP, 3 SP37, 158—60 v

Hutchinson, Ward *and*
Riding, Laura
Photography.
EP, 1 Au35, 236—45 c

Hutchison, Isobel Wylie
Bogoslof.
JG, 42 Au37, [8, 11] v
Creation of life.
DD, ix 33 My—Je32, 46 v
Light from darkness.
DD, x 38 M—A33, 35 v
McLeish.
JG, 24 Sp33, [14—16] v
Song for moneses uniflora.
JG, 41 Su37, [8] v
see also Kibkarjuk; Qerraq

Hutt, George Allen
Flint and steel English.
LR, i 4 J35, 130—35 c
Jolas' julep [*Transition*,
no. 23].
LR, i 12 S35, 528, r
The postwar history of the
British working class
rev. by I. Robertson

This final crisis
rev. by S. Jameson

Huxley, Aldous
Paris Congress speech.
LR, i 11 Ag35, 472 c
Two sonnets.
BB, vii 2 M30, 18 v
Brave new world
rev. by G. Pendle
Ends and means
rev. by E. Waugh
Eyeless in Gaza
rev. by G. West
see also Spender,
S. An open letter to
Aldous Huxley

Huxley, Julian Sorrell
On education:
the biological approach.
TC, v 25 M33, 33—35 c
The voice in the night.
HR, 5 1932, 59 v
A scientist among the Soviets
rev. by F. R.

Hyde, F. Austin
Depper, awd meer:
an East Riding dialect poem.
HR, 6 1933, 46 v

Hyde, Lawrence
The prospects of humanism
rev. by G. West

Hyman, Marcus
The adventures of the white
girl in her search for knowledge
rev. by A. Brown

Hyne, Charles John Cutliffe
The original of Captain Kettle.
HR, 4 1931, 16 c

I

I see what I want in Russia.
LR, ii 11 Ag36, 542 p

Ibbotson, William
Trifle.
DD, xi 46 Jy—Ag34, 63 v

Ibsen, Henrik
Extract from a tr. of 'Peer Gynt',
by R. Swingler.
GTP, 6 D36, [5—6] v

Ignatieff, George
Transatlantic contrasts, I.
The undergraduate.
FB, ii 4 25J37, 14, 22 c

Ilin, M. *pseud.*
Moscow has a plan rev. by J. R. Evans
Turning night into day
rev. by F. Le Gros Clark

Ince, Richard B.
Lipstick.
WW, i 2 A30, 14—41; WW, i 3 Jy30,
32—58; WW, i 4 Oc30, 25—77 c

Incitement to disaffection.
LR, i 1 Oc34, 37 c

Incog *pseud.*
Cad's colloquy.
K, i 2 D39—J40, 36 v
A parent's prayer to the proctors.
K, i 1 17N39, 24 v

Indian Progressive Writers Association
Manifesto.
LR, ii 5 F36, 240 c

Inge, William Ralph
Epilogue.
HR, 5 1932, 70 c

Ingilby, J.
Meadow flowers.
JG, 71 W39, [26] v
Two trees.
JG, 70 Au39, [21] v
The wind song.
DD, xi 45 My—Je34, 35 v

Inglis, Daniel
Why not the Tyrol?
LD, ii 2 D37, 30 p

Ingliss, Charles A.
Sequence.
LD, i 4 Je37, 26 v

Inkster, Leonard
A spring rondeau.
PQ, i 1 Sp39, 13 v

Innes, Geoffrey
O tempora! O movies!
VP, i 1 A—Je34, 4—8 c

Innes, Michael *pseud.*
Hamlet, revenge!
rev. by H. Read

International Association of Writers,
2nd congress
Manifesto.
LR, iii 8 S37, 445—46 c

International Student Congress
Against war and fascism.
CL, ii 1 Au34, 16—18 c

The invitation, tr. from the Low German
by A. G.
MS, i 4 J31, 24 v

Irvine, J. L.
Derek: or tittle by tattle.
OB, i 1 M—A34, 10—22 d
Escape ladder.
RM, 2 D34, 43—49 p
Films.
PR, 4 5M35, 9, 11—12 t
Proper geese.
PR, 2 12F35, 12 r

Irvine, John
Documentary film [by P. Rotha].
FB, i 1 4F36, 21—22 r

Isaacs, Susan
Original sin.
TC, v 30, Ag33, 337—42 c

Isherwood, Christopher William
Bradshaw
A Berlin diary (Autumn 1930).
NW, 3 Sp37, 11—26 p
A day in Paradise.
PS, 7 A—My35, 6—7 p
The first journey.
ND, 12 16S37, 10, 12
The Landauers.
NW, 5 Sp38, 5—41 p
The Nowaks.
NW, 1 Sp36, 8—37 p
Some notes on Auden's early poetry.
NV, 26/27 N37, 4—9 c
Goodbye to Berlin
rev. by NV, i 2 My39, 52
Lions and shadows rev. by G. Grigson
The memorial rev. by G. Rees
see also Auden, Wystan Hugh

Isserlis, Leon John
Poetry and the war.
PP, 15 N39, 1—2 c
3.1.39.
PP, 10 A39, 12 v
The unconscious
[*The dangers of being human,*
by E. Glover].
LR, ii 13 Oc36, 726 r

J

J., F.
Review [*The necessity of communism,*
by J. M. Murry].
TC, iii 14 A32, 26—27 r

J., J. *see* Winocour, Jack

Jacks, Lawrence Pearsall
Groups and their ways.
NO, i 2 N33, 154—60 c

Jackson, Ada
The widow rev. by A. D. Hawkins

Jackson, Frank
China strikes back [film].
LR, iii 13 F38, 808—9 r
Films for labour.
LR, ii 9 Je36, 477 r
For peace or war [*Peace of Britain*].
LR, ii 8 My36, 413 r
Land without bread.
LR, iii 14 M38, 855 r
New Russian films.
LR, iii 16 My38, 1004—6 r
Soviet cinema.
LR, iii 11 D37, 679—81 c

Jackson, J. Dawson
Five poems.
OO, x 51 F30, 430 v
Poem.
OO, x 52 My30, 502 v
Poem.
OO, x 53, N30, 607 v

Jackson, Michael
The machine.
ST, i 1 F33, 3—4 p

Jackson, Thomas Alfred
The Conzological method of trusting
[*The scientific method of thinking,*
by E. Conze].
EY, 2 Oc35, 3 r
A cure for headaches
[*Thinking,* by H. Levy].
LR, ii 10 Jy36, 528—29 r
Dickens the radical.
LR, iii 2 M37, 88—95 c
Four veterans
[*Sir James Sexton, agitator:
an autobiography; Tom Mann,*
by D. Torr; *My life of revolt,*
by D. Kirkwood; *Revolt on the Clyde,*
by W. Gallacher].
LR, ii 9 Je36, 466—67 r
Marxism: pragmatism: surrealism.
LR, ii 11 Ag36, 565—67 c
The Moscow trial
[*Report of court proceedings in the case
of the Anti-Soviet Trotskyite centre*].
LR, iii 2 M37, 116—18 r
This Freudian ballyhoo
[*Freud and Marx,* by R. Osborn].
LR, iii 4 My37, 233—37 r
Charles Dickens rev. by E. Cook
Dialectics rev. by H. Read

Jacob, Alaric
Peter Pan Coward.
DV, 3 My32, 92—94 c

Jacob, Lewis
Crumbs.
CV, 1 Su34, 14 v

Jacquot, J. *see* Breton, A.; Eluard, P.

James, Cyril Lionel Robert
World revolution, 1917—1936
rev. by R. F. Andrews

James, John
Two teachers.
LR, ii 7 A36, 310—12 p

James, Laurel
Aldershot tattoo.
VP, i 2 Jy—S34, 36—37 p

James, Montague Rhodes
The malice of inanimate objects.
M, i 1 Je33, 29—32 p

Jameson, Margaret Storm
Circa 1942.
LR, ii 4 J36, 148—54 p
Crisis [*This final crisis,*
by G. A. Hutt].
LR, ii 4 J36, 156—59 r
Extract from a book of views.
HR, 6 1933, 17—20 p
To a Labour party official.
LR, i 2 N34, 29—34 c
In the second year rev. by A. Brown
The moon is making
rev. by T. L. Hodgkin
None turn back rev. by A. L. Morton

Jamieson, Morley
Night light.
NA, i 1 Au39, 57—60 p

Jaques *pseud.*
Review [*Eva Gay,* by E. Scott;
Magpie, by L. Vidal;
*Further extracts from the notebooks
of Samuel Butler;
The Indian theatre,* by R. K. Yajnik].
LS, i 1 F34, 55—64 r

Jaquet, Frida
Friendship.
DD, x 39 My—Je33, 54 v
The plain.
DD, vii 26 S—Oc30, 410 v

Jardelle, Hugues
The philosophy of the Intelligent
Educated Person.
TC, i 1 M31, 5—7 c

Jardine, Robin
Buddha the nationalist
[*Gautama Buddha,* by I. Singh].
LR, iii 12 J38, 754—56 r
Living newspaper, no. 1: Busmen.
LR, iii 15 A38, 922—23 dr
The mixed populations
[*Half-caste,* by C. Dover].
LR, iii 5 Je37, 310 r
Paris — Xmas 1937.
LR, iii 13 F38, 791—93 p
Twentieth anniversary
[*History of the Civil War in the U.S.S.R.,*
ed. by M. Gorki *and others;
Twenty years after,* by H. Lee;
Russia — with open eyes, by
P. Winterton;
History of anarchism in Russia,
by E. Yaroslavsky]. LR,
iii 10 N37, 615—17 r

Jardine, Rupert
Across the beaches.
CM, i 4 Sp34, 165—67 p
Fragment from a journal.
CM, i 3 Au33, 108—9 p
The heater.
CM, i 1 Sp33, 22—23 p
Teaparty.
CM, i 2 Su33, 83—91 p
The two passengers.
CM, i 4 Sp34, 158—60 p

Jarrett, Bede
'The hound of heaven' as a retreat
book.
CA, 5 M31, 105—14 c
The poetry of St. Thomas Aquinas.
CA, 12 1932, 360—67 c

Jarry, Alfred
Fable, tr. by A. L. Lloyd.
CPP, 2 Je36, 32—33 v
Sonnet, tr. by F. Scarfe.
CPP, 9 Sp37, 28 v

Jakovski, Anatole
Brancusi.
AX, 3 Jy35, 3—9 c
Inscriptions under pictures.
AX, 1 J35, 14—20 c
Wassily Kandinsky.
AX, 2 A32, 9—12 c

**Jawarharlal Nehru's campaign for
Indian liberties.**
LR, ii 12 S36, 624—26 c

Jay, Douglas Patrick Thomas
Mr T. S. Eliot: after Lambeth
[*Thoughts after Lambeth*].
OO, xi 55 Je31, 78—85 r
The 'Oxford' groups criticised
[*For sinners only,* by A. J. Russell].

NO, i 1 My33, 77—85 r
Socialism and planning.
NO, i 2 N33, 140—47 c
A testament of autumn.
F, 1 F30, 3—9 c

James, Edwin Stanley
Cigarette,
DD, viii 28 J—F31, 7 v

Jeans, *Sir* James
Eos rev. by R. Graves
The mysterious universe
rev. by TC, iv 20 Oc32, 21—23

Jeans, Ronald
The theatre's news reel.
R, i 3 A34, 4—5 c

Jeffers, Robinson
Answers to an enquiry.
NV, 12 D34, 18 p
Dear Judas rev. by L. MacNeice

Jefferson, Thos. G.
Tryst.
DD, vii 26 S—Oc30, 397 v

Jeffery, Gordon
The apprentices binge.
LR, iii 4 My37, 224—26 p
In the welding bay.
NW, 5 Sp38, 169—73 p

Jeffrey, William
The Galleys (1547—1549).
MS, iv 4 J34, 290—93 v
The grassy place.
MS, i 4 J31, 43—44 v
The satyr said.
MS, i 2 Su30, 12 v
Sea glimmer.
MS, iv 3 Oc35, 218—19 v
The senses.
MS, iv 2 Jy33, 122—25 v
Stanzas from 'An elegy written in an
industrial town'.
MS, iii 2 Ag32, 124—32 v
Supernymph.
MS, ii 1 A31, 13 v

Jellinek, Frank
Writers and artists in the Commune.
LR, i 3 D34, 83—86 c
The Paris Commune of 1871
rev. by A. L. Morton

Jenkinson, Editha
A December rose.
JG, 71 W39, [31] v
Fox-gloves.
JG, 68 Sp39, [32—33] v
Garden solitude.
JG, 63 W37, [22] v

Jenkinson, Editha (cont.)
Saint Francis.
JG, 66 Au38, [11] v
The sea.
JG, 69 Su39, [8] v
Speedwells.
JG, 64 Sp38, [6] v

Jenner, *Mrs* Henry
The tabernacle lights.
CA, 8 1931, 252 v

Jennings, Humphrey
An apple a day.
DE, 1 New year 1932, 4 c
Eliot and Auden and Shakespeare.
NV, 18 D35, 4—7 c
The iron horse.
LB, 3 Je38, 22, 27—28 c
In Magritte's paintings.
LB, 1 A38, 15 c
Notes on Marvell's 'To his coy mistress'.
EX, 5 F30, 14—19 c
Prose poem [also tr. by E. L. T. Mesens].
LB, 2 My38, 8 v
Report on the industrial revoltuion.
CPP, 9 Sp37, 41—42 p
Reports.
CPP, 4/5 Ag36, 94—95 p
Study for a long report
'The boyhood of Byron'.
CPP, 8 D36, 146—47 p
Surrealism [by H. Read].
CPP, 8 D36, 167—68 r
Three reports.
CPP, 2 Je36, 39—41 p
Two American poems;
The boyhood of Byron.
LB, 12 15M39, 7—8 v, p
Two poems.
LB, 11 M39, 19 v
Who does that remind you of?
LB, 6 Oc38, 21—22 c
see also Breton, A.; Mesens, E. L. T.;
Peret, B.

Jennings, Humphrey *and* Madge, Charles
Poetic description and Mass-Observation,
NV, 24 F37, 1—6 p

Jennings, Humphrey *and* Noxon, G. F.
Rock painting and *La jeune peinture*.
EX, 7 Sp31, 37—40 c

Jennings, Humphrey *and* Reeves, J. M.
A consideration of Herrick.
EX, 7 Sp31, 50—56 c

Jennings, J.
Oil in Mexico.
PP, 4 Oc38, 10 v

Jennings, Richard
At the theatre.

ND, 14 30S37, 37 dr
Let's stagger Christmas.
ND, 21 18N37, 16 p

Jennings, W. N.
Sedition.
TC, vi 35 Je34, 265—71 c

Jerrold, Douglas
The catholic view of art and letters.
CA, 7 Je31, 204—13 c
They that take the sword rev. by J. D.

Joad, Cyril Edwin Mitchinson
The advocacy of peace.
TC, v 29 Jy33, 273—78 c
Liberalism (small L) re-stated.
FB, i 1 4F36, 4—5 c
The need for co-operation.
TC, iv 24 F33, 26—27 c
Speech at the High Leigh conference.
TC, iv 20 Oc32, 26—28 c
World crisis: unity against war.
TC, v 27 My33, 172—75 c
Guide to modern thought
rev. by G. West
Philosophical aspects of modern science
rev. by TC, v 29 Jy33, 305—8 r
Under the fifth rib rev. by G. West

Johansen, Marguerite
After Calvary.
JG, 39 W36, [32] v
The curtained hour.
JG, 38 Au36, [10] v
Far, far as the eye can see.
JG, 69 Su39, [30] v
Fool's paradise.
JG, 42 Au37, [18—19] v
A gull's cry.
JG, 31 W34, [20] v
Herzchen mein.
JG, 35 W35, [28—29] v
Hunter's vale.
JG, 34 Au35, [22] v
It was at Michaelmas.
JG, 36 Sp36, [27—29] p
A little while.
JG, 66 Au38, [31—32] v
Outgoing.
JG, 37 Su36, [19—20] v
Precious.
JG, 33 Su35, [28—29] v
Revelation.
JG, 64 Sp38, [14] v
Sanctuary.
JG, 40 Sp37, [33—34] v
The unpredictable.
JG, 71 W39, [29] v
Witch-hazel.
JG, 32 Sp35, [13—14] v

John Dory.
T, 4 Je37, [12] v

Johnes, Edith M.
Abestos.
JG, 26 Au33, [14] v
Ballad.
JG, 13 Su30, [23—24] v
Bracken.
JG, 20 Sp32, [23] v
The butterfly.
JG, 35 W35, [22] v
Children of time.
JG, 14 Au30, [19—20] v
Company of jongleurs.
JG, 39 W36, [9] v
Courage.
JG, 66 Au38, [7] v
The daring minx.
JG, 42 Au37, [36] v
Dead leaves.
JG, 23 W32, [11—12] v
Echoes.
JG, 30 Au34, [14—15] v
Errant Persephone.
JG, 70 Au39, [8] v
The fortune teller.
JG, 64 Sp38, [36] v
An ivory elephant.
JG, 19 W31, [11—12] v
Little heaven.
JG, 63 W37, [21] v
Moods.
JG, 17 Su31, [19] v
The moon.
JG, 40 Sp37, [33] v
The old mother.
JG, 18 Au31, [12—13] v
Oldholmston.
JG, 15 W30, [7] v
One gone before.
JG, 67 W38, [34] v
Ours.
JG, 21 Su32, [9] v
The portrait.
JG, 34 Au35, [30] v
Sea-port.
JG, 41 Su37, [20—21] v
The sifting.
JG, 24 Sp33, [12—13] v
Song of the Moujic.
JG, 16 Sp31, [20—21] v
The star.
JG, 29 Su34, [27] v
The sumach tree.
JG, 38 Au36, [19] v
The travellers.
JG, 32 Sp35, [17] v
Treasury.
JG, 25 Su33, [26] v
Triolet.
DD, vii 26 S—Oc30, 413 v

Johns, Carmichael
Insomnia.
C, iii 57 23J37, 29 v

Johnson, Alan Campbell
West end Hamlet.
PR, 1 1F35, 3—4 dr

Johnson, Geoffrey
The bat,
RR, 10 Je39, [13] v
Building estate.
JG, 65 Su38, [13] v
Celery-carters.
BB, vii 2 M30, 41 v
The challenge.
JG, 69 Su39, [11] v
The explanation.
JG, 68 Sp39, [15] v
The highland bull.
JG, 39 W36, [6] v
House in the gale.
JG, 38 Au36, [27—28] v
Irrelevant.
JG, 70 Au39, [12] v
The lovely land.
JG, 42 Au37, [14—15] v
March morning.
JG, 37 Su36, [10—11] v
Morning vista.
JG, 63 W37, [6—7] v
The night-light.
JG, 67 W38, [23] v
The reactionary rebels.
JG, 64 Sp38, [7] v
Roadmakers.
JG, 36 Sp36, [18—19] v
The sower.
JG, 69 Su39, [2] v
The three graces.
JG, 66 Au38, [26] v
Twilight.
JG, 40 Sp37, [32] v
The weaver.
JG, 71 W39, [12] v

Johnson, Hewlett
Greetings on May day.
LR, iii 16 My38, 962—63 c

Johnson, J.
Simonstown rev. by S. Blumenfeld

Johnson, Pamela Hansford
The fugitive.
C, i 1 7D35, 3 p
Old mole.
ND, 6 5Ag37, 11—12, 14—15 p
Poem.
C, ii 35 22Ag36, 54 v
Riverside pub.
LR, ii 7 A36, 322—25 p
Suddenly a woman.
NS, i 5 Oc34, 365—70 p
'There's a breathless hush . . . '
ND, 9 26Ag37, 31 c
Here to-day

rev. by A. Calder-Marshall
World's end rev. by E. Waugh

Johnson, R. J. G.
Lyric.
CM, i 1 Sp33, 14 v

Johnston, George
Scottish culture and politics.
VS, i 2 S—N38, 6—9 c

Johnstone, George Harcourt
3rd lord Derwent
see Derwent, George Harcourt
Johnstone
3rd lord

Johnstone, William
Credo [and] Four paintings.
TO, i 1 J38, 25 p, i
Creative art in England
rev. by O. Blakeston

Jolas, Eugene
I have seen monsters and angels
rev. by H. Treece

Jolly, Reginald G.
May day 1939.
PP, 11 My39, 5 v
Struggle,
PP, 2 Ag38, 5 v

Jones, A. G. Prys-
see Prys-Jones, A. G.

Jones, Alan Pryce-
see Pryce-Jones, Alan

Jones, Allan Gwynne-
see Gwynne-Jones, Allan

Jones, Archibald Creech
This nationalism.
DV, 3 My32, 73—76 c

Jones, Carel Ramsay
Review [*My life,* by L. D. Trotsky].
OO, x 53 N30, 632—35 r

Jones, Charles Garrett
Poem.
TC, vi 31 S—Oc33, 7 v

Jones, D. Gwenallt
Saunders Lewis.
W, 4 M38, 141 v

Jones, D. Rocyn- *see* Rocyn-Jones, D.

Jones, David
In parenthesis
rev. by W. Griffith and N. Heseltine;

C. W. E. Shelley; J. Stead; V. Watkins;
E. Waugh

Jones, E. Odwyn
The pedlar's song.
PQ, i 1 Sp39, 7 v

Jones, Frederick Elwyn
German universities under the Nazi
regime.
LR, iii 14 M38, 842—44 c
Mussolini's career
[*Mussolini in the making,*
by G. Megaro; *Goliath,*
by G. A. Borgese;
Government in fascist Italy,
by H. A. Steiner].
LR, iii 16 My38, 1010—13 r
Reporter in central Europe
[*South of Hitler,* by M. W. Fodor].
LR, iii 15 A38, 941—42 r

Jones, George Aubrey
In Somerset.
JG, 71 W39, [30] v
Spite.
JG, 70 Au39, [26] v
These mortals.
JG, 68 Sp39, [27] v

Jones, Glyn
An afternoon at Uncle Shad's.
WR, i 1 F39, 8—15 p
Easter.
NV, 9 Je34, 3 v
Eden tree.
NS, ii 1 F35, 30—34 p
The four headed man.
W, 3 Au37, 110—14 p
Night.
PL, i 2 A39, [24] v
Park.
W, 4 M38, 154 v
Poem.
W, 6/7 M39, 197 v
Porth-y-Rhyd.
NS, ii 3 Je35, 168—74 p
Review [*The map of love,*
by D. Thomas].
WR, ii 3 Oc39, 179—80 r
Scene.
W, 1 Su37, 7—8 v
Satiric eye.
T, 6/7 N37, [42] c
Shadow; Gull.
T, 3 A37, [12] v
The slum-world.
W, 11 W39, 302 v
Town.
W, 10 Oc39, 274 v
Tree; Choirs.
W, 3 Au37, 87—89 v
Two poems.

73

Jones, Glyn (cont.)
NV, 10 Ag34, 12 v
The blue bed
rev. by M. Evans; J. Lindsay

Jones, Gwyn
The buttercup field.
WR, ii 1 Ag39, 15—22 p
Copy.
P, 2 1938, 108—20 p
Editorial.
WR, i 1 F39, 3—7; WR, ii 1 Ag39, 3—5;
WR, ii 2 S39, 63—65; WR, ii 3 Oc39,
123—27; WR, ii 4 N39, 183—84 c
Review
[*The loneliest mountain and other
poems,*
by W. H. Davies].
WR, ii 4 N39, 232—34 r
The ripening Davies
[*A time to laugh,* by Rhys Davies].
W, 1 Su37, 30—31 r
An unpublished poem of Charles
Kingsley.
WR, ii 3 Oc39, 165 c
Times like these rev. by E. Evans

Jones, Herbert
Page me; Layout for a poem.
S, 2 A—Jy33, 27—28 v

Jones, Jack
Shoni in Shaftesbury avenue.
WR, ii 1 Ag39, 40—44 c
Rhondda roundabout
rev. by D. A. Willis
Unfinished journey rev. by E. Evans

Jones, Lewis
Oxford from Rhondda.
TU, 1 1933, 5—6 c
The people of Wales
[*My Wales,* by R. Davies].
LR, iii 9 Oc37, 568—69 r
Tonypandy.
LR, iii 3 A37, 157—59 p
Tory coal-miner [*Coal miner,*
by G. A. W. Tomlinson].
LR, iii 7 Ag37, 439—41 r
Cwmardy rev. by E. Evans; W. H.
Williams

Jones, Percy Mansell
French introspectives
rev. by H. L. R. Edward

Jones, Percy Thoresby *and others*
Welsh border country rev. by M. Evans

Jones, S. Beryl
At my sister's.
NS, ii 5 Oc35, 394—98 p
The woman at the well.
NS, ii 1 F35, 70—80 p

Jones, Tom
Man mind thyself.
LR, i 5 F35, 166-68 p
Safety first.
LR, i 12 S35, 492—96 p
The survivor.
ST, i 2 A33, 3—7 p
Writers international.
LR, i 3 D34, 77—78 c

Jopson, Norman Brook *tr.*
see Bozhovitch, G.; Nalkowska, Z.

Josephs, Laurence
Life's pilgrim.
I, i 2/3 15S31, 38 v
The sun spirit.
I, i 2/3 15S31, 85 i
Three poems.
I, i 1 15Je31, 5 v
Two poems.
I, i 2/3 15S31, 95 v
Two poems.
I, i 4 15D31, 116 v

Joyce, James
From *Work in progress.*
EX, 7 Sp31, 27—29 p
Ulysses rev. by S. Spender

Judd, Michael T.
Art atrophied in Oxford.
LD, i 3 My37, 6 c

Jukes, Joan
On the floor.
NS, i 6 D34, 405—19 p

K

K., E. M.
Anacreon 22.
LS, i 1 F34, 45 v

Kabir, Humayun
The Film society.
OO xi 55 Je31, 136—37; OO, xi 56 N31,
221—23 c

Kabraji, Fredoon
The patriots.
LR, ii 12 S36, 638—39 v

Kaestlin, John
Berdyaev and the spirit of Dostoievski.
CM, ii 1 Su35, 254—73 c
Joyce by candlelight.
CM, 1 2 Su33, 47—54 c
T. F. Powys.
CM, i 3 Au33, 110—23 c

The tyranny of self; Michel
de Montaigne.
CM, i 1 Sp33, 1—5 c
What have they done since Dunbar.
CM, i 4 Sp34, 180—94 c

Kafka, Franz
Aphorisms, tr. by W. and E. Muir.
MS, iii 3 Oc32, 202—8 p
First sorrow, tr. by W. Muir.
EQ, i 1 My34, 46—49 p
Two fragments, tr. by G. H. Roberts.
W, 6/7 M39, 194—95 p
The trial rev. by H. Howarth

Kahn, Derek
Andrew Marvell.
NO, i 1 My33, 116—24 c
Anthropology begins at home
[*Mass observation,*
by C. Madge and T. Harrisson].
LR, iii 6 Jy37, 373 r
Country bus strike.
LR, iii 5 Je37, 276—78 p
End of an epoch
[*Aspects of modernism,*
by J. Lavrin].
LR, ii 7 A36, 347 r
Fear and hope.
TU, i 2 1934, 35—36 v
International writers in London.
LR, ii 10 Jy36, 481—90 c
The Italian dictatorship
[*Under the axe of fascism,*
by G. Salvemini].
LR, ii 14 N36, 785 r
Low company [by M. Benney].
LR, iii 1 F37, 59 r
Magic of liberalism
[*The magic of monarchy,* by K. Martin]
LR, iii 4 My37, 241 r
A man of feeling.
LR, ii 12 S36, 639—41 p
A monograph a month
[*Fact,* no. 1].
LR, iii 4 My37, 255 r
The morality of W. B. Yeats.
LR, ii 6 M36, 252—58 c
Myth and history
[*The burning cactus,* by S. Spender].
LR, ii 9 Je36, 463—64 r
Number one [*New writing,* no. 1].
LR, ii 9 Je36, 464 r
Realist films.
LR, ii 7 A36, 348 c
The road to Wigan pier
[by G. Orwell].
LR, iii 3 A37, 186—87 r
The social roots of thought.
[*Ideology and Utopia,* by K. Mannheim]
LR, iii 1 F37, 55—57 r
The Stratford festival.
LR, ii 12 S36, 652—53 dr

Theatre notes.[*Where's that bomb*,
by R. Gullan and B. Roberts;
Spain, by R. Swingler;
The Agamemnon of Aeschylus].
LR, ii 15 D36, 833 dr
Two poems.
F, 6 Je31, 206—7 v
Wara waratonga.
LD, i 2 M37, 5—7 p
What is culture?
LR, ii 16 J37, 891—94 c

Kahn, Derek *and* **Aragon**, Louis
French writers and the people's front.
LR, ii 8 My36, 378—80 c

Kahn, Milton
The anatomy of spirit
[by J. Lindsay].
LR, iii 8 S37, 494—95 r
But how [*War can be averted*,
by E. Rathbone]?
LR, iii 15 A38, 949—50 r
Dubious colours [*In letters of red*,
ed. by E. A. Osborne].
LR, iii 16 My38, 1018—19 r
Jewish culture.
LR, iii 16 My38, 996—99 c
The problems of adolescence
[*Commonsense and the adolescent*,
by E. Mannin].
LR, iii 12 J38, 763 r
The Soviet Union versus barbarism
[*For peace and friendship*].
LR, iii 9 Oc37, 569 r
A waiter's autobiography
[*Coming, sir!* by D. Marlowe].
LR, iii 9 Oc37, 567—68 r

Kalicstein, Daniel
Park scene.
P, 4 1938 53—59 p

Kandinsky, Vassily
Abstract and concrete art; preface.
LB, 14 My39, 2 c
Line and fish.
AX, 2 A35, 6 c

Kantorowicz, Alfred
A Madrid diary, tr, by J. Cleugh.
NW, 4 Au37, 40—58 p
Paris Congress speech.
LR, i 11 Ag35, 469 c
To the Western front.
NW, 1 Sp36, 61—64 p

Karinthy, Frederick
The moral.
ND, 20 11N37, 16 p

Kataev, Valentin
Squaring the circle [play]
rev. by C. C. Doggett

Kay, A.
Illegal children's papers in Austria.
LR, ii 8 My36, 370—73 c
One year after.
LR, i 6 M35, 234—35 c
We remember.
LR, i 2 N34, 12 v

Kay, Vera
Little old woman.
LR, i 9 Je35, 374—76 p

Kelly, Alison
Lôches by moonlight.
LS, ii 1 My35, 9—12 p

Kelly, Bernard W.
The boy poet of the Great War
[Edward Wyndham-Tennant].
CA, 10 1931, 309—15 c

Kelly, Clare
Poem.
PR, 7 12Je35, 12 v

Kemp, H. V.
Beauty be reasonable.
CL, i 1 Su33, 4 v
Criticism of 'Scrutiny'
[*For continuity*, by F. R. Leavis].
RM, 1 Je34, 19—24 r
On Lucilla going to the wars.
CM, i 1 Sp33, 35 v
On the 13th plenum.
CL, i 3 Sp34, 59 v
Winter and spring.
CL, i 2 W33, 21—22 v
see also Davis, H.

Kemp, H. V. *and* **Davis**, H.
The rise and fall of bourgeois poetry.
CL, i 4 Su34, 93—100 c

Kemp, Harry Hibbard
Poems.
EP, 3 Sp37, 131—37 v
see also Riding, Laura *and others*

Kemp, Jonathan
Britain today
[*The condition of Britain today*,
by G. D. H. and M. I. Cole].
LR, iii 4 My37, 246 r
A history of the people
[*Man's worldly goods*, by L. Huberman].
LR, iii 5 Je37, 310 r
Diderot, interpreter of nature
rev. by S. Swingler

Kendall, L.
Humanity.
PP, 13/14 Jy—Ag39, 12 v
To the heroes of the International

Brigade in Spain.
PP, 4 Oc38, 7 v

Kennedy, Adam *pseud.*
The mourners.
MS, iii 4 J33, 287—319; MS, iv 1 A33,
24—37; MS, iv 2 Jy33, 141—56; MS,
iv 3 Oc33, 215—34 p
Number 249 of the catalogue.
MS, i 1 Sp30, 11—17 p
One bright day.
MS, ii 2 Jy31, 118—22 p
Orra boughs.
MS, i 3 Au30, ii, 93 p
Review [*The turn of the day*,
by M. Angus].
MS, ii 1 A31, 87—89 r
see also Hesse, Herman

Kennedy, T.
The strangling of a modern state.
MS, i 2 Su30, 24—30 c

Kennedy, Walter P.
Plaint of the tormentor.
SM, 3 1932, 49 v

Kerr, James Lennox
The fool and the tractor
rev. by A. L. Morton

Kerr, W. R.
The man who got on and where he got
off!
ST, i 2 A33, 18—21 p

Kerr, William
A prayer for peace.
HR, 5 1932, 48 v

Kersh, Gerald
Birth of a love song.
ND, 23 2D37, 15—16 p
The drunk and the blind.
P, 4 1938, 61—70 p
The extraordinarily horrible dummy.
P, 6 1939, 138—43 p
What for a tiger!
ND, 2 8Jy37, 15—17 p

Kershaw, Victor
Cuban Jane.
P, 3 1938, 118—42 p
Outback.
P, 5 1939, 135—54 p

Kessler, Jean
Deo gratias.
JG, 68 Sp39, [17] v
Fragment.
JG, 19 W31, [12] v
Marching song.
JG, 37 Su36, [16—17] v
Rozinante.

LR, ii 11 Ag36, 600 r
Clerical labour in Britain
rev. by T. H. Wintringham

Klinger, Godfrey
Abstraction.
CV, 4 1935, 8—9 p

The knave.
T, 4 Je37, [4] v

Knickerbocker, Hubert Renfro
Germany—Fascist or Soviet?
rev. by J. R. Evans
Revolutionary art criticism
rev. by R. Fox
Soviet trade and world depression
rev. by W. N. Warbey

Knight, Eric
Time for the pie-boy.
P, 5 1939, 102—12 p
Song on your bugles
rev. by T. L. Hodgkin

Knight, George Wilson
Kubla Khan: an interpretation.
PR, 9 23Oc35, 4—9 c
Principles of Shakespearian production
rev. by F. Berry

Knight, Gilbert
Fog.
LD, i 3 My37, 7, 9 p

Knights, Lionel Charles
Mr Knights replies to Alick West.
LR, iii 9 Oc37, 566—67 c
Drama and society in the age of Jonson
rev. by D. A. Traversi; A. West
How many children had Lady Macbeth?
rev. by W. H. Auden

Knowland, Garry
A critic's propositions.
J, 2 My36, 10 c
Images of a day.
Y, i 2 My39, 59 v
Poem.
J, 2 My36, 21 v
Poetry [*Twelve noon,*
by R. Church;
Songs and initiations,
by W. J. Turner; *Harlem,*
etc. by W. R. Benet].
J, 2 My36, 25 r

Knowles, Kenneth Guy Jack Charles
Portrait 1928.
F, 3 Oc30, 183 i
Portrait of my father, 1927.
F, 1 F30, 44 i

Knox, Penelope
Conversation in war-time.
K, i 2 D39—J40, 39 p

Knox, Ronald
The last absence.
M, i 1 Je33, 39—40 v

Ko Fu-hua
Achinese woman's poem,
tr. by Z. L. Yih and C. Doyle.
JG, 70 Au39, [13] v

Koerber, Lenka von
Soviet Russia fights crime
rev. by A. Brown; C. D. Rackham

Koestler, Arthur
Spanish testament
rev. by S. T. Warner

Kohn, Hans
Nationalism in the Soviet Union
rev. by W. N. Warbey

Kohn-Bramstedt, Ernst
*Autocracy and the middle-classes in
Germany*
rev. by A. Henderson

Koike, Takesai
The road of flowers; Glassy hour.
TO, i 1 J38, 6—7 v

Kollerstrom, Oscar G.
The tale of any prophet.
I, i 4 15D31, 116 v

Kollontai, Aleksandra Mikhailovich
Free love rev. by E. M. Barraud

Komai, Gonnoske
Let us think seriously.
FB, iii 6 21Oc37, 10—11 c
On Japanese poetry.
FB, i 3 9My37, 61—62 c

Konrad, Edmund
The wizard of Menlo, tr. by P. Selver.
SM, 5 1934, 13—108 d

Kosztolanyi, Deszo
The pleasure of stealing.
ND, 16 14Oc37, 14—15 p

Kramer, Jacob
C. J. Cutliffe Hyne, Esq.
HR, 4 1931, 40 i
Gandhi.
HR, 5 1932, 14 i
Herbert Read.
HR, 4 1931, 23 i
J. B. Priestley.
HR, 4 1931, 32 i

To the heroic dead of the R101.
HR, 4 1931, 7 i

Krasny
Lower rents.
PP, 11 My39, 12 v

Kraus, Florence Lee
Rough edges.
NS, ii 1 F35, 27—29 p

Krishnaswami, A.
The Indian mind.
CM, i 3 Au33, 137—39 c

Krklec, Gustav
Two poems, tr. by P. Selver.
SM, 4 1933, 112—13 v

Krymov, V.
He's got a million
rev. by H. O. Whyte

Kubka, Frantisek
A complicated affair,
tr. by P. Selver.
SM, 3 1932, 57—92 p

Kujar, E. *see* Uraon marriage sermon

Kunitz, Joshua
Lenin as a revolutionary writer.
TC, iii 18 Ag32, 17—20 c

Kuo Chia
New Year's eve,
tr. by Z. L. Yih and C. Doyle.
JG, 71 W39, [17] v

Kuo Tzeh-hsiung
The Far Eastern crisis.
DV, 2 A32, 43—46 c

Kurella, Alfred
The taking of Pskhu, tr. by J. L.
NW, 4 Au37, 192—97 p

L

L, E.
War.
TU, 3 Je34, 14—22 c

L, I.
Review [*The islands of Scotland,*
by H. MacDiarmid].
NA, i 1 Au39, 100—102 r

Ll., M.
Review [*Selected poems,*
by H. MacDiarmid].
PR, 7 12Je35, 14—15 r

L,-C., F. *see* Lafitte-Cyon, François

Labeyrie, Francis Dufau-
see Dufau-Labeyrie, Francis

Laer, Theodore
Forty years rev. by M. Henshaw

Lafage, Leon
Poulou, wife of Maluque,
tr. by R. Cooke.
P, 4 1938, 144—52 p

Lafitte-Cyon, François
Paris, May day 1931.
TU, 3 Je34, 39—42 p
Review [*Karl Marx,*
by E. H. Carr].
LS, i 3 N34, 64—67 r

Laforgue, Jules
The defeat of Baudelaire
rev by. E. Starkie

Lagden, Mervyn
Green peas.
NS, ii 2 A35, 91—96 p
The ride.
NS, i 6 D34, 420—25 p
Vixen.
NS, i 5 Oc34, 357—63 p
The beginning rev. by L. A. Pavey

Laidlaw, A. K.
Book reviews.
VS, i 2 S—N38, 16—21 r
Three wars.
VS, i 1 Je—Ag38, 14 v
What has been may be again.
VS, i 4 M—My39, 1—2 v

Laird, John
Recent philosophy
rev. by D. J. B. Hawkins

Lambert, Constant
Music notes.
ND, 22 25N37, 28 c
An objective self portrait.
T, 6/7 N37, [30—32] c
Positively the last on the Promenades.
ND, 17 21Oc37, 35—36 c
Music ho! rev. by R. G. Adams

Lambert, Richard Stanton
On education: adult education.
TC, v 25 M33, 37—40 c

Lancaster, Osbert
An art critic in Paris.
ND, 18 28Oc37, 26—27 c
Art in the headlines.
ND, 23 2D37, 27 c
Kultur-Bolschevismus.
ND, 6 5Ag37, 24—25 c
Lord Bountiful.
ND, 2 8Jy37, 26—27 c
Those stately homes, I. Osborne House.
ND, 10 2S37, 25—26 c
Tourists guide to art.
ND, 12 16S37, 26 c

Landells, Alan
Poem.
C, iii 54 2J37, 4 v

Landor, Walter Savage
Landor on the Royal Georges.
LR, i 8 My35, 296 v

Landry, A. *see* Kline, M.

Lane, Allen
Books for the million.
LR, iii 16 My38, 968—70 c

Lang, Erda
Armistice.
JG, 15 W30, [26] v
An Autumn dawn.
JG, 18 Su31, [8] v
The flail.
JG, 13 Su30, [17] v
Grace.
JG, 14 Au30, [28—29] v
Immortality.
DD, vii 26 S—Oc30, 404 v
Life.
JG, 17 Su31, [11] v
The precious stones of dusk.
JG, 25 Su33, [18] v
Sanctuary.
JG, 19 W31, [26—27] v
Speech between friends.
JG, 22 Au32, [26—27] v
Stars.
JG, 20 Sp32, [17] v
Treading out flames.
JG, 16 Sp31, [26] v
Uncovetous nights.
JG, 23 W32, [15] v
Wind.
JG, 29 Su34, [29] v

Langdon-Davies, John L.
Behind the Spanish barricades
rev. by V. Ackland

Larg, David
Bluestocking and mist.
MS, vi 4 J36, 330—37 p
Diagnosis of a poet.

MS, iv 2 Jy33, 109—17 c
Fragments from a biography.
MS, iii 4 J33, 320—24; MS, iv 1 A33,
53—56 p

Larkin, D. Freeman
To the beloved, in a pause.
C, iii 55 9J37, 12—13 v

Lasch, Robert
Review [*The city keep,*
by R. Malam].
OO, xi, 55 Je31, 152—54 r

Laski, Harold Joseph
Political prosecutions.
TC, iv 24 F33, 12, 21—22 c
Democracy in crisis
rev. by W. N. Warbey
Law and justice in Soviet Russia
rev. by B. Pritchard
The rise of European liberalism
rev. by S. Graves

Laski, Marghanita
Allegory.
LS, i 1 F34, 13—15 p
The quest of Meadowsweet Smythe.
PR, 2 12F35, 2—4 p
Recipe for conversation.
PR, 2 12F35, 11 v
The sneeze.
LS, ii 1 My35, 35—41 p

Lassen, Nina
Nocturne; The quiet land.
DD, viii 30 Au31, 106 v

Lassie and laddie.
T, 4 Je37, [9—10] v

The late duty porter, by a Hotel Porter.
LR, i 6 M35, 207—9 p

Laughlin, James IV
A natural history.
CV, 2 D34, 1—13 p
Portraits of two dogs.
CV, 3 Su35, 8—9 v
The Spanish beauty.
SV, 4A Sp39, 16—17 p

Laurence, Julia Mary
Discarded.
JG, 67 W38, [6—7] v
Fire play.
JG, 30 Au34, [21] v
Progress.
JG, 21 Su32, [14] v
To tobacco.
JG, 63 W37, [28—29] v

Laurier, Roy
The morning train.
LR, i 9 Je35, 371 i

Lautréamont, Isidor Lucien Ducasse
comte, pseud.
see Ducasse, Isidor Lucien
comte de Lautréamont, pseud.

Laver, James
The modern movement in stage design.
R, i 4 My34, 4—5 c
The laburnum tree rev. by G. West

Lavery, Ursula
Poems.
WR, ii 1 Ag39, 12—13 v

Lavrin, Janko
The dervish.
EQ, i 4 F35, 223—29 p
The riddle of Rimbaud.
EQ, i 3 N34, 172—82 c
Sergei Essenin.
EQ, i 1 My34, 23—24 c
Sex and eros: on Rozanov, Weininger
and D. H. Lawrence.
EQ, i 2 Ag34, 88—96 c
Zimin.
NS, i 2 A34, 124—40 p
Aspects of realism rev. by D. Kahn
see also Vazov, Ivan

Law, Alice
Lines on looking upon an early
portrait of Christ.
DD, x 39 My—Je33, 46—47 v
No songs come to me now.
DD, xi 43 J—F34, 3—4 v

Lawrence, Lettice Ada and **Gelder,**
Stuart
The early life of D. H. Lawrence
rev. by A. D. Hawkins

Lawrence, David Herbert
Two letters.
TC, iv 23 J33, 1—3 p
A collier's Friday night
rev. by C. Slater
Lady Chatterley's lover
rev. by TC, iii 15 My32, 25—26
Last poems rev. by I. A. Richards
Letters, ed. by A. Huxley
rev. by A. D. Hawkins
The man who died rev. by A. D. Hawkins
Nettles rev. by S. Spender
New poems rev. by A. D. Hawkins
Phoenix rev. by S. Spender

Lawrence, Frieda
Not I, but the wind rev. by D. Garman

Lawson, Jack
Under the wheels rev. by D. A. Willis

Laxness, Haldor
Salka Valka rev. by G. West

Leahy, Maurice
Alfred Noyes' epic of science.
CA, 4 N30, 65—69 c
The catholic revival in English literature,
CA, 1 Ag30, 1—4 c
The cross and the thorns.
CA, 11 1932, 321—27 c
Ernest Dowson and his poetry.
CA, 3 Oc30, 33—39 c
A poet of the catholic school
[D. M. Dolben].
CA, 2 S30, 1—5 c
Poetry and the lady poverty.
CA, 12 1932, 353—59 c
The poetry of Gilbert Chesterton.
CA, 5 M31, 97—104 c
The poetry of Lionel Johnson.
CA, 10 1931, 289—94 c
The poetry of martyrs.
CA, 9 1931, 257—63 c
The poetry of Padraic Colum.
CA, 7 Je31, 193—97 c
The poetry of the Blessed Eucharist.
CA, 8 1931, 225—29 c

Leavis, Frank Raymond
Reply.
RM, 1 Je34, 24—25 c
Determinations rev. by A. D. Hawkins
For continuity
rev. by H. V. Kemp; A. C. Sewter
How to teach reading rev. by W. H.
Auden
Revaluations rev. by R. Todd

Leavis, Frank Raymond and
Thompson, Denys
Culture and environment
rev. by W. H. Auden

Le Breton, Louis
Another world [Un autre monde,
by J. G. Grandville].
V, 5 F30, 222—26 c
Landscape.
V, 6 Je30, 278 i

Lecky, Jane
Spring in a suburban garden.
DD, x 41 S—Oc33, 83 v

Lecomte, Marcel
Chirico, Max Ernst et Turin.
LB, 14 My39, 10—12 c

Lee, Auriol
New York and London.
R, i 7 N34, 5—6 c

Lee, Caroline
First and only.
P, 6 1939, 73—82 p

Lee, G. M.
The butterfly.
JG, 32 Sp35, [30—31] v

Lee, Hubert
Twenty years after rev. by R. Jardine

Lee, Kathleen
A dialogue between flesh and spirit.
CA, 2 S30, 13 v
Richard Crashaw.
CA, 1 Ag30, 19—21 c

Lee, Olga
Blue hours.
PQ, i 2 Su39, 46 v

Lee, Robert
A forgotten Yorkshire pottery
[Linthorpe].
HR, 7 1934, 37—40 c

Lees, Aubrey
Autumn.
PQ, i 1 Sp39, 12 v
Autumn gold.
JG, 65 Su38, [17] v
Francis Thompson.
JG, 70 Au39, [15] v
A garden close.
JG, 67 W38, [17] v

Lefebure, Victor
Scientific disarmament.
TC, i 4 Je31, 7—10 c

Left Review
Contributor's conference.
LR, i 9 Je35, 366—69 c
End of the first year.
LR, i 12 S35, 481 p

Legg, Stuart
A note on locomotive names.
LB, 4/5 Jy38, 20, 25 c

Legge, Sheila
I have done my best for you.
CPP, 8 D36, 165 p

Lehmann, Beatrix
Crime in our village.
NW, ns2 Sp39, 95—100 p
Massacre of the innocents.
Y, i 1 M39, 24—26 p
The two-thousand-pound raspberry.
NW, 5 Sp38, 187—92 p

Lehmann, John
After this.

Lehmann, John (cont.)
LR, i 12 S35, 505 v
Batum beach; His hands.
LR, ii 6 M36, 249—50 v
Epic and the future of the soviet arts.
LR, iii 10 N37, 580—83 c
Gradual spring.
V, 6 Je30, 288—89 v
Grey granite [by L. G. Gibbon].
LR, i 5 F35, 190—91 r
Letter from Tiflis.
LR, iii 1 F37, 8—15 p
Our girls [*Daughters of Albion,*
by A. Brown].
LR, ii 3 D35, 140—41 r
Review [*Fontamara,* by I. Silone;
Storm in Shanghai, by A. Malraux].
LR, i 4 J35, 140—42 r
The separator.
NW, 3 Sp37, 193—202 p
The seven soviet arts [by K. London].
LR, iii 9 Oc37, 558—60 r
Should writers keep to their art?
LR, ii 16 J37, 881—85 c
Three sketches.
NS, i 3 Je34, 187—93 p
Three sketches.
LR, i 4 J35, 99—101 p
Via Europe: scenes from a travel
sequence, 1934—35.
NW, 1 Sp36, 193—202 p
The walnut tree.
V, 5 F30, 238—39 v
Woodcut. V, 5 F30, 198 i
Woodcut design for a binding paper.
V, 5 F30, 237 i
A garden revisited and other poems
rev. by C. B. Spencer
Prometheus and the Bolsheviks
rev. by G. Graham
see also Kurella, A.; Roberts, Denys
Kilham; Spender, Stephen; Tabidze, T.

Leighton, Clare
The bread line.
LR, ii 2 N35, 59 i
The women mend them . . .
LR, ii 2 N35, 77 i

A Leja, or love song, of the Murias of
the Amabal Pargana of Bastar state,
tr. by W. V. Grigson.
NV, 24 F37, 17—19 v

Lejeune, Caroline Alice
Cinema rev. by W. A. Reynolds

Lench, Rous
Sonnet (for Maxwell Bodenheim).
DD, vii 26 S—Oc30, 386 v

Lenin, Vladimir Il'ich
Down with literary supermen.
ST, i 3 1933, 4—5 c

Leonard, S. G.
The labour of love.
W, 8/9 Ag39, 235—38 p

Leonhard, Rudolf
A fairytale for Christmas.
NW, ns1 Au38, 124—33 p
El Hel, tr. by J. Cleugh.
NW, 3 Sp37, 52—62 p

Lepper, John
Conscience is a funny thing.
NW, ns3 C39, 255—59 p

Leroux, Karel
Poem.
DD, x 41 S—Oc31, 85 v

Lerroux, Alexandro
Like a rebel.
LR, ii 2 N35, 55—56 c

Lester, Barbara F.
Windmills.
HR, 7 1934, 54—57 p

Le Strange, V.
The dead tree.
DD, xi 44 M—A34, 30 v

Levidov, Mikhail Yul'evich
Three Shakespears.
EQ, i 4 F35, 230—40 c

Levstik, Vladimir
The Holy Ghost and John Dolt.
DV, 2 A32, 60—62 p

Levy, Hyman
A philosophy for modern man
rev. by R. Swingler
Thinking rev. by T. A. Jackson

Lewin, Pauline
From morning till night.
NW, ns3 C39, 179—97 p

Lewinsohn, Richard
The profits of war rev. by L. W.

Lewis, Alun
The wanderers.
WR, ii 3 Oc39, 128—39 p

Lewis, Cecil Day *see* Day Lewis, Cecil

Lewis, Clive Staples
A metrical suggestion.
LS, ii 1 My35, 13—24 c

Lewis, Dominic Bevan Wyndham-
see Wyndham-Lewis, Dominic Bevan

Lewis, Frank
Mrs Robinson at Tregunter.
WR, ii 3 Oc39, 149 p

Lewis, John
Sex in Soviet Russia.
TC, v 29 Jy33, 279—83 c

Lewis, John *and others*
Christainity and the social revolution
rev. by A. West

Lewis, Percy Wyndham
Answers to an enquiry.
NV, 11 Oc34, 7—8 p
The artist as crowd.
TC, iii 14 A32, 12—15 c
A letter to the editor.
T, 6/7 N37, [3—5] p
W. B. Yeats.
NV, i 2 My39, 45—46 c
The apes of God rev. by H. G. Porteus
Blasting and bombardiering
rev. by G. Grigson
The diabolical principle
rev. by H. G. Porteus
The doom of youth
rev. by H. G. Porteus
The enemy of the stars
rev. by TC, iv 19 S32, 28
Filibusters in Barbary
rev. by R. S. Forrist;
TC iv 19 S32, 28
Hitler rev. by H. G. Porteus
The lion and the fox
rev. by T. S. Eliot
The mysterious Mr Bull
rev. by J. Symons
The old gang and the new gang
rev. by H. G. Porteus
One-way song
rev. by G. Armitage; F. Prince;
TC, vi 34 M34, 249—50
Snooty baronet rev. by S. Spender

Lewis, Sinclair
Ann Vickers rev. by G. West
It can't happen here
rev. by C. Ashleigh

Leyland, Morland
Spotlight on unemployed clubs.
W, 2 Ag37, 53—55 c

Li Ho
A poem, tr. by B. Mellor and
H. Y., Yang.
K. i 2 D39—J40, 48 v

Liam, Sean
Man in the street.
C, ii 43 17Oc36, 124 p
Poem.
PR, 7 12Je35, 5 v

Liamog, Eithne Nic
Abend in Böhmen.
LS, i 2 My34, 69 v
Dining with Maximilian.
PR, 4 5M35, 5 v
In Europam.
LS, i 1 F34, 36—40 c
Poem.
PR, 2 12F35, 4 v
Rondeau; März.
LS, i 1 F34, 47 v
$2\pi p^2$; And so on.
RM, 2 D34, 61, 63 v
Variation on a theme by Heine.
LS, i 3 N34, 63 v

Licht, Hans *pseud.*
Sexual life in ancient Greece
rev. by E. M. Barraud

Liepmann. Heinrich
Fires underground rev. by R. S.

Light and dark, vol.2 no.3.
rev. by G. Grigson

Liliev, Nikolay
Autumn, tr. by P. Selver.
SM, 4 1933, 114 v

Lincoln, Tom
Flood.
ST, i 3 1933, 1—3 p
Heroism? Adventure? Glory?
[*Dogs of war,* by F. Yeats-Brown;
The first war in the air,
by R. H. Kiernan; *One's company,*
by P. Fleming]
LR, i 2 N34, 47—48 r
Odd John [by O. Stapledon].
LR, ii 2 N35, 96 r
Redemption from futility
[*The Fascist quarterly*].
LR, i 6 M35, 238—40 r
War [*The citizen faces war,*
by R. and B. Donington;
Footsteps in warfare, by R. L Worrall].
LR, ii 8 My36, 401—2 r

Lindow, D. K.
The discontented woman.
PP, 4 Oc38, 16 v

Lindsay, Jack
Aesthetics and Marxism
[*A note on literary criticism,*
by J. T. Farrell].
LR, ii 13 Oc36, 725 r
Capitalists and workers.
[*Devil take the hindmost,*
by F. Tilsley;
Brittlesnaps, by E. A. Hibbitt;
A penny for the poor, by B. Brecht;
The tomato field, by S. Engstrand;

The Trojan horse, by P. Nizan].
LR, iii 3 A37, 178—80 r
Cradle song.
CPP, 8 D36, 157—58 v
Editorial.
PP, 2 Ag38, 1—4; PP, 5 N38, 1—3 c
England.
PP, 4 Oc38, 4—5 v
Man in society [*Major operation,*
by J. Barke; *The lovely girl,*
by A. Brown; *The big money,*
by J. Dos Passos; *Bread and wine*
by I. Silone; *The brothers Ashkenazi,*
by I. J. Singer].
LR, ii 15 D36, 837—40 r
Marxism and the novel
[*The novel and the people,*
by R. Fox; *The novel today,*
by P. Henderson; *Famine,*
by L. O'Flaherty].
LR, iii 1 F37, 51—53 r
The May day tradition.
LR, iii 16 My38, 963—66 c
Neglected aspects of poetry,
parts 1—3, 5.
PP, 1 Jy38, 14—20; PP 2 Ag38, 6—13;
PP 3 S38, 3—11; PP, 7 J39, 6—8 c
Not English?
LR, ii 8 My36, 353—57 v
On guard for Spain: a poem for mass
recitation.
LR, iii 2 M37, 79—86 v
A plea for mass declamation.
LR, iii 9 Oc37, 511—17 c
Questionnaire.
PP, 12 Je39, 3 v
The seed-plot of the European lyric.
PP, 5 N38, 5—11 c
Shakespeare.
LR, iii 6 Jy37, 333—39 c
Socialists in fiction
[*Pie in the sky,* by A. Calder-Marshall;
The brimming lake, by A. Smith;
The blue bed, by G. Jones;
The making of a hero, by N. Ostrovski].
LR, iii 2 M37, 107—9 r
Song for wedding 1600,
CPP, 9 Sp37, 43—44 v
Songs of the Irish struggle
[*Good-bye twilight,* by L. H. Dalkeith].
LR, iii 2 M37, 121 r
The swamp.
NW, 5 Sp38, 203—9 p
Three novels [*May day,*
by J. Sommerfield; *Inhale and exhale,*
by W. Saroyan; *Salavin,*
by G. Duhamel].
LR, ii 16 J37, 915—16 r
Writer and society
[*Crisis and criticism,* by A. West].
LR, iii 2 M37, 115—16 r
Adam of a new world
rev. by A. Calder-Marshall
The anatomy of spirit rev. by M. Kahn

John Bunyan rev. by E. Rickword
Marc Antony rev. by G. T.

Lindsay, Noel
Before a fire.
F, 5 F31, 109 v
Daedalus.
F, 6 Je31, 159—61 v
Insomnia.
NO, i 1 My33, 107—8 v

Lindsay. T. F.
The Lady of Gattaiola.
F, 6 Je31, 175—83 p

Lindsey, John *pseud.*
Stricken gods rev. by R. G. T.

Linklater, Eric Robert Russell
Kind Kitty.
MS, vi 3 Oc35, 192—207 p
Preamble to a satire.
MS, iv 1 A33, 18—22 v
God likes them plain
rev. by L. A. Pavey

Lipton, Julius
By the dancing needles.
LR, i 6 M35, 214—15 p
A few remarks about proletarian poetry.
PP, 3 S38, 12—18 c
I am glad.
PP, 2 Ag38, 15 v
Jewish poet of the war
[*Collected works of I. Rosenberg*].
LR, iii 9 Oc37, 563—64 r
Left Book Club writers and readers group.
LR, iii 15 A38, 937—39 c
Poetry 1935 [*The year's poetry,*
ed. by G. Gould and others].
LR, ii 5 F36, 236 r
Twenty five workers' songs
[*The workers song book,*
ed. by A. Bush and R. Swingler].
LR, iii 15 A38, 953—54 r
Worker writers [*Seven shifts,*
ed. by J. Common; *Let me tell you,*
by L. Halward].
LR, iii 16 My38, 1019—20 r
Poems rev. by J. B. Harvey
Poems of strife
rev. by NV, 21 Je36, 17

Lisky, I. A. *pseud.*
'Productivisation'.
LR, ii 2 N35, 57—62 p

Lister, Frederick William
Shadow over Spennylam
rev. by A. Calder-Marshall

Little, Lawrence
The graves at Harpenden; Scene.
NV, i 2 My39, 36—37 v

Little Musgrave.
CPP, 1 My36, 7—9 v

The little review [periodical]
rev. by R. Todd

Livingston, William
Ireland weeping, tr. from the Gaelic.
VS, i 2 S—N38, 14—15 v

LLewellyn, Peter
Bath Theatre Royal.
R, i 7 N34, 14 c

Lloyd, Albert Lancaster
Lorca: poet of Spain.
LR, iii 2 M37, 71—72 c
New novels reviewed
[*His Worship the Mayor,*
by W. Greenwood;
Lean men,
by R. Bates].
LR, i 2 N34, 46 r
Our Jameses [*A calendar for 1936*
with drawings by J. Fitton, J. Boswell,
and J. Holland].
LR, ii 4 J36, 184—85 r
The red steer.
LR, i 1 Oc34, 26—30 p
Surrealism and revolutions
[*Surrealism*, ed. by H. Read].
LR, ii 16 J37, 895—98 r
see also Alberti, R.; Cross, C.; Dali, S.;
Dieste, R.; Eluard, P.; Garcia Lorca, F.;
Gonzalez Tunon, R.; Herrera Petere, J.;
Jarry, A.; Nukarpiartekak; St. John
Perse;
Traditional country ballads; Zozulya, E.

Lloyd, Geoffrey
To the word our God.
C, i 4 28D35, 32 v
Unsent letter to a non-Aryan.
C, i 14 7M36, 112 v

Lloyd, J. William
Eneres.
TC, i 2 A31, 8—11; TC, i 3 My31,
13—16 c
Why monogamy?
TC, i 6 Ag31, 18—19 c

Llywelyn-Williams, Alun
Gwyr catraeth.
W, 5 Su38, 172 v

Locherbie-Goff, Margaret
Moth.
C, iii 58 30J37, 36 v

Loder, John de Vere
Bolshevism in perspective
rev. by H. G. Porteus

Lodge, *Sir* Oliver Joseph
Mr Gosse and Professor Collins.
AC, i 1 C39, 7—11 c

Lodge, Oliver William Foster
Poems.
CD, 1—3 1938—39, v

Loewenstein, Hubertus
Friedrich M. J. L. L.
The tragedy of a nation
rev. by G. West

Loewy, Herta
Day by day.
SM, 1 Je31, 36—43 p

London, Keith
The seven Soviet arts
rev. by J. Lehmann

London Bulletin [periodical]
rev. by M. Scott

London mercury [periodical]
rev. by J. C. Hall

Long, Herbert Kingsley
see McArthur, Alexander

Lopez y Fuentes, Gregorio
They that reap rev. by T. L. Hodgkin

Lorca, Federico Garcia
see Garcia Lorca, Federico

Lord, Douglas
Juan Gris.
AX, 7 Au36, 9—12 c
Rappel à l'ordre.
LB, 4/5 Jy38, 39 c

Lovejoy, Ritchie
The short road.
NW, ns3 C39, 120—26 v

Low, David
Blake's wood engravings.
LQ, i 1 N36, [11—17] c
The ten spiritual designs of Edward
Calvert.
LQ, i 2 D36, [7—21] c

Low, David *cartoonist*
George Bernard Shaw.
R, i 1 N33, 2 i

Low, David *cartoonist and*
Thoroughgood, H.
Low and Terry rev. by M. Black

Lowbury, Edward
The crying shame.

PP, 12 Je39, 3 v
Moving picture.
PQ, i 1 Sp39, 10 v

Lowry, Malcolm
Goya the obscure.
V, 6 Je30, 270—78 p
Port Swettenham.
EX, 5 F30, 22—26 p
Punctum indifferens skibet gaar videre.
EX, 7 Sp31, 62—75 p

Lubbock, Phyllis M.
April.
JG, 33 Su 35, [31] v
Bryn Mynael.
JG, 63 W37, [17] v
The climbers.
JG, 20 Sp32, [21—22] v
Contrast.
JG, 35 W35, [21—22] v
The death of a small bird.
JG, 29 Su34, [16—17] v
Duality.
JG, 28 Sp34, [14] v
Early green.
JG, 26 Au33, [9—10] v
Farewell to Thirza.
JG, 38 Au36, [29] v
From the dark corners.
JG, 36 Sp36, [32] v
Haworth.
JG, 30 Au34, [17] v
Here is this quiet lane.
JG, 16 Sp31, [15] v
The hill.
JG, 17 Su31, [18—19] v
Holidays.
JG, 14 Au30, [6—7] v
Impress.
JG, 41 Su37, [27] v
Incident.
JG, 21 Su32, [11] v
The little shrine.
JG, 23 W32, [18—19] v
Night show.
JG, 27 W33, [9] v
The old country.
JG, 18 Au31, [22] v
On looking out of a bedroom window.
JG, 15 W30, [6] v
The outcast.
JG, 19 W31, [15] v
Sonnet.
JG, 37 Su36, [26—27] v
Star song.
JG, 34 Au35, [25] v
The stars are out.
JG, 22 Au32, [14—15] v
Sun set on Rydal water.
JG, 39 W36, [30—31] v
Tone poem.
JG, 32 Sp35, [21—22] v
Vision.

JG, 24 Sp33, [17−18] v
The way out.
JG, 40 Sp37, [29−31] p
When life in me.
JG, 31 W34, [28] v

Lucas, Barbara
Love's animus.
CA, 4 N30, 91 v
Love's insubstantiality.
CA, 10 1931, 307 v

Lucas, Frank Laurence
A song of two cities.
FB, i 1 4F36, 18 v
The criticism of poetry
rev. by G. Grigson

Lucas, P. B.
Gossiping about golf.
LD, i 4 Je37, 29−30 c

Lucas, Paul H.
The bewitched.
OO, xi 54 M31, 3 v
Goldfish.
OO x 53 N30, 565 v

Luce, Morton
Quotation.
CPP, 9 Sp37, 46 p

Ludendorff, Friedrich Wilhelm Erich
The nation at war
rev. by L. E. O. Charlton

Ludwig, Emil
The Davos murder
rev. by C. Madge

Lugard, Edward Aylmer
The gifts of the bells.
PQ, i 1 Sp39, 20−21 v

Lulham, Edwin Percy Habberton
Fate's weaving.
DD, ix 34 Jy−Ag32, 58 v
The patrin.
DD, ix 32 M−A32, 22 v
To a young artist.
DD, ix 35 S−Oc32, 78−79 v

Lushington, Roland
Women are difficult.
ND, 17 21Oc37, 13−14, 16 p

Lushington, S.
Lines by a madman.
M, i 1 Je33, 16 v

Lye, Len
Essential honesty.
DE, 1 New year 32, 4 v

Hungry for love.
DE, 2 Su32, 1 v

Lye, Len *and* **Riding**, Laura
Film-making.
EP, 1 Au35, 231−35 c

M

M.
Benjamin Sink.
M, i 1 Je33, 26−28 p

M., A.
For Mussolini, God, Moscow
and Major Douglas
[*Jefferson and/or Mussolini,*
by E. Pound;
Alfred Venison's poems,
by E. Pound;
Essential communism,
by H. Read].
NV, 16 Ag35, 18−20 r

M., H. *see* **A., S. H. V.**

M., H. M.
The Douglas A+B theorem.
MS, ii 2 Jy31, 178−35 c
Social credit: the hope of
the world.
MS, i 4 J31, 12−19 c

M., J.
Australian verse: the other half.
PP, 6 D38, 7−10 c

M., J. D.
Review [*Mad house,*
by B. Niles].
FB, 1 4F36, 23 r
A visit to the Paris
exhibition.
ND, 2 8Jy37, 18 p

M., J. S.
Poem.
CM, 1 2 Su33, 59 v

M., M.
*The benefits moral and secular
of assassination*
rev. by A. D. Hawkins

Maas, W.
The kind look.
T, 12/13 Oc38, 106 v

Macalastair, Somhairle
Ballyseedy befriends Badajoz.
LR, ii 15 D36, 817 v

McAlmon, Robert
Being geniuses together
rev. by J. Symons

McArthur, Alexander *and*
Long, Herbert Kingsley
No mean city
rev. by J. F. Hendry

Macartney, Wilfred Francis
Pennington
Walls have mouths
rev. by C. Craven

Macaulay, Ian
A Brontë story.
FB, i 2 3M36, 28−30 p

Macaulay, Rose
The affectionate book of
the week
[*Little lion,* by B. Whitlock].
ND, 15 7Oc37, 30 r
In defence of the home.
ND, 1 1Jy37, 11 p

Macaulay, T. E.
Marxian criticism [*Literature,*
by P. Henderson].
MS, vi 2 Jy35, 147−49 r

MacCaig, Norman
Poem.
VS, i 4 M−My39, 23 v
Poems.
SV, 4 Su39, 39−40 v
Two poems.
SV, 2 Au38, 15 v

MacCance, William
Idea in art.
MS, i 2 Su30, 13−16 c

McClaskey, K.
Repression and revolt in
American universities.
TU, 4 F35, 38−43 c

McClymont, Murray
A Scottish theatre:
the need for a new form.
MS, i 4 J31, 5−9 c

MacColla, Fionn
'Rebellious Scots to crush':
a chapter from a novel.
MS, v 4 J35, 276−89 p
The Albannach rev. by E. Muir

McCoy, Horace
No pockets in a shroud
rev. by A. Calder-Marshall;
E. Waugh

McDean, Anthony
Good-bye to introspection.
VP, i 2 Jy—S34, 30—32 v

MacDiarmid, Hugh
Answers to an enquiry.
NV, 11 Oc34, 18—19 c
The antlered stag.
PR, 8 19Je35, 6 v
The arts of Scotland
[by J. Tonge].
VS, i 4 M—My39, 21—22 r
The back of beyond.
MS, iii 3 Oc32, 208 v
By Wauchopeside.
MS, iii 1 A32, 50—51 v
The case of Alice Carruthers.
NW, ns2 Sp39, 227—31 p
Charles Doughty and the need
for heroic poetry.
MS, vi 4 J36, 308—18 c
Diamond body:
the cave of the sea.
WR, ii 4 N39, 193—96 v
Crowdie knowey;
music by F. G. Scott;
The eemis stane. MS, v 1/2 Je34,
39—43, 62—66 v
Direadh, [I].
VS, i 3 D38—F39, 13—21 v
Domhnull Mac-na-Ceardaich
[Donald Sinclair].
MS, iii 3 Oc32, 237—43 c
Editorial note.
VS, i 3 D38—F39, 32 c
The English literary left.
VS, ii 1 Je—Ag39, 1—6 c
Four Scots poems.
NA, i 1 Au39, 36—37 v
From work in progress.
MS, ii 2 Jy31, 107—10 v
The glen of silence.
VS, i 1 Je—Ag38, 1—3 v
A golden wine in the
Gaidhealtachd.
VS, i 2 S—N38, 4—5 v
Happy on Heimaey.
SV, 7 C39, 19—20 v
Killing no murder.
LR, i 1 Oc34, 19 v
Love, set to music by F. G. Scott.
MS, iii 1 A32, 56—57 v, m
Lyrics.
MS, iv 1 A33, 47—48 v
Lyrics from 'Clann Albann'.
MS, ii 3 Oc31, 205—6 v
My sailor son comes home.
MS, vi 4 J36, 318 v
Moonstruck;

music by F. G. Scott.
MS, iv 1 A33, 49—52 v, m
Nekrassov.
MS, vi 1 A35, 16 v
Nemestes.
MS, vi 1 A35, 51 v
New poems.
MS, iv 2 Jy33, 104—8 v
Notes of the quarter.
VS, i 1 Je—Ag38, 24—32;
VS, i 2 S—N38, 27—32;
VS, i 3 D38—F39, 1—6;
VS, i 4 M—My39, 26—32;
VS, ii 1 Je—Ag39, 11—14 c
Notes on our forerunners.
VS, i 4 M—My39, 3—12;
ii 1 Je—Ag39, 25—32 c
On reading Professor Ifor
Williams's 'Canu Aneurin'
in difficult days.
W, 8/9 Ag39, 232—34 v
The parrot cry.
MS, i 2 Su30, 31—32 v
Poetry like the hawthorn.
W, 11 W39, 296—97 v
A reply to T. A. Jackson.
VS, i 3 D38—F39, 24—31 c
To Alasdair MacMaighstir
Alasdair.
MS, i 1 Sp30, 18—19 v
Two poems.
MS, iv 3 Oc33, 185—87 v
Two poems in Scots.
MS, vi 3 Oc35, 108—9 v
Two Scottish poems
[*Human voice,*
by G. R. Malloch; *Conflict,*
by W. Soutar].
MS, ii 1 A31, 89—90 r
Welcome to the P E N
delegates.
MS, v 1—2 Je34, 20—23 v
Wheesht, wheesht;
music by F. G. Scott.
MS, iv 4 J34, 320—24, v, m
Whuchulls.
MS, iii 4 J33, 340—44 v
Why I became a Scots
nationalist; The back of beyond.
DD, ix 35 S—Oc32, 66 v
Writers international.
LR, i 5 F35, 182 c
*First hymn to Lenin and
other poems* rev. by A. R. Orage
The islands of Scotland
rev. by I. L.
Second hymn to Lenin
rev. by G. Grigson; J. A. Scott
Selected poems rev. by M. Ll.
To circumjack cencrastus
rev. by G. Bottomley; P. Hole;
D. Saurat
see also MacDonald, A.;
MacIntyre, D.; Grieve, C. M.

MacDonagh, Donagh
He is dead and gone, lady.
VS, i 3 D38—F39, 7 v

MacDonald, Alexander
Birlinn Chlann-Raghnaill,
tr. by H. Macdiarmid.
MS, v 4 J35, 230—47 v

McDonald, Arthur
Men who mock at a lover.
F, 5 F31, 78 v
Triolet 'June'.
F, 4 D30, 39 v

McDonald, Hilda
A moment; Dawn.
DD, viii 28 J—F31, 11—12 v
Quest.
DD, vii 26 S—Oc30, 406—7 v

MacDougall, Ursula
Titty's dead and Tatty weeps.
NS, ii 6 D36, 426—32 p

McElwee, Patrick
The fantasy.
NO, i 1 My33, 109—15 p

McGavin, Lawrie
Ode on the funeral of Earl Haig.
DD, vii 27 N—D30, 440—41 v

Mac Gill'Eathain, Somhairle
Ban-ghaidheal.
VS, i 1 Je—Ag38, 4—5 v

M'Gonigle, George Cuthbert
Mura *and* **Kirby**, J.
Poverty and public health.
rev. by F. Le Gros Clark

McGrath, Raymond
From a woodcut.
V, 6 Je30, 266 i
Woodcut.
V, 6 Je30, 299 i

McGreevy, Thomas
Epithalamium.
W, 8/9 Ag39, 244 v
T. S. Eliot: a study
rev. by C. M. Grieve

Macintyre, Alison
Robert McLellan, playwright.
VS, i 2 S—N38, 11—13 c

Macintyre, Christian
To the muse.
PQ, i 1 Sp39, 14—15 v

Macintyre, Duncan
The praise of Ben Dorain,

tr. by H. Macdiarmid.
MS, vi 2 Jy35, 101—15 v

Mackay, Alexander Leslie Gordon
*Experiments in educational
self-government*
rev. by K. Arnold

Mackay, David
The Board of Control.
TC, i 6 Ag31, 21—23 c

McKay, Dermot
Quandary.
NV, 20 A36, 6 v
Where are the children?
NV, 21 Je36, 13 v

Mackenzie, Agnes Mure Scobie
The muse with two masks.
MS, ii 1 A31, 6—12 c
The wheel chair.
P, 1 1938, 60—75 p

Mackenzie, Compton
The National Party.
MS, i 4 J31, 25—29 c

Mackenzie, Margaret
Every year.
CA, 9 1931, 286—87 v
Hymns, old and new.
CA, 2 S30, 17—18 c

Mackenzie, Orgill
Extract from the diary of a
shell-shocked man.
NS, i 4 Ag34, 247—52 p
The tree.
NS, i 1 F34, 15—18 p

Mackereth, James Allan
And so I think.
JG, 69 Su39, [28] v
Ballerina.
HR, 7 1934, 30—31 v
The basket weaver.
JG, 32 Sp35, [18—19] v
Hands.
JG, 27 W33, [11—12] v
Hush.
JG, 66 Au38, [15] v
An inscription.
JG, 33 Su35, [5] v
Mercy.
JG, 24 Sp33, [6] v
Morning.
JG, 39 W36, [18—20] v
Poet unheard.
JG, 65 Su38, [5] v
The re-christening.
JG, 31 W34, [16—18] v
Soul in its own hell.
JG, 25 Su33, [14—15] v

Summer night.
HR, 4 1931, 54—55 v
Too-hoo.
JG, 41 Su37, [7] v
Twelve o'clock.
JG, 37 Su36, [7—8] v

Mackeson, *Mrs* Peyton
And God made the best of the
earth.
DD, x 40 Jy—Ag33, 63—64 v
Ars victoria.
DD, x 42 N—D33, 96 v

Mackesy, Marjorie
A dance; The north-west frontier;
Maize.
DD, vii 26 S—Oc30, 385 v
The deserted room;
Riding song; Reality.
DD, vii 26, S—Oc30, 393—95 v
Evening in Afghanistan.
DD, vii 27 N—D30, 450 v

Mackie, Albert D.
Sonnet.
MS, iv 1 A33, 57 v

McLaverty, Michael
Pigeons.
NS, ii 8 A36, 561—69 p

Maclean, Donald
Poem.
CM, i 3 Au33, 136 v
Puppet.
CM, i 2 Su33, 60 p
Review
[*Contemporary literature and
social revolution*,
by R. D. Charques].
CL, i 2 W33, ii—iii r

Maclean, Murdoch
Wind and stream.
JG, 69 Su39, [26] v

MacLeish, Archibald
Answers to an enquiry.
NV, 12 D34, 17—18 c
In vocation to the social muse.
NV, 4 Jy33, 2—4 v
Conquistador rev. by G. Grigson
The fall of the city
rev. by K. Allott
Panic rev. by C. Madge
Poems rev. by G. Grigson

McLellan, J. Borland
The unknown warrior.
P, 5 1939, 134 i

MacLeod, John
Is social credit sound?
MS, ii 1 A31, 26—31 c

MacLeod, Joseph Gordon
Earthscape.
NV, 3 My33, 15—18 v
Notes on the contemporary
theatre.
CM, i 3 Au33, 100—102 c
Prayer in the fens.
PR, 3 19F35, 7—8 v
Today's non-commercial
theatre
[*The family reunion*, by T. S. Eliot].
TO, ii 6 A39, 16—17 r
To-day's non-commercial theatre
[*On the frontier*,
by W. H. Auden and
C. Isherwood].
TO, ii 5 J39, 22—24 r
Wayside station.
NV, 1 J33, 5—6 v
The ecliptic
rev. by R. H. Goodman

MacLeod, M. J.
Louisiana bonfire.
P, 5 1939, 85—101 p

MacLeod, Norman
Beautiful women in
Montgomery.
MS, ii 4 J32, 300 v
'Black Alabama':
the historic necessity.
MS, ii 3 Oc31, 216—17 v
C. M. Grieve speaks of ancestors.
W, 8/9 Ag39, 245 v
The eyes on the potatoes.
VS, i 3 D38—F39, 7 v
Journey to the waterfront.
MS, vi 2 Jy35, 142 v
Montage for a newsreel.
CV, 1 Su34, 18—20 v
Sing sing.
TO, i 4 Oc38, 7 v
Horizons of death
rev. by C. M. Grieve

MacMurray, John
The disintegration of European
culture.
TC, v 27 My33, 151—57 c
Mr Sloan and Marxism.
TC, v 28 Je33, 225—26 c
Interpreting the universe
rev. by A. D. Hawkins

MacNab, Angus
Memorandum.
RR, 5 J38, [16] v
Translations.
RR, 6 Jy38, [10] v

MacNab, Angus (cont.)
Translations from the Greek.
RR, 5 J38, [9] v

MacNab, Ian
The sardine fishers.
MS, vi 2 Jy35, 147 i

McNabb, Vincent
Love's utter loss.
CA, 8 1931, 249 v
To a dead mother.
CA, 12 1932, 381 v

McNally, C. E. *and*
McNally, Anne
Biography of John Smith.
LR, ii 2 N35, 89—91 p

MacNeice, Frederick Louis
Answers to an enquiry.
NV, 11 Oc34, 7 c
Bagpipe music.
NV, 28 J38, 2—3 v
Birmingham.
NV, 7 F34, 3—4 v
A comment [on Hopkins].
NV, 14 A35, 26—27 c
Cuckoo.
NV, 16 Ag35, 9 v
An eclogue for Christmas
NV, 8 A34, 3—7 v
Everyman his own Pygmalion.
NV, 1 J33, 10—11 v
Final chorus from a play.
GTP, 6 D36, [6] v
First chorus from the Hippolytus
of Euripides.
PL, i 2 A39, [8—9] v
Four poems.
NW, ns3 C39, 78—81 v
Homage to clichés.
NV, 19 F36, 2—4 v
Iceland.
NV, 23 C36, 8—9 v
Insidiae.
NV, 15 Je35, 7 v
June thunder.
NW, 4 Au37, 6 v
Letter to the Editor.
NV, 28 J38, 18 c
Letter to W. H. Auden.
NV, 26/27 N37, 11—13 c
Lyrics from a play.
NV, 23 C36, 10—13 v
Miss Riding's Death
[*The life of the dead,*
by L. Riding].
NV, 6 D33, 18—20 r
Mr Empson as a poet
[*Poems,* by W. Empson].
NV, 16 Ag35, 17—18 r
Neurospastoumenos.
OO, x 51 F30, 421—29 v

The newest Yeats
[*A full moon in March,*
by W. B. Yeats].
NV, 19 F36, 16 r
Painters and poets.
NV, i 2 My39, 58—60 p
Perchists.
NV, 28 J38, 12—13 v
Poem.
NV, 2 M33, 14—15 v
Poem.
NV, 6 D33, 6—7 v
Poem; August à la Poussin.
NV, 5 Oc33, 6—7 v
Poems by Edwin Muir
[*Variations on a time theme,*
by E. Muir].
NV, 9 Je34, 18—20 r
The prodigal son.
OO, x 52 My30, 489—90 v
Review [*Poems,* by W. H. Auden].
OO, xi 54 M31, 59—61 r
Reviews [*The Lysis,* by Plato,
tr. by K. A. Matthews;
Deserted house, by D. Wellesley;
Dear Judas, by R. Jeffers;
This experimental life,
by R. Snow;
The signature of pain,
by A. Porter].
OO, xi 55 Je31, 146—49 r
Section two of 'Autumn journal'.
PL, i 1 F39, [16—17] v
Some notes on Mr Yeat's plays.
NV, 18 D35, 7—9 c
A statement.
NV, 31/32 Au38, 7 C
Three poems.
NW, ns1 Au38, 98—101 v
Train to Dublin.
NV, 13 F35, 2—3 v
Turn again Worthington.
NV, 1 J33, 2—3 v
Two poems.
NV, 12 D34, 12—13 v
Autumn journal
rev. by R. Garioch
The earth compels
rev. by G. S. Fraser; G. Grigson;
J. Symons
I crossed the Minch
rev. by G. Grigson; J. Symons
Modern poetry rev. by K. Allott
Out of the picture
rev. by H. G. Porteus; M. Wilson
Poems rev. by S. Spender
Zoo rev. by K. Allott
see also Aeschylus; Auden,
Wystan Hugh

MacNeice, Frederick Louis *and*
Doone, Rupert
Extracts from a dialogue on the
necessity for an active tradition

and experiment.
GTP, 6 D36, [3—5] c
A parable.
GTP, 7 J37, 2—3 c

MacNeice, Patrick
Forethought.
PR, 13 5F36, 11 v
Poem.
PR, 21 1M37, 3 v
Poem.
PR, 22 Je37, 16 v

McNulty, John H.
Browning as a catholic poet.
CA, 3 Oc30, 51—54 c
Keeping the night watches.
CA, 4 N30, 94 v

McPherson, Aimée Semple
I view the world rev. by H. Read

MacPherson, Anne
Silence.
DD, x 37 J—F33, 15 v
Spring.
DD, x 42 N—D33, 107 v

MacPherson, Ian
Alive-oh!
MS, iv 4 J34, 277—83 p
The cage in Benalder.
MS, vi 4 J36, 297—306 d
The Cailleach Ban.
MS, vi 2 Jy35, 116—27 p
Vive le sport!
MS, v 1/2 Je34, 81—87 p

McTaggart, Morna
The estuary.
NS, ii 4 Ag35, 241—51 p

Maddox, Conroy
Note [on Picasso]
LB, 15/16 15My39, 35—36 c

Madge, Charles
Air gun
[*A short survey of surrealism,*
by D. Gascoyne].
NV, 18 D35, 20—21 r
America's lead
[*American writers congress,*
ed. by H. Hart].
LR, ii 8 My36, 404—6 r
Apprehending.
NV, 4 Jy33, 6 v
Architecture at the R. A.
LR, iii 2 M37, 124 c
Bourgeois news.
NV, 19 F36, 7—10 p
Comment on Auden.
NV, 26/27 N37, 27—28 c
Cryptogram in flower

[*The seventeenth century background*, by B. Willey; *The rock*, by T. S. Eliot].
NV, 9 Je34, 14—18 r
Delusions.
NV, 20 A36, 2—5 v
Flight margarine.
PL, i 2 A39, [16—18] v
From 'Five stages of political consciousness'.
CM, i 1 Sp33, 14 v
The hours of the planets.
NV, 10 Ag34, 2—7 v
In memoriam T.S.E.
NV, 31/32 Au38, 18—21 c
Instructions.
NV, 2 M33, 4—7 v
Last days of the bourgeoisie.
PR, 10 6N35, 13—14 v
Magic and materialism.
LR, iii 1 F37, 31—35 c
May Day.
CL, i 1 Su33, 3 v
The meaning of surrealism
[*Petite anthologie poétique du surréalisme*].
NV, 10 Ag34, 13—15 r
Modern hero [*Panic*, by A. MacLeish].
LR, ii 11 Ag36, 593—94 r
New verse.
NV, 3 My33, 12 V
News.
TU, 1 1933, 48 v
Nth philosopher's riddlemeree.
NV, i 2 My39, 38—39 v
Oxford collective poem.
NV, 25 My37, 16—19 c
Pens dipped in poison.
LR, i 1 Oc34, 12—17 c
Poem.
LB, 4/5 Jy38, 19 v
Poetry and politics.
NV, 3 My33, 1—4 c
The press and social consciousness.
LR, iii 5 Je37, 279—86 c
Revolutionary poem.
CL, i 2 W33, 24 v
Some reflections on popular poetry.
NW, ns3 C39, 65—75 c
Struggle in Germany
[*Death without battle*, by L. Renn;
Men without mercy, by A. Döblin; *The Davos murder*, by E. Ludwig].
LR, iii 3 A37, 182—83 r
Surrealism for the English.
NV, 6 D33, 14—18 c
Three fragments from Alanus;
Two poems.
NV, 12 D34, 8—9 v

Three poems.
NV, 9 Je34, 11—12 v
Three poems.
NW, ns1 Au38, 44—46 v
Two poems.
NV, 5 Oc33, 5—6 v
Vocabulary; Great West road.
CM, i 2 Su33, 80—81 v
What is all this juice?
NV, 14 A35, 17—21 c
Writers under two flags
[*Problems of Soviet literature*, by M. Gorki and others].
LR, ii 5 F36, 228—30 c
The world of love.
TC, vi 36 S34, 346 v
The disappearing castle
rev. by A. E. Darbyshire;
P. O'Connor; S. Spender;
X *pseud*.
Mass observation rev. by D. Kahn
see also Jennings, Humphrey

Madge, John *and* **Cox**, Anthony
M.A.R.S. exhibition of the new architecture.
LR, iii 13 F38, 805—7 c

Madol, Hans Roger
Das Sommerschloss.
DD, ix 34 Jy—Ag32, 59 v
Das Traumgesicht.
DD, x 42 N—D33, 104 v

Maenchen-Helfen, O. *see*
Nicolaievsky, B.

Maginnis, John
The winning entry.
LR, ii 4 J36, 179 c

Magritte, René *and*
Nougé, Paul
Colour-colours, tr. by I. Singh.
LB, 17 15 Je39, 9—12 c

Magritte, René *and*
Scutenaire, Jean
L'art bourgeois.
LB, 12 15M39, 13—14 c

The maiden's dream.
T, 4 Je37, [8—9] v

Maillart, Ella Kini
Forbidden journey
rev. by E. Waugh

Maines, C. R.
Aubade.
DD, vii 26 S—Oc30, 407—8 v

Mair, John
Review

[*Some versions of pastoral*, by W. Empson].
J, 2 My36, 23—24 r
Reviews
[*Pied piper of lovers*, by L. Durrell;
The year's poetry 1935, ed. by G. Gould and others].
J, 1 J36, 29 r
Sense and abstraction.
LT, i 1 N36, 4—5 c
Sketch for a love story.
J, 1 J36, 22—23 p
Theatre reviews
[*The dog beneath the skin*, by W. H. Auden and C. Isherwood;
Murder in the cathedral, by T. S. Eliot].
J, 2 My36, 30 dr
Tribute.
J, 2 My36, 13—15 p

Maitland, Patrick Francis
viscount
Cambridge lawn tennis prospects.
FB, i 3 9My36, 65 c

Makarenko, Anton Semenovich
Road to life
rev. by C. D. Rackham

Malam, Robert
The city keep
rev. by P. Hartnoll; R. Lasch

Malfatti, Dora T.
Comment on situation.
C, i 25 23My36, 195—96 p

Malham-Dembleby, J.
Wer Gwennie Lossin.
HR, 5 1932, 15 v

Mallalieu, H. B.
Agamemnon.
W, 4 M38, 138 v
Ballad of the dutiful son.
T, 10 My38, 32—34 v
Bruges,
C, i 28 27Je36, 227 v
Lament for a lost life.
NV, i 2 My39, 42—43 v
The lover's world.
C, i 7 18J36, 54 v
The marsh:
an excerpt from a prose work.
C, i 15 14M36, 115—16 p
The philologist.
T, 17 A39, 13 v
The photograph.
PL, i 2 A39, [3] v
Poem.
LR, ii 7 A36, 314 v

Mallalieu, H. B. (cont.)
Poem.
C, ii 34 15Ag36, 51 v
Poem.
C, ii 50 5D36, 191 v
Poem.
LT, i 11 J37, 16 v
Poem.
NW, 4 Au37, 89 v
Poem.
W, 5 Su38, 165 v
Poem.
NW, ns2 Sp39, 173—74 v
Poem in autumn.
T, 14 D38, 121 v
Poem two for symphony.
C, i 1 5D35, 7 v
Renewal; Poem from a sequence.
T, 1 J37, [10—11] v
Review [*Devil's dyke*,
by C. Hassall;
The emperor heart,
by L. Whistler] .
T, 2 M37, [19] r
Review [*Poetry and anarchism*,
by H. Read] .
T, 11 Jy38, 76, 78 r
Social force.
T, 6/7 N37, [44] c
Two preludes.
T, 3 A37, [13] v
Two young poets
[*The autumn world*,
by D. S. Savage] .
T, 15/16 F39, 167—69 r
Welcome in August.
LR, ii 13 Oc36, 692 v
Winter afternoon.
T, 17 A39, 16—17 v
see also Symons, J.

Mallalieu, Joseph Percival
William
Means test murder.
ST, i 2 A33, 27—30 d

Malleson, Miles
Yours unfaithfully
rev. by J. Chance

Mallett, Richard
Horse.
LT, i 4 Je36, 12—13 p

Malloch, George Reston
Human voices
rev. by H. MacDiarmid

Malraux, André
Our cultural heritage.
LR, ii 10 Jy36, 491—96 c
Paris Congress speech.
LR, i 11 Ag35, 475 c
Days of contempt

rev. by E. Rickword
Storm in Shanghai
rev. by J. Lehmann

Maltby, Henry Francis
The future of the theatre.
R, i 5 Je34, 8 c

Maltz, Albert
Private Hicks rev. by B. Nixon

Mamet, Louis
Episode from life.
NS, i 3 Je34, 228—33 p

Mangan, Kate
Newspapermen in the Civil
War.
ND, 20 11N37, 10—12 p

Mangan, Sherry
Walk do not run.
NO, ii 2 J35, 125 v

Mangeot, Sylvain
Fencing.
ND, 26 23D37, 32 p
A job in a million.
ND, 17 21Oc37, 20, 22—23 p
Judo and kendo.
ND, 18 28Oc37, 32 p
Take my cue.
ND, 15 7Oc37, 40 c

Manhood, Harold Alfred
Love at ease.
NS, i 3 Je34, 217—20 p
Fierce and gentle
rev. by G. West

Manifold, John
Complaint of N. C.;
Elegy in a country cinema.
PP, 8 F39, 8, 17 v
Ballad of the missing masses.
PP, 12 Je39, 18 v
Night piece II.
PP, 10 A39, 7 v
Village Sunday evening.
P, 5 1939, 177 v

Mann, Erika
School for barbarians
rev. by NV, i 2 My39, 52

Mann, Heinrich
Paris Congress speech.
LR, i 11 Ag35, 472 c
King Wren rev. by S. Blumenfeld

Mann, John
Commonsense.
I, i 2/3 15S31, 52 v

Mann, Klaus
Journey into freedom
rev. by A. L. Morton

Mann, Margaret
Seed.
FB, v 2 My39, 29—30 p

Mann, Merlyn
Village idiot.
P, 3 1938, 48 i

Mann, Thomas
Hour of labour,
tr. by J. M. Smith.
MS, vi 2 Jy35, 156—62 p
Stories of three decades
rev. by S. N. Hampshire

Mann, Tom
Georgi Dimitroff.
EY, 2 Oc35, 2 c
Message,
TU, 3 Je34, 2 c
Rolling stonemason
[*The autobiography of
Fred Bower*] .
LR, ii 10 Jy36, 526—27 r

Mannheim, Karl
Ideology and Utopia
rev. by D. Kahn

Mannin, Ethel Edith
Oxford revisited.
LD, i 2 M37, 19, 21—22 c
*Common sense and the
adolescent* rev. by M. Kahn

Manning, C. Kathleen
Without malice.
C, iii 54 2J37, 5 v

Manning, Frederic
[Private 19022 *pseud.*]
Her privates we rev. by F. H.

Manning, Hugo
Poem.
C, ii 45 31Oc36, 147—48 v
Poem.
C, iii 54 2J37, 4 v
Portrait of a financier.
C, i 20 18A36, 159 v
When twilight comes.
C, ii 48 21N36, 168—71 p

Manning, Olivia M.
A change of mood.
NS, ii 2 A35, 117—22 p
Portrait of a Hungarian doctor.
NS, ii 6 D36, 409—18 p
A scantling of foxes.
NS, i 5 Oc34, 340—47 p

Mannington, Edyth
Peace.
DD, viii 29 Su31, 77 v
Vision.
DD, viii 28 J—F31, 24 v
Words.
DD, xi 45 My—Je34, 43 v

Manwaring, George Ernest
and Dobrée, Bonamy
The floating republic
rev. by T. H. Wintringham

Maraini, Yoi
Letters from abroad.
BB, vii 2 M30, 109—12 c

March, Hilton
The pyre.
C, iii 57 23J37, 31 v

March, Richard
Meditation at a book fair.
TO, ii 5 J39, 20—21 p
Review
[*New directions, 1938*;
In dreams begin responsibilities,
by D. Schwartz;
Complete collected poems,
by W. C. Williams].
TO, ii 6 A39, 18—19 r
Review [*The turning path*,
by F. J. R. Bottrall].
TO, ii 7 Ag39, 22—24 r
The sorcerers.
TO, ii 7 Ag39, 15—18 c
Two periodicals
[*British Union quarterly*;
Regains].
TO, ii 7 Ag39, 24—25 r

March, William
The little wife and other stories
rev. by E. J. O'Brien

Margetson, Pamela
Psyche.
JG, 64 Sp38, [29] v

Marien, Marcel
La charpente des mirages.
LB, 3 Je38, 21 c
Le masque du chair.
LB, 8/9 J39, 2—4 v

Maritain, Jacques
Art and scholasticism
rev. by M. C. d'Arcy

Mark, Enid, W.
Aspects of death.
PP, 12 Je39, 10—11 v

Markland, Russell
Eskdale.
DD, viii 30 Au31, 105 v

Marks, J. H. P.
Bailadoras: notes on Spanish
dancers.
V, 5 F30, 246—51 c

Marks, John
Cinema.
ND, 20 11N37, 30—31 r

Marks, M. J.
Effet des nuages.
M, i 1 Je33, 16 v

Marlow, Louis
Welsh ambassadors
rev. by J. Hanley

Marlowe, Dave
Coming, sir! rev. by M. Kahn

Marmoset *pseud.*
The occupants of a house.
LD, ii 3 F38, 26 v

Marsden, Albert Walter
Clerks wanted.
LR, i 6 M35, 216 p

Marsden, Christopher Alexander
The bricklayer and the
washerwoman.
NO, i 2 N33, 189—97 c

Marsh, Edward
A number of people
rev. by NV, i 2 My39, 52

Marsh, Philip
Poem.
J, 1 J36, 24 v

Marshall, Alan
Australian picture-book.
LR, iii 10 N37, 607—8 p
Australian picture-book II.
LR, iii 12 J38, 705—7 p
An encounter.
LR, ii 11 Ag36, 557—60 p

Marshall, Arthur Calder-
see Calder-Marshall, Arthur

Marshall, Francis Dunbar-
see Dunbar-Marshall, Francis

Marshall, Herbert
Soviet poetry.
LR, iii 10 N37, 596—602 c
The unemployed.
PP, 4 Oc38, 17 v

Yessenin and Mayakovsky.
LR, iii 11 D37, 651—56 c
see also Mayakovsky, Vladimir

Marston, Jeffrey Eardley
No middle way rev. by A. West

Martelli, George
As the world goes round.
ND, 24 9D37, 9—10;
ND, 25 16D37, 9—10;
ND, 26 23D37, 9—10 c
France revisited.
ND, 19 4N37, 15—16 p

Martin, Alexander
Mexican night.
P, 4 1938, 37—52 p

Martin, Dorothy
Print.
LS, i 2 My34, 13—14 c

Martin, E. M.
All souls' day.
JG, 34 Au35, [7] v
Avenues of time.
JG, 38 Au36, [8—9] v
The ball.
JG, 39 W36, [22—23] v
By Paradise gate.
JG, 63 W37, [20] v
A 'charm' song.
JG, 40 Sp37, [21] v
Down Poplar way.
JG, 32 Sp35, [26] v
The flying man.
JG, 37 Su36, [30] v
In Hampshire.
JG, 64 Sp38, [13] v
Island men.
JG, 23 Su35, [9—10] v
Lady day.
JG, 26 Au33, [10] v
Leporello's last service.
JG, 66 Au38, [28—29] v
A lost god.
JG, 42 Au37, [13] v
The magic maker.
JG, 35 W35, [8—9] v
Marshland and sea.
JG, 29 Su34, [19—20] v
The nightmare's foal.
JG, 30 Au34, [8] v
An old song.
JG, 41 Su37, [28] v
Old time's new bride.
JG, 31 W34, [12—13] v
A puzzled mind.
JG, 27 W33, [25—27] v
The sapling.
JG, 36 Sp36, [20] v
To the dreamers of dreams.
JG, 65 Su38, [21] v

Marten, E. M. (cont.)
What the tramp sang.
JG, 28 Sp34, [15] v

Martin, Eva
The storm on the lake.
DD, ix 31 J—F32, 15 v

Martin, Kingsley
The significance of the
Reichstag trial.
TC, vi 32 N33, 72—77 c
The magic of monarchy
rev. by D. Kahn

Martin, Marjorie
CH.33.
TC, v 25 M33, 19—21 c

Martin, Philip
Organisational.
PP, 15 N39, 15 c

Martin, William
French painting
[by R. H. Wilenski;
An account of French painting,
by C. Bell].
OO, xi 56 N31, 213—20 r
French painting and the
exhibition.
OO, xii 57 F32, 50—59 c
Notes on landscape painting
in Europe.
OO, xi 54 M31, 18—27 c
Understand the Chinese
rev. by S. Wang
see also Spencer, C. Bernard

Martindale, Cyril Charles
The lavender league; Christocosm;
La belle au bois dormant.
CA, 12 1932, 382—84 v
Transfiguration.
CA, 12 1932, 367—78 d

Martyn, Marjorie Jeannette
The forgotten people.
JG, 26 Au33, [26—27] v
The hilltop.
JG, 25 Su33, [19] v
The ships of Esmer.
JG, 29 Su34, [23—24] v
The singing tree.
JG, 30 Au34, [30] v
The wall speaks.
JG, 27 W33, [6] v
When beauty passing by.
JG, 31 W34, [27] v

Marx, Karl *and*
Engels, Friedrich
Correspondence
rev. by T. H. Wintringham

Marx! Hear your answer!
LR, i 1 Oc34, 47—48 c

Mary Benvenuta
The anniversary.
CA, 2 S30, 24 v
The contemplative.
CA, 1 Ag30, 11 v
From 'A rosemary of hosts'.
CA, 3 Oc30, 59 v
Paschal moon.
CA, 5 M31, 104 v
The penitent.
CA, 7 Je31, 214 v

Mary Jane *pseud.*
School-teacher.
LR, ii 15 D36, 829 p

Marzani, Carla A.
German hitch-hike.
LD, ii 2 D37, 25—29 p
Manhattan idyll.
LD, i 2 M37, 25—26 p

Masefield, John Edward
Comment on Auden.
NV, 26/27 N37, 29 c
William Butler Yeats.
AW, Su39, 5—6 c
The trial of Jesus
rev. by W. R. Childe
The witch rev. by J. Paris

Masefield, Lewis Crommelin
Atonal romance.
F, 5 F31, 85—90 c
The commercial novel.
NO, ii 2 J35, 142—52 c

Masereel, Franz
Moscow scenes.
LR, ii 8 My36, 385 i

Mason, Eudo Colecastra
Rilke's apotheosis
rev. by H. R.

Mason, S. A.
Bleistein to Calvary.
FB, iii 9 6Je39, 66 v
The lovers.
B, 1 Su38, 9 v
What shall give profit?
PR, 15 11M36, 4 v

Mass Observation
Mass Observation day survey
rev. by M. Richardson
May the twelfth
rev. by E. Waugh

Massingham, Harold John
The lonely humanist.

[*Views and reviews:
second series, 1920—1932*,
by H. H. Ellis].
TC, iv 21 N32, 25—26 r

Mathew, David
Autumn in Nauplia.
AR, i 2 Jy37, 95—97 p

Matthewman, Sydney
At apple trees.
JG, 20 Sp32, [10] v
A ballad of Martha.
JG, 31 W34, [14—15] v
He addresses his muse after a
long silence.
JG, 65 Su38, [8, 11] v
Ode in May.
JG, 13 Su30, [27—28] v
The plum, the cherry and the
the sloe.
HR, 6 1933, 42 v
A triumvir.
JG, 23 W32, [17—18] v
Wet grass at evening.
JG, 38 Au36, [6] v

Matthews, Bache
A little bit about myself.
R, i 2 F34, 12 c

Matthews, Thomas
Homiletic studies: praise.
EP, 3 Sp37, 54—62 p
Poems.
EP, 1 Au35, 55—59 v

Matthews, Thomas *and*
Riding, Laura
The idea of God.
EP, 1 Au35, 6—54 c

Mauriac, François
'The outstretched hand'.
AR, i 3 Oc37, 164—166 c

Maurois, André
A private universe
rev. by G. Pendle

Maurras, Charles
Chorus to Cypris.
RR, 10 Je39, [14—17] v
Oedipus and Cypris.
RR, 9 A39, [14—16] v
On a Venetian cup;
The vain ballad;
Je ne redirai plus; Summer.
RR, 11 S39, [11—15] v
Reliquiae foci.
RR, 7 Oc38, [21—23] v
Theme from Cicero's Somnium
Scipionis;
Colloquy of the dead.

RR, 12 D39, [11—14] v
Unpublished poem; Beauty;
The reign of grace.
RR, 8 J39, [17—19] v

Mavor, Osborne Henry
see Bridie, James *pseud.*

Maxtone-Graham, Joyce
see Struther, Jan *pseud.*

Maxwell, Bertram Wayburn
The Soviet state rev. by R. Bishop

Maxwell, J. D.
On an island.
RM, 2 D34, 49—55 p

Maxwell, John
Modern literature for non-
starters.
C, i 1 17N39, 18 v

Maxwell, William
River in Venezuela.
?, 4 1938, 162—68 p

May, Peter D.
A gardener's lament.
G, 63 W37, [30] v

Mayakovsky, Vladimir
At the top of my voice,
tr. by H. Marshall.
LR, ii 13 Oc36, 699—704 v

Mayer, Gustav
Friedrich Engels
rev. by D. Torr

Mayo, *pseud.*
On taking politics seriously.
LR, iii 12 J38, 712—14 p

Mayor, Flora Macdonald
The room opposite
rev. by L. A. Pavey

Mealand, Richard
I swept up gold.
ND, 9 26Ag37, 10, 12—14 p

Measor, Beryl
On lying, or the art of acting.
R, i 5 Je34, 14 c

Mechtilde, Maria
An anthem of life.
CA, 3 Oc30, 50—51 v
The child and the shells.
CA, 8 1931, 255—56 v

Medley, Robert
Hitler's art in Munich.

AX, 8 W37, 28—29 c
The surrealist exhibition.
GTP, 2 Ag36, [4] c

Mednikoff, Reuben
In the moon's light.
C, iii 56 16J37, 21 v
Victor B. Neuberg reading
Swinburne.
J, 1 J36, 27 i

Megaro, Gaudence
Mussolini in the making
rev. by F. E. Jones

Megroz, Rodolphe Louis
Reality.
I, i 2/3 15S31, 77 v
Sir Ronald Ross as a satirical
poet.
TC, i 4 Je31, 16—20 c
Modern English poetry
rev. by G. Grigson
Rhys Davies: a critical study
rev. by G. West

Mehring, Franz
Karl Marx rev. by D. Torr

Melliar, R. A. Foster-
see Foster-Melliar, R. A.

Mellor, B. *and* **Yang**, H. Y. *trs.*
A poem from Li Ho.
K, i 2 D39—J40, 48 v

Melville, Robert
Suburban nights, II.
LB, 8/9 J39, 49 p

Memor et fidelis.
DD, viii 30 Au31, 116 v

Menai, Huw
As time the sculptor.
WR, i 1 F39, 17—18 v

Mendes, Alfred H.
Afternoon in Trinidad.
NW, 2 Au36, 97—107 p
Lulu gets married.
NS, ii 5 Oc35, 328—58 p

Mendilov, Adam Abraham
Fool's mate; Erinnys;
Mayfair pastoral.
SM, 2 S31, 43—46 v

Meng Yueh
A Chinese literary lady,
tr. by Z. L. Yih and C. Doyle.
JG, 70 Au39, [2] v

Menon, Aubrey
Genesis II
rev. by C. C. Doggett

Meredith, Anne *tr.*
Prague.
PP, 15 N39, 8—9 v

Merrill, Frances *and*
Merrill, Mason
Among the nudists
rev. by J. R. Evans

Mesens, Edouard L. T.
Chanson nette.
LB, 12 15M39, 15—16 v
Le moyen d'en finir.
LB, 10 F39, 19 v
Trois poèmes.
LB, 4/5 Jy38, 26—28, 31 v
Two poems, tr. by H. Jennings
and R. Todd.
CPP, 2 Je36, 27—28 v
see also Jennings, Humphrey

Metcalfe, John
Cheap sarmons.
HR, 5 1932, 31 p

Meyerstein, Edward Harry
William
The alchemist.
DD, viii 29 Su31, 76 v
[*see* DD, viii 30, 117]
The astronomer.
DD, xi 48 N—D34, 94 v
Autumn.
JG, 67 W38, [19] v
Before a picture; Hallucination;
Song; John Selden.
DD, vii 27 N—D30, 423—24 v
Dirge; An epitaph;
Before a picture.
DD, vii 26 S—Oc30, 387—88 v
February; Chatterton at
Shoreditch; The first Christmas.
DD, viii 28 J—F31, 29—30 v
Fish clouds.
JG, 69 Su39, [8] v
The gate.
JG, 68 Sp39, [6] v
One hour; Sussex sunset.
DD, viii 29 Su31, 64 v
[*see* DD, viii 30, 117]
Plane trees after rain.
DD, ix 33 My—Je32, 45 v
The self-satisfied.
DD, x 37 J—F33, 11 v
Sounds.
DD, xi 44 M—A34, 29 v
The starlings.
JG, 70 Au39, [6—7] v
To C. J. Arnell.
DD, ix 32 M—A32, 20 v

Meyerstein, Edward Harry (cont.)
To one killed in the last war.
JG, 71 W39, [13] v
Vision.
DD, viii 30 Au31, 99 v

Meynell, Francis
Review [*Dogs of war*,
by F. Yeats-Brown].
TC, vi 36 S34, 376—81 r
The Meerut case.
TC, iv 24 F33, 22—24 c
World crisis: the debunking
of patriotism.
TC, v 27 My33, 182—84 c

Meynell, Wilfred
Joseph Mary Plunkett.
CA, 5 M31, 122 v

Miatlev, Adrian
Louis Marcoussis.
LB, 13 15A39, 5—9 c

Michaelis.
RM, 1 Je34, 12—13 p

Micinski, Tadeusz
Lucifer, tr. by P. Selver.
EQ, i 4 F35, 273 v

Mickiewicz, Adam
Forefathers, tr. by
Count Potocki de Montalk.
RR, 5 J38, [10—13] v

Middleditch, G. E.
Can Shakespearian comedy
be entertaining?
R, i 7 N34, 4—5 c

Mikhailovsky, Stoyan
Fin de siècle, tr. by P. Selver
SM, 4 1933, 114 v

Mikhaylov, Nikolai Nikolaevich
Soviet geography
rev. by E. Rickword

Miles, Hamish
Review
[*And lastly the fireworks*,
by J. Pudney].
NS, ii 7 F36, 559 r
Review [*Moving pageant*,
by L. A. Pavey].
NS, ii 6 D36, 482 r
A war museum, 1914—18
rev. by G. West

Miles, Rex
November.
C, iii 58 30J37, 36 v

Oboe for grieving.
C, i 23 9My36, 181—82 p

Miles *pseud.*
Socialism's new start
rev. by G. West

Miličič, Sibe
La côte dalmatique.
DD, xi 43 J—F34, 8—9 v
Nuit d'engloutissement,
tr. by P. H.
DD, ix 36 N—D32, 95—97 v
La nuit étoilée.
DD, ix 33 My—Je32, 36;
DD, xi 45 My—Je34, 37 v

Mill, Samuel
The rebellious needleman
Tom Paine.
LR, iii 4 My37, 202—7 c

Millar, Robins
Dream island
rev. by J. H. Whyte

Miller, Alastair William Rowsell
From 'Stages of pursuit'.
RM, 1 Je34, 14—16 v
Poem.
RM, 2 D34, 62 v
Poem.
PR, 4 5M35, 4—5 v
Stages of pursuit
rev. by H. S. B.

Millar, Douglas
The Theatre Royal, Bristol.
R, i 1 N33, 16 c

Miller, Henry
The Brooklyn bridge.
SV, 1 Su38, 4—10 p
Chez Benno.
LB, 3 Je38, 11—12, 18 c
Peace! It's wonderful.
SV, 3 W38, 18—22 p
Portrait of General Grant.
ND, 26 23D37, 20—21 p

Miller, Henry S.
Camoens, dying.
JG, 29 Su34, [26] v
Change.
JG, 32 Sp35, [31] v
Derelict.
JG, 28 Sp34, [29] v
Homage.
JG, 22 Au32, [25] v
A last wish.
JG, 26 Au33, [15] v
The old and the new.
DD, vii 26 S—Oc30, 411 v

Samson.
JG, 21 Su32, [15] v
Spring.
JG, 24 Sp33, [10] v
The stoic.
JG, 33 Su35, [29] v
A theft.
JG, 17 Su31, [16—17] v
To Sylvia.
JG, 31 W34, [6] v
To Violet.
JG, 27 W33, [22] v

Miller, Margaret J.
A job in a million: 2.
ND, 2 8Jy37, 19—20 p
A job in a million: 17.
ND, 24 9D37, 15—16 p
On ice.
ND, 21 18N37, 40 p
Plain and milk,
ND, 12 16S37, 28 c
Robots at Earls Court.
ND, 14 30S37, 34 c

Miller, Patrick
Let there be light.
DD, xi 45 My—Je34, 36 v
My mother.
DD, xi 43 J—F34, 10 v

Miller, Ray.
Elegy.
PR, 12 4D35, 4—6 v

Mills, James W.
The verger's romance.
FB, ii 5 5M37, 34—36 v

Mills, Sidney
The band.
C, i 27 20Je36, 216—17 p

Mills-Francis, Catherine
The symbolistic school and
the English mind.
PR, 6 31My35, 5—7 c

Milne, Alan Alexander
Peace with honour
rev. by D. Garman

Milne, Charles Ewart
Caravanserai.
C, ii 31 25Jy36, 27 v
Hieroglyph.
C, ii 48 21N36, 166 v
Mediaeval duologue.
C, ii 53 26D36, 215 v
O quam te memorem.
C, i 23 9My36, 183 v
Poet's corner.
C, i 4 28D35, 30 v

Sierran vigil.
NW, ns2 Sp39, 34—35 v
Sporting piece.
C, ii 38 12S36, 83—84 v
Storm over Wicklow.
C, i 9 1F36, 71 v
The unfading dream;
C, ii 44 24Oc36, 138 v
An unknown warrior.
C, ii 44 24Oc36, 131 v

Mirsky, Dimitri Petrovich
Suyatopolk
Correspondence.
OO, xi 56 N31, 224—25 c
Intelligentsia,
tr. by A. Brown.
LR, i 4 J35, 117—22 c
*The intelligentsia of Great
Britain* rev. by A. West

Mitchell, James Leslie
The diffusionist heresy.
TC, i 1 M31, 14—16 c
The Prince's placenta and
Prometheus as god.
TC, ii 12 F32, 16—18 c

Mitchell, Ronald Elwy
The new Welsh stage —
a vision.
W, 3 Au37, 123—28 c
Deep waters rev. by M. Evans

Mitchison, Naomi
Beginning of a new order.
K, i 1 17N39, 7—8 p
Breaking up the home.
TC, iii 17 Jy32, 1—3 c
Chapter from an unpublished
novel.
NO, i 3 F34, 274—87 p
Comment on the basis of
the Sexology group.
TC, iv 21 N32, 19—20 c
Eviction in the Hebrides.
LR, iii 1 F37, 20 v
Fascism in Austria.
TC, vi 35 Je34, 257—61 c
In time of trouble.
PR, 5 17My35, 15 v
Interlude (from an unpublished
novel).
MS, iv 2 Jy33, 100—4 p
Marxist love poem.
LS, i 2 My34, 70 v
The N. U. W. M. against
Lord Trenchard.
TU, i 2 1934, 61 v
New Cloud-Cuckoo-Borough.
MS, v 1/2 Je34, 30—38 c
Pages from a Russian diary.
MS, iii 3 Oc32, 229—36;
CL, i 1 Su33, 16—20 p

The reluctant feminist
[*Women*, by W. Holtby].
LR, i 3 D34, 93—94 r
Sex and politics.
TC, vi 33 D33—J34, 139—48 c
A socialist plan for Scotland.
MS, iii 1 A32, 25—30 c
To some young communists
from an older socialist.
NV, 1 J33, 9 v
Vase room at the Louvre.
I, i 2/3 15S31, 61 v
White nights.
MS, vi 3 Oc35, 226 v
An outline for boys and girls
rev. by P. Cyon
We have been warned
rev. by T. H. Wintringham

Moffat, David
A.R.P.; Materfamilias.
PP, 6 D38, 6, 13 v

Molière, Jean Baptiste Poquelin
The love-tiff,
tr. by F. Spencer.
rev. by S. Spender

Mollison, Amy
My first cross-country flight.
HR, 7 1934, 16 p

Moncrieff, George Scott-
see Scott-Moncrieff, George

Monk, Una
Poem.
PR, 21 1M37, 11 v
The Spanish gentlewoman.
C, iii 57 23J37, 30 v

Mont, J. L.
Afraid to die.
NS, ii 8 A36, 608—24 p
Ten minutes from town.
NS, ii 6 D36, 401—8 p

Montagu, Mary Wortley
Letters rev. by R. S. Forrist

Montech, P.
In Freiburg, tr. by J. Rodker.
NW, 2 Au36, 227—45 p

Montgomerie, William
The foundation.
PP, 5 N38, 12—13 v
Glasgow.
PP, 7 J39, 13 v
Kinfauns castle.
MS, iii 1 A32, 39—40 v
Mental pyramid.
MS, v 3 Oc34, 183 v
The mountain.

MS, iv 4 J34, 313—15 v
The primitives.
MS, vi 4 J36, 338 v

Montgomery, Niall
Eyewash.
CPP, 8 D36, 158—59 v

Montherlant, Henry de
Love in the Sahara,
tr. by C. Fitzgibbon.
Y, i 1 M39, 19—23 p

Moody, Irene H.
Sky-passion.
JG, 67 W38, [28] v
Wanderlust.
JG, 63 W37, [18—19] v

Moon, Eve
Glamour.
DD, ix 32 M—A32, 31 v

Moore, Eldon
Some modern problems of
population.
TC, i 2 A31, 1—4 c

Moore, Henry
Carving in Ancaster stone.
I, i 4 15D31, 107 i
Wood engraving.
I, i 1 15Je31, 7 i
Wood engraving.
I, i 1 15Je31, 14 i

Moore, John
Fragments from a scheme;
The birds.
CM, ii 1 Su35, 242—43 v

Moore, M. F.
The cathedral windows.
LS, i 1 F34, 33—35 p

Moore, Marianne
Answers to an enquiry.
NV, 11 Oc34, 16 p
Answers to an enquiry.
T, 12/13 Oc38, 114 p
Selected poems rev. by A. Hodge

Moore, Merrill
People fill this world; Seers
SV, 3 W38, 38 v

Moore, Nicholas
Dr Magnus and the blackbirds.
K, i 2 D39—J40, 51—52 p
The five candles.
SV, 4 Su39, 6—7 p
Favour; The big city.
TH, 1 27J39, 3—4 p, v
I'm David Greer.

Moore, Nicholas (cont.)
LD, ii 3 F38, 17—18 p
The innocent;
The man of nothing.
T, 17 A39, 15 v
Poem.
TH, 1 27J39, 1 v
Poem.
TH, 3 24F39, 1 v
Poem.
SV, 6 Au39, 2 v
Poem.
TO, ii 8 N39, 8 v
Poem.
K, i 1 17N39, 32 v
Poem.
RR, 12 D39, [10] v
Poem.
K, i 2 D39—J40, 56 v
Poem; No epilogue but death.
FB, v 1 F39, 7—9 v, p
Poem for Sheila; Poem.
SV, 4 Su39, 15 v
The rare poet; It is better.
PL, i 1 F39, [25] v
The wind flew down the
valley.
LD, ii 2 D37, 10—11 p
Wood of devils.
K, i 1 17N39, 11—12 p

Moore, Olive
Fugue rev. by A. Bristow

Moore, Thomas Sturge
Endymion's prayer.
DD, x 37 J—F33, 6 v
Fashion in art and literature.
LR, iii 15 A38, 897—900 c
Two sonnets.
DD, x 40 Jy—Ag33, 58 v

Morand, Paul
Mr. U, tr. by D. Flower.
ND, 4 22Jy37, 10—12 p

Morang, Alfred
A good marriage for Bee.
NS, ii 6 D36, 455—63 p
Tangled with darkness.
CPP, 8 D36, 162—64 p
Two stories.
NS, i 3 Je34, 199—208 p

Moray-Williams, Alan
Virginity: an epitaph.
FB, iii 6 21Oc37, 9 v

Mordaunt, Geoffrey
Television.
IP, i 1 6A39, 14—17 c

Mordaunt, Myles
Carson the British fascist

94

[*Carson,* by I. Colvin].
LR, i 3 D34, 95—96 r

Moreno Villas, José
Madrid front,
tr. by S. Richardson.
NW, ns1 Au38, 34—35 v

Moreton, B. J. R.
The calm breaks.
FB, v 1 F39, 7 v

Moreton, Jock
For you, Odysseus.
TH, 3 24F39, 4 v
Poem.
TH, 2 10F39, 1 v
Salmon.
K, i 2 D39—J40, 36 v

Morgan, Alun
Review
[*Reply to reason and other
poems,* by N. C. Yendell;
Selected poems,
by R. C. Trevelyan].
PR, 8 19Je35, 15 r

Morgan, Edna Hylda
Annunciation.
LR, i 4 J35, 137—40 p

Morgan, Evan Frederic
And even then.
CA, 12 1932, 383 v
Babylon.
CA, 3 Oc30, 40 v
The catholic renascence.
CA, 7 Je31, 198—200 c
A cenotaph to beauty.
CA, 10 1931, 306—7 v
The dragonfly.
CA, 4 N30, 82 v
Eternity and the clock.
CA, 2 S30, 20—21 p
The interior litany.
CA, 8 1931, 254—56 v
An Italian nocturne.
CA, 2 S30, 26 v
A lyric.
CA, 5 M31, 125 v
The serpent of doom.
CA, 9 1931, 272—74 v
To dress and to keep.
CA, 1 Ag30, 12—13 v
A toast.
CA, 11 1932, 327 v

Morland, Harold
London street game.
TC, iv 22 D32, 9 v
Arabesque rev. by A. D. Hawkins

Morland, Nigel
see Barwell, Peggy

Morley, John Royston
Ankles and trousers.
J, 2 My36, 19—21 c
New books
[*The Jacobean drama,*
by U. Ellis-Fermor;
In defence of Shelley,
by H. Read].
J, 2 My36, 22—23 r
Review
[*Selected passages from
The dawn in Britain,*
by C. Doughty;
The book of Job,
ed. by A. Nairne;
First day, by C. Dyment].
J, 1 J36, 28—29 r
Theatre reviews
[*A doll's house,*
by H. Ibsen;
The lady from the sea,
by H. Ibsen;
King Lear, by W. Shakespeare;
Lysistrata, by Aristophanes.
J, 2 My36, 28—29 dr
Two episodes.
J, 1 J36, 18—20 p

Morley, S.
The flowers on the hillside
green.
DD, xi 44 M—A34, 18 v
Immutability.
DD, xi 45 My—Je34, 35 v

Morris, Edita
Evening in Spring.
NS, i 4 Ag34, 270—75 p
Frail sister.
NS, ii 4 Ag35, 294—307 p
Mrs Lancaster-Jones.
NS, i 1 F34, 4—14 p

Morris, Helen
A Cornish fantasy.
DD, xi 44 M—A34, 25—26 v

Morris, I. V.
Marching orders.
NS, ii 8 A36, 574—600 p

Morris, John *tr.*
see Tureck, Ludwig

Morris, Margaret
Men in the rigging.
P, 3 1938, 243 i

Morrison, B.
see Corbett, Mary

Morrison, Donald R.
Commonsense.
TC, ii 11 J32, 21—23 c
Commonsense: for Prometheus.
TC, i 4 Je31, 10—13 c
The greatest war.
PR, 19 20Oc36, 3 v
Review
[*The ascent of humanity;*
The social substance of religion;
The emergence of man;
all by G. Heard].
TC, ii 11 J32, 23—24 r
Storm.
PR, 23 N37, 13 v
The superman.
TC, i 2 A31, 25—26 c

Morrison, Elizabeth
The position of the woman
student.
NO, i 3 F34, 270—73 c

Morse, Benjamin Joseph
Eventual birth of thought.
W, 5 Su38, 178 v

Morse, Samuel French
Prelude to the long sleep.
T, 9 M38, 12—14 v
Man with imagination
[*The man with the blue guitar,*
by W. Stevens].
T, 8 J38, [15—19] r
Quaking bog.
T, 12/13 Oc38, 102 v
The rabbit, the fox, the snake.
T, 15/16 F39, 150 v

Mortimer, Charles Gordon
Beauty.
DD, xi 45 My—Je34, 38 v
The bee; The rose.
DD, ix 36 N—D32, 98 v
Compassion.
DD, ix 32 M—A32, 29 v
The first snowdrop;
To a shell.
DD, x 42 N—D33, 93 v
The golden age.
DD, ix 31 J—F32, 4 v
The market women,
Blackburn.
DD, x 39 My—Je33, 49 v
Memory.
DD, x 38 M—A33, 32 v
Phantasy; The sun-dial.
DD, xi 48 N—D34, 96 v
Reverie.
DD, viii 29 Su31, 61—63 v
Rivers; The hammock of dreams.
DD, viii 30 Au31, 111—12 v
Science; Scribes and Pharisees.
DD, ix 34 Jy—Ag32, 60 v

Morton, Arthur Leslie
Adam.
EQ, i 4 F35, 264—65 v
Blow, blow.
TC, v 29 Jy33, 283 v
Chesterton:
the man of Thermidor.
TC, vi 36 S34, 327—30 c
The coming world war
[by T. H. Wintringham].
LR, ii 16 J37, 918 r
Commander
[*King-Hall survey 1936,*
by S. King-Hall].
LR, iii 1 F37, 61 r
E. M. Forster and the
classless society.
TC, v 26 A33, 89—96 c
Fascism.
LR, ii 15 D36, 796 v
Giant harvest.
TC, vi 31 S—Oc33, 33 v
Historical moralism
[*Only one battle,*
by R. Acland;
The first American revolution,
by J. Hardy].
LR, iii 13 F38, 813—17 r
Introduction to English history
[*A history of English life,*
by A. Williams-Ellis and
F. J. Fisher].
LR, ii 16 J37, 917 r
New novels
[*None turn back,*
by S. Jameson;
Summer will show,
by S. T. Warner;
I am death, by R. Connor;
Journey into freedom,
by K. Mann].
LR, ii 13 Oc36, 719—21 r
New novels [*The friendly tree,*
by C. Day Lewis;
In dubious battle,
by J. Steinbeck;
Manhattan side street,
by J. Dratler;
Death of a man, by K. Boyle;
The king sees red,
by A. Bertram;
The fool and the tractor,
by L. Kerr].
LR, ii 14 N36, 787—88 r
Night pieces for Vivien.
C, i 5 4J36, 37 v
Review
[*Goldsworthy Lowes*
Dickinson, by E. M. Forster].
TC, vi 35 Je34, 306—8 r
Review [*New country,*
ed. by M. Roberts;
The magnetic mountain,
by C. Day Lewis].

TC, v 27 My33, 185—88 r
Review [*Mutiny,*
by T. H. Wintringham].
C, iii 56 16J37, 18 r
Simple or compound?
TC, vi 31 S—Oc33, 34—36 v
So I became.
LR, i 3 D34, 69—70 v
Their London and ours.
[*The spirit of London,*
by P. Cohen-Portheim;
Odd jobs, by P. Binder].
LR, i 8 My35, 333—34 r
Twilight song.
TC, iv 24 F33, 19—20 v
Two poems.
C, ii 30 18Jy36, 20 v
'What an admirable people'
[*The Paris Commune of 1871,*
by F. Jellinek].
LR, iii 2 M37, 113—14 r

Mosbacher, Eric *tr. see* Silone, I.

Moses, W. R.
Angina pectoris;
Hunter's evening.
T, 12/13 Oc38, 102—3 v
Oregon coast.
T, 15/16 F39, 154 v
Scenery of anger.
NV, 10 Ag34, 10—11 v

Mott, E. Bentley-
see Bentley-Mott, E.

Mott, Elizabeth
The room.
JG, 21 Su32, [18] v

Mottram, C. F.
For they know not.
LR, i 4 J35, 135—37 p
Friend of ours.
LR, iii 3 A37, 143—47 p
Traces of opium.
LR, i 2 N34, 39—40 p

Mottram, Ralph Hale
Epilogue.
HR, 7 1934, 67 c

Mouilpied, Helen de
Review
[*The fool of Venus,*
by G. Cronyn].
LS, i 3 N34, 68—70 r
see also Bolgar, Bryan
pseud.

Moult, Thomas
Best poems of 1936.
rev. by R. Todd

Moulton, L.
In the Tuileries.
DD, xi 48 N–D34, 99 v

Moulton, Matthew
Notes on Scots literature.
NA, i 1 Au39, 5–15 c

Moung, Daphne Aye
All the birds of the air.
LD, ii 1 Oc37, 16–17 p
Armageddon.
LD, i 4 Je37, 10 p

Moung, Margaret Aye
Les précieux ridicules.
LD, i 3 My37, 16–17 c

Mourant, Joe
Like Father.
ST, i 3 1933, 12 p

Mowrer, Edgar
Germany puts the clock back
rev. by G. West

Moynihan, Martin
Prelude to jubilee celebrations
in the East End.
PR, 20 17N36, 16 v

Muehsam, Erich
Erich Mühsam fund.
LR, i 3 D34, 70 p
Erich Mühsam's death and an
appeal.
LR, i 2 N34, 36–37 c
Mühsam in prison.
LR, i 7 A35, 273–75 p

Muggeridge, Malcolm
Epic book of the week
[*Memoirs*, by J. R. Clynes].
ND, 15 7Oc37, 31–32 r
Letter.
R, i 5 Je34, 16 c
A newspaper is a fearsome thing.
ND, 26 23D37, 18–19 p
One day cruise.
ND, 13 23S37, 20–21 p
The Soviet stage.
R, i 4 My34, 6 c
The theatre.
ND, 11 9S37, 29 dr
see also Kingsmill, Hugh

Muir, Edwin
Answers to an enquiry.
NV, 11 Oc34, 17 c
Bolshevism and Calvinism.
EQ, i 1 My34, 3–11 c
Burns and Holy Willie.
LR, ii 14 N36, 762–64 c

Chapter from a novel.
MS, iii 1 A32, 9–13 p
Comment on Auden.
NV, 26/27 N37, 23 c
The contemporary novel.
EQ, i 2 Ag34, 70–76 c
A death.
MS, ii 4 J32, 270–76 p
The decline of the novel.
MS, iv 4 J34, 284–90 c
The fall.
MS, i 4 J31, 10–11 v
The harvest.
MS, v 4 J35, 266–67 v
Hermann Broch.
MS, iii 2 Ag32, 103–10 c
Hölderlin.
NV, 30 Su38, 13–16 c
Hölderlin's *Patmos*.
EQ, i 4 F35, 241–55 c
In the wilderness.
MS, iv 2 Jy33, 138–40 v
A new Scottish novelist
[*The Albannach*,
by F. Mac Colla].
MS, iii 2 Ag32, 166–67 r
Oswald Spengler,
EQ, i 3 N34, 143–52 c
Pages from a Scottish journey.
MS, vi 1 A35, 18–28 p
Parallels.
MS, i 1 Sp30, 6–10 c
Poem.
NV, 28 J38, 3 v
The refugees.
NA, i 1 Au39, 61–65 v
Review
[*Land everlasting*;
The endless furrow,
both by A. G. Street].
EQ, i 3 N34, 208 r
Robert Louis Stevenson.
MS, ii 3 Oc31, 196–204 c
Scott and tradition.
MS, iii 2 Ag32, 118–20 c
The stronghold.
MS, v 3 Oc34, 159 v
Three fold time.
NV, 6 D33, 3–4 v
Poor Tom
rev. by H. G. Porteus.
The three brothers
rev. by R. West
Variations on a time theme
rev. by D. Botterill; L. MacNeice

Muir, Kenneth
The babe.
JG, 65 Su38, [12] v
Beethoven sonata.
JG, 67 W38, [14, 17] v
The dry bones.
JG, 41 Su37, [20] v
Extract.

JG, 34 Au35, [11–12] v
Extract from 'The garden'.
JG, 30 Au34, [23] v
For Muriel.
MS, vi 2 Jy35, 128–30 v
From 'The nettle and the flower'.
MS, iv 1 A33, 38–39 v
From 'The nettle and the flower'.
JG, 25 Su33, [5–6] v
Ikhnaton's psalm.
JG, 32 Sp35, [29] v
In the broad spectrum.
JG, 38 Au36, [21] v
The island.
JG, 35 W35, [15] v
Letter I.
MS, iv 3 Oc33, 234–36 v
Light.
JG, 42 Au37, [12–13] v
Lilies.
JG, 27 W33, [23] v
Loving not me.
JG, 68 Sp39, [28] v
Lyric.
JG, 66 Au38, [7] v
Marina's song.
JG, 64 Sp38, [9] v
No disaster can fall.
JG, 29 Su34, [15] v
Now when the sun.
JG, 39 W36, [21] v
Orpheus.
JG, 28 Sp34, [8–10] v
Poppies.
JG, 31 W34, [6] v
Prologue.
MS, v 1/2 Je34, 44–45 v
Seek not.
JG, 71 W39, [5] v
Southern sea bathers.
JG, 36 Sp36, [19] v
Tempus fugit.
JG, 66 Au39, [13] v
To James Mackereth.
JG, 33 Su35, [17–18] v
Versicles.
JG, 26 Au33, [19–20] v
Who hath despised?
JG, 63 W37, [9] v

Muir, Willa
Chapter from a novel.
MS, iii 3 Oc32, 198–201 p
Clock-a doodle-doo.
MS, v 1/2 Je34, 46–50 p
Images and writers.
NA, i 1 Au39, 51–56 c
Mrs Grundy comes to Scotland.
MS, vi 4 J36, 289–96 c
The new education
[*The problem parent*,
by A. S. Neill].
MS, iii 1 A32, 74–75 r
Women in Scotland.

LR, ii 14 N36, 768—70 c
see also Kafka, Franz

Mulciber *pseud.*
The future of the industrial
novel in Britain.
WR, ii 3 Oc39, 154—58 c

Mulhern, James
Irish spirit.
ST, i 1 F33, 25—30 p

Munby, A. N. L.
see Flower, D. J. N.

Munro, Edward
The knifegrinder.
P, 4 1938, 154—61 p

Munro, Francis
The boulder.
P, 6 1939, 83—89 p

Munro, Nan
Open letter to the audience.
R, i 7 N34, 11 c

Munson, G. B.
Sorel.
TC, iv 20 Oc32, 11—13 c

Murgatroyd, James
Life without a shoehorn.
ND, 19 4N37, 20—21 p

Murgatroyd, Vera
First spring.
JG, 30 Au34, [11] v
Flight of the swallows.
JG, 63 W37, [15] v
Interlude.
JG, 28 Sp34, [21] v
June Gale.
JG, 34 Au35, [14] v
Machines.
JG, 39 W36, [24] v
Oxfordshire in April.
JG, 17 Su31 [22—23] v
Prayer.
JG, 22 Au32, [20—21] v
Resurrection.
JG, 70 Au39, [33] v
Shot in the dark.
JG, 36 Sp36, [22] v
Sonnet.
JG, 14 Au30, [9] v
Throstle song.
JG, 37 Su36, [28—29] v
To a young recruit.
JG, 67 W38, [30] v

Murphy, Gwendolen *ed.*
The modern poet
rev. by G. Taylor

Murphy, Vera M.
A masterpiece.
DD, viii 28 J—F31, 38 v

Murray, A. J. J.
Violin.
PR, 20 17N36, 9—10 v

Murray, A. M. St. L. Ramsay
Poppycock politics.
FB, iii 7 25N37, 35 p
Three years at Shangri-La.
FB, iii 8 3M38, 50 p
An undergraduate delirium.
FB, iii 6 21Oc37, 16—17 p

Murray, Andrew
Advent,
B, 2 W38, 9 v
Arthur's evening out.
K, i 1 17N39, 24—29 p
Don Juan.
K, i 2 D39—J40, 45—48 p
Elegy for the passing of 1936.
PR, 21 1M37, 10—11 v
Lights out.
FB, iii 9 6Je38, 67—68 p
Other Eden.
FB, iv 10 N38, 8—11 p
Poem.
T, 8 J38, [10] v
Poem.
T, 10 My38, 39 v
Poem.
B, 1 Su38, 8 v

Murrill, Herbert
The bachelor.
F, 2 Je30, 90—91 m
Stravinsky and the return to
classicism in music.
F, 4 D30, 17—21 c

Murry, John Middleton
Comment on the report.
TC, ii 10 D31, 9—10 c
Communism and the
universities.
OO, xii 58 My32, 79—88 c
Communist tactics.
TC, iii 15 My32, 26 c
Essays.
WA, 1—13 D33—N34, c
Is there a point of focus for
progressives?
TC, vi 32 N33, 68—70 c
Myself and the I.L.P.
TC, v 29 Jy33, 309—10 c
Notes on communism.
TC, ii 13 M32, 3—5 c
War — pure and simple.
K, i 2 D39—J40, 49—50 c
The necessity of communism
rev. by F. J.; H. G. Porteus; G. West

Reminiscences of D. H. Lawrence
rev. by J. P. Hogan
Son of woman
rev. by H. G. Porteus
William Blake
rev. by G. Barker; S. Spender

Musgrave, Noel
Art critic,
LR, ii 3 D35, 126 i

Music of democracy in China.
LR, iii 12 J38, 737—39 c

Muskett, Netta
Middle mist rev. by E. Waugh

Mussolini, Benito
No dynamite?
LR, ii 5 F36, 196 p

My best story for boys
rev. by J. Hayward

Myer. Michael
To Marie.
ND, 21 18N37, 36 v

Myers, Elizabeth
Lost.
NS, i 5 Oc34, 386—93 p

Myers, Leopold Hamilton
Strange glory rev. by R. Wright

N

N., B.
Willa and Edward Muir: caricature.
VS, i 2 S—N38, 10 i

N., J.
Boots.
LR, ii 8 My36, 392—93 p

Nachsen, Doria
All God's chillun got wheels.
LR, i 7 A35, 271 i

Nadin, Russell
Going to the devil.
BB, vii 2 M30, 19—26 p

Naga, Syuiti
A back sigh.
TO, i 3 Jy38, 6 v

Nairne, Campbell
Full moon.
MS, v 3 Oc34, 160—72 p

Nakamura, Tio
The end of evil fortune.
TO, i 1 J38, 6 v

Nalkowska, Zofja
Motherhood, tr. by N. B. Jopson.
EQ, i 2 Ag34, 97—105 p

Narayan, R. K.
Fellow-feeling.
ND, 7 12Ag37, 10, 12—14 p

Nash, Paul
F. E. McWilliam.
LB, 11 M39, 11—12 c
For, but not with.
AX, 1 J35, 24—26 c
John Piper.
LB, 2 My38, 10 c
Souvenir of Florence; The pond.
OO, xi 56 N31, 157, 209 i

National Farmers Union
The farmers manifesto
rev. by H. Swabey

Natusch, J. A.
Snow.
DD, ix 32 M—A32, 32 v

Naylor, Bernard
Albert Lortzing.
F, 3 Oc30, 190—99 c
Fires of heaven, by R. Bridges.
F, 4 D30, 32—34 m
My eyes for beauty pine, by R. Bridges.
F, 1 F30, 38—39 m
A night in May.
F, 6 Je31, 200—206 p, c

Neale, Ralph
One taste of heaven.
SM, 4 1933, 39—56 p

Neame, Derek
The new order.
ND, 21 18N37, 36 v

Nearing, Scott
Will Roosevelt go Fascist?
TC, vi 34 M34, 200—4 c

Nehru, Jawaharlal
An autobiography
rev. by M. Slater
India and the world
rev. by M. Slater

Neill, Alexander Sutherland
Masturbation.
TC, vi 36 S34, 347—54 c
Masturbation in childhood.
TC, vi 35 Je34, 291—96 c
The new education.

TC, ii 11 J32, 1—4 c
On education: the free school.
TC, v 25 M33, 40—43 c
Review [*Education and the social order*,
by B. Russell].
TC, iv 20 Oc32, 20—21 r
The problem parent
rev. by K. A.; W. Muir

Nemilov, Antony
The biological tragedy of woman
rev. by D. Ramsay

Nenni, Pietro
Ten years of tyranny in Italy
rev. by J. R. Evans

Neruda, Pablo *pseud.*
Almeria, tr. by N. Cunard.
LR, iii 7 Ag37, 407 v
To the mothers of the dead militia,
tr. by N. Cunard.
LR, iii 3 A37, 140—41 v
Walking around,
tr. by A. C. and A. Boyd.
NV, 22 S36, 2—3 v

Nesbitt, Marian
The bells of Innisfallen.
CA, 8 1931, 256 v

Nettlefold, William T.
Epigram.
PP, 7 J39, 3 v
Fan mail for a poet.
NV, 30 Su38, 11—12 v
Hints to the prospective poets who
would rather write than earn an honest
living.
PP, 7 J39, 8—10 c
The law and the order.
PP, 12 Je39, 6 v
Poem for May Day.
PP, 11 My39, 4 v
Reality; Warning.
PP, 4 Oc38, 9 v
Remembrance day; A lullaby for a baby
born in 1937.
LR, iii 11 D37, 661—62 v
Society notes.
PP, 8 F39, 4 v
Song for a choir of agricultural workers
to sing at Covent Garden.
PP, 9 M39, 6 v
Spring also stirs.
LR, iii 14 M38, 868 v

Neuberg, Victor B.
The Atys of Catullus.
C, i 8 25J36, 60—61 v
Bridging it over.
OO, x 51 F30, 442—48 c
The nemesis of wit
[*Notes on English verse satire*,

by H. Wolfe].
OO, x 51 F30, 458—60 r
Perdita
[*Memoirs of the life of the late
Mrs P. Robinson*].
OO, x 52 My30, 546—48 r

Neumark, Peter
Max Hansen.
FB, ii 4 25J37, 13—14 c
The Paris theatre.
FB, i 3 9My36, 55—57 c

Neustatter, Walter Lindesay
Nihilism and Neillism.
TC, iv 21 N32, 24—25 c

Nevinson, Christopher Richard Wynne
The adventure of modern art in England.
I, i 4 15D31, 112—14 c

Nevinson, Henry Wood
Snakes.
DD, xi 47 S—Oc34, 75 v
Vipers.
DD, xi 48 N—D34, 90 v
New directions, 1938
rev. by R. March

New directions, IV
rev. by R. Todd

New Indian literature,
[no.1] rev. by P. Henderson

New stories, vol.1, no.1
rev. by A.D.W.

New writing, no. 1
rev. by A. Hodge; D. Kahn

New writing, no.2
rev. by S. Spender

New writing, no.3
rev. by S. T. Warner

New writing, no.4
rev. by M. Slater

New writing, no.5
rev. by R. Fuller

New writing, n.s. 1
rev. by NV, i 2 My39, 52

Newbolt, Sir Henry
The young reader.
M, i 1 Je33, 3—5 c

Newbury, K.
Milk — before breakfast.
LR, i 6 M35, 213—14 p

News of the month.
TC, v 25 M33, 65—80; TC, v 27 My33,
197—208; TC, v 29 J 33, 325—36;
TC, v 30 Ag33, 385—400 c

Newsom, John
On the other side
rev. by D. A. Sington

Newsom, Sam
How Cambridge saved the Festival
Theatre.
R, i 2 F34, 5 c

Newson-Smith, Peter
Oxford's chances at the White City.
FB, i 2 3M36, 42 c

Newton, Elsie
The hope of England; The enemy.
PP, 6 D38, 11, 18 v

Nicholas, Thomas Evan
I gofio Cymro.
VS, i 4 M—My39, 22 v
I gofio Cymro.
W, 8/9 Ag39, 244 v
Writers international.
LR, i 3 D34, 78—79 c

Nicholl, Clare
Compensations of autumn.
DD, x 37 J—F33, 14 v
'Life is very sweet, brother'.
DD, ix 33 My—Je32, 44 v
Poem.
DD, x 40 Jy—Ag33, 62 v
Things of dear delight.
DD, x 39 My—Je33, 39—41 v

Nicholls, Elizabeth
Daily Express.
ND, 15 7Oc37, 11 v
Poem.
ND, 14 30S37, 15 v
Politics.
ND, 16 14Oc37, 34 v

Nichols, Beverley
Jacob Epstein.
HR, 5 1932, 11—14 c
A message from Beverley Nichols.
TC, vi 32 N33, 77 c

Nicholson, B. D.
The dead manufacturer talks to Gabriel.
F, 3 Oc30, 149—58 p

Nicholson, E. M.
National planning: a speech at High
Leigh conference.
TC, iv 20 Oc32, 28—29 c

Nicholson, Hubert

Lizard shoes.
NS, i 3 Je34, 236—44 p
White man's city.
NS, i 6 D34, 452—60 p

Nicholson, Norman
Behead a god; Poem beside a war
memorial.
B, 2 W38, 14—15 v
Carol for Holy Innocents day.
K, i 2 D39—J40, 50 v
Poem for declamation.
B, 3 Sp39, 2—3 v
Poem on Thursday.
B, 1 Su38, 4 v
Tree of knowledge.
FB, iii 9 6Je38, 77—78 p

Nickels, Arthur
Sonnet.
JG, 24 Sp33, [20] v

Nicolaievsky, B. *and* **Maenchen-Helfen**, O.
Karl Marx rev. by D. Torr

Nicolson, Harold
Edwardian Oxford.
FB, i 1 4F36, 9—10 c
On disliking school.
M, i 1 Je33, 43—45 c
Helen's tower rev. by E. Waugh

Niles, Blair
Mad house
rev. by J. D. M.

Nin, Anais
Fragment from a diary.
SV, 1 Su38, 26—27 p
Mischa's confession to the analyst.
SV, 4A Sp39, 31—33 p
Rag-time.
SV, 2 Au38, 2—4 p

Nisbet, Norah
Lovers in tapestry.
CV, 1 Su34, 24 v

Nitti, Giuseppe
Order in revolution.
tr. by G. Pendle.
TC, iii 14 A32, 15—16 c

Nixon, Barbara
Clifford Odets: playwright
[*Three plays*].
LR, ii 8 My36, 406—7 r
Has Ibsen dated?
LR, ii 7 A36, 326—29 c
Plays about trade unionism.
LR, i 2 N34, 42—44 c
Plays of the month
[*Return to yesterday*,
by C. Vildrac;

Bees on the boat deck,
by J. B. Priestley;
Ah, wilderness,
by E. O'Neill].
LR, ii 9 Je36, 479 r
Realist films
[*Housing problem; Night mail*].
LR, ii 7 A36, 348 r
Theatre [*The ascent of F6*,
by W. H. Auden and C. Isherwood].
LR, iii 4 My37, 254 r
Theatre now.
LR, ii 3 D35, 105—7 c
Toller's drama and ideas
[*Seven plays*].
LR, ii 3 D35, 136—38 r
Unity Theatre Group
[*Private Hicks*, by A. Maltz;
Waiting for Lefty,
by C. Odets].
LR, ii 8 My36, 415 r

Nizan, Paul
About Theseus,
tr. by J. Rodker.
NW, 5 Sp38, 71—76 p
Paris Congress speech.
LR, i 11 Ag35, 473 c
The trojan horse
rev. by J. Lindsay

Noble, George
I met a youth.
JG, 63 W37, [21] v
Silhouettes.
JG, 65 Su38, [26] v

Nock, Albert Jay
A journal of these days
rev. by R. Fox

Noel, Conrad
Life of Jesus
rev. by H. Holorenshaw

Norbury, K.
A start in life.
LR, ii 2 M36, 269—70 p

Norden, Charles
Obituary notice.
ND, 11 9S37, 8, 10—12 p

Norman, Clarence Henry
The neutrality of God
rev. by A. D. Hawkins

Norman, John
The relation of the sexual ethic to
the economic system.
LS, i 1 F34, 23—32 c

North, Gordon Allen
One for sorrow.
PP, 4 Oc38, 15 v
Yahhoo!
PP, 13/14 Jy—Ag39, 11 v

North, Sterling
Night outlasts the whippoorwill
rev. by A. Calder-Marshall

Northcote, M. A.
A toast.
DD, viii 29 Su31, 56 v

Northe, James Neill
Formula left for youth.
JG, 64 Sp38, [32] v
When time lies dead.
JG, 64 Sp38, [8—9] v

Norton, Arthur
Food — for thought.
SM 2 S31, 39—42 p
Nancy. SM, 3 1932, 93 v

Norton, Eleanour
Twilight piece.
DD, xi 48 N—D34, 97 v

Nott, Kathleen
Poem.
NO, i 3 F34, 305—6 v

Nottingham, Muriel
'And cease to be'.
JG, 69 Su39, [23] v
The Banffshire coast.
JG, 39 W36, [16] v
The blarney stone.
JG, 64 Sp38, [10] v
From the valley.
JG, 66 Au38, [12] v

Nougé, Paul
Final advice.
LB, 1 A38, 5—6 p
see also Magritte, René

Nowell-Smith, Simon
Ballade.
F, 1 F30, 54 v

Noxon, G. F.
Conflict in the Russian cinema.
EX, 6 Oc30, 43—47 c
Francis Bruguière.
EX, 5 F30, 47—49 c
From Fall conversation.
EX, 5 F30, 2—3 p
see also Jennings, Humphrey

Noyes, Alfred
Ad astra.

DD, vii 27 N—D30, 420 v
Alice Meynell.
CA, 1 Ag30, 5—11 c
Poetry, old and new.
CA, 2 S30, 6—13 c

Nukarpiartekak,
tr. by A. L. Lloyd.
CPP, 3 Jy36, 62—63 p

Nunn, Judith
Two poems.
PP, 6 D38, 16—17 v

Nuptials.
SM, 4 1933, 7—15 p

Nussbaum, Hilary
Review
[*The intelligent man's guide through
world chaos,*
by G. D. H. Cole;
Economic tracts for the times,
by G. D. H. Cole].
TC, iv 20 Oc32, 23—25 r
Review
[*The ABC of technocracy,*
by F. Arkwright].
TC, v 25 M33, 50—52 r
Social credit examined.
TC, iii 17 Jy32, 23—24 c

Nyabongo, Akiri K.
Africa answers back
rev. by N. Cunard

O

O., G. E.
Year of jubilee.
LR, i 8 My35, 306 v

O., J.
Notes on Kafka.
Y, i 1 M39, 43—47 c

Obey, Andre
Noah rev. by G. S. Sayer

O'Brien, Desmond
There was nothing else to do.
P, 1 1938, 194—241 p

O'Brien, Edward Joseph Harrington
Review
[*The little wife and other stories,*
by W. March; *Captain Patch,*
by T. F. Powys].
NS, ii 3 Je35, 238—39 r

Review [*What the sweet hell?*
by P. Chamberlain].
NS, ii 4 Ag35, 319 r
Review
[*The Marchesa and other stories,*
by K. Swinstead-Smith;
Mirages,
by R. B. Cunningham-Grahame].
NS, ii 8 A36, 640 r
The best short stories of 1935
rev. by G. West
The best short stories of 1937
rev. by D. Gillespie

O'Brien, Flann *pseud.*
At swim two-birds
rev. by N. Heseltine

O'Brien, Ruth
An accident.
NS, i 1 F34, 22—23 p

O'Callaghan, Dennis S.
Politics: Oxford and Cambridge.
FB, i 1 4F36, 14—15 c
The union: Oxford.
FB, i 1 4F36, 16 c

O'Callaghan, Maeve
Where some people live.
BB, vii 2 M30, 60—63 p

O'Casey, Sean
Greetings on May day.
LR, iii 16 My38, 961 c

O'Connor, Armel
A poet's ambition.
CA, 1 Ag30, 22—24 c

O'Connor, Frank
The wild geese.
NA, i 1 Au39, 38—50 p
Bones of contention
rev. by L. A. Pavey

O'Connor, Philip
'Blue bugs in liquid silk'.
NV, 25 My37, 12 v
Children.
PL, i 1 F39, [28—29] v
Fag-end.
T, 8 J38, [11] v
Man addresses milkbottle.
NV, 29 M38, 10—11 v
Personalities, and a deduction from
their conflict.
SV, 4 Su39, 16—17 p
Poem.
NV, 28 J38, 5 v
Poem.
SV, 3 W38, 41 v
Poem,
T, 14 D38, 123 v

Poem.
W, 11 W39, 300 v
Poems.
NV, 24 F37, 11—15 v
The raspberry in the pudding.
T, 9 M38, 18 v
Review [*The black book*,
by L. Durrell].
SV, 3 W38, 55—56 r
Review [*The disappearing castle*,
by C. Madge].
T, 4 Je37, [22—23] r
Slays for love.
W, 5 Su38, 175—77 v
Society notes.
T, 15/16 F39, 151—54 v
Three peoms.
T, 5 S37, [10—11] v
Told to shun monkey dances;
Democratic chants.
SV, 7 C39, 12—15 v
Useful letter.
T, 11 Jy38, 67—68 v

O'Connor, Violet
Singer of a noble poem
[A. A. Proctor].
CA, 1 Ag30, 30—32 c

Oddy, G. S.
Divina commedia.
JG, 42 Au37, [26] v
A return.
JG, 64 Sp38, [16] v

Odets, Clifford
Three plays
rev. by H. Howarth; B. Nixon
Waiting for Lefty
rev. by G. Buchanan; B. Nixon

O'Donnell, Peadar
The Irish struggle today.
LR, ii 7 A36, 296—300 c
Salud rev. by L. H. Daiken

O'Duffy, Eimar Ultan
The leisure state.
MS, iii 2 Ag32, 155—62 c
Machinery: captor or liberator.
MS, ii 3 Oc31, 222—27 c
The vitalist implications of the new
economics.
MS, ii 4 J32, 325—32 c

O'Faolain, Sean
Ossian — the sow's ear of Celtic
literature.
MS, vi 1 A35, 44—51 c
A purse of coppers
rev. by D. Gillespie
The silver branch
rev. by NV, 29 M38, 24

O'Flaherty, Liam
A cure for unemployment
rev. by A. D. Hawkins
Famine rev. by J. Lindsay
Short stories
rev. by D. Gillespie

Ogden, Charles Kay
Basic English.
DV, 3 My32, 79—82 c

Ognev, N, *pseud.*
Sour grapes — and sweet.
NW, 1 Sp36, 38—45 p

Oke, Richard
Other Mexicos.
LS, i 1 F34, 5—12 p
India's coral strand
rev. by A.D.W.

An Old Blue *pseud.*
Dead or dying.
FB, ii 4 25J37, 12 c

Old man.
LR, i 9 Je35, 376—77 p

Oldag, John
Capricorn.
P, 2 1938, 180 i

Olden, Ika
'A stench in the nostrils of the world'
[*The yellow spot*].
LR, ii 8 My36, 411 r

Oldershaw, Peter
The moon.
DD, vii 26 S—Oc30, 412, 414 v
To a child.
DD, viii 30 Au31, 100 v

Olson, Lawrence
Colonel Putnam.
TO, ii 8 N39, 9 v
Walkers.
TO, ii 7 Ag39, 18 v

Olver, Brian
The divine keyhole.
C, ii 32 1Ag36, 32 p
Divine serie.·
C, ii 30 18Jy36, 16 v
Elder sister.
C, ii 45 31Oc36, 144 p
In the hour glass darkly.
C, ii 39 19S36, 91—92 v
Myth.
C, i 21 25A36, 165—66 p
Reveille.
C, ii 36 29Ag36, 66 v

Olyesha, Yuri
Liompa, tr. by A. Wolfe.
NW, 5 Sp38, 117—20 p
Love, tr. by A. Wolfe.
NW, 3 Sp37, 113—21 p

O'M., M. G.
Silence.
LS, i 1 F34, 22 v
Translations from Sappho.
LS, ii 1 My35, 12 v

O'Malley, Ernie
On another man's wounds
rev. by C. Donnelly

O'Neill, Brian
Dublin strike episode.
LR, i 9 Je35, 339—40 p

O'Neill, Eugene Gladstone
Ah, wilderness
rev. by B. Nixon

Ongley, Philip
Editorial.
PP, 9 M39, 2—4 c
The future development of the Group;
Appeal to all readers.
PP, 1 Jy38, 10, 12 c

Oppé, Armide
Anacreon Carmen XX.
F, 6 Je31, 199 v
Folly.
F, 6 Je31, 170 v

Oppen, George
Discrete series
rev. by G. Grigson

Orage, Alfred Richard
Review
[*First hymn to Lenin and other poems*.
by H. MacDiarmid].
MS, ii 4 J32, 341—43 r
Political and economic writings
rev. by A. Goldschmidt

Oras, Ants
A glimpse of the Scottish literary
renaissance.
MS, v 3 Oc34, 153—56 c

O'Reilly, Montagu
The influence of harps and laundry
on railway commitments.
SV, 3 W38, 33—37 p

Ormiston, Margaret *pseud.*
Dahlias.
DD, viii 28 J—F31, 8 v
Distance,
JG, 68 Sp39, [16] v

Dog day.
NO, i 3 F34, 334—38 p

Owen, Wilfrid
Dulce et decorum est; Apologia pro
poemate meo.
LR, i 11 Ag35, 437—40 v

Oxford poetry, 1930
rev. by M. C. d'Arcy

Oxford poetry, 1931
rev. by E. Blunden

Ozenfant, Amadée
Foundations of modern art
rev. by H. G. Porteus

P

P., A. B.
To a boy whom his father dreamed dead.
CA, 1 Ag30, 27 v

P., D.
Spanish war [*Boadilla,*
by E. Romilly].
LR, iii 14 M38, 885—86 r

P., J.
Encounter in the Pyrenees.
LR, ii 2 N35, 75—78 p

P.-O., R.
Review
[*Song through space and other poems,*
by T. White].
PR, 7 12Je35, 13 r

Paalen, Alice
Multra.
LB, 10 F39, 20 v

Padwick, Nita H.
Springtime.
DD, x 39 My—Je33, 54 v

Page, Harold
Fighting spirit.
ST, i 3 1933, 20—22 p

Pailthorpe, Grace Winifred
Letter to the Editor.
LB, 17 15Je39, 22—23 c
The scientific aspect of surrealism.
LB, 7 D38, 10—16 c

Pain, Peter Richard
The present position.
NO, i 3 F34, 266—69 c

A reply to R. G.
TU, i 2 1934, 44—48 c

Pain, S.
The unknown.
DD, xi 47 S—Oc34, 77 v

Painter, George
Extracts from a Cambridge journal;
FB, ii 5 5M37, 31—32 p
For R. B.
FB, iii 6 21Oc37, 9 v
Poem.
FB, ii 4 25J37, 22 v
Poem.
FB, ii 4 25J37, 16 v
Poem.
FB, ii 4 25J37, 8 v
Poem.
FB, ii 5 5M37, 43 v
Poem.
FB, iii 6 21Oc37, 7 v
Poem; Sonnet.
FB, i 3 9My36, 58, 60 v

Pakenham, Frank
De Valera.
NO, i 1 My33, 52—67 c

Pakenham, Mary
No sex, please.
ND, 19 4N37, 12, 14 c

Pakington, Mary
About 'Wuthering heights'.
R, i 1 N33, 14 c

Palliser, Farquhar
Love; Pity; Music.
DD, viii 30 Au31, 115 v
Poem.
DD, ix 36 N—D32, 103 v

Palmer, Aileen
Thaelmann battalion.
PP, 12 Je39, 12 v

Palmer, Herbert Edward
Letter for publication — if you dare.
NV, i 2 My39, 62 p
Maps, plans, blueprints and reform.
TC, i 2 A31, 17—19 c
The armed muse
rev. by R. H. Goodman
Post-Victorian poetry
rev. by R. Fuller; G. Grigson

Palmer, J. Wood
The waterfall.
P, 6 1939, 46—61 p

Pangloss, Dr. *pseud.*
Checking the mate.
LR, ii 16 J37, 867—69 c

Pape, Alfred Garbutt
The New Political Fellowship.
MS, ii 1 A31, 66—70 c

Papineau, Roderic
Chicago day.
C, iii 55 9J37, 13—14 p
Dismember, dismember.
C, ii 52 19D36, 202 v
Films of the month.
LT, i 10 D36, 10—13 c
Films of the quarter
LT, i 8 Oc36, 9—10 c
Mr T. S. Eliot, in adolescence, prays.
LT, i 11 J37, 16 v

Pares, Bernard
Moscow admits a critic
rev. by G. Graham

Paris, John
Love, o love!
PR, 1 1F35, 8 v
Review [*The witch,*
by J. Masefield].
PR, 2 12F35, 9 dr

Park, Bertram *and* **Gregory,** Yvonne
Eve in the sunlight
rev. by G. Greene

Parker, Agnes Miller
Fish; Barbary sheep.
MS, v 1/2 Je34, 36, 82 i

Parker, Frank
A Crimean holiday.
TU, 1 1933, 49—51 p

Parker, Philip
A new lead for democratic socialism
in France.
NO, ii 3 N35, 272—75 c

Parker, Ralph
Blackpool belle.
ND, 14 30S37, 22 p
The sand artist.
V, 6 Je30, 294—98 p
see also Arnoux, Alexandre

Parker, Richard
Moon on the orchard.
NS, ii 4 Ag35, 308—11 p
Potato Jones; Let the landlord fret.
PP, 8 F39, 11, 17 v

Parkinson, Lucy
A Christmas carol.
JG, 31 W34, [22] v
Christmas Eve in Washburndale.
JG, 35 W35, [17] v
Cowslips.
JG, 17 Su31, [10—11] v

Parkinson, Lucy (cont.)
Fragments.
JG, 26 Au33, [25—26] v
Law hill, 1936.
JG, 40 Sp37, [22] v
Nicodemus.
JG, 70 Au39, [19] v
Once upon a time.
JG, 16 Sp31, [11] v

Parks, Mercedes
Introduction to Keyserling
rev. by G. Pendle

Parraton, Walter
Ethnology.
DD, xi 44 M—A34, 20 v

Parry, R. Williams-
see Williams-Parry, R.

Parsons, Geoffrey
Allen Tate [*Selected poems*].
T, 8 J38, [23—24] r
Antagonists.
NW, ns2 Sp39, 180 v
Europe a wood.
T, 9 M38, 11 v
The inheritor.
T, 11 Jy38, 64 v
Let her stay — let them marry.
PP, 7 J39, 17—18 v
Love on the dole.
PP, 9 M39, 12—13 v
Pretty pidgy.
NW, ns3 C39, 117—19 p
Suburban cemetery; Crookbarrow.
T, 3 A37, [8—9] v

Parsons, Ian *ed.*
The progress of poetry
rev. by G. Grigson

Partridge, Eric Honeywood
The war comes into its own: a note on
some war books.
WW, i 1 J30, 72—104 c
The war continues.
WW, i 2 A30, 62—85 c

Partridge, John
The last straw.
NS, ii 6 D36, 445—54 p

Pascal, Roy
Erasmus and peace.
LR, ii 11 Ag36, 544—48 c

Pascale, Geraldine
Brother and sister.
NS, ii 7 F36, 507—16 p

Pascin, Jules
Brush drawing.
J, 1 J36, 7 i

Pasternak, Boris
Four poems, tr. by G. Reavey.
EX, 6 Oc30, 18—20 v
The high malady, tr. by R. Young.
SV, 4A Sp39, 34—39 v
1905, tr. by A. Brown.
NW, 1 Sp36, 159—70 v

Patchen, Kenneth
The fox.
VS, i 3 D38—F39, 22 v

Pater, Walter
Leonardo da Vinci.
LQ, ii 1 My37, 20—32 c

Patmore, Derek
The poetry of Coventry Patmore.
CA, 9 1931, 264—72 c

Paul, John
Sketch.
FB, iii 7 25N37, 31 i

Paul, Leslie Allen
Pears.
NS, ii 5 Oc35, 386—93 p

Paul, Louis
Hallelujah I'm a bum
rev. by M. Benney

Pavey, L. A.
Artists.
SM, 5 1934, 109—11 p
Carbon copy.
NS, i 2 A34, 115—23 p
The fete.
NS, ii 3 Je35, 161—67 p
Film over the eyes.
P, 1 1938, 85—105 p
Parkinson.
SM, 2 S31, 25—38 p
Review
[*Forsytes, Pendyces and others,*
by J. Galsworthy;
The proceedings of the society,
by K. M. Willans; *The room opposite,*
by F. M. Mayor; *Dip Lizzie dip,*
by J. Blumenfeld;
Half-way east, by D. Footman].
NS, ii 4 Ag35, 316—17 r
Review [*Polly Oliver,*
by A. E. Coppard].
NS, ii 5 Oc35, 399—400 r
Review [*God likes them plain,*
by E. Linklater; *Fate cries out,*
C. Dane].
NS, ii 7 F36, 558—59 r
Review [*Bones of contention,*

by F. O'Connor].
NS, ii 8 A36, 638 r
Review [*The beginning,*
by M. Lagden].
NS, ii 6 D36, 481—82 r
Moving pageant
rev. by H. Miles

Pavlenko, Petr Andreevich
Red planes fly east
rev. by A. West
Peace on earth [play]
rev. by A. W. F.

Peacock, C. H.
Poems
rev. by G. Grigson; J. Symons

Peacock, Herbert Leonard
Ballad of the fen.
PP, 10 A39, 12—13 v
In memoriam.
PP, 11 My39, 10—11 v
Ship for Spain.
PP, 6 D38, 5—6 v
To Sir John Anderson from a friend.
PP, 8 F39, 18 v

Peacock, Marion
Experience.
PQ, i 1 Sp39, 9 v
Winter's silhouette.
DD, viii 29 Su31, 60 v

Peers, Edgar Alison
Catalonia infelix
rev. by J. Hawthorne

Pell, Mike
Kong Kong road.
LR, i 7 A35, 275 v

Pember, William Leonard
Art, ideology and Lionell Britton.
TC, ii 10 D31, 25—27 c
Credo.
TC, i 6 Ag31, 11—13 c

Pemberton, *Sir* Max
That good Samaritan.
M, i 1 Je33, 50—52 p

Pemberton-Pigott, D.
Review
[*Six characters in search of an author,*
by L. Pirandello].
LD, i 4 Je37, 25—26 dr

Pendle, George
About it and about.
TC, iii 17 Jy32, 25—26 c
Apropos of *Brave new world.*
TC, ii 13 M32, 27—28 c
Argentine perspectives.

TC, i 6 Ag31, 5—7 c
The artist in isolation.
TC, iii 15 My32, 3—5 c
The daughter-mothers: being an
introduction to the method of José
Ortega y Gasset.
TC, i 1 M31, 7—9 c
Dons play bowls,
TC, v 30 Ag33, 358—61 c
A future for Oxford.
TC, v 27 My33, 170—71 c
Genteel-ity.
TC, iii 18 Ag32, 22—23 c
God bless Lord Winterton!
TC, ii 13 M32, 5—7 c
God: or the unending muddle in
Miguel de Unamuno.
TC, i 2 A31, 11—13 c
Greece without monuments.
TC, iv 21 N32, 11—14 c
I am I and my world.
TC, v 26 A33, 98—101 c
The in-break of the south.
TC, iv 24 F33, 4—7 c
Jolly old world.
TC, iii 14 A32, 10—12 c
Literature and revolution.
TC, iii 16 Je32, 5—8 c
M. Maurois and Emile Herzog.
TC, iii 17 Jy32, 4—6 c
Ortega y Gasset's contribution to the
Spanish republic.
TC, i 5 Jy31, 5—7 c
Perspectives.
TC, v 25 M33, 14—18 p
Ramon Gomez de la Serra.
TC, ii 7 S31, 15—18 p
Reinterpreting André Gide.
TC, ii 11 J32, 17—20 c
Review [Mirabeau o el politico,
by J. Ortega y Gasset].
TC, ii 7 S31, 22 r
Review
[Inquiètude et reconstruction,
by B. Crémieux].
TC, ii 9 N31, 27—29 r
Review
[Regards sur le monde actuel,
by P. Valéry].
TC, ii 12 F32, 27—28 r
Review [How to read,
by E. Pound;
Traps for unbelievers,
by M. Butts].
TC, iii 15 My32, 29—30 r
Review [A private universe,
by A. Maurois].
TC, iii 16 Je32, 28—29 r
Review [Letter to a young poet,
by V. Woolf].
TC, iii 18 Ag32, 27 r
Review [People in the south,
by A. Pryce-Jones].
TC, iv 19 S32, 24—25 r

Review
[The adventures of the black girl in
her search for God,
by G. B. Shaw; Argentine tango,
by P. Guedalla].
TC, iv 23 J33, 28—29 r
Review
[Les chemins de la mort,
by M. Galvez;
Impressions of South America,
by A. Siegfried].
TC, v 28 Je33, 249—51 r
Review
[Introduction to Keyserling,
by G. Parks].
TC, vi 35 Je34, 303—4 r
Revolution for realists.
TC, vi 34 M34, 205—8 c
Samuel Insull.
TC, iv 22 D32, 10—12 c
Spain goes pink.
TC, ii 12 F32, 9—14 c
Strange poetry
[Pigeon Irish, by F. Stuart].
TC, iii 14 A32, 30—31 r
Tango.
DV, 2 A32, 62—63 p
Too Shaw to be true.
TC, iv 19 S32, 12—15 c
Much sky rev. by A. D. Hawkins
see also Nitti, G.; Ortega y Gasset, J.

Pennywhistle, Peter
Any old iron.
PP, 11 My39, 5 v

Penrose, Roland Algernon
Notes on the Ratton exhibition of North
Western American art exhibition, Paris.
AX, 4 N35, 18—19 c
Review
[A short survey of surrealism,
by D. Gascoyne].
AX, 5 Sp36, 28—30 r
The road is wider than long.
LB, 7 D38, 16—22; LB, 8/9 J39,
50—[56] p, i
The transplanted mirror.
LB, 2 My38, 24 c
see also Eluard, P.; Picasso, P.;
Scutenaire, J.

Penrose, Valentine
To a woman to a path.
CPP, 7 N36, 131—33 v

Penton, Charles Antony
Some aspects of the colour problem.
TC, i 3 My31, 11—13 c

Peret, Benjamin
Four poems, tr. by D. Gascoyne,
R. Todd, and H. Jennings.
CPP, 2 Je36, 23—25 v

Making feet and hands.
CPP, 3 Jy36, 56—57 v
Portrait of Max Ernst,
tr. by G. Reavey.
LB, 7 D38, 6, 8 v
The staircase with a hundred steps,
tr. by D. Gascoyne.
CPP, 4/5 Ag36, 90—91 v

Perez de Ayala, Ramon
Incipit historia.
DV, 1 M32, 7—10 c

Perkoff, H. L.
Advice before a journey.
T, 17 A39, 16 v
Review [Karl Marx,
by E. H. Carr].
VP, i 2 Jy—S34, 54—55 r

Perlès, Alfred
The death of Messrs. S & R.
SV, 2 Au38, 29—30 p
The gay source.
SV, 4A Sp39, 40—42 p
Le quatuor en Ré majeur
rev. by A. White

Perse, St-John pseud.
see St.-John Perse [i.e. Aléxis Saint-
Leger Leger]

Peter the Painter pseud.
The miner.
LR, i 7 A35, 245 i

Petere, J. H. see Herrera Petere, J.

Peters, E. Curt
Asylum.
JG, 69 Su39, [26, 29] v
Time and substance.
JG, 71 W39, [26] v
To a very gallant friend.
JG, 70 Au39, [15] v
Transition.
JG, 68 Sp39, [13] v

Peters, Paul and **Sklar**, George
Stevedore rev. by A.W.E.

Petersen, Jan
Overtime on aero engines.
LR, ii 2 N35, 66—68 p
The skier's return,
tr. by C. Ashleigh.
NW, ns3 C39, 20—28 p
Travellers, tr. by J. Cleugh.
NW, 5 Sp38, 43—50 p
Our street
rev. by A. Henderson

Petite anthologie poètique de surréalisme
rev. by C. Madge

Petre, Maud Dominica Mary
Ave maris stella.
CA, 12 1932, 379 v
Translation of breviary hymns.
CA, 8 1931, 247; CA, 11 1932, 351 v

Pettet, Ernest Charles
Architect of peace.
PP, 9 M39, 9—10 v
In church.
LR, iii 4 My37, 226 v
Now Saturday night.
LR, iii 9 Oc37, 524—28 p
To Ernest Brown.
PP, 11 My39, 19 v

Petts, R. John
Dance of life.
WR, ii 3 Oc39, 143 i
see also Chamberlain, Brenda

Phare, Elsie Elizabeth
Extract from an essay on the devotional
poetry of T. S. Eliot.
EX, 6 Oc30, 27—32 c
Open door; Life, by P. Eluard.
EX, 5 F30, 13 v

Phelan, Jim
Among those present.
NW, ns2 Sp39, 163—69 p
Pupils of empire.
LR, iii 11 D37, 647—50 p
The slip.
NW, ns3 C39, 266—71 p
Lifer rev. by A. West

Philipps, W.
An ambulance man in Spain.
NW, ns1 Au38, 28—33 p

Phillips, Ewan
Nijinsky's drawings.
LR, iii 11 D37, 667 c

Phillips, M. A.
A basis for a new economic system.
TC, ii 7 S31, 7—10 c

Phillpotts, Eden
Death and sleep; Secret wealth.
DD, vii 26 S—Oc30, 367 v
Dreaming; Waking; The pixies plot.
DD, viii 28 J—F31, 3—4 v
Nicky Pool.
DD, viii 29 Su31, 52 v
Song to silver eyes; Evolution.
DD, vii 27 N—D30, 421 v
The Spanish main.
DD xi 45 My—Je34, 39 v

Picasso, Pablo
Poème, tr. by R. Penrose.
LB, 15/16 15My39, 1—3 p

Six poems, tr. by G. Reavey.
CPP, 4/5 Ag36, 75—79 v

Pickles, Arnold
Jonas Murgatroyd.
HR, 6 1933, 32—33 p
Round and about with Jonas
Murgatroyd.
HR, 7 1934, 46—49 p

Pictorial art [in China].
LR, iii 12 J38, 740—42 c

Pigott, D. Pemberton
see Pemberton-Pigott, D.

Pijet, G.
Justice in Vienna.
ST, i 3 1933, 6—9 p

Pilcher, Velona
Another November.
I, i 1 15Je31, 25—28 p
A play of light.
I, i 2/3 15S31, 91—95; I, i 4 15D31,
126—28 p
Suggia.
I, i 1 15Je31, 6—9 c

Pinchos
Pressers in a knitting factory.
LR, i 8 My35, 299 i

Pine, Edward
Farewell in storm.
TC, vi 35 Je34, 261 v

Pinhorn, Elisabeth
Poem.
NO, i 2 N33, 153 v

Pinto, Vivian de Sola
The poetry of Rochester.
NO, i 3 F34, 339—47 c

Piper, John
Picasso at the Tate.
AX, 1 J35, 27—28 c
Picasso belongs where?
AX, 6 Su36, 30—31 c
Prehistory from the air.
AX, 8 W37, 5—7 c
see also Grigson, Geoffrey

Pirandello, Luigi
The old god, tr. by J. Purves.
MS, iv 1 A33, 58—62 p
Six characters in search of an author
rev. by D. Pemberton-Pigott

Pirosmanishvili, Niko
Niko Pirosmanishvili.
EQ, i 4 F35, 256—58 c, i

Pitcairn, Frank
[*pseud.* Francis Claud Cockburn]
The Sedition Bill and political censorship
VP, i 2 Jy—S34, 39—41 c
Reporter in Spain
rev. by V. Ackland

Pittaway, Thomas
The ark of God.
JG, 64 Sp38, [19] v
Bath abbey.
JG, 42 Au37, [19] v
The Christmas gift.
JG, 67 W38, [10] v
The meeting.
DD, xi 46 Jy—Ag34, 61 v
My ship.
JG, 68 Sp39, [29] v
Sunset in the cathedral.
JG, 66 Au38, [32] v
True alchemists.
JG, 70 Au39, [31] v

Pitter, Ruth
Times's fool.
FB, iii 7 25N37, 27 v
A trophy of arms
rev. by J. Symons

Plato
The lysis,
tr. by K. A. Matthews
rev. by L. MacNeice

Platter, Thomas
Thomas Platter's travels in England
rev. by E. Waugh

Playing ball.
PP, 13/14 Jy—Ag39, 20 v

Plomer, William Charles Franklyn
Actors at Blackfriars.
ND, 10 2S37, 32 c
The eccentric compass.
SV, 2 Au38, 7 v
French Lisette: a ballad of Maida Vale.
NW, ns3 C39, 76—77 v
A letter from the seaside.
NW, 3 Sp37, 104—12 p
Notes on a visit to Ireland.
NW, 1 Sp36, 107—12 p

Plowman, Alan William
Sonnet to J.M.F.
FB, i 2 3M36, 43 v
To E.M.D.
FB, i 1 4F36, 10 v
There let him die.
LD, i 1 J37, 7—8 p

Plowman, Max
The necessity of war-resistance.
TC, v 26 A33, 81—88 c

Where there is no vision.
TC, ii 13 M32, 10—13 c

Plumbe, Herbert J.
In the wind.
JG, 69 Su39, [24—25] v

Plumbe, Wilfred John
Below the rocks.
JG, 65 Su38, [19] v
Moorhens.
JG, 63 W37, [11] v
Solitude.
JG, 66 Au38, [16—17] v
Sun.
JG, 41 Su37, [37] v
The willow-wren.
DD, xi 47 S—Oc34, 83 v
Words are partly meaning.
JG, 69 Su39, [9] p
Youth.
JG, 70 Au39, [17] v

Plunkett, Edward John Moreton Drax-
Lord Dunsany see Dunsany, Edward
John Moreton Drax Plunkett *Lord*

Plunkett, *Count* George Noble
Aspiration.
CA, 10 1931, 303 v
Love's clairvoyance.
CA, 12 1932, 379 v
A personal note on Joseph Mary
Plunkett.
CA, 9 1931, 276—77 c
Thalassa.
CA, 8 1931, 252 v

Plunkett, Joseph Mary
An unpublished poem.
CA, 9 1931, 276 v

Plutynski, Antoni
The German paradox
rev. by G. West

Poetry London [vol.1, no.1]
rev. by J. C. Hall

The poisoned kiss
[by R. Vaughan Williams].
FB, i 3 9My36, 57 dr

Polanovskaya, Fania *tr.*
see Zoschenko, Michael

Pollard, Marjorie
Review [*Man and technics,*
by O. Spengler].
TC, iii 17 Jy32, 26—27 r
Review [*The coloured dome,*
by F. Stuart].
TC, iv 19 S32, 26—27 r

Review [*Try the sky,*
by F. Stuart].
TC, iv 24 F33, 32 r

Pollard, Robert Spence Watson
The thin end of the wedge.
TC, v 29 Jy33, 313—14 c

Pollett, Geoffrey
Dedication.
C, i 10 8F36, 79 v
Ecstasy.
C, ii 30 18Jy36, 14 v
Marx.
C, i 23 9My36, 180 v
Northern November.
C, iii 57 23J37, 30 v
Robin.
C, i 6 11J36, 46 v
Silhouette.
C, ii 41 3Oc36, 111 v
Street musicians.
LT, i 8 Oc36, 13 v
To certain poets.
LT, i 10 D36, 22 v
Waking.
C, ii 36 29Ag36, 66 v

Pollitt, Harry
Building the people's front.
LR, ii 15 D36, 797—803 c

Pollok, N.
Shoes.
JG, 70 Au39, [35] v

Polson, Philippa
Feminists and the woman question.
LR, i 12 S35, 500—2 c
Monstrous regiment
[*Towards sex freedom,*
by I. Clephane;
Seven women against the world,
by M. Goldsmith].
LR, ii 6 M36, 286 r
Review [*New Babylon*].
LR, ii 3 D35, 144 r

Pomerai, Ralph de
Aphrodite rev. by G. Trease

Pool, Brenda A.
Descensus Averno.
RM, 2 D34, 63 v
Editorial.
LS, ii 1 My35, 3—4 c

Pool, Phoebe
Salzburg since Dolfuss.
LS, i 3 N34, 9—14 c

Poole, Leonard
He lies there with unlifted head.

DD, ix 31 J—F32, 6 v
I once aspired.
DD, x 37 J—F33, 11 v
Summer.
DD, x 39 My—Je33, 44 v
Winter begone.
DD, ix 34 Jy—Ag32, 55 v

Popham, Hugh
And old men shall dream dreams.
FB, v 2 My39, 38—39 p

Porter, Alan
The signature of pain
rev. by L. MacNeice

Porter, Katharine Anne
Pale horse, pale rider.
P, 5 1939, 179—240 p

Porter, Neil
Reply to Ronald Gow.
R, i 8 D34, 16 c

Porteus, Hugh Gordon
Aldous Huxley.
TC, i 6 Ag31, 7—10 c
'Art for art's sake': programme notes for
the Arts Group of the Prometheans.
TC, i 5 Jy31, 9—10 c
Art for politicians.
TC, iii 16 Je32, 19—24 c
Auden now [*Look stranger!*
and *The ascent of F6,*
by W. H. Auden and C. Isherwood].
T, 1 J37, [12—16] r
Bombs for Bloomsbury.
TC, ii 11 J32, 4—6 c
Bombs for Bloomsbury, II
[*The apes of god,*
by P. W. Lewis; *The Georgiad,*
by R. Campbell].
TC, ii 12 F32, 14—16 c
Doomsday data
[*The doom of youth,*
by P. W. Lewis].
TC, iii 17 Jy32, 20—22 r
Exhibition of abstract painting at the
Experimental Theatre.
AX, 1 J35, 27 c
Eyes from (Ideogram).
T, 6/7 N37, [10—15] c
Ezra Pound.
TC, iii 14 A32, 7—9 c
A few lines.
AX, 7 Au36, 13—15 c
Herbert Read.
TC, v 25 M33, 25—29 c
Homage to Don Roberto.
TC, iv 23 J33, 6—8 c
Julien Benda.
TC, ii 13 M32, 7—9 c
Letter.
TC, ii 11 J32, 28 c

Porteus, Hugh Gordon (cont.)
The lost race.
T, 17 A39, 5 v
Modern Chinese poetry
[tr. by H. Acton and Ch'en,
Shih-Hsiang].
LT, i 2 A36, 6—8 c
New planets.
AX, 3 Jy35, 22—23 c
Observations of X
[*Several observations,*
by G. Grigson; *Confusions about X,*
by J. Symons].
SV, 4 Su39, 24—31 r
Piper and abstract possibilities.
AX, 4 N35, 15—16 c
Political indifference.
TC, vi 36 S34, 341—46 c
Prayer.
TC, iv 21 N32, 14 v
Public examples.
TC, iv 20 Oc32, 9—10 c
Reading and riding
[*Collected poems,* by L. Riding].
T, 14 D38, 130—33 r
Review [*Son of woman,*
by J. M. Murry].
TC, i 5 Jy31, 24 r
Review [*Hitler,* by P. W. Lewis;
The diabolical principle,
by P. W. Lewis].
TC, i 6 Ag31, 24—25 r
Review
[*Foundations of modern art,*
by A. Ozenfant].
TC, ii 9 N31, 30—31 r
Review
[*The necessity of communism,*
by J. M. Murry].
TC, iii 14 A32, 26 r
Review
[*Bolshevism in perspective,*
by J. de V. Loder].
TC, ii 13 M32, 29—30 r
Review [*Leonardo da Vinci,*
by C. Bax].
TC, iv 19 S32, 26 r
Review [*As a man grows older,*
by I. Svevo].
TC, iv 20 Oc32, 25—26 r
Review
[*Fanfare for tin trumpets,*
by M. Sharp; *Poor Tom,*
by E. Muir].
TC, iv 22 D32, 27—28 r
Review
[*The old gang and the new gang,*
by P. W. Lewis].
TC, v 25 M33, 54—58 r
Review [*Light in August,*
by W. Faulkner].
TC, v 26 A33, 122—24 r
Review [*Reconstruction,*
by R. Swingler].

TC, v 30 Ag33, 377—78 r
Richard Aldington.
TC, v 27 My33, 158—61 r
Stop press.
TC, v 30 Ag33, 362—66 c
Straws in the wind
[*Straw in the hair,*
by D. K. Roberts].
PL, i 2 A39, [27—28] r
T. E. Hulme.
TC, ii 10 D31, 11—14 c
T. S. Eliot.
TC, ii 8 Oc31, 7—11 c
T. S. Eliot, II.
TC, ii 9 N31, 10—13 c
The twittering machine.
TC, vi 34 M34, 223—25 c
Two twentieth century fragments
[*Sweeney Agonistes,* by T. S. Eliot].
TC, iv 19 S32, 15—18 c
Ulterior motives.
AX, 5 Sp36, 20—23 c
W. H. Auden.
TC, iv 24 F33, 14—16 c
Words and pictures
[*Out of the picture,*
by L. MacNeice].
T, 5 S37, [17—19] r
Wyndham Lewis.
TC, ii 7 S31, 4—6 c
Wyndham Lewis rev. by A. D.
Hawkins

Portheim, Paul Cohen-
see Cohen-Portheim, Paul

Posegate, Mabel
Rural graveyard.
PQ, i 2 Su39, 36 v

Post, Mary Brinker
The deer.
NS, i 4 Ag34, 285—89 p

Potocki, *Count* Cedric
Sonnet.
J, 1 J36, 30 v

Potocki de Montalk,
Geoffrey Wadislas Vaile *Count*
Right review *passim*

Potter, Stephen
D. H. Lawrence rev. by S. Spender

Potts, Paul
Beyond the barricades.
PP, 8 F39, 12 v
Michael Gold to Thornton Wilder;
Twentieth century god; Inside.
PL, i 2 A39, [6—7] v
People walking down a street.
PP, 11 My39, 8—10 v

A poet on the theory of revolution;
The making of a poem; Thanks for
strawberries.
SV, 4A Sp39, 13—15 v
Two poems; A poet's testament.
VS, ii 1 Je—Ag39, 18—24 v, p

Pound, Ezra Loomis
Abu Salammamm; Slice of life.
TO, ii 5 J39, 4—5 v
Comment on Auden.
NV, 26/27 N37, 28 c
Communications.
TO, ii 6 A39, 12—13 p
The coward surrealists.
CPP, 7 N36, 136 c
Condensare [quoted from T. E.
Hulme].
TO, i 1 J38, 24 c
'Heaulmiere' from the opera Villon.
TO, i 2 A38, 12—18 m, c
Janequin, Francesco da Milano.
TO, i 1 J38, 18 c
A letter.
CM, i 2 Su33, 92 c
M. Pom-Pom.
TO, i 1 J38, 3 v
Message to Oxford.
PR, 6 31My35, 3 c
Musicians, god help 'em.
TO, i 4 Oc38, 8—9 c
Muzik, as mistaught.
TO, i 3 Jy38, 8—9 c
Religio; Ecclesia.
TO, ii 8 N39, 4—5 c
Statues of gods.
TO, ii 7 Ag39, 14 p
This Hulme business.
TO, i 5 J39, 15 c
VOU club.
TO, i 1 J38, 4 c
ABC of reading
rev. by D. Botterill
Alfred Venison's poems
rev. by A.M.
A draft of XXX cantos
rev. by J. Drummond; G. Grigson
A draft of cantos XXXI—XLI
rev. by A. Hodge
The fifth decad of cantos
rev. by S. Spender
Guide to culture
rev. by D. Thompson
How to read
rev. by G. Pendle; W. M. Stewart
Jefferson and/or Mussolini
rev. by A.M.
Polite essays
rev. by J. Beevers; A. Hodge
Social credit
rev. by J. A. Scott
Ta hiao,
by Confucius
rev. by A. Hodge

Povey, Ronald
Spring wind.
DD, xi 46 Jy—Ag34, 64 v

Powell, Anthony
I was a territorial.
ND, 2 8Jy37, 12—13 p
A reporter in Los Angeles.
ND, 7 12Ag37, 28; ND, 8 19Ag37, 22 p
The worldly book of the week
[*Outrage in Manchukuo*,
by V. Gielgud].
ND, 15 7Oc37, 30—31 r

Powell, Dilys
Descent from Parnassus
rev. by G. Grigson

Powell, Selwyn
Motor racing.
ND, 11 9S37, 31 c
The motor show.
ND, 16 14Oc37, 34 c
On and off the road.
ND, 23 2D37, 28; ND, 14 30S37, 32 c

Power, N.S.
The sentimentalist.
FB, iii 6 21Oc37, 19 v

Power, William
John Davidson: the doom of an exile.
MS, i 2 Su30, 20—23 c
Scotland's greatest men of letters:
Andrew Lang in the perspective of 1931.
MS, i 4 J31, 37—42 c
Should auld acquaintance
rev. by J. Barke

Powys, John Cowper
Answer to questionnaire.
W, 10 Oc39, 280—81 c

Powys, Laurence
Cock-crow; The unbidden silence; Life;
The forbidden song; The thief;
The battlefield.
SM, 1 Je31, 44—47 v
The garden.
WW, i 4 Oc30, 11—12 v
Ghost of Marseilles.
SM, 2 S31, 16—24 v
Poverty.
BB, vii 2 M30, 6 v

Powys, Theodore Francis
Ask and ye shall have.
SM, 5 1934, 112—16 p
The dove and eagle.
SM, 1 Je31, 48—55 p
The gramophone.
SM, 4 1933, 57—62 p
Like paradise.
WW, i 3 Jy30, 6—12 p

The red petticoat.
SM, 2 S31, 11—15 p
Rosie Plum.
WW, i 2 A30, 7—13 p
Soppit's Sabbath.
ND, 10 2S37, 12—14 p
A suet pudding.
SM, 3 1932, 94—99 p
Uncle Dottery.
Y, i 2 My39, 69—76 p
Captain Patch
rev. by E. J. O'Brien

Prassinos, Gisèle
Story, tr. by D. Gascoyne.
CPP, 2 Je36, 38—39 p

Pratt, Wallace
To capitalism.
PP, 10 A39, 14 v

A prefatory note.
NS, i 1 F34, 1—3 c

Preston, John M.
Beacons.
JG, 40 Sp37, [22—23] v
Boughs.
JG, 37 Su36, [11] v
Bridge, an intellectual pastime.
JG, 64 Sp38, [36] v
Thorp cloud.
JG, 36 Sp36, [21] v

Preston, Muriel
Fog.
JG, 40 Sp37, [14] v
Greeting.
JG, 38 Au36, [29] v
Lines.
JG, 42 Au37, [16] v
Spring in the yellow room.
JG, 65 Su38, [16] v
The troubled wood.
JG, 36 Sp36, [14] v

Preston, Richard
End of Cornwall
rev. by S. Blumenfeld

Preston, William Easterbrook
Heaton Royds.
HR, 4 1931, 24 c

Prestwich, Mark Fiennes
A doubt about Mr [Christopher]
Dawson.
CM, ii 1 Su35, 214—20 c
A note on Irving Babbitt.
CM, i 4 Sp34, 144—53 c

Price, Evadne
The angel of Balham.
DD, xi 43 J—F34, 5 v

Price, Marion
Down in Hell; As a child calls.
DD, viii 28 J—F31, 13 v

Price, R. G.
The passionate film agent to his love.
ND, 13 23S37, 31 v

Prichard, John
Bachelors three.
SV, 1 Su38, 37—42 p
The beloved.
W, 10 Oc39, 262—64 p
The green navies.
W, 4 M38, 140 v
King Pantygwydr.
W, 3 Au37, 100—7 p
Love in a window.
Y, i 2 My39, 84—88 p
Poem.
W, 3 Au37, 84 v
Poem.
W, 1 Su37, 9 v
Swansea bay.
W, 6/7 M39, 198—99 v
The visitor.
W, 1 Su37, 23 v

Priday, N. H.
The fifth author.
BB, vii 2 M30, 83—87 p

Priestley, John Boynton
Bradford.
HR, 4 1931, 7—9 c
Writers and war.
LR, i 1 Oc34, 5 p
Bees on the boat deck
rev. by B. Nixon
Eden end rev. by E. Bannister
Time and the Conways
rev. by A. van Gyseghem

Priestley, Winifred
The Bradford Civic Playhouse.
R, i 6 Oc34, 14 c

Prieto, Carlos
Spanish front
rev. by V. Ackland

Prince, Frank Templeton
Cefalù.
NO, i 2 N33, 208—9 v
Four poets [*Collected poems*,
vol.1, by V. Sackville-West;
One way song, by P. W. Lewis;
The end of a war, by H. Read;
The dance of death,
by W. H. Auden].
NO, i 3 F34, 61—66 r
Proposal.
PR, 5 17My35, 6—7 v

Prince, Frank Templeton (cont.)
Review [*The return,*
by J. R. Young].
LS, i 3 N34, 76–77 r
Scene with an echo.
PR, 10 6N35, 5–7 v
Stanze.
LS, i 3 N34, 15 v
Poems
rev. by D. I. Dunnett; G. Grigson

Pringle, Gerald
Abbey Theatre country.
R, i 6 Oc34, 10–11 c

Pringle, K.
Thriftless.
F, 6 Je31, 171 v

Pritchard, Beryl
Review
[*Lectures on political economy,*
vol.1, by K. Wicksell;
Law and justice in the Soviet Union,
by H. J. Laski].
LS, ii 1 My34, 49–50 r

Pritchett, Victor Sawdon
The ape who lost his tail.
NW, ns1 Au38, 233–40 p
Father and the bucket shop.
ND, 13 23S37, 12–15 p
Many are disappointed.
NW, 4 Au37, 93–101 p
The sailor.
NW, ns3 C39, 1–19 p
Sense of humour.
NW, 2 Au36, 16–30 p
Upstairs, downstairs.
ND, 1 1Jy37, 13–15 p

Pritt, Denis Nowell
Free speech: an illusion.
LR, i 6 M35, 195–98 c

Private 19022 *pseud.*
see Manning, Frederic

Probo *pseud.*
The country is behind you, sir!
LR, iii 16 My38, 991 i
Gangster government.
LR, iii 14 M38, 833 i

Procter, John C.
The new tradition [in architecture].
HR, 7 1934, 41–42 c

Prokosch, Frederic
Ballad.
T, 14 D38, 120–21 v
The Baltic shore.
NV, 19 F36, 11 v
The bridge; Song.

SV, 1 Su38, 20–21 v
Comment on Auden.
NV, 26/27 N37, 24 c
The festival.
NV, 25 My37, 5–6 v
Ode.
NV, 29 M38, 2–8 v
Past and present: the business of a poet.
NV, 31/32 Au38, 8–9 c
The piazza.
PR, 16 6My36, 3 v
Poem.
NV, 16 Ag35, 7–8 v
Poem.
NV, 17 Oc35, 2–3 v
Poet to audience.
T, 18 Je39, 32–34 c
Port Said.
NV, 19 F36, 14 v
Three songs.
LD, ii 3 F38, 3–4 v
The assassins
rev. by NV, 22 S36, 16
The carnival
rev. by K. Allott; G. S. Fraser;
G. Grigson

Proletarian literature in the U.S.A.:
an anthology
rev. by A. Calder-Marshall; R. Wright

Promethean Society
A survey.
TC, i 1 M31, 23–24 c

Promethean Society.
Political and Economic Group
Report on financial policy.
TC, ii 10 D31, 5–8 c
Report on politics and economics.
TC, iii 18 Ag32, 7–12 c

Promethean Society. Sexology group
Basis.
TC, ii 11 J32, 31–32 c
Basis.
TC, iv 19 S32, 29–30 c

Protest against the Jubilee.
LR, i 8 My35, 291 c

Proteus *pseud.*
Far Eastern notes.
LR, iii 13 F38, 768–72 c
Palestine pictures.
LR, iii 16 My38, 973–76 p

The proud lamkin.
CPP, 3 Jy36, 57–60 v

Pryce, Marion
The dark room; Hill fairies; A song.
DD, vii 27 N–D30, 427–28 v

Pryce, Myfanwy
When I am old.
DD, vii 27 N–D30, 429 v

Pryce-Jones, Alan
People in the south
rev. by G. Pendle

Prys, John
The excursion.
F, 4 D30, 43–62 p

Prys-Jones, A. G.
Shepherd-poet.
WR, ii 3 Oc39, 141 v

Pudney, John Sleigh
Armistice day; Winter landscape.
TC, vi 32 N33, 100–1 v
Building.
NV, 4 Jy33, 9 v
Chance.
NV, 4 Jy33, 11 v
'Day that I have loved'.
S, 2 A–Jy33, 23 v
First drums heard.
NV, 2 M33, 7–8 v
Generals.
LR, iii 4 My37, 223 v
The heirs.
P, 3 1938, 49–108 p
Lodging.
TC, vi 31 S–Oc33, 36 v
No dreams.
CV, 5 M36, [16] v
Poem.
TC, vi 31 S–Oc33, 15 v
Poem.
J, 2 My36, 15 v
Saturday heroes.
TC, vi 35 Je34, 285 v
The Thames near its source.
NV, 3 My33, 14 v
To lick our small fire; Song.
T, 2 M37, [5–6] v
Two poems.
J, 1 J36, 12 v
And lastly the fireworks
rev. by H. Miles
Spring encounter
rev. by G. Grigson; A. D. Hawkins

Pulman, Clement B.
Quest.
HR, 6 1933, 43 v
Woodland trespass.
HR, 7 1934, 65 v

Purpose [periodical]
rev. by M. Scott

Purves, John *tr.*
see Pirandello, Luigi; Ungaretti,
Giuseppe

Putnam, Phelps
Political lyric.
T, 12/13 Oc38, 93 v

Q

Qerraq
A simpleton's song,
tr. by Isobel W. Hutchison.
JG, 69 Su39, [12—13] v

Queneau, Raymond
Oak and dog, tr. by F. Scarfe.
NV, 30 Su38, 2—3 v

Quentin, Cecil
Orpheus: experimental fragments.
K, i 1 17N39, 6 p

Quiller-Couch, *Sir* Arthur
Studies in literature: third series
rev. by F. H.

Quinn, Kerker
Morality play.
CPP, 3 Jy36, 56 v

Quirk, Charles J.
The mother of Judas.
CA, 10 1931, 308 v

R

R., C.
Music in Scotland.
MS, vi 1 A35, 60—61 c

R., F.
Review [*Seeing Soviet Russia*,
by H. Griffith;
A scientist among the Soviets,
by J. Huxley].
TC, iii 16 Je32, 30 r

R., H.
Rilke and his critics
[*Rainer Maria Rilke*,
ed. by W. Rose and G. C. Houston;
Rilke's apotheosis,
by E. C. Mason].
NV, 30 Su38, 23—25 r

R., R. A.
'Opium of the people'.
ST, i 3 1933, 11 v

Rabinowitch, Joseph
To a mother singing to her child.
CV, 2 D34, 23 v

Rackham, Clara D.
Changing man in Soviet Russia
[*Soviet Russia fights crime*,
by L. von Koerber;
Road to life,
by A. S. Makarenko;
*Changing man: the Soviet education
system*,
by B. King].
LR, ii 15 D36, 852—53 r

Radcliffe, T. A.
The dog in the sky.
WR, ii 3 Oc39, 144—47 p

Radek, Karl
The position of women in the U.S.S.R.
[*Women in Soviet Russia*,
by F. Halle].
LR, ii 3 D35, 131—35 r
We Soviet writers.
EY, 1 S35, 1 c

Rae, George H.
Death and Mr Lovelock.
C, ii 37 5S36, 71—72 p
The return.
C, i 20 18A36, 157, 160 p

Rafferty, John
The command.
MS, ii 4 J32, 299 v
Johnny Twa.
MS, vi 2 Jy35, 131—41 p
Passages towards a portrait.
MS, i 4 J31, 45—49 p
The return to Wittenberg.
MS, iii 2 Ag32, 141—44 v
Salon, Edinburgh, 1934.
MS, vi 1 A35, 35—43 p
The visit.
MS, iv 3 Oc33, 188—91 p

Raine, Kathleen J.
Advice to a gentleman.
NV, i 2 My39, 44—45 v
Attalus.
EX, 6 Oc30, 50 v
The crystall skull.
LB, 12 15M39, 18—19 v
Easter poem.
NV, 30 Su38, 12 v
Fata morgana.
NV, 25 My37, 7—9 v
George Chapman.
NV, 10 Ag34, 17—19 c
1. Lyric. 2. Strophe. 3. Word.
NV, 17 Oc35, 10—11 v
Maternal grief.
NV, 20 A36, 15 v

Poem.
NV, 8 A34, 10 v
The rushes.
NV, 23 C36, 13—14 v
Shortness of memory.
NV, 10 Ag34, 11 v
Temptation.
NV, 24 F37, 16 v
Three poems.
NV, 9 Je34, 4—5 v
Three poems.
NV, 13 F35, 9—10 v
Two poems.
NV, 7 F34, 2—3 v
Waking.
NV, 12 D34, 2—3 v

Rake, Leona
New York book-hunt.
ND, 11 9S37, 21—22 p

Ralphs, Lincoln *ed.*
Young minds for old
rev. by R. Abercrombie

Ramaniah, S. V.
Pamela.
FB, v 2 My39, 35—37 p

Ramsay, David
Review
[*The biological tragedy of women*,
by A. Nemilov].
TC, iii 18 Ag32, 26—27 r

Ramsay, Mary Paton
Contemporary France: Alphonse de
Chateaubriand.
MS, iv 4 J34, 325—33 c

Ramsey, T. Weston
Atlantis.
JG, 67 W38, [25] v
Berlioz, requiem mass.
JG, 68 Sp39, [29] v
Death of intellectuals.
JG, 71 W39, [6] v
Fugue.
JG, 69 Su39, [16] v
'Ne transeat...'
JG, 66 Au38, [6] v
Poet to reader.
JG, 68 Sp39, [11] v
Prelude and fugue in A minor.
JG, 70 Au39, [23] v
To poets.
JG, 68 Sp39, [26] v

Randall, A. E.
Nocturne; On an urgent theme.
PP, 12 Je39, 6, 11 v

Ransom, John Crowe
Prelude to an evening.

Ransom, John Crowe, (cont.)
NV, 10 Ag34, 9—10 v
The world's body
rev. by K. Allott

Ransome, Patrick
The promenaders.
ND, 15 7Oc37, 36 c

Rao, Raja
Kanthapura
rev. by M. R. Anand

Raskova, Marina Mikahilovna
An airwoman over Mayday, tr. by
S. Garry.
NW, ns3 C39, 250—54 p

Raspin, Elsie Harriet
Evening mist.
JG, 13 Su30, [31] v
Magic.
JG, 15 W30, [20] v
Marigolds.
HR, 5 1932, 22 v
The pelicans.
JG, 22 Au32, [5—6] v
Seacoast of Cumberland.
JG, 16 Sp31, [7—8] v
The shrew.
JG, 17 Su31, [5] v

Ratcliffe, Dorothy Una
African tropics.
JG, 32 Sp35, [14] v
All or nowt.
JG, 29 Su34, [23] v
April in Wensleydale; Dale courtin'.
DD, viii 30 Au31, 113—14 v
Autumn tryst.
JG, 14 Au30, [8] v
Bird calls.
JG, 68 Sp39, [9] v
Brough hill fair.
JG, 71 W39, [18—19] v
Builders.
JG, 69 Su39, [7] v
T'calf.
JG, 30 Au34, [9] v
Charity.
HR, 4 1931, 36—38 p
Cranesbills of Wensleydale.
JG, 67 W38, [9] v
T'dancin' star.
JG, 27 W33, [7] v
T'dancin' star;
The moorland daughter-in-law.
HR, 7 1934, 11, 44 v
Defiance.
JG, 13 Su30, [8] v
80° in the shade.
HR, 6 1933, 36 v
The farmer's daughter;
A Yorkshire charm against rainbows.

JG, 70 Au39, [7, 9] v
Finna.
JG, 42 Au37, [7—8] v
From Leslie of Winpenie.
JG, 16 Sp31, [16] v
Granny Mat to her grand-daughter
Matilda.
DD, x 41 S—Oc33, 78 v
Gypsies at Barden Brig.
HR, 4 1931, 10 v
Home-coming.
JG, 25 Su33, [22] v
Home-sickness.
HR, 5 1932, 16 v
Independence day in Greece.
JG, 41 Su37, [17] v
The island wood: inner Hebrides.
JG, 40 Sp37, [13] v
Lament.
JG, 18 Au31, [7] v
The last lover.
JG, 23 W32, [13] v
Let's go once more a-gypsying.
JG, 35 W35, [7—8] v
Lines.
JG, 66 Au38, [8] v
Mad old Mike.
JG, 19 W31, [13—14] v
Mrs Buffey on music.
HR, 7 1934, 50—51 p
The new kettle.
HR, 6 1933, 44—45 p
October moors.
JG, 26 Au33, [8] v
Prayer for caravaners.
JG, 24 Sp33, [20] v
Resurrection.
JG, 37 Su36, [5] v
Review [*Reaching for the stars,*
by N. Waln].
JG, 70 Au39, [36] r
Roads.
JG, 22 Au32, [9] v
Rosemary Land.
JG, 31 W34, [9—10] v
Sea-faring ship.
JG, 63 W37, [12] v
Sea-worthy.
JG, 39 W36, [15] v
Shepherd agnostic.
JG, 34 Au35, [6] v
The ship model.
JG, 38 Au36, [13—15] v
Ships.
JG, 15 W30, [25] v
Song.
JG, 21 Su32, [16] v
Song: Bonnie boat.
DD, vii 26 S—Oc30, 368 v
Thoo!
DD, ix 31 J—F32, 7 v
Tides.
JG, 28 Sp34, [6] v
To a stray cat.

JG, 17 Su31, [20] v
To England.
JG, 65 Su38, [6] v
To a veteran yachtsman.
JG, 33 Su35, [8] v
Wallflowers.
JG, 64 Sp38, [30] v
Warning.
JG, 20 Sp32, [9] v
When John O'Dick comes a'coutin'.
JG, 36 Sp36, [13] v

Rathbone, Eleanor Florence
War can be averted
rev. by M. Kahn

Raverat, Gwendolen
Woodcut.
P, 1 1938, 106 i

Ravilious, Eric
Wood engraving.
F, 2 Je30, 121 i

Rawnsley, Hardwicke Drummond
The two springs.
DD, vii 27 N—D30, 431—32 v

Ray, Man
Dessin pour 'Les mains libres'.
LB, 12 15M39, 16 i
La tour fendue.
LB, 17 15Je39, 5 i
see also Eluard, Paul

Raymond, Ernest
Recognition; At the elevation of the host.
DD, ix 34 Jy—Ag32, 52 v

Read, Herbert Edward
Abstract art: a note for the uninitiated.
AX, 5 Sp36, 3 c
Answers to an enquiry.
NV, 11 Oc34, 10 c
The anonymous king.
HR, 7 1934, 24 v
Answer to Lord Peter's prayer
[*Busman's honeymoon,*
by D. L. Sayers; *Hamlet, revenge!*,
by M. Innes].
ND 2 8Jy37, 25—26 r
An art of pure form.
LB, 14 My39, 6—9 c
Ben Nicholson's recent work.
AX, 2 A35, 15—16 c
Blood wet and dry.
ND, 26 23D37, 26 r
Bombing casualties: Spain.
P, 1 1938, 176 v
The brown book of the Hitler terror.
NV, 6 D33, 2 v
Comment on Auden.
NV, 26/27 N37, 28 c
Croce the deaf

[*The defence of poetry*,
by B. Croce].
NV, 6 D33, 20—22 r
The development of Ben Nicholson.
LB, 11 M39, 9—10 c
Emblem.
PL, i 1 F39, [10] v
The future of fiction.
PR, 5 17My35, 3, 5 c
The G-man and the dames.
ND, 7 12Ag37, 27 r
Herschel Grynsban.
LB, 7 D38, 25 v
In what sense 'living'?
LB, 8/9 J39, 5—7 c
Jean Helion.
AX, 4 N35, 3—4 c
Literature, nationalism and revolution.
MS, iii 3 Oc32, 216—24 c
The long poem.
MS, ii 4 J32, 301—11 c
Magritte.
LB, 1 A38, 2 c
The map of love [by D. Thomas].
SV, 6 Au39, 19—20 r
The marshal.
LR, ii 9 Je36, 424—25 v
Night's affirmation is day's negation.
HR, 4 1931, 22 v
Not so tough.
ND, 13 23S37, 26 r
On hearing a legend played on the viola.
NV, 2 M33, 2—3 v
An open letter to the new Director of the
British Broadcasting Corporation.
NV, 31/32 Au38, 10—11 p
Our terminology.
AX, 1 J35, 6—8 c
Picasso's 'Guernica'.
LB, 6 Oc38, 6 c
Poetry and belief in Gerard Manley
Hopkins.
NV, 1 J33, 11—15 c
A primer of dialectics
[*Dialectics*, by T. A. Jackson].
LR, ii 10 Jy36, 518—20 r
The prophetic book of the week
[*I view the world*, by A. S. McPherson].
ND, 15 7Oc37, 23—34 r
Pursuits and verdicts.
ND, 17 21Oc37, 31—32 r
Surrealism — the dialectic of art.
LR, ii 10 Jy36, ii—iii c
Art now rev. by K. Allott
Collected essays rev. by J. Symons
The end of a war rev. by F. Prince
Essential communism rev. by A.M.
Five on revolutionary art
rev. by D. Garman
In defence of Shelley
rev. by W. H. Auden; J. R. Morley
Poetry and anarchism
rev. by G. Grigson; H. B. Mallalieu;
D. Thompson

Surrealism
rev. by K. Allott; H. Jennings;
A. L. Lloyd; R. Todd
Unit one rev. by C. H. Rowe

Read, Herbert Edward *and* **Davies**,
Hugh Sykes
Surrealism: reply to A. L. Lloyd.
LR, iii 1 F37, 47—48 c

Read, Robert G.
For Morris R. Cohen.
TO, i 4 Oc38, 4—6 v

Reavey, George
Bodas de Sangre.
LB, 4/5 Jy38, 43 v
Charles Howard.
LB, 13 15A39, 13—15 c
The endless chain.
LB, 2 My38, 23 p, v
First essay towards Pasternak.
EX, 6 Oc30, 14—17 c
Gear van Velde.
LB, 2 My38, 16 c
Hic jacet.
LB, 12 15M39, 11—12 v
Hippolytus.
EX, 7 Sp31, 41—42 v
Icarus.
EX, 5 F30, 46 v
The parliament of Faust.
EX, 6 Oc30, 40—41 v
Prolegomenon.
PL, i 1 F39, [10] v
The rape of Europe.
LB, 6 Oc38, 11 v
Review of reviews
[*Seven*, nos. 1—3].
LB, 12 15M39, 21—22 r
Roundabout Ben Nicholson.
LB, 12 15M39, 19 c
Soviet literature, 1917—1932.
TC, iv 21 N32, 1—5 c
Quixotic perquisitions
rev. by M. J. Tambimuttu
see also Babel, I.; Eluard, P.;
Pasternak, B.; Peret, B.; Picasso, P.

Reckitt, Eva C.
Ten years ago.
LR ii 8 My36, 359—61 c

Red Army song [from the film
'China strikes back'].
LR, iii 13 F38, 809—10 v

Red Scotland group
The Red Scotland thesis.
VS, i 1 Je—Ag38, 7—14 p

Redgrave, Michael
Four poems in couplets.
V, 6 Je30, 290—93 v

The shoot.
V, 5 F30, 240—45 p
Sporting club for metaphysicals.
V, 6 Je30, 309 v
Why Lamb was wrong.
R, i 6 Oc34, 12, 16 c

Redmayne, Mary
The old homestead.
DD, vii 26 S—Oc30, 396—97 v

Rees, George Edward
Bluff: an ass's dream.
JG, 69 Su39, [34] v
Compensation.
JG, 29 Su34, [21] v
Din.
JG, 32 Sp35, [16—17] v
The empty punchbowl.
JG, 26 Au33, [8—9] v
Entre nous.
JG, 23 W32, [24] v
Fuimus.
JG, 71 W39, [16] v
Ich dien.
JG, 38 Au36, [27] v
Musk.
JG, 35 W35, [20] v
To a maiden.
JG, 30 Au34, [28—29] v
Old age.
JG, 22 Au32, [16—17] v
The reviewer.
JG, 21 Su32, [13] v
The umptieth letter.
JG, 25 Su33, [20] v

Rees, Morgan Goronwy
Boguslavitz, July 1929.
F, 2 Je30, 123 v
The colliers.
OO, xi 56 N31, 199 v
Degeneration.
F, 1 F30, 45 v
Going to bed.
NO, ii 1 My34, 27—30 p
Mr Eliot and some others
[*Sweeney agonistes*,
by T. S. Eliot; *The orators*,
by W. H. Auden; *Poems*,
by S. H. Spender;
The magnetic mountain,
by C. Day Lewis; *New signatures*,
ed. by M. Roberts; *New country*,
ed. by M. Roberts].
NO, i 2 N33, 243—47 r
Point-to-point.
F, 2 Je30, 112—13 v
Politics on the London stage.
NW, ns2 Sp39, 103—12 c
Review [*The memorial*,
by C. Isherwood].
OO, xii 58 My32, 139—42 r
Two poems for———

Rees, Morgan Goronwy (cont.)
F, 5 F31, 119—20 v
View of Cardiff.
F, 1 F30, 10—11 v
A bridge to divide them
rev. by S. Blumenfeld; E. Evans

Rees, R. J.
Michaelangelo in the Sistine.
CM, ii 1 Su35, 224 v

Rees, Richard
D. H. Lawrence and communism.
TC, v 28 Je33, 209—18 c

Reeves, James [*i.e.* John Morris]
The committal.
EX, 6 Oc30, 42 v
The place; New year notes.
EX, 7 Sp31, 24—26 v
Poems.
EP, 1 Au35, 208—12 v
Poems.
EP, 2 Su36, 108—9 v
Poems.
EP, 3 Sp37, 149—50 v
The romantic habit in English poets.
EP, 1 Au35, 175—200 c
Sirventes.
EX, 5 F30, 41 v
The natural need
rev. by K. Allott; C. B. Spencer
see also Jennings, Humphrey

Reeves, James *and* **Riding,** Laura
Humour and poetry as related themes.
EP, 3 Sp37, 173—90 c

Reeves, John Baptist
What is poetry — the reply of
St. Thomas Aquinas.
CA, 10 1931, 295—303 c

Reeves, Joseph
I am for the People's Front.
LR, ii 16 J37, 860 c

Regains [periodical]
rev. by R. March;
TO, ii 7 Ag39, 24 [also by R. March]

Reid, Janet
Coming event.
LR, iii 6 Jy37, 342—45 p

Reid, John
Bric-a-brac.
ND, 14 30S37, 19; ND, 16 14Oc37, 12 c

Reid, John MacNair
A big fish.
MS, i 1 Sp30, 25—28 p
The tune, Kilmarnock.
MS, ii 1 A31, 14—19 p

Reid, Meta Mayne
Death of policeman.
P, 6 1939, 130—37 p

Renn, Ludwig *pseud.*
Death without battle
rev. by C. Madge

Repard, Theodore *see* Gannes, Harry

Retinger, Josef Hieronim
Royal menus.
ND, 25 16D37, 18, 20 c

Return.
M, i 1 Je33, 25 v

Reynolds, Ernest
Lazelot.
CM, i 1 Sp33, 6 v
Poem.
CM, i 2 Su33, 82 v
Tyranny; Poem; Orion; Pavane for a
drowned bride.
CM, i 4 Sp34, 154—57 v

Reynolds, Reginald Arthur
Social democracy and the empire.
TC, v 30 Ag33, 347—51 c
What price peace?
TC, iv 23 J33, 11—13 c

Reynolds, W. A.
Achievement in the sound film.
TC, ii 13 M32, 18—21 c
Actor material in the sound film.
TC, ii 11 J32, 15—17 c
Impressionism in the sound film.
TC. ii 8 Oc31, 22—26; TC, ii 9 N31,
23—25 c
Review [*Cinema,*
by C. A. Lejeune; *Celluloid,*
by P. Rotha].
TC, ii 10 D31, 29—30 r
Sound and the film;
TC, i 2 A31, 15—17; TC, i 4 Je31,
13—15 c
Towards the starless cinema.
TC, i 6 Ag31, 16—18 c

Rhind, John Gray
Immanuel.
PQ, i 2 Su39, 37 v

Rhodes, Henry Taylor Fowkes
The criminals we deserve
rev. by M. Richardson

Rhodes, Margaret Elizabeth
Alloy.
LD, ii 3 F38, 18 v
Pause at the well.
B, 1 Su38, 13 v

Rhys, Ernest
Aubade.
DD, x 41 S—Oc33, 79 v
Black pilgrimage.
WR, ii 2 S39, 91—97 p
Broom Hall.
DD, x 42 N—D33, 92—93 v
The house by the cree.
DD, x 37 J—F33, 2—3 c
Transfiguration.
DD, xi 47 S—Oc34, 73 v
Song of the sun
rev. by K. Etheridge

Rhys, Keidrych
Air pageant.
RR, 2 F37, [13] v
Barddoniaeth; Interlude.
T, 14 D38, 126—27 v
Cartoon done in Something will be
done week; Socialites.
W, 1 Su37, 25—27 v
Celtic view.
T, 6/7 N37, [40—41] c
Death-dance; The van pool.
W, 10 Oc39, 270—71 v
Ephemerae for Bruska.
W, 6/7 M39, 201 v
The fire sermon; or democracy burned.
W, 2 Ag37, 69 v
Homage to a split man.
PL, i 1 F39, [21] v
Laugharne pastoral.
W, 10 Oc39, 274—75 v
Letter from Wales.
T, 18 Je39, 58—61 c
Letter to Lord Beaverbrook.
SV, 7 C39, 27 v
Notes for a new editor.
W, 8/9 Ag39, 246—50 c
Poem for a neighbour; Rip Van
Winkle;
Building job.
T, 3 A37, [6—7] v
St. David's day.
W, 3 Au37, 99—100 p
Spin; Landmark.
T, 8 J38, [9—10] v
Tenement.
C, ii 49 28N36, 182—83 v
Tri englyn.
RR, 6 Jy38, [8] v
Triads during lambing season;
The last supper.
T, 10 My38, 40 v
Tryst.
SV, 1 Su38, 36 v
Understood by Boadicea and
King Arthur.
VS, i 3 D38—F39, 8 v
The van pool: Tichrig.
W, 11 W39, 292—93 v
War-baby.
C, iii 54 2J37, 4—5 v

Ribemont-Dessaignes, Georges
Sliding trombone.
tr. by D. Gascoyne.
NV, 6 D33, 7 v

Ricardo, Henry
The waiting grove.
F, 4 D30, 10—13 p

Rice, Elmer
Other plays
rev. by J. B. Harvey

Richards, A. Edward
Worthy is the lamb.
WR, ii 4 N39, 206—17 p

Richards, Ivor Armstrong
Lawrence as a poet
[*Last poems*] .
NV, 1 J33, 15—17 r

Richards, James Maude
London shows.
AX, 4 N35, 21—24 c

Richards, Susan
Lands End to John O'Groats.
R, i 2 F34, 7 c

Richardson, Dorothy Miller
Ordeal.
WW, i 4 Oc30, 2—10 p

Richardson, Edward
tr. see Fogazzaro, A.;
Valle Inclan, R. M. del

Richardson, Harriet Dale
Winter night.
PQ, i 2 Su39, 38 v

Richardson, Matthew
Overture to a jazz dance.
CA, 3 Oc30, 58 v
Rex Iudaeonom, rex coelestis.
CA, 2 S30, 19—20 v
The sepulchre.
CA, 1 Ag30, 26 v

Richardson, Maurice
The bottle-party belt.
ND, 1 1 Jy37, 22—23 p
Mass-Observation
[*Mass-observation day survey;*
The criminals we deserve,
by H. T. F. Rhodes].
LR, iii 10 N37, 625—26 r

Richardson, Maurice Lane
The bad companions
rev. by R. Wright

Richardson, Norah

An old gown; Kilmington.
DD, vii 27 N—D30, 425—26 v

Richardson, Stanley
Afternoon performance.
CM, i 1 Sp33, 10—11 p
Andulucia; Poem; Francisco;
To F. L. dead, August 1932.
CM, i 1 Sp33, 24—25 v
Et ego in Arcadia; Poem; Sea burial.
CM, i 2 Su33, 56—57 v
Flight of a don.
CM, i 2 Su33, 66—70 p
From Sonnets to a Victorian godmother.
CM, i 4 Sp34, 163—64 v
Ophelia by the dark water; Way into life;
Extract from Songs of my home;
The traveller.
CM, i 3 Au33, 103—5 v
Sick harvest.
CM, i 4 Sp34, 141—43 p
Spanish poetry, 1935.
CM, ii 1 Su35, 129—41 c
Triptych for youth; Poem; Spinsters.
CM, ii 1 Su35, 244—45 v
see also Garcia Lorca, F.; Moreno Villa, J.

Rickword, Edgell
And this time
[*We did not fight,*
ed. by J. Bell] ?
LR, ii 3 D35, 114—18 r
Andre Malraux: the path to humanism.
NW, ns1 Au38, 147—64 c
Art and propaganda
[*Prefaces,* by G. B. Shaw;
Mammonart, by U. Sinclair] .
LR, i 2 N34, 44—45 r
Auden and politics.
NV, 26/27 N37, 21—22 c
Criticism at sea
[*Literature and society,*
by D. Daiches].
LR, iii 14 M38, 889—90 r
Editorial.
LR, ii 16 J37, 857—59; LR, iii 1 F37,
1—2; LR, iii 2 M37, 65—66; LR, iii 3
A37, 129—32; LR, iii 4 My37, 193—95;
LR, iii 5 Je37, 257—59 c
In defence of culture: the second con-
gress of the International Association of
Writers.
LR, iii 7 Ag37, 381—83; LR, iii 8 S37,
446—54 c
John Bunyan [by J. Lindsay] .
LR, iii 12 J38, 758—59 r
Labour and reaction.
LR, ii 11 Ag36, 537—38 c
National liberties.
LR, ii 12 S36, 601—2 c
Nazi and anti-Nazi
[*Days of contempt,*
by A. Malraux; *Once your enemy,*
by H. Hauser] .

LR, ii 12 S36, 659—60 r
Reply to reaction.
LR, ii 13 Oc36, 665—67 c
Review [*Swift,* ed. by J. Hayward] .
LR, i 6 M35, 236—37 r
Review [*Literature,* by P. Henderson] .
LR, ii 1 Oc35, 41—44 r
Scottish problems; Jew baiting.
LR, ii 14 N36, 729—31 c
Social creativity
[*Soviet geography,*
by N. Mikhaylov] .
LR, ii 6 M36, 283 r
Stalin on the national question.
LR, ii 14 N36, 746—49 c
Stephen Spender
[*The destructive element,*
by S. Spender] .
LR, i 11 Ag35, 479—80 r
Straws for the wary: antecedents to
Fascism.
LR, i 1 Oc34, 19—25 c
To the wife of any non-intervention
statesman.
LR, iii 14 M38, 834—36 v
The turn of the tide.
LR, ii 15 D36, 793 c
When writers unite
[*The writer in a changing world*] .
LR, iii 14 M38, 881—84 r
Who is this Noah
[*Noah and the waters,*
by C. Day Lewis] ?
LR, ii 7 A36, 339—40 r
Workers' writing.
LR, ii 9 Je36, 417—18 c

Riding, Laura
Advertising: the justifications of
advertising.
EP, 3 Sp37, 246—55 c
Answers to an enquiry.
NV, 11 Oc34, 3—5 c
Crime.
EP, 2 Su36, 8—56 c
The end of the world, and after.
EP, 3 Sp37, 1—5 c
A film scenario.
EP, 2 Su36, 162—89 p
Homiletic studies: in defence of anger.
EP, 2 Su36, 90—107 c
In apology.
EP, 2 Su36, 1—7 c
Letter.
NV, i 1 J39, 30 p
A letter to England from Majorca.
EP, 3 Sp37, 227—29 p
Marginal themes: the bull-fight.
EP, 2 Su36, 193—207 c
Marginal themes:
the literary intelligence.
EP, 2 Su36, 221—30 p
Picture making.
EP, 1 Au35, 213—19 c

Riding, Laura (cont.)
Poems.
EP, 1 Au35, 220—27 v
Poems.
EP, 2 Su36, 250—52 v
Poems.
EP, 3 Sp37, 140—48 v
Poems and poets.
EP, 1 Au35, 144—56 c
Preliminaries.
EP, 1 Au35, 1—5 c
Collected poems
rev. by G. Grigson; H. G. Porteus
The life of the dead
rev. by L. MacNeice
Progress of stories
rev. by A. Calder-Marshall
see also Hodge, A.; Hutchinson, W.;
Lye, Len; Matthews, T.; Reeves, J.

Riding, Laura *and* **Graves**,
Robert von Ranke
The exercise of English.
EP, 2 Su36, 110—36 c
From a private correspondence on
reality.
EP, 3 Sp37, 107—30 c

Riding, Laura *and* **Vara**, Madeleine
The cult of failure.
EP, 1 Au35, 60—86 c

Riding, Laura *and others*
Germany, by L. Riding, J. Cullen,
M. Vara.
EP, 1 Au35, 93—129 c
Drama, by L. Riding, A. Hodge,
R. Graves.
EP, 3 Sp37, 193—226 c
Politics and poetry, by L. Riding,
R. Graves, H. Kemp, A. Hodge, M. Vara.
EP, 3 Sp37, 6—23 c

Ridler, Anne
Bunhill fields; Death and the lady; Poem.
SV, 4 Su39, 17—19 v

Ridley, Francis A.
Libertatia.
RR, 10 Je39, [9—12]; RR, 11 S39
[7—10]; RR, 12 D39, [4—7] c

Ridley, Joyce *and* **Scarfe**, F. H.
see Ducasse, I. L.

Ridout, Ronald
Night hath her spell.
C, iii 56 16J37, 21—22 p

Rigby, Vera
Along the Walsgrave road.
JG, 70 Au39, [14] v
On ambition.
JG, 67 W38, [18] v

116

Right review [periodical]
rev. by M. J. Tambimuttu

Rilke, Rainer Maria
Autumn day, tr. by P. Selver.
SM, 4 1933, 109 v
Orpheus; Erydice; Hermes,
tr. by S. Spender.
NV, 5 Oc33, 2—4 v
Sonnets to Orpheus
rev. by NV, 23 C36, 16

Rimbaud, Arthur
The drunken boat,
tr. by J. N. Cameron.
NV, 21 Je36, 9—12 v
From The deserts of love,
tr. by D. Gascoyne.
CPP, 9 Sp37, 39—41 p

Rivera, Diego *see* Breton, A.

Rivers, Charles E.
Memories of poets, past and present.
CA, 1 Ag30, 24—26 c

Rivers, Jean
Artichokes and republics.
CV, 1 Su34, 21—23 p
Excerpt.
CV, 2 D34, 17—21 p
October the tenth.
CV, 5 M36, [10] p
Poetry reviews.
CV, 1 Su34, 27—30; CV 2 D34, 31;
CV 4 1935, 21—22 r

Robert, Rudolf
A London swallow.
DD, xi 46 Jy—Ag34, 60 v

Roberts, Alec
Classes.
TU, 1 1933, 41—47 c

Roberts, Buckley *see* Gullan, Roger

Roberts, Carl Eric Bechofer
Little Green Riding Hood, by Cami.
ND, 5 29Jy37, 10, 12 d
Secrets of the Tower, by Cami.
ND, 1 1Jy37, 20 p
The timid husband, by Cami.
ND, 26 23D37, 16 d

Roberts, David
Love at the piano.
NS, ii 8 A36, 625—28 p

Roberts, Denys Kilham
Gallantry on the Downs.
ND, 6 5Ag37, 32 c
Mid-day sunset.
ND, 12 16S37, 32 c

The century's poetry
rev. by M.F.E.
Straw in the hair
rev. by H. G. Porteus

Roberts, Denys Kilham *and* **Lehmann**,
John *eds.*
The year's poetry, 1936
rev. by C. Day Lewis; G. Ewart; R. Todd

Roberts, Denys Kilham *and* **Grigson**,
Geoffrey Edward Harvey *eds.*
The year's poetry, 1937
rev. by NV, 28 J38, 23; J. Symons
The year's poetry, 1938
rev. by NV, i 1 J39, 26: J. Symons

Roberts, G. Humphreys *tr.*
see Kafka, Franz

Roberts, Harry
The economics of morality.
TC, ii 10 D31, 23—24 c

Roberts, Lynette
Enough acid for 'the etching' to bite
[*Jubilee blues*, by R. Davies].
W, 6/7 M39, 207—8 r
Poem.
W, 11 W39, 302 v
Poem without notes.
W, 6/7 M39, 200—1 v
To Keidrych Rhys.
W, 10 Oc39, 279—80 v
Song of praise.
WR, ii 3 Oc39, 141 v

Roberts, Michael [*i.e.* William Edward]
A knack to know a knave.
TC, iv 23 J33, 8—10 c
Night climbing.
ND, 19 4N37, 32 c
Review [*Soviet education*,
R. D. Charques].
TC, iv 22 D32, 23—24 r
Sirius B.
TC, iv 24 F33, 17 v
Temperance festival: Town moor,
Newcastle.
T, 14 D38, 122—23 v
Critique of poetry
rev. by A. D. Hawkins
The Faber book of modern verse
rev. by G. Grigson; G. S. Sayer
The modern mind
rev. by D. J. B. Hawkins
New country
rev. by A. T. Cunninghame; G. Grigson;
A. L. Morton; G. Rees
New signatures
rev. by A. T. Cunninghame; G. Grigson;
TC, iii 14 A32, 29
Poems
rev. by J. B. Harvey

T. E. Hulme
rev. by D. I. Dunnett

Roberts, R. E.
Welsh folk-songs.
WR, ii 2 S39, 98—100 c

Roberts, Rosemary
Evensong.
LS, i 1 F34, 44 v
Lines to H.M.
RM, 1 Je34, 29 v

Roberts, Wilfrid
Films for the countryside.
LR, iii 14 M38, 852—53 c

Robertson, Archibald
About it and about.
TC, iv 21 N32, 23—24 c
Philosophers on holiday
rev. by G. West

Robertson, Eileen Arnot
How 'they' have changed.
ND, 9 26Ag37, 19—20 p

Robertson, Ian
The last twenty years
[*The post-war history of the British working-class,*
by A. Hutt].
LR, iii 8 S37, 491—93 r

Robeson, Paul
National cultures and the Soviet Union.
LR, iii 10 N37, 577—79 c

Robey, John
Dance suite.
FB, i 2 3M36, 34—36 p

Robins, Joan
My life as an actress.
R, i 7 N34, 16 c

Robinson, Joan
Mr Keynes and socialism
[*Mr Keynes and the labour movement,*
by A. L. Rowse].
LR, ii 15 D36, 853 r

Robinson, Lennox
As man of the theatre
[W. B. Yeats].
AW, Su39, 20—21 c

Robinson, Perdita
Memoirs of the life
rev. by V. O. Neuberg

Robinson, T. O.
Fatal accident.
LR, ii 10 Jy36, 515 v

Neurosis; Now threat of action;
Useless to compare history;
The mirror makes two rooms.
T, 17 A39, 6—9 v

Roca, Bartolomé
The bender, tr. by J. Rivers.
CV, 1 Su34, 15—17 p

Rockwood, Flozari
Compensation.
JG, 66 Au38, [8] v

Rocyn-Jones, D.
Public health in Wales: a survey.
WR, i 1 F39, 19—26 c

Rodd, Ralph
The monkey puzzle.
HR, 4 1931, 56—63 p

Roditi, Edouard
Culture, communism and fascism.
TC, iv 22 D32, 2—4 c
Poem.
OO, xi 56 N31, 212 v

Rodker, John *see* Chamson, A.;
Giono, J.; Guilloux, L.; Montech, P.;
Nizan, P.; Sartre, J. P.; Storm over
Canicatti; Triolet, E.

Roebuck, John
An illuminated page.
C, iii 57 23J37, 29 v

Roethke, Theodore
Academic.
NV, i 2 My39, 41 v
The victims.
T, 12/13 Oc38, 105 v

Rogers, Grace E.
Composition.
I, i 4 15D31, 121 i
Exodus.
I, i 4 15D31, 100 c
Juvenilia.
I, i 2/3 15S31, 64—66 p
Phantasmagoria.
I, i 1 15Je31, 18—19 v, i
Poem.
I, i 1 15Je31, 31 v
Wood engraving.
I, i 2/3 15S31, 96 i
Wood engraving.
I, i 4 15D31, 103 i

Roley, A. P.
Boots, boots, boots.
ST, i 3 1933, 28 p
Good-bye Gallipoli.
ST, i 1 F33, 14—16 p

Roll, Erich
A text-book of socialism
[*The theory and practice of socialism,*
by J. Strachey].
LR, ii 16 J37, 910—11 r
Spotlight on Germany
rev. by G. West

Rolland, Romain
Beethoven's politics,
tr, by J. Stewart.
LR, ii 10 Jy36, 497—502 c
Gorky.
TC, iv 21 N32, 9—11 c
I will not rest
rev. by J. Stewart

Romains, Jules
January 22nd,
tr. by J. H. Whyte.
MS, v 1/2 Je34, 54—61 p
Dr Knock rev. by C. E. Eland

Romanov, Panteleiman Sergeyeevich
Diary of a Soviet marriage
rev. by O. Blakeston

Romilly, Esmond Mark David
The case against fascism.
OB, i 1 M—A34, 30—32 c
Gangsters or patriots?
OB, i 2 Je—Jy34, 23—25 c
Modern schools.
OB, i 3 W34, 12—15 c
Boadilla rev. by D.P.

Romilly, Giles Samuel Bertram
Julius Caesar and all that:
English in Public Schools.
OB, i 3 W34, 35—37 c
The gate — obituary.
OB, i 1 M—A34, 25—26 c
Morning glory (sex in Public Schools).
OB, i 2 Je—Jy34, 32—34 c
Peace and the Public Schools.
OB, i 4 Je35, 24—29 c

Ronvers *pseud.*
Breezes.
LR, ii 7 A36, 308—10 p ·

Rood, John
This, my brother
rev. by O. Blakeston

Rook, Alan
For a new friend; Winter willows;
Overture to time.
B, 3 Sp39, 13—15 v
Night in the Chilterns.
K, i 1 17N39, 30—31 v
Songs from a cherry tree
rev. by J. Waller

Rope, Henry Edward George
At home in exile.
CA, 7 Je31, 224 v
England's vocation.
CA, 2 S30, 23 v
King Henry VI.
CA, 4 N30, 83 v
Human respect.
CA, 8 1931, 229 v
Mediaeval England.
CA, 9 1931, 228 v
Suffolk byways.
CA, 3 Oc30, 56—58 v

Rops, Henry Daniel-
see Daniel-Rops, Henry

Roscoe, Theodora
In Bunhill fields.
JG, 68 Sp39, [30] v
The martinet.
JG, 69 Su39, [31—32] v

Rose, William *and* **Houston,**
Gertrude Craig
Rainer Maria Rilke
rev. by H.R.

Rosenberg, Isaac
Collected works
rev. by J. Lipton

Rosenblatt, Benjamin
Sacrifice.
NS, ii 2 A35, 129—42 p

Rosey, Guillaume Jean Hector du
André Breton,
tr. by D. Gascoyne.
CPP, 2 Je36, 30—31 v

Roskolenko, Harry
Reflection on violence.
CV, 1 Su34, 25—26 v
Synopsis.
W, 8/9 Ag39, 245 v
Sequence on disorder
rev. by H. Treece

Ross, Anthony
The yellow-bush.
DD, xi 43 J—F34, 3 v

Ross, Jean
Film stories wanted.
LR, i 11 Ag35, 440 p

Ross, Margaret
Poem.
TU, 1 1933, 4 v

Ross, *Sir* Ronald
Facing truth.
TC, i 5 Jy31, 17—18 v

Ross, Sam
A pair of shoes.
NW, ns3 C39, 202—11 p
You're coming for a walk.
NW, 4 Au37, 172—76 p

Ross, William Lloyd
The Lunenberg blockade.
LR, iii 14 M38, 862—67 p

Rotha, Paul
The cinema today.
TC, i 1 M31, 18—21 c
Celluloid rev. by W. A. Reynolds
Documentary film rev. by J. Irvine

Rothenstein, *Sir* William
Bradford revisited.
HR, 6 1933, 7—8 c, i
Foreword.
HR, 5 1932, [5] c
W. B. Yeats.
AW, Su39, 16—17 c

Rothstein, Andrew F.
see Andrews, R. F. *pseud.*

Roughton, Roger
Animal crackers in your croup.
CPP, 2 Je36, 36 v
Building society blues.
CPP, 9 Sp37, 45 v
Censored!
CPP, 9 Sp37, 2—3 c
Eyewash, do you? a reply to Mr Pound.
CPP, 7 N36, 137—38 c
Fascism murders art.
CPP, 6 Oc36, 106 c
Final night of the bath.
CPP, 8 D36, 166 p
The foot of the stairs.
CPP, 10 Au37, 28—29 v
From The largest imaginary ballroom in
the world.
CPP, 9 Sp37, 33—39 p
The journey.
CPP, 8 D36, 152—54 p
Lady Windermere's fan dance.
CPP, 6 Oc36, 117 v
Many happy returns.
PR, 17 27My36, 8 v
New York.
PR, 17 27My36, 15—16 v
Soluble noughts and crosses.
CPP, 3 Jy36, 55 v
Surrealism and communism.
CPP, 4/5 Ag36, 74—75 c
Watch this space.
CPP, 1 My36, 7 v

Roumain, Jacques
Madrid, tr. by N. Cunard.
LR, iii 15 A38, 909—10 v

Round, Dora *tr.*
see Brezina, Otakar

Routier, Simone
Je m'en vais.
DD, xi 44 M—A34, 28 v
Neige et nostalgie.
DD, x 40 Jy—Ag33, 62 v

Rowdon, Maurice
Sonnet.
PL, i 1 F39, [8] v

Rowe, C. H.
The position of art today.
VP, i 1 A—Je34, 17—19 c
Unit one [ed. by H. Read].
VP, i 2 Jy—S34, 44 r

Rowe, Eileen
The seventh son.
DD, vii 26 S—Oc30, 399—400 v

Rowe, Joyce T.
The small man.
JG, 71 W39, [23] v

Rowntree, Kenneth
Drawing.
LS, i 2 My34, 2 i

Rowse, Alfred Leslie
Extempore memorial.
NO, ii 3 N35, 264—66 v
Shaw and democracy
[*The apple cart*].
OO, xi 54 M31, 8—15 c
War and the psychological argument.
NO, ii 3 N35, 204—31 c
Mr Keynes and the labour movement
rev. by J. Robinson

Royde-Smith, Naomi
Two Christmas trees — a confession.
R, i 8 D34, 4—5 p

Rudas, Laszlo
*Dialectical materialism and
communism*
rev. by C. Day Lewis

Rudd, Maxwell Billens
Poems.
RR, 2 F37, [11, 14] v
Poems.
Rr, 3 My37, [15] v
Poems.
RR, 4 S37, [11] v
Poems.
RR, 5 J38, [15—16] v
Zebu; Mozambique.
RR, 1 Oc36, 17—18 v

Ruddock, Margot
The lemon tree
rev. by J. Symons

Rudge, Olga
Music and a process.
TO, i 1 J38, 21—22 c
Music chronicle.
TO, i 3 Jy38, 10 c

Rudwin, Maximilian Josef
Les écrivains diaboliques de France
rev. by G. M. Turnell

Rueff, A. M.
A story.
CM, i 3 Au33, 131—33 p

Rugeley, Doris M.
Christ and the law.
JG, 35 W35, [31—32] v
Conclusion.
JG, 26 Au33, [13] v
Life.
JG, 25 Su33, [9—10] v
Like God.
JG, 28 Sp34, [18] v
Market day.
JG, 38 Au36, [24] v
My fear.
JG, 29 Su34, [27—28] v
Refuge.
JG, 63 W37, [5] v
The virgin's lament.
JG, 42 Au37, [17] v

Russell, Arthur James
For sinners only
rev. by D. P. T. Jay

Russell, Bertrand Arthur William
Comment on the basis of the Sexology
group.
TC, iv 21 N32, 22 c
Education and the social order
rev. by A. S. Neill
The scientific outlook
rev. by J. R. Evans

Russell, C. J. and **Hendry,** J. F. *eds.*
Albannach rev. by R. Garioch

Russell, Dora
On education: state, army and church.
TC, v 25 M33, 35—37 c
Sex in women.
TC, vi 34 M34, 216—22 c

Russell, Eileen
English miss.
TC, v 30 Ag33, 352—56 p

Russell, J. L.
Religion and the scientific worker.
AR, i 2 Jy37, 138—44 c

Russell, John
Felix Weingartner.
LD, ii 3 F38, 4—5 c
Pitoeff is dead.
K, i 1 17N39, 19—20 p

Russell, Thomas
Colonne orchestra in London.
LR, iii 12 J38, 715—16 c
Music betrayed.
LR, iii 9 Oc37, 520—23 c

Rutherston, Albert
Drawing.
OO, xii 58 My32, 79 i
Drawing.
HR, 6 1933, 20 i
Girl's head.
F, 2 Je30, 69 i

Rutter, Owen
From natural causes.
P, 2 1938, 181—88 p
The man in the moon.
DD, ix 35 S—Oc32, 73 v
Triumphant pilgrimage
rev. by E. Waugh

Ryan, Desmond
The sword of light
rev. by J. L. Campbell
Unique dictator
rev. by C. Donnelly; B. Souvis

Rylands, George
Poems rev. by C. B. Spencer

S

S. *pseud.*
The pawn of Prague.
LD, i 1 M37, 24 v

S.
Vienna, Amsterdam, Madrid.
CL, ii 1 Au34, 3 v

S., A.
Creation.
M, i 1 Je33, 42 v

S., D.
Weight the scales.
TC, v 30 Ag33, 374—75 c

S., H. C.
Review [*The medium of poetry,*
by J. Sutherland] .
LS, i 1 F34, 58—60 r

S., J. M. E. H.
Salome.
FB, i 3 9My36, 63 v

S., P. P.
Caucasus.
PR, 8 19Je35, 7 v

S., R.
Misfires underground
[*Fires underground,*
by H. Liepmann] .
LR, ii 11 Ag36, 597—98 r

S., R. W.
Concerts.
TC, vi 33 D33—J34, 190—91 r

S., W.
The style and the man.
FB, iii 6 21Oc37, 7 v

S.-K., I. S.
Sins of the fathers; Ego I.
TH, 3 24F39, 2, 4 v, p

Sackville, *Lady* Margaret
Epigrams.
DD, viii 29 Su31, 51 v
For a blind man; Consummation;
The handicap; Memorial; Dream
fulfilled.
DD, viii 28 J—F31, 2 v
How comes it, song?
C, i 3 21D35, 22 v
Memorial.
CA, 9 1931, 285 v
Pride; Joy; Songless sleep;
A sigh; The accident.
DD, vii 27 N—D30, 419 v
The stranger; On woman;
Content; Arrogance.
DD, vii 26 S—Oc30, 366 v

Sackville-West, Edward Charles
Ski-run.
NW, ns3 C39, 278—83 p

Sackville-West, Victoria Mary
The censorship question.
R, i 5 Je34, 5 v
Collected poems, vol. 1
rev. by F. Prince
Pepita rev. by E. Waugh

Sade, Donatien Alphonse
François *Marquis de*
Sur l'imagination.
LB, 17 15Je39, 5—6 c

Sadleir, Michael
Blessington d'Orsay
rev. by C. H. Gibbs-Smith

Sadler, *Sir* Michael Ernest
Foreword.
HR, 6 1933, [5—6] c
Leeds.
HR, 5 1932, 7—10 c

Sainsbury, Geoffrey
But not for freedom.
TC, iv 23 J33, 23—24 c
Capitalism and the denial
of force.
TC, vi 32 N33, 83—86 c
Comment on Promethean
Society report.
TC, iii 18 Ag32, 13—14 c
Materialism and revolution.
TC, iv 21 N32, 5—9 c
Materialism and revolution, 2.
TC, iv 22 D32, 17—21 c
The dictatorship of things
rev. by K. E. Barlow

Saint-Genois, *Countess*
Deine stimme.
DD, x 37 J—F33, 12 v

St.-John Perse
[i.e. Aléxis Saint-Léger Leger]
Amity of the prince,
tr. by A. L. Lloyd.
CPP, 9 Sp37, 3—7 p
Song, tr. by A. L. Lloyd.
CPP, 8 D36, 160 v
Anabasis tr. by T. S. Eliot
rev. by D. I. Dunnett

St. Paul, F.
Curiosity.
PP, 13/14 Jy—Ag39, 9 v
Heard in street; Overtime.
PP, 10 A39, 16, 18 v

Saklatvala, Beram Shapurji
Presage; Before the world.
SM, 2 S31, 10 v

Salaman, Michael
The circus.
F, 4 D30, 29 i

Salkeld, Cecil Ffrench-
see Ffrench-Salkeld, Cecil

Salkeld, James
For a song.
F, 4 D30, 34 v
Two poems.
F, 1 F30, 35 v

Sallé, Marguerite
Danäe.
RR, 4 S37, [10] i
Tiki.
RR, 4 S37, [20] i
Winter: Regent's park.
RR, 2 F37, [12] i

Salt, Sydney
Children of tomorrow.
CV, 2 D34, 24—29 p
The new land.
CV, 3 Su35, 18—19;
CV, 4 1935, 14—15 v
So far gone.
CV, 1 Su34, 3—7 p

Salter, Charles Henry
Younger British painters.
K, i 2 D39—J40, 40 c

Salter, Roy
Winter sunset.
PQ, i 1 Sp39, 8 v

Saltmarshe, Christopher
Cavalcade for the general.
DE, 1 New year 1932, 1 v
A job in a million.
ND, 1 1Jy37, 16—18;
ND, 4 22Jy37, 17, 19;
ND, 10 2S37, 18—20;
ND, 19 4N37, 18—19;
ND, 23 2D37, 17—18 p

Salvemini, Gaetano
Under the axe of Fascism
rev. by D. Kahn

Salwey, Reginald Ernest
From Penn Hill, Yeovil.
DD, xi 46 Jy—Ag34, 64 v

Sambrook, Joyce
Dead day.
DD, vii 26 S—Oc30, 406 v
The house on the harbour.
DD, viii 28 J—F31, 32 v
Ideas for promoting the
circulation of The Decachord.
DD, vii, S—Oc30, 414 c

Sargent, G. R.
Song.
DD, x 42 N—D33, 102 v
The suppliant.
DD, xi 45 My—Je34, 42 v

Sargeson, Frank
An affair of the heart.
NW, ns3 C39, 85—91 p
White man's burden.
NW, ns1 Au38, 1—3 p

Saroyan, William
Further news of the world
from California.
TO, i 4 Oc38, 2—3 p
News of the world from
California.
TO, i 3 Jy38, 15—16 p
The poor world turning.
SV, 2 Au38, 24—27 p
Six bits.
TO, i 2 A38, 29 p
*The daring young man on the
flying trapeze*
rev. by A. Calder-Marshall
Inhale and exhale
rev. by A. Hodge; J. Lindsay
The trouble with tigers
rev. by G. S. Fraser

Sartre, Jean Paul
The room, tr. by J. Rodker.
NW, ns2 Sp39, 6—28 p

Sasajima, Toshio
Young swan; Love's
magnetism.
TO, i 1 J38, 7 v

Sassoon, Siegfried Loraine
Survivors; Base details;
Lamentations; The general;
Glory of women; Fight to a
finish.
LR, i 11 Ag35, 435—36 v
Writers and war.
LR, i 1 Oc34, 6 v

Saunders, Kingsley
Music and the machine.
PR, 22 Je37, 12—16 c

Saunders, Roy
Love song of the gold crests.
WR, ii 1 Ag39, 37—39 p

Saurat, Denis
Review
[*To circumjack cencrastus*,
by H. Macdiarmid].
MS, i 4 J31 64—66 r

Savage, Derek Stanley
Absent creation.
PL, i 1 F39, [24] v
Dirge.
PR, 22 Je37, 7 v
Epitaph; Harvest.
W, 2 Ag37, 68 v
Galahad.
SV, 1 Su38, 2—3 v
Landscape 2.
T, 9 M38, 11 v
The last miner.
RR, 9 A39, [17—18] v

Lewis and Lawrence.
T, 6/7 N37, [39] c
Lines composed on looking
through a volume of British
poets.
RR, 8 J39, [12] v
The mask; At Conway Hall.
RR, 7 Oc38, [19—20] v
Mr Idris Davies
[Gwalia deserta].
W, 6/7 M39, 208 r
October.
T, 14 D38, 129 v
Phoenix.
LT, i 11 J37, 16 v
Poem.
C, ii 53 26 D36, 213 v
Poem.
W, 3 Au37, 85—86 v
Poetry and Life.
PL, i 1 F39, [31] c
Prelude.
W, 5 Su38, 166 v
Review
[Walking through Merioneth,
by H. Hewett].
W, 10 Oc39, 286—87 r
Rhapsody.
C, ii 48 21N36, 173 v
Seaside.
W, 4 M38, 140 v
Solstice.
T, 2 M37, [6] v
Song.
RR, 6 Jy38, [9] v
The autumn world
rev. by C. Dyment;
H. B. Mallalieu
Don Quixote rev. by H. Treece

Saward, Jack
Spring term.
P, 5 1939, 24—43 p

Sayer, George S.
Auden's wild beast show
[The dog beneath the skin,
by W. H. Auden and
C. Isherwood].
PR, 6 31My35, 11—13 r
The chair.
PR, 1 1F35, 5 v
Contemporary poets, 1:
Laura Riding.
PR, 3 19F35, 9, 11—14 c
Editorial.
PR, 7 12Je35, 1 c
For J. E.
PR, 8 19Je35, 6 v
Noah [by A. Obey].
PR, 10 6N35, 11—13 dr
A note on style.
PR, 17 27My36, 12—14 c
Review.

PR, 1 1F35, 7 dr
Review
[The Faber book of modern
verse, ed. by M. Roberts].
PR, 15 1M36, 23—24 r
To a lady.
PR, 11 27N35, 8 v
see also Hodge, A.

Sayers, Dorothy Leigh
Busman's honeymoon
rev. by H. Read

Sayers, Michael
The jew in the moon.
NS, ii 8 A36, 629—36 p
Story of a revolutionary.
NS, ii 7 F36, 517—24 p

Scarfe, Francis Harold
Defence of gothic.
CPP, 9 Sp37, 27—28 v
Easter; Progression.
T, 10 My38, 31 v
Holiday.
CPP, 10 Au37, 27 v
A myth.
CPP, 8 D36, 144—46 p
No morning.
PR, 20 17N36, 14 v
Notes on Guillaume
Apollinaire.
PR, 17 27 My36, 3—7 c
Ode in honour.
CPP, 7 N36, 133—34 v
Palms.
T, 11 Jy38, 68 v
Peter Pan's other half.
NV, i 1 J39, 13 v
Poem; Beauty, boloney.
T, 15/16 F39, 144—46 v
Review
[Hölderlin's madness,
by D. Gascoyne].
T, 11 Jy38, 75—76 r
Serenade.
PR, 17 27My36, 15 v
Tats.
PR, 18 17Je36, 11 v
Two poems.
CPP, 4/5 Ag36, 89—90 v
see also Ducasse, I.; Jarry, A.;
Queneau, R.; Tzara, T.

Scheffer, Paul
Seven years in Soviet Russia
rev. by J. R. Evans

Schmalhausen, Samuel Daniel
The new road to progress
rev. by N. K. Cecil

Schnack, Anton
The abbey, tr. by P. Selver.
SM, 5 1934, 119—20 v

Schneider, Isidor
The grandmother speaks.
NW, ns1 Au38, 122—23 v

Schofield, E. Percy
The imprisoned soul.
DD, vii 27 N—D30, 428 v

Schoon, George E.
'Laycocks'.
HR, 4 1931, 48—49 p

Schreiner, Olive
Message to the SDF,
Cape Town, 1905.
LR, iii 10 N37, 594—95 p

Schrire, David
Nzonda.
LR, ii 6 M36, 266—68 p

Schwartz, Delmore
From Coriolanus and his
mother.
TO, ii 6 A39, 2—3 v
Imitation of a fugue.
T, 12/13 Oc38, 97 v
In dreams begin responsibilities
rev. by R. March

Scotland and the cinema.
MS, i 1 Sp30, 53 c

Scott, A. C. Dawson-
see Dawson-Scott, A. C.

Scott, Evelyn
Eva Gay rev. by Jaques pseud.

Scott, Francis George
The auld man's mear's dead.
MS, iii 4 J33, 336—39 m
Crowdieknowe,
by H. Macdiarmid;
The Eemis stane.
MS, v 1/2 Je34, 39—43,
62—66 m
Cupid and Venus.
MS, iii 2 Ag32, 145—48 m
Love, by H. Macdiarmid.
MS, iii 1 A32, 56—57 m
Moonstruck, by H. Macdiarmid.
MS, iv 1 A33, 49—52 m
My luve is like a red, red rose,
by R. Burns; Amang the trees,
by R. Burns; Of ane Blackamore,
by W. Dunbar.
MS, vi 4 J36, 319—29 m
Phillis, by W. Drummond;

Scott, Francis George (cont.)
O, were I an Parnassus' Hill,
by R. Burns.
MS, v 4 J35, 271—75 m
Rorate caeli desuper,
by W. Drummond.
MS, iv 2 Jy33, 133—37 m
St. Brendan's graveyard.
MS, iii 3 Oc32, 225—28 m
Scroggan, by R. Burns;
O dear minny, what shall I do,
by R. Burns;
Fare ye well, my auld wife.
MS, vi 3 Oc35, 235—41 m
The tailor fell thro' the bed,
by R. Burns.
MS, v 3 Oc34, 173—77 m
The twa kimmers, by W. Dunbar.
MS, vi 1 A35, 30—34 m
Twist ye, twine ye.
MS, iv 3 Oc33, 207—14 m
Wheesht, wheesht,
by H. Macdiarmid.
MS, iv 4 J34, 320—24 m
When I think on the happy days;
My wife's a wanton wee thing,
by R. Burns.
MS, vi 2 Jy35, 150—55 m

Scott, George
Command, master, and I obey!
LR, iii 16 My38, 972 i
Drawing.
LR, iii 11 D37, 669 i
The Führer appoints a
correspondent for 'The Times'.
LR, iii 8 S37, 487 i
In England's green and pleasant
land.
LR, ii 12 S36, 627 i
Patriot.
LR, iii 1 F37, 16 i

Scott, Harold
Eastbourne and the Earl's
Court exhibition.
Y, i 1 M39, 11—17 p
Pantomime.
LR, iii 11 D37, 641—43 c

Scott, J. A.
Review
[*Second hymn to Lenin,*
by H. Macdiarmid;
Social credit, by E. Pound].
PR, 10 6N35, 17—18 r

Scott, J. Creagh
The casus belli.
TO, ii 8 N39, 3—4 c

Scott, John Waugh
*Self-subsistence for the
unemployed*
rev. by D. Garman

Scott, Leonard
Some remarks on the cruel
dilemma of the post-Wagnerian
composer.
Y, i 2 My39, 97—102 c

Scott, Malcolm
'Of what importance is personal
stuff?'
TO, i 4 Oc38, 15 r
Periodicals
[*Purpose*; *London bulletin*;
The examiner].
TO, ii 7 Ag39, 26—27 r
Three periodicals.
TO, ii 6 A39, 15 c

Scott-Moncrieff, George
5 years.
NA, i 1 Au39, 19—22 p
Goat and child.
MS, vi 1 A35, 9—16 p

Scouller, Edward
A broken Apollo.
MS, vi 3 Oc35, 227—34 p
Lobsters.
MS, v 4 J35, 248—59 p
Murdoch's bull.
MS, v 3 Oc34, 184—87 p
My redeemer liveth.
LR, ii 14 N36, 750—58 p

Scovell, Edith Joy
A dancer.
NO, ii 2 J35, 153 v
Three poems.
NO, ii 2 J35, 169—70 v

Scrannel, Orpheus *pseud.*
see Gawsworth, John

Scriven, Ronald Charles
Any lady to any poet.
JG, 36 Sp36, [7] v
Consolation.
JG, 16 Sp31, [18] v
Epitaph.
JG, 13 Su30, [32] v
From 'Lament for the living'.
JG, 26 Au33, [28—29] v
I wove a dream.
JG, 34 Au35, [13] v
Ilarion, loquitur.
JG, 15 W30, [10—11] v
The jongleur.
JG, 18 Au31, [5—6] v
The Levite.
JG, 19 W31, [22—24] v
Makers of dreams.
JG, 31 W34, [24—27] v
Night mood of provincial spring.
JG, 28 Sp34, [22—25] v
On Doris.

JG, 35 W35, [16] v
The temptation of St. Ilarion.
JG, 21 Su32, [29—30] v
'There shall not remain to thee
one of all'.
JG, 17 Su31, [27—28] v
There's beauty in industry,
you know.
JG, 30 Au34, [18—19] v
To the quite impossible she.
JG, 35 W35, [27—28] v
Turn not your face.
JG, 14 Au30, [27—28] v
Upon the ill effects of
adverse reviews.
JG, 17 Su31, [29—30] v
Woe for Apollo.
JG, 25, Su33, [8] v

Scroop, John
Putsch and Judy show.
OB, i 4 Je35, 10—16 p

**The 'Scrutiny' movement in
education.**
OB, i 4 Je35, 58—61 c

Scrutiny, nos. 1—3
rev. by G. Ewart, D. C. Thomson;
OB i 4 Je35, 58—61

Scurfield, George B.
Party going [by H. Green].
SV, 7 C39, 28—29 r
The wood.
FB, v 2 My39, 33—34 p

Scutenaire, Jean
Cour naturel, par P. Eluard.
LB, 2 My38, 17 c
Paul Delvaux,
tr. by R. Penrose.
LB, 3 Je38, 7—8 c
La poésie
[*Une écriture lisible,*
by G. Hugnet and K. Seligmann].
LB, 11 M39, 16—17 r
La poésie
[*Oeillades ciselées en branche,*
by G. Hugnet].
LB, 14 My39, 13—14 r
see also Magritte, Rene

Seal, Pulin
The Indian people's victory.
LR, iii 3 A37, 147—50 c

Searle, Humphrey
Sibelius: the position reviewed.
NO, ii 2 J35, 177—83 c

Sedgwick, Peter
Review

[*Die Heilung durch den Geist*,
by S. Zweig].
TC, ii 11 J32, 25—26 r

See-saw; People in large houses.
LT, i 1 M36, 13, 15 v

Seferis, George
Message in a bottle;
Untitled poem.
SV, 7 C39, 21 v

Seghers, Anna *pseud.*
The Lord's prayer:
an episode of 1933.
NW, 1 Sp36, 69—71 p
The rescue,
tr. by C. Ashleigh.
NS, ns1 Au38, 5—24 p

Seligmann, Kurt
see Hugnet, Georges

Selver, Paul
Three outrageous sonnets.
SM, 1 Je31, 56—57 v
Three topical sonnets.
SM, 5 1934, 117—118 v
The unprecedented case of
Dr Murdoch.
SM, 4 1933, 63—107 p
see also Bach, R.; Balmont, K. D.;
Brezina, O.; Dehmel, R.; Gall, I.;
Hlaváček, K.; Kubka, F.;
Konrad, E.; Krklec, G.; Liliev, N.;
Micinski, T.; Mikhailovsky, S.;
Rilke, R. M.; Schnack, A.;
Tuwin, J.; Vrchlicky, J.;
Zech, P.

Sen, Jatindranath
The Indian question.
TU, 4 F35, 43—47 c

Sender, Ramon José
Seven red Sundays
rev. by R. Wright
The war in Spain
rev. by V. Ackland

Senior, H. L.
Milton at Horton.
PQ, i 1 Sp39, 5 c

Serpell, Christopher H.
Poem.
OO, x 52 My30, 488 v

Serraillier, Ian L.
Christian's vision of the cross;
the first days; City on a hill.
RM, 1 Je34, 9—12 i, v
House two.
RM, 2 D34, 37—43 p

Landscape; High wind.
LS, i 2 My34, 61, 71 i
Two poems.
NO, ii 2 J35, 139 v

Seton, Marie
The evolution of the Soviet
theatre, and the Festival
Theatre — a comparison.
CL, i 4 Su34, 101—6 c
In search of material.
VP, i 2 Jy—S34, 43 c
Propaganda in the theatre:
right and left.
VP, i 1 A—Je34, 8—11 c
The theatre of Palestine.
VP, i 2 Jy—S34, 51 c

Seven, nos. 1—3
rev. by G. Reavey;
M. J. Tambimuttu; J. M. Todd

Sewter, Albert Charles
Review
[*Beauty looks after herself*,
by E. Gill; *Unemployment*,
by E. Gill].
TC, v 29 Jy33, 318—20 r
Review
[*Contemporary literature and
social revolution*,
by R. D. Charques].
TC, vi 32 N33, 118—20 r
Review [*For continuity*,
by F. R. Leavis].
TC, vi 33 D33—J34, 187—88 r
Review [*Nature in design*,
by J. Evans].
TC, vi 35 Je34, 308—9 r

Sexton, *Sir* James
An autobiography,
rev. by T. A. Jackson

Seyfoollina, Lydia
Pavlovshkin's career,
tr. by H. Brennan.
MS, iii 4 J33, 333—35 p

Seymour, William Kean
The dragon of Nu-Yir.
ND, 26 23D37, 15 v
Ghost in garden.
DD, x 37 J—F33, 5 v
I might have said.
DD, xi 44 M—A34, 30—31 v
Ivor Innes Cox.
DD, ix 35 S—Oc32, 72 v
Memory.
DD, x 39 My—Je33, 42 v
Rooms.
DD, ix 32 M—A32, 19 v
Son and heir.
DD, xi 46 Jy—Ag34, 55 v

Words.
DD, x 41 S—Oc33, 77 v

Sforza, Carlo
European dictatorships
rev. by J. R. Evans

Shall the poor be angry?
LR, i 10 Jy35, 407—10 p

Shand, Philip Morton
Capital considerations.
MS, i 4 J31, 30—36 c
D. O. Hill:
master photographer.
MS, vi 3 Oc35, 220—26 c
The Scottish larder considered.
MS, ii 2 Jy31, 155—62 c
We Anglo-Scots.
MS, i 2 Su30, 33—37 c

Sharp, Margery
Fanfare for trumpets
rev. by H. G. Porteus

Sharrock, Roger
Urban evening.
FB, v 2 My39, 34 v

Shaw, George Bernard
Britain and the U.S.S.R.
LR, ii 4 J36, 145—47 c
Comment on the report
[of the Political and Economic
group of the Promethean
society].
TC, ii 10 D31, 8 c
G.B.S.'s message.
R, i 1 N33, 8 p
Lenin extempore.
LR, i 3 D34, 51—52 p
Mr G. B. Shaw and Bradford.
HR, 4 1931, 10 c
Writers and war.
LR, i 1 Oc34, 6 p
*The adventures of the black
girl in her search for God*
rev. by G. Pendle
The apple cart
rev. by A. L. Rowse
Cymbeline
rev. by A. van Gyseghem
Prefaces rev. by E. Rickword

Shawe-Taylor, Desmond
The assault on Wagner.
F, 1 F30, 13—18 c

Shayler, Hugh
The countryside.
TC, iv 24 F33, 24—25 c

Sheldon, Michael
Education.
LD, i 1 J37, 11—13 p

Shelley, C. W. E.
Review
[*In parenthesis,* by D. Jones].
AR, i 3 Oc37, 253—55 r

Shepherd, S. d'Horne
Edwin Muir.
MS, vi 2 Jy35, 130 i
Francis George Scott.
MS, vi 4 J36, 316 i
James Bridie.
MS, vi 3 Oc35, 208 i
John Rafferty.
MS, vi 1 A35, 40 i

Sherry, J. M.
Memory canyon.
CV, 2 D34, 30—31 v

Shih Ming *pseud.*
Meeting.
NW, 5 Sp38, 51—55 p

Shipp, Horace
Breviaire de Belleville.
DD, ix 33 My—Je32, 35 v

Sholokhov, Mikhail Aleksandrovich
The father.
NW, 4 Au37, 185—91 p
Sholokhov: an interview.
LR, i 6 M35, 193—94 p

Shoolman, Regina Lenore
Canary yellow.
NS, ii 1 F35, 40—53 p

Shore, Clifford Bower-
see Bower-Shore, Clifford

Short, John
At a wrestling match.
FB, iii 8 3M38, 49 v
Carol for Corpus-Christi-tide.
PR, 22 Je37, 11—12 v
Cemetery song; In vacation.
PR, 21 1M37, 12—13 v
English garden.
LD, i 3 My37, 25—26 p
A lament for Dido.
K, i 1 17N39, 19 v
Manifesto from Westmorland.
FB, iii 8 3M38, 55 v
Meditation after reading
Traherne.
LD, ii 3 F38, 22 v
Que j'aime les fôrets,
from the French of
François de Maynard.
K, i 2 D39—J40, 59 v

Skeltonicks for Mistress
Margaret Douthwaite.
K, i 1 17N39, 12 v
The testament (1911—1938); Me.
B, 1 Su38, [2—3] v
Walter de la Mare
[*Memory and other poems*].
B, 1 Su38, 10—11 r
Westmorland folk play.
PR, 22 Je37, 3—6 c

Shortridge, Enid
Tantal'sing.
DD, viii 29 Su31, 57 v

Shostakovitch, Dmitri
Lady Macbeth of Mzensk
rev. by J. F. Hendry

Shove, Fredegond
Night in Chartres.
CA, 3 Oc30, 48 v

Shrapnel, Norman
Rocks to roses.
TO, i 3 Jy38, 17—19 c

Shrensky, Lazarus
Ah! when I was a boy.
LR, iii 5 Je37, 287—88 p

Shukla, J. K.
One day.
NW, ns2 Sp39, 184—92 p

Shull, Virginia
University women in
England and America.
LS, i 2 My34, 49—58 c

Sib *pseud.*
Song of a nuit blanche.
PP, 11 My39, 13—15 v

Sibanyone, John
Tshaka.
PP, 9 M39, 17 v

Siddall, Anne Elizabeth
Gateway to a dream.
JG, 42 Au37, [22—23] v

Sidgwick, Elizabeth
Poem.
CM, i 3 Au33, 136 v
Two poems.
CM, i 1 Sp33, 26 v

Sidgwick, Maude C.
Creation.
DD, x 40 Jy—Ag33, 71 v
Design.
DD, x 38 M—A33, 35 v

Siegfried, Andre
Impressions of South America
rev. by G. Pendle

Silone, Ignazio
The fox,
tr. by G. David and
E. Mosbacher.
NW, 4 Au37, 18—35 p
Journey to Paris,
tr. by E. Mosbacher.
NW, 2 Au36, 108—30 p
Mobilisation day,
tr. by E. Mosbacher.
LR, ii 11 Ag36, 549—56 p
Bread and wine
rev. by J. Lindsay
Fontamara
rev. by CL, ii 1 Au34, 30;
J. Lehmann

Simeon, Eleanor B.
Outside.
JG, 29 Su34, [28] v
A penny for dreams.
JG, 27 W33, [10] v

Simmons, Bayard
This other Eden.
C, iii 57 23J37, 30 v

Simon *pseud.*
The house opposite.
LT, i 5 Jy36, 17—19 p
Rat room.
LT, i 11 J37, 48 p
Tied up.
LT, i 5 Jy36, 35 v

Simon, *Sir* Ernest Darling
and others
Moscow in the making
rev, by M. Best

Simon, Henry
Peace on earth.
CV, 5 M36, [20] v

Simpson, Henry
Aeroplanes.
DD, ix 35 S—Oc32, 77 v
Chant of morning.
DD, xi 47 S—Oc34, 71 v
The journey.
DD, xi 43 J—F34, 2 v
Legend of Noel.
JG, 71 W39, [24—25] v
Melody.
DD, ix 33 My—Je32, 43 v
North sea.
JG, 40 Sp37, [8] v
Perdita.
DD, xi 45 My—Je34, 40 v
Sea quiet.
DD, x 38 M—A33, 31 v

Simpson, Margaret Winefride
Joan of France.
MS, i 4 J31, 19 v

Sinclair, Donald
The path of the old spells,
tr. from the Gaelic.
VS, i 3 D38—F39, 11—12 p

Sinclair, Upton
Mammonart rev. by E. Rickword
Manassas rev. by G. West
Upton Sinclair presents
William Fox rev. by G. West
The way out rev. by G. West

Singer, Israel Joshua
The brothers Ashkenazi
rev. by J. Lindsay

Singh, Iqbal
Gautama Buddha
rev. by R. Jardine
When one is in it
rev. by P. Henderson
see also Magritte, René *and*
Nougé, Paul

Sington, D. A.
Review [*On the other side*,
by J. Newsom].
OO, x 51 F30, 463—64 r

Sinha, Sasadhar *see*
Chatterjee, Sarat Chandra

Sinko, Ervin
Love.
NW, 5 Sp38, 200—2 p

Sir Hugh Le Blond.
T, 4 Je37, [13—16] v

Sitwell, Edith
Two songs.
CV, 5 M36, [8] v
Aspects of modern poetry
rev. by G. Grigson
Collected poems
rev. by C. B. Spencer
I live under a black sun
rev. by T. L. Hodgkin;
E. Waugh

Sitwell, Osbert
The next war.
LR, i 5 F35, 160 v

Skae, Hilda
The chapel in the glen.
PQ, i 1 Sp39, 19—20 v

Skelton, G. D.
A new life.
NW, ns3 C39, 139—47 p

Sklar, George *see* Peters, Paul

Skyeman *pseud.*
Highland development.
VS, i 1 Je—Ag38, 18—20 c

Slack, F.
Ineffable mantle.
C, i 18 4A36, 140 p

Slamkin, Jake Lee
Red bastards.
LR, iii 14 M38, 873—77 p

Slater, Charles
The heart of learning
[*A collier's Friday night*,
by D. H. Lawrence].
LR, i 7 A35, 285—86 r
In the beginning.
LR, i 1 Oc34, 30—33 v
Poem.
LR, i 8 My35, 296 v

Slater, Montagu
Art right and left.
LR, ii 2 N35, 83—87 c
Artist's international exhibition
1935.
LR, ii 4 J36, 161—64 c
Charles Donnelly.
LR, iii 6 Jy37, 318—19 c
The fog beneath the skin
[*Collected poems, 1930—1933*,
by C. Day Lewis;
A time to dance,
by C. Day Lewis;
The dog beneath the skin,
by W. H. Auden and
C. Isherwood].
LR, i 9 Jy35, 425—30 r
Forty months on trial
[*Conspiracy at Meerut*,
by L. Hutchinson].
LR, ii 5 F36, 233—34 r
Human nature changes
[*New writing*, no. 4].
LR, iii 13 F38, 817—19 r
Nehru and Gandhi
[*An autobiography*,
by J. Nehru;
India and the world,
by J. Nehru].
LR, ii 12 S36, 654—56 r
Prologue for Punch.
LR, i 3 D34, 59—61 d
Prometheus unbound
[*The mind in chains*,
ed. by C. Day Lewis].
LR, iii 6 Jy37, 363—65 r

The purpose of a *Left Review*.
LR, i 9 Je35, 359—65 c
A story everybody knows.
LR, i 6 M35, 227—33 c
The thing happens.
LR, i 8 My35, 328—29 c
The turning point
[*Problems of Soviet literature*,
by A. Zhdanov *and others*;
The poet's tongue,
ed. by W. H. Auden and
J. Garrett;
Poetry of tomorrow,
ed. by J. A. Smith].
CL, ii 1 Oc35, 15—23 r
Vienna, February days
[*Vienna*, by S. Spender].
LR, i 5 F35, 184—87 r
Writers International
LR, i 4 J35, 125—28 c
Easter rev. by D. Garman
Haunting Europe
rev. by D. A. Willis
Stay down miner
rev. by A. Brown; L. A. Butts;
G. Buchanan
see also Ajax *pseud.*

Sloan, Patrick Alan
Letter.
TC, ii 11 J32, 29 c
Problems of Soviet planning.
TC, iv 19 S32, 18—21 c
Professor MacMurray and
Marxism.
TC, v 28 Je33, 219—24 c
Red herrings on the left wind.
DV, 3 My32, 83—86 c
The Soviet Union and the world.
DV, 2 A32, 39—43 c
The two André Gides
[*Back from the U.S.S.R.*,
by A. Gide].
LR, iii 4 My37, 242—44 r
Soviet democracy
rev. by S. Webb

Smale, Edith
November.
DD, xi 47 S—Oc34, 85 v

Small, Victor
The banality of recent English
films.
LR, iii 15 A38, 935—37 c
Demarche of time.
LR, iii 16 My38, 1001—4 r

Smirnov, Aleksi Aleksandrovich
Shakespeare rev. by A. West

Smith, Arthur James Marshall
Answers to an enquiry.
NV, 11 Oc34, 9—10 p

Smith, Arthur James Marshall (cont.)
Arp's randy rant in the comfy
confession box;
Quietly to be quickly, or to be
ether: a song or a dance.
NV, 18 D35, 11—12 v
Ballade un peu banale.
NV, 9 Je34, 13—14 v
The face; Chorus;
Noctambule.
NV, 22 S36, 7—8 v
The faithful heart.
RR, 9 A39, [13] v
Far west.
T, 15/16 F39, 148 v
Political note.
CPP, 7 N36, 130—31 v
Poor innocent.
NV, 28 J38, 5 v
Resurrection of Arp.
NV, 8 A34, 2—3 v
Son-and-heir.
NV, 15 Je35, 3—4 v
Two poems.
NV, 6 D33, 10 v

Smith, Ashley
Brothers.
NS, i 1 F34, 19—21 p
The dust of freedom.
NS, ii 7 F36, 497—506 p
The brimming lake
rev. by J. Lindsay
Children with fire
rev. by G. West

Smith, Edith M.
White Mary.
DD, x 42 N—D33, 107 v

Smith, Howard W.
Flower of Cuba.
DD, x 42 N—D33, 105 v

Smith, Janet Adam *ed.*
Poems of tomorrow
rev. by G. Grigson; M. Slater

Smith, Jessie Maclellan *tr.*
see Britting, G.; Mann, T.

Smith, K. Swinstead-
see Swinstead-Smith, K.

Smith, Naomi Royde-
see Royde-Smith, Naomi

Smith, Peter Heriz-
see Heriz-Smith, Peter

Smith, Peter Newson-
see Newson-Smith, Peter

Smith, Simon Nowell
see Nowell-Smith, Simon

Smith, S. Sydney
At least we were together to the
end.
SV, 4 Su39, 13—14 p
Neuropath; Dive plummet-wise
darling; Powdered lackeys should
receive one; Once I was adrift;
The caverned hand.
SV, 3 W38, 12—16 v

Smith, Stevie
A portrait.
ND, 24 9D37, 16 v
Portrait; Villains.
ND, 11 9S37, 31 v
Salon d'Automne;
Sigh no more.
ND, 11 9S37, 16 v
Sterilization.
ND, 17 21Oc37, 12 v
Via Media Via Dolorosa.
ND, 8 19Ag37, 11 v

Smythe, Barbara E.
Harbour.
JG, 22 Au32, [15] v
I shall not seek.
JG, 41 Su37, [21] v
If fate ordains.
JG, 18 Au31, [20—21] v
The lonely hunter sings
his love.
JG, 20 Sp32, [17—18] v
1914—1918—1930.
JG, 16 Sp31, [8] v
Song in March.
JG, 24 Sp33, [22—23] v
Song in July.
JG, 25 Su33, [10—11] v
A song of living.
JG, 14 Au30, [15] v
Thanksgiving.
JG, 66 Au38, [19] v
Threefold biography.
JG, 63 W37, [10] v

Snow, Edgar
Red star over China
rev. by R. Goodman

Snow, Royall
This experimental life
rev. by L. MacNeice

Soap and clothes.
LR, i 6 M35, 212—13 p

Soboleff, Leonid Sergeevich
Storm warning
rev. by T. H. Wintringham

Soddy, Frederick
Comment on Promethean
Society report.
TC, iii 18 Ag32, 12—13 c

Soderberg, Hjalmar Emil
Frederick
Selected stories
rev. by H. E. Bates

Södergran, Edith Irene
The portrait,
tr. by G. Ewart.
CPP, 2 Je36, 34 v

Solicitor *pseud.*
English justice
rev. by A. Craig

Somerset, Basil
The bishop's retreat.
F, 2 Je30, 93—96 p
'But it shouldn't go on'.
F, 4 D30, 25—29 p

Somerville, J. Baxter
Revivals.
R, i 1 N33, 9 p

Sommerfield, John
The escape.
NW, 5 Sp38, 59—67 p
From a Spanish diary.
LR, iii 2 M37, 75—78 p
A personal matter.
NW, ns1 Au38. 184—92 p
To Madrid.
NW, 3 Sp37, 43—48 p
Two novels
[*Between two men,*
by F. Le Gros Clark;
Untouchable, by M. R. Anand].
LR, i 10 Jy35, 423—25 r
May day rev. by J. Lindsay

Sonnet.
M, i 1 Je33, 52 v

Soutar, William
Aphorisms.
MS, vi 4 J36, 346—47 p
The auld horse.
VS, i 1Je- Ag38, 6 v
The auld tree.
MS, iii 1 A32, 14—24 v
The children.
VS, i 2 S—N38, 22 v
Epigrams.
MS, vi 1 A35, 52—53 v
Faith in the vernacular.
VS, i 1 Je—Ag38, 22—23 c
A moment for desire.
MS, ii 2 Jy31, 154 v
Poem.

LR, ii 14 N36, 761 v
The silent moment.
CA, 10 1931 315 v
Star swarm.
MS, v 1/2 Je34, 67 v
Three lyrics.
MS, vi 3 Oc35, 257—58 v
Two sonnets.
MS, iii 4 J33, 325 v
Two sonnets.
MS, iv 3 Oc33, 196 v
Uniquity.
TC, vi 33 D33—J34, 153 v
Why the worm feeds on death.
MS, v 1/2 Je34, 24—29 v
Worker's broadcast.
PP, 10 A39, 17 v
Brief words
rev. by C. M. Grieve
Conflict rev. by H. Macdiarmid

South, A. E.
Spareroom.
NS, ii 7 F36, 530—40 p

Southern review [periodical]
rev. by J. Symons

Southwart, Elizabeth
The god.
HR, 5 1932, 49—50 p

Souvis, Barbara
The living and the dead
[*Unique dictator,*
by D. Ryan].
LD, i 1 J37, 13—14 r

Sowerby, Benn
The migrant.
P, 6 1939, 102—29 p

Spanish folk song,
tr. by A. L. Lloyd.
CPP, 2 Je36, 33 v

Sparrow, John Hanbury Angus
Dr Beddoes.
F, 3 Oc30, 135—48 c
The new criticism.
F, 1 F30, 22—34 c
Practical criticism:
a reply to Mr Empson.
OO, x 53 N30, 598—607 c
Reply.
F, 2 Je30, 128—30 c
Sense and poetry
rev. by A. D. Hawkins

Spate, Oskar Hermann Khristian
Last days of.
CL, i 1 Su33, 1 v

Spear, Thelma

Before a Peter Breughel
picture.
I, i 4 15D31, 106 v

Speare, Sorrelle
The black-haired girl.
PE, 3 Oc36, 68—74 p
Episode of a journey.
PE, 1 Ag36, 10—20 p
A red handkerchief.
PE, 2 S36, 35—38 p
The witch of Enderby street.
PE, 4 N36, 134—38 p

Speight, Rose E.
Mes boeufs.
JG, 38 Au36, [18] v

Spencer, Anne
Haworth moor.
JG, 66 Au38, [27] v
Land of the Navajo.
JG, 70 Au39, [18] v

Spencer, C. Bernard
Allotments: April.
NV, 21 Je36, 4—5 v
A cold night; Going to the
country; Ill; Part of plenty.
NV, 24 F37, 8—11 v
Dylan Thomas
[*Twenty five poems*].
NV, 23 C36, 19—21 r
Four poems.
NV, 15 Je35, 2—3 v
A hand; Evasions;
Poem.
NV, 17 Oc35, 4—6 v
Keeping up traditions.
OO, x 51 F30, 439—41 c
Picked clean from the world.
NV, 28 J38, 4 v
Poem.
OO, xii 58 My32, 132 v
Reminiscent poetry
[*The natural need,*
by J. Reeves].
NV, 20 A36, 25 r
Review [*Vale and other poems,*
by A. E.].
OO, xi 55 Je31, 143—44 r
Review
[*A garden revisited and other
poems,* by J. Lehmann;
Poems, by G. Rylands].
OO, xii 57 F32, 71—72 r
Review [*The poet's progress,*
by W. d'Arcy Creswell;
A dream in the Luxembourg,
by R. Aldington].
OO, x 52 My30, 543—45 r
Review [*Collected poems,*
by E. Sitwell;

Early poems, by H. Wolfe].
OO, x 53 N30, 630 r
Suburb factories;
A thousand killed; The house.
NV, 20 A36, 10—11 v
Three poems.
NV, 13 F35, 4—5 v
Two poems.
OO, xii 57 F32, 42—43 v
Waiting.
NV, 29 M38, 12 v

Spencer, C. Bernard *and*
Martin, William
Art chronicle.
OO, xi 54 M31, 44—48 c

Spencer, Theodore
Eclogue.
NV, 2 M33, 12—13 v
Eclogue.
NV, 9 Je34, 5—6 v
Eclogue.
T, 12/13 Oc38, 91 v
Song.
NV, 2 M33, 9 v

Spender, John Alfred
Men and things
rev. by E. Waugh

Spender, Stephen Harold
Beethoven's death mask.
OO, x 53 N30, 578 v
The burning cactus.
NO, i 1 My33, 24—42 p
By the lake.
NS, i 1 F34, 52—80 p
D. H. Lawrence: *Phoenix.*
LR, ii 16 J37, 902—4 r
De La Mare
[*The fleeting and other poems*].
NV, 4 Jy33, 16—17 r
Easter Monday.
NV, 17 OC35, 16 v
Fable and reportage
[*The ascent of F6,*
by W. H. Auden and
C. Isherwood;
Look, stranger! by W. H. Auden;
New writing, no.2].
LR, ii 14 N36, 779—82 r
Five notes on W. H. Auden's
writing.
TC, iii 17 Jy32, 13—15 c
Four poems.
NW, 1 Sp36, 113—17 v
The haymaking.
OO, x 53 N30, 579—97 p
The human situation.
PL, i 2 A39, [22—24] v
The landscape near an
aerodrome.
TC, iii 15 My32, 15 v

Spender, Stephen Harold (cont.)
The left-wing orthodoxy.
NV, 31/32 Au38, 12—16 c
Mr MacNeice's poems.
NV, 17 Oc35, 17—19 r
Murry on Blake
[*William Blake*,
by J. M. Murry].
NV, 6 D33, 22—24 r
Music and decay
[*Ulysses*, by J. Joyce].
LR, ii 15 D36, 834—36 r
New poetry
[*Calamiterror*, by G. Barker;
Poems, by R. Warner;
The disappearing castle,
by C. Madge;
Spain, by W. H. Auden;
The fifth decad of cantos,
by E. Pound].
LR, iii 6 Jy37, 358—61 r
A new writer
[*Thirty preliminary poems*,
by G. Barker].
NV, 6 D33, 20 r
New year.
NV, 7 F34, 8 v
On looking at a book of
death masks.
OO, x 53 N30, 627 v
An open letter to Aldous
Huxley.
LR, ii 11 Ag36, 539—41 c
Oxford to communism.
NV, 26/27 N37, 9—10 c
Poem.
OO, x 51 F30, 413 v
Poem.
OO, xi 55 Je31, 77 v
Poem.
NO, i 2 N33, 186 v
Poem.
NV, 22 S36, 3—4 v
Poems.
OO, x 51 F30, 448, 452 v
The poetic dramas of
W. H. Auden and
Christopher Isherwood.
NW, ns1 Au38, 102—8 c
Review [*Near and far*,
by E. Blunden].
OO, x 51 F30, 462—63 r
Review [*The waves*,
by V. Woolf].
OO, xi 56 N31, 226—27 r
Review [*Snooty baronet*,
by P. W. Lewis].
TC, iv 21 N32, 27 r
Review [*The red front*,
by L. Aragon].
NV, 3 My33, 24—25 r
Review [*Adamastor*,
by R. Campbell;
Nettles, by D. H. Lawrence;

D. H. Lawrence, by S. Potter;
The love-tiff,
by J. B. Moliere
tr. by F. Spencer].
OO, x 52 My30, 557—58 r
Sonnet.
NV, 29 M38, 9 v
Spain invites the world's
writers.
NW, 4 Au37, 245—51 p
Tangiers and Gibraltar then
and now.
LR, iii 1 F37, 17—19 c
Three poems.
NW, ns1 Au38, 25—27 v
Two poems.
NW, ns3 C39, 55—57 v
Two speeches from a play.
NW, 3 Sp37, 9—10 v
The uncreating chaos.
NV, 17 Oc35, 11—14 v
Variations on my life;
Two kisses.
PL, i 1 F39, [11—15] v
Writers and manifestoes.
LR, i 5 F35, 145—50 c
Written whilst walking down
the Rhine; The swan.
OO, x 52 My30, 479—80 v
The burning cactus
rev. by D. Kahn
The destructive element
rev. by G. Grigson;
E. Rickword
Forward from liberalism
rev. by R. C. Swingler
Poems rev. by G. Barker
Trial of a judge rev. by K. Allott;
G. Ewart; G. S. Fraser;
J. Symons
Vienna rev. by A. Hope;
M. Slater; D. Thomas
see also Brecht, B.; Rilke, R. M.

Spender, Stephen Harold
and **Lehmann**, John *eds.*
Poems for Spain
rev. by NV, i 2 My39, 52; R. Todd

Spender, Stephen Harold *and*
Spender, I. *trs. see*
Hernandez, M.

Spengler, Oswald
The hour of decision
rev. by G. West
Man and technics
rev. by M. Pollard

Spero, Leonard
A job in a million, 12.
ND, 14 30S37, 20—21 p

Spivak, John L.
see Ashleigh, Charles

Spottiswoode, Raymond
The cinema today.
TO, i 2 A38, 25—28 c

Sprigg, Christopher St. John
see Caudwell, Christopher *pseud.*

Sprigge, Sylvia
Friends; Littlehampton,
January 1939.
AC, i 1 C39, 3—4 v

Stanley, Perdita
As Miss Stein says.
ND, 19 4N37, 28 c
Bouquets for the Colonel.
ND, 4 22Jy37, 28 r
A triumph for Lichine.
ND, 14 30S37, 36 c

Stanley, Sydney
Between the lines of a 'Times'
leader.
OB, i 4 Je35, 17—20 c

Stanley-Wrench, Margaret
Arcady.
C, i 23 9My36, 183—84 v
Circus.
C, ii 48 21N36, 173 v
Descent from the Pyrenees.
B, 1 Su38, 12 v
The dryad.
DD, x 39 My—Je33, 51 v
Listener.
LD, i 4 Je37, 18 v
Lost.
FB, iii 9 6Je38, 70 v
Mirror.
PR, 23 N37, 8 v
Moment transfixed.
C, i 5 5J36, 39 v
News reel.
LD, ii 3 F38, 5—6 v
Our words the wind.
PR, 20 17 N36, 3 v
Parable.
FB, iv 10 N38, 2 v
Spring frost.
B, 2 W38, 10 v
Wistaria.
C, ii 34 15Ag36, 51—52 v
The Lyceum book of verse
rev. by P. Hole
News reel rev. by J. Symons

Stanton, Blair Hughes-
see Hughes-Stanton, Blair

Stapledon, William Olaf
Odd john rev. by T. Lincoln

Star maker rev. by S. Blumenfeld
Waking world
rev. by A. Williams-Ellis

Starkie, Enid
Baudelaire psycho-analysed
[*The defeat of Baudelaire,*
by J. Laforgue].
OO, xii 58 My32, 123—31 r
Arthur Rimbaud rev. by H.A.B.

Stead, Christina
The writers take sides.
LR, i 11 Ag35, 453—63 c
The beauties and the furies
rev. by G. West

Stead, Philip John
Anubis and Osiris.
FB, iii 9 6Je38, 73 v
Aubade.
B, 1 Su38, 17 v
Bomber.
B, 2 W38, 12 v
Disinheritance.
B, 1 Su38, 3 v
Easter 1937.
LD, i 3 My37, 21 v
The encounter.
LD, ii 3 F38, 17 v
The farm.
LD, ii 2 D37, 17—18 p
The friends.
LD, ii 1 Oc37, 11 v
October fair.
LD, i 3 My37, 30—31 p
Poem.
K, i 1 17N39, 16 v
The poems of Louis MacNeice.
B, 1 Su38, 14—15 c
Review [*In parenthesis,*
by D. Jones].
PR, 23 N37, 15 r
Saturday night: mining town;
April poem.
FB, iii 7 25N37, 33, 34 v
The sentinel.
LD, ii 2 D37, 10 v
Two seaside poems.
PR, 23 N37, 4 v

Steedman, George
Surrealism: or is this the key
of the kingdom?
FB, iii 8 3M38, 57—58 c

Steel, James
Pantheism.
DD, x 40 Jy—Ag33, 68 v
The rebels.
DD, xi 44 M—A34, 33 v
The sower.
DD, xi 48 N—D34, 95 v

Steele, James
The conveyor rev. by J. Stewart

Steer, George
The fall of Balbao.
ND, 6 5Ag37, 17—19 p

Stein, Gertrude
A portrait of the Abdys.
J, 2 My37, 15 p
Procession.
PR, 8 19Je35, 8—9, 11 p

Stein, J. H.
Frosty moonlight.
DD, viii 28 J—F31, 37 v
Winter mists.
DD, ix 34 Jy—Ag32, 65 v

Steinbeck, John
In dubious battle
rev. by A. L. Morton

Steinberg, Isaac
Spiridonova
rev. by A. Williams-Ellis

Steiner, Harold Arthur
Government in Fascist Italy
rev. by F. E. Jones

Steni, L. *pseud.*
Mère deux oeufs.
NS, i 2 A34, 81—91 p

Stephens, James
The living torch, by A. E.
rev. by G. Grigson
Vale and other poems, by A. E.
rev. by C. B. Spencer

Stephenson, Robert
Lament for the flycatchers.
JG, 67 W38, [30—31] v

Stern, James
Ladies and gentlemen.
NW, 5 Sp38, 142—62 p
The man from Montparnasse.
P, 1 1938, 177—93 p
Next door to death.
NW, ns1 Au38, 110—21 p
Our mother.
NS, i 6 D34, 426—36 p
A stranger among miners.
NW, 3 Sp37, 1—8 p

Stevens, Wallace
Answers to an enquiry.
NV, 11 Oc34, 15 p
Answers to an enquiry.
T, 12/13 Oc38, 112 p
The blue buildings in the
summer air.

SV, 3 W38, 5 v
Connoisseur of chaos.
T, 12/13 Oc38, 90 v
Farewell to Florida.
CPP, 3 Jy36, 52—53 v
Inaccesible Utopia;
The place of poetry.
T, 3 A37, [3] v
The man with the blue guitar.
T, 5 S37, [2—7] v
Thunder by the musician.
SV, 4 Su39, 7—8 v
Ideas of order rev. by G. Grigson
The man with the blue guitar
rev. by S. F. Morse

Stevenson, Lionel
Pagan prayer.
DD, ix 33 My—Je32, 46 v
Revelation.
DD, x 39 My—Je33, 53 v
Summer interlude.
DD, ix 32 M—A32, 29 v

Stewart, Douglas
The white cry
rev. by M. J. Tambimuttu

Stewart, Gervase
Fire.
SV, 4A Sp39, 43 v
Hints to astronomers;
Poem for John.
FB, v 1 F39, 7, 9 v
Obituary notice for the squire.
FB, v 2 My39, 28 v
Poem.
SV, 4 Su39, 33—34 v
Poem.
K, i 2 D39—J40, 53 v

Stewart, Jean
Claudel and Valéry on poetry.
V, 5 F30, 199—207 c
English intellectual and
American proletarian
[*Men adrift,* by A. Bertram;
The conveyor, by J. Steele].
LR, ii 6 M36, 285 r
Romain Rolland
[*I will not rest*].
LR, ii 6 M36, 277—78 r
see also Rolland R.

Stewart, John Anderson
Caradoc's monument.
DD, x 42 N—D33, 103 v
Conscience.
DD, x 38 M—A33, 34 v
The night journey.
DD, xi 48 N—D34, 103 v
Star-gazing.
DD, xi 45 My—Je34, 41 v

Stewart, William M'Causland
Review [*Ash Wednesday*,
by T. S. Eliot].
MS, i 3 Au30, 98—100 r
Review [*How to read*,
by E. Pound].
MS, ii 4 J32, 347—49 r
see also Valéry, P.

Stinson, Gertrude Sheila
Awareness.
PQ, i 2 Su39, 46 v

Stoker, E. M.
The downs.
DD, xi 46 Jy—Ag34, 65 v

Stokes, Stanley
Fog; Fish.
DD, viii 30 Au31, 117 v
The reason; Belief.
DD, viii 28 J—F31, 22 v
Transformation;
Artists.
DD, vii 26 S—Oc30, 392 v

Stone, George
The Little Theatre,
Bournemouth.
R, i 3 A34, 11 c

Stone, Isobel
A Welch tapestry.
JG, 17 Su31, [28] v

Stone, Myrtle
Ager: a harvest hymn.
DD, x 40 Jy—Ag33, 67 v

Stonier, George Walter
Patricia.
SV, 4 Su39, 23 v
Poetry and the individual.
T, 3 A37, [14—18] c
That taxi-driver.
T, 6/7 N37, [22—24] c

Stopes, Marie Carmichael
Youth.
K, i 1 17N39, 5 v

Storm over Canicatti,
tr. by J. Rodker.
NW, 1 Sp36, 132—46 p

Storrs, Ronald
Orientations rev. E. Waugh

Stowell, Gordon
From an imaginary diary.
HR, 6 1933, 47—49 p

Strachey, Evelyn John St. Loe

130

The American scene.
LR, i 9 Je35, 347—58 c
The education of a communist.
LR, i 3 D34, 63—69 p
A 'New Statesman' pamphlet
[*Abyssinia*, by Vigilantes].
LR, ii 2 N35, 51—54 r
On the organisation of authors.
LR, iii 1 F37, 46—47 c
Paris Congress speech.
LR, i 11 Ag35, 472 c
Should John Strachey be
deported [quotations].
LR, i 8 My35, 307—11 c
The coming struggle for power
rev. by W. N. Warbey
The menace of fascism
rev. by W. N. Warbey
*The theory and practice of
socialism* rev. by E. Roll

Straker, S. Christine
Embrace,
JG, 42 Au37, [24—25] v
First snow.
JG, 31 W34, [10] v
The forest.
JG, 40 Sp37, [15—16] v
Friendship.
JG, 34 Au35, [19] v
Gethsemane.
JG, 68 Sp39, [24] v
The half of life.
JG, 37 Su36, [17] v
I be thine.
JG, 30 Au34, [9] v
Life and death.
JG, 32 Sp35, [7] v
Love song.
JG, 29 Su34, [18] v
My garden.
JG, 38 Au36, [32—33] v
Sanctuary.
JG, 64 Sp38, [24] v

Strawinsky, Soulima
Words and music.
TO, ii 6 A39, 8—10 c

Street, Arthur George
The endless furrow
rev. by E. Muir
Land everlasting
rev. by E. Muir

Strick, John Richard
Correspondence.
TO, ii 5 J39, 17 c

Strohbach, Hans
Pelléas and Mélisande.
F, 6 Je31, 137 i

Strong, Leslie Arthur George

Bank holiday.
FB, v 2 My39, 25—28 p
The escape.
NS, i 2 A34, 92—97 p
Tuesday afternoon
rev. by G. West

Struther, Jan *pseud.*
The curious phenomenon of the
militarist's sister.
ND, 23 2D37, 11—12 p
Miss Beverley feeds the birds.
ND, 8 19Ag37, 8, 10—11 p
The poet and the sage.
ND, 3 15Jy37, 17, 19 p
R.I.P.
ND, 24 9D37, 24 v

Struve, Gleb
Soviet Russian literature
rev. by A. Brown

Stuart, Francis
Post-war portrait.
TC, iv 19 S32, 8—10 p
The coloured dome
rev. by M. Pollard
Pigeon Irish
rev. by G. Pendle
Try the sky
rev. by M. Pollard

Stuart, Gwendolen
Poem.
T, 3 A37, [11] v

Stuart, Muriel
Pagan.
I, i 2/3 15S31, 87 v
Unknown warrior.
I, i 2/3 15S31, 52 v

Stubbs, H. W.
Blackshirt's lament.
OB, i 1 M—A34, 24 v

Subramaniam, Alagru
This time the fan.
LR, iii 8 S37, 463—67 p

Suckling, Norman *and*
Hodge, Alan
The Scioliad.
PR, 15 1M36, 8—10 v

Summers, Montague
Joris-Karl Huysmans.
OO, x 52 My30, 514—21 c

Summerson, John Newenham
Those stately homes:
Wilton and the earls.
ND, 26 23D37, 27—28 c
Where starlings rest:

those stately homes, 2:
Seaton Deleval.
ND, 14 30S37, 30—31 c

Sutcliffe, Harry
Renunciation.
PQ, i 2 Su39, 39 v

Sutherland, James
The medium of poetry
rev. by H.C.S.

Sutherland, Robert Garioch
see Garioch, Robert *pseud.*

Sutton, Denys
On the school of painting for 1938.
Y, i 1 M39, 38—42 c

Sutton, Lance
To an organ.
DD, ix 31 J—F32, 12—13 v
The wild ducks.
DD, x 37 J—F33, 15 v

Svetlov, Michael
Granada.
LR, iii 13 F38, 798—800 v

Svevo, Italo
As a man grows older
rev. by H. G. Porteus

Swaab, Jack S.
The coffee ritual; The tree.
FB, iii 7 25N37, 29 p, v
A modern Parnassus.
FB, iii 6 21Oc37, 14—15 p
The rape of the Sabines.
FB, iii 8 3M38, 51 p
The river.
FB, iii 7 25N37, 24 v
Sonnet.
FB, iii 6 21Oc37, 20 v
Sonnet.
FB, ii 8 3M38, 57 v
Wondering.
FB, iii 6 21Oc37, 2 v

Swabey, Henry
Notes.
TO, ii 8 N39, 5—6 c
Review
[*The farmers' manifesto*;
The compensated price;
both by the National Farmers
Union].
TO, ii 7 Ag39, 25—26 r

Swart, E. V.
Casey Jones.
NV, 21 Je36, 3—4 v
Two poems.
NV, 18 D35, 12—14 v

Sweeney, A.
Poem.
FB, ii 4 25J37, 16 v

Sweeney, J. L.
Poem. W, 5 Su38, 177—78 v
Poem.
T, 8 J38, [9] v
Poem.
SV, 1 Su38, 32 v
Potwan.
W, 4 M38, 139 p

Swick, Helen
The hour off.
NS, ii 7 F36, 525—29 p

Swift, Jonathan
Swift, ed. by J. Hayward
rev. by E. Rickword

Swingler, Randall Carline
Angelus.
F, 2 Je30, 75—79 v
Beauty's freedom;
The eagle's feather.
TC, iv 24 F33, 19 v
Before morning.
LR, i i Oc34, 17 v
Bird rock.
F, 1 F30, 19 v
Chorus and audience:
notes on a new form.
GTP, 3 S36, 3—4 c
Chorus from a play:
'Crucifixus'.
TC, iv 20 Oc32, 5 v
Diary of a revolutionary;
The swans.
NO, i 1 My33, 75—76 v
Editorial.
LR, iii 6 Jy37, 317—18;
LR, iii 9 Oc37, 509—10;
LR, iii 10 N37, 573—76;
LR, iii 11 D37, 637—40;
LR, iii 12 J38, 701—3;
LR, iii 13 F38, 765—67;
LR, iii 14 M38, 829—32;
LR, iii 15 A38, 893—95;
LR, iii 16 My38, 957—60 c
Elegy.
T, 5 S37, [15] v
Good Friday in Spain.
PP, 15 N39, 12—13 v
Hard march; The gulls;
Ascent into power.
NO, ii 1 My34, 46—48 v
History and the poet.
NW, ns3 C39, 47—54 c
The imputation of madness:
a study of William Blake and
literary tradition.

LR, iii 1 F37, 21—28 c
Last stage.
NS, i 3 Je34, 211—16 p
Mind's exploration; Dancer;
Morning pride; Cloud.
F, 4 D30, 14—16 v
MSS from the mountains.
NS, ii 2 A35, 148—60 p
On the development of poetry.
PP, 1 Jy38, 4—9 c
Philosophy is science
[*A philosophy for the modern
man*, by H. Levy].
LR, iii 14 M38, 887—88 r
Poem.
NV, 4 Jy33, 9 v
Poem.
LR, ii 10 Jy36, 514 v
Poem.
PP, 1 Jy38, 11—12 v
A seat in the dress circle.
LD, i 4 Je37, 23, 25 c
'Something will be done'
[*The problem of the distressed
areas*, by W. Hannington].
LR, iii 12 J38, 752—54 r
Speech from a play.
GTP, 5 N36, 4 v
Spender's approach to
communism
[*Forward from Liberalism*,
by S. Spender].
LR, iii 2 M37, 110—13 r
Three poems.
MS, vi 1 A35, 29 v
Triumphal song for the
peacemaker.
PP, 5 N38, 4 v
Two pastorals.
LT, i 1 M36, 40—41 v
Two poems.
TC, v 25 M33, 22—23 v
Two poems.
NW, 5 Sp38, 197—99 v
Two sonnets.
CV, 5 M36, [17] v
What is the artist's job?
LR, iii 15 A38, 930—32 c
Writers international.
LR, i 3 D34, 78 c
Difficult morning
rev. by G. Grigson; A. D.
Hawkins
No escape rev. by T. L. Hodgkin
Reconstruction
rev. by H. G. Porteus
Spain rev. by D. Kahn
see also Bush, Alan Dudley;
Ibsen, H.

Swingler, Stephen
Diderot: a living force
[*Diderot, interpreter of nature*,

Swingler, Stephen (cont.)
ed. by J. Kemp].
LR, iii 6 Jy37, 372—73 r

Swinnerton, Frank Arthur
Authors and the book trade
rev. by G. West

Swinstead-Smith, K.
The Marchesa and other stories
rev. by E. J. O'Brien

Sykes, Hugh *later* H. S. Davies
see Davies, Hugh Sykes

Sykes, J. A.
Autumn of the mood,
words by C. Day Lewis.
F, 5 F31, 110—11 m

Sylander, Gordon
Apocalypse; Five parts of
wholly dying.
SV, 4 Su39, 12 v

Symes, Gordon
A detective story.
FB, iii 7 25N37, 36—38 p
The djongleur and the djinn.
FB, iii 8 3M38, 60—61 p
'. . . et praeterea nihil'.
FB, iii 9 6Je38, 74—75 p
A fairy story.
FB, iii 6 21Oc37, 5—7 p
The traveller who found
himself.
FB, iv 10 N38, 18—19 p

Symons, Alphonse
James Albert
An episode in the life of the
Queen of Sheba.
F, 3 Oc30, 183—89 p
A forgotten dinner party.
FB, i 1 4F36, 12—14 c
The novelist.
T, 6/7 N37, [18—21] c
Review
[*English poetical autographs,*
ed. by D. Flower and A. N. L.
Munby].
T, 14 D38, 139—40 r
Round the restaurants.
ND, 12 11S37, 27—28;
ND, 18 28Oc37, 28;
ND, 25 16D37, 28 c

Symons, Julian
About frontiers
[*Collected essays in literary
criticism,* by H. Read;
The mysterious Mr. Bull,
by P. W. Lewis;

On the frontier, by W. H. Auden
and C. Isherwood;
Collected poems, by R. Graves;
Being geniuses together,
by R. McAlmon;
The year's poetry, 1938,
ed. by D. K. Roberts and
G. Grigson].
T, 15/16 F39, 163—67 r
Against surrealism.
T, 3 A37, [2] c
Aiken, Pitter
[*Time in the rock,*
by C. Aiken;
A trophy of arms,
by R. Pitter].
T, 2 M37, [16—17] r
Briefly [*The Southern review;
Wales,* no.1].
T, 5 S37, [19] r
Briefly [*The Southern review;
The year's poetry, 1937,*
ed. by D. K. Roberts and
G. Grigson].
T, 9 M38, 19—20 c
Briefly.
T, 10 My38, 44—45;
T, 14 D38, 141—42 c
Change of season.
C, i 8 25J36, 63 v
Construction and invention
[*Hawk among the sparrows,*
by D. Hawkins;
Over the mountain,
by R. Todd;
Happy valley, by P. White].
T, 17 A39, 22—23 r
Everyman's poems
[*I crossed the Minch,*
by L. MacNeice;
The earth compels,
by L. MacNeice].
T, 11 Jy38, 69—71 r
Exclusiveness, politics,
etc.
T, 2 M37, [2] p
The family reunion,
[by T. S. Eliot]
T, 18 Je39, 44—48 r
The half and half.
C, ii 45 31Oc36, 146—47 v
Hart Crane.
T, 8 J38, [20—23] c
How wide is the Atlantic:
or, Do you believe in
America?
T, 12/13 Oc38, 80—84 c
The journey, parts 1 and 2.
W, 5 Su38, 162—64 v
Mr Wyndham Lewis.
T, 6/7 N37, [2] c
Notes on 'One-way song'.
T, 6/7 N37, [27—29] c
Poem.

NV, 16 Ag35, 11 v
Poem.
PR, 13 5F36, 7 v
Poem.
C, ii 38 12S36, 83 v
Poem.
T, 14 D38, 128 v
Poem.
SV, 3 W38, 42 v
Poem; Prologue; This year.
T, 5 S37, [12—13] v
Poems for a sequence.
C, i 26 13Je36, 205 v
Prelude to poems.
T, 9 M38, 16—17 v
Programme 1938.
T, 8 J38, [2] p
Review [*The lemon tree,*
by M. Ruddock;
Euripides Ion tr. by H.D.].
T, 4 Je37, [22] r
Review [*The ascent of F6,*
by W. H. Auden and C. Isherwood].
T, 3 A37, [19—20] r
Review [*Poems,*
by K. Allott].
T, 14 D38, 136—38 r
Review
[*New verse: an anthology,*
ed. by G. Grigson].
W, 11 W39, 308 r
The romantic speaking.
T, 1 J37, [11] v
Sonnet.
W, 6/7 M39, 206 v
Tuttifrutti: or the worse for poetry.
T, 17 A39, 19 c
Twentieth century verse.
T, 1 J37, [2] c
Two poems.
NV, 16 Ag35, 5 v
Words as narrative
[*Twenty-five poems,*
by D. Thomas].
T, 1 J37, [17—19] r
X, Y and Z [*Poems,*
by C. H. Peacock;
News reel, by M. Stanley-Wrench;
The garden of disorder,
by C. H. Ford].
T, 11 Jy38, 78 r
Confusions about X
rev. by R. Fuller; H. G. Porteus;
M. J. Tambimuttu
see also Ewart, G.

Symons, Julian *and* **Mallalieu,** H. B.
Conversation after dinner.
T, 18 Je39, 28—31 p

Syrett, Netta
The sheltering tree
rev. by J. Gawsworth

T

T., E.
D. H. Lawrence's literary debut.
EQ, i 3 N34, 159—68 c
D. H. Lawrence's student days.
EQ, i 2 Ag34, 106—14 c
The literary formation of D. H.
Lawrence.
EQ, i 1 My34, 36—45 c

T., G.
Class struggles in the Roman world
[*Marc Antony*, by J. Lindsay].
LR, iii 3 A37, 185—86 r

T., G. H.
Review [*Letters from Iceland*,
by W. H. Auden and L. MacNeice].
PR, 23 N37, 14 r

T., J.
A parting.
PR, 6 31My35, 7 v

T., R. G.
Review [*Stricken gods*,
by J. Lindsay].
TC, iii 15 My32, 32 r

Tabidze, Titsian
Festival song, tr. by J. L.
NW, 4 Au37, 198 v

Taggard, Genevieve *and* **Fitts**, Dudley
Ten introductions
rev. by G. Grigson

Tagore, Rabindranath
The son of man.
HR, 6 1933, 29 v

Taig, Thomas
Swansea little theatre.
WR, i 1 F39, 51 c

Tait, Stephen
see Allot, Keith

Tallis, Eric
A tale of a hero.
PP, 2 Ag38, 17—18 v

Tambimuttu, M. J.
First letter.
PL, i 1 F39, [1—4] c
Four Ceylonese love songs.
PL, i 2 A39, [12—13] v
My Symons in his nursery
[*The white cry*, by D. Stewart;
Confusions about X,
by J. Symons; *The right review*,

January 1939; *Seven*].
PL, i 2 A39, [28—30] r
Review [*Quixotic perceptions*,
by G. Reavey].
PL, i 1 F39, [32] r
Second letter.
PL, i 2 A39, [2] c

Tansley, Ronald
In the summer.
NS, i 2 A34, 98—104 p

Tarr, John Charles
Cotswold picnic.
P, 4 1938, 170 i

Taseer, M. D.
Correspondence: the Indian problem.
CM, i 4 Sp34, 195—98 c

Tate, John Orley Allen
Aenaes at Washington.
NV, 7 F34, 4—5 v
Answers to an enquiry.
NV, 11 Oc34, 20—22 p
Answers to an enquiry.
T, 12/13 Oc38, 112 p
Comment on Auden.
NV, 26/27 N37, 27 c
Eclogue of the liberal and the
liberal poet.
T, 12/13 Oc38, 85—86 v
The meaning of life.
NV, 2 M33, 9—10 v
The Mediterranean.
NV, 5 Oc33, 8—9 v
A new artist [*Poems*,
by S. Spender].
NV, 3 My33, 21—23 r
Reactionary essays
rev. by A. Hodge
Selected poems
rev. by G. Parsons

Taviton town.
DD, xi 44 M—A34, 17 v

Tayler, Herbert
The Paris exhibition.
AX, 8 W37, 19—22 c

Taylor, Allan N.
All God's chillun.
DV, 1 M32, 10—13 c
Perspective.
DV, 2 A32, 63 v
U.S.E.
DV, 3 My32, 26—29 c

Taylor, Basil
Commonplace words.
DE, 2 Su32, 3 p
Pictures.
EP, 3 Sp37, 190 i

Taylor, Dorothy
To T.H.T.
DD, xi 45 My—Je34, 47 v
To T.H.T.
DD, xi 47 S—Oc34, 82 v

Taylor, E. L. S.
William Burrough: a study of a Quaker
personality.
HR, 5 1932, 40—42 c

Taylor, Geoffrey Gordon
At the play; Desiccated poem;
Mistakes cannot be rectified.
T, 8 J38, [8] v
Conceit; Black beauty.
T, 11 Jy38, 66 v
Epigrams.
NV, 13 F35, 14—15 v
On a vain poet.
NV, i 2 My39, 41 v
Portrait 1936; Epigram of straw;
To the builder; In the street.
T, 1 J37 [4—5] v
She mocks at time; Farewell to art;
Ambition; Oil painting and sculpture
in wood; From the French of a poem
picked up in the Bois de Boulogne.
NV, 15 Je35, 8—11 v
Six poems.
NV, 13 F35, 6—8 v
The triumph; The nightmare.
T, 15/16 F39, 149—50 v
Three anthologies •
[*The modern poet*,
ed. by G. Murphy;
Cassell's anthology of English poetry,
ed. by M. and D. Flower;
A treasury of unfamiliar lyrics,
ed. by N. Ault].
T, 14 D38, 133—36 r
Two epitaphs; Abdication.
T, 2 M37, [13] v
Vision of Eden; Dead months.
W, 5 Su38, 166—67 v

Taylor, Jack
Song of revolt.
PP, 8 F39, 16 v
The unemployed.
PP, 12 Je39, 13—14 v

Taylor, Peter
Quatrains.
DD, xi 47 S—Oc34, 86 v

Taylor, R. S.
Running.
LR, ii 2 M36, 270—71 p

Tchang T'ien-yih
Hatred.
NW, 1 Sp36, 203—18 p

Tchikvadze, P.
The road to affluence.
NW, 3 Sp37, 248—56 p

The tea party, by a seven-year-old girl.
CPP, 2 Je36, 39 p

Teeling, William
Our continental correspondent.
ND, 25 16D37, 32 p

Teesdale, E. B.
Olympic games.
FB, i 1 4F36, 8 c

Telco, Paul
The birth control racket.
TC, ii 7 S31, 11—15; TC, ii 8 Oc31,
16—19 c

Temple, William *Archbishop of York*
Epilogue.
HR, 4 1931, 71 c

Ten Uraon poems.
NV, 22 S36, 9—10 v

Teng Kwei
Industrialism and art [in China].
I, i 2/3 15S31, 84 c

Tennant, Peter Frank Dalrymple
The themes of Ibsen's plays.
FB, i 2 3M36, 30—32, 59—60 c

A terrible battle fought on the fifty-
twelfth day of rotten sticks.
Found! The young man who has been
missing since the 21st of October last.
Attractive sale, A wonderful receipt for
whiskers.
NV, 23 C36, 3—7 p

Terry, C. P.
Toynbee defies Tolstoy.
LD, ii 3 F38, 27—29 c

Tessimond, Arthur Seymour John
Any man speaks;
Epitaph on a disturber of the age.
S, 1 J33, 11 v
England.
NW, ns3 C39, 83—84 v
Invitation to dance; Portrait of J.M.'s
hands.
PR, 4 5M35, 2—3 v
Poem.
P, 2 1938, 179 v
Song of the city.
ND, 13 23S37, 31 v
Steel April.
TC, iii 18 Ag32, 21 v
To a lover of living; In that cold land.
T, 1 J37, [6] v

The walls of glass
rev. by G. Grigson; D. A. Willis

Tew, David
The Cornish landscape.
PP, 9 M39, 19 v

Thackeray, William Makepeace
It happened before: 1714.
LR, iii 4 My37, 199—200 p

The theatre in Cambridge.
FB, i 3 9My36, 58 c

Thesiger, Ernest
The Dauphin and how I approached the
part.
R, i 1 N33, 4 c
Restaurant.
IP, i 1 6A39, 13—14 c

Thoma, Richard
On the sowing of the wind.
S, 2 A—Jy33, 26 v
Green chaos
rev. by R. Burford
The promised land
rev. by R. Burford

Thomas, Arthur Spencer Vaughan-
see Vaughan-Thomas, Arthur Spencer

Thomas, Dylan Marlais
An adventure from a work in progress.
SV, 4A Sp39, 45—48 p
Answers to an enquiry.
NV, 11 Oc34, 8—9 p
The burning baby.
CPP, 1 My36, 10—14 p
Comment on Auden.
NV, 26/27 N37, 25 c
The dress.
C, i 5 4J36, 35 p
The enemies.
NS, i 3 Je34, 194—98 p
The enemies.
Y, i 1 M39, 32—37 p
Fey, Dollfuss, Vienna
[*Vienna*, by S. Spender].
NV 12 D34, 19—20 r
The holy six.
CPP, 9 Sp37, 18—26 p
The horse's ha.
J, 2 My36, 4—9 p
In the direction of the beginning.
W, 4 M38, 147—48 p
January 1939.
T, 15/16 F39, 148 v
Just like little dogs.
W, 10 Oc39, 255—60 p
The map of love.
W, 3 Au37, 116—23 p
Patricia, Edith and Arnold.

SV, 7 C39, 4—11 p
Poem.
NV, 8 A34, 11—12 v
Poem.
NV, 10 Ag34, 8—9 v
Poem.
NV, 12 D34, 10—12 v
Poem.
PR, 9 23Oc35, 2—3 v
Poem.
PR, 9 23Oc35, 10, 12 v
Poem.
C, i 9 1F36, 66 v
Poem.
CV, 5 M36, [15] v
Poem (For Caitlin).
T, 8 J38, [3—4] v
Poem.
W, 4 M38, 138 v
Poem (For Caitlin).
W, 5 Su38, 179—81 v
Poem.
VS, i 3 D38—F39, 12 v
Poem; poem.
W, 6/7 M39, 196 v
Poem.
PL, i 2 A39, [25] v
Poem in the ninth month.
PL, i 1 F39, [26—27] v
Poem, part 1.
T, 1 J37, [3] v
A poem in three parts.
NV, 16 Ag35, 2—5 v
Prologue to an adventure.
W, 1 Su37, 1—6 p
Review [*Night wood*,
by D. Barnes].
LD, i 2 M37, 27, 29 r
The school for witches.
CPP, 4/5 Ag36, 95—100 p
Three poems.
NV, 18 D35, 15—17 v
To others than you.
SV, 6 Au39, 5—7 v
The true story; The vest.
Y, i 2 My39, 60—67 p
Two poems.
NV, 9 Je34, 6—9 v
Two poems.
CPP, 1 My36, 2—3 v
Two poems.
SV, 3 W38, 17 v
Two poems towards a poem.
CPP, 3 Jy36, 53 v
We lying by seasand.
W, 3 Au37, 82 v
Eighteen poems rev. by A. Hodge;
NV, 13 F35, 21—22
The map of love
rev. by D. Aberpennar; G. Jones;
H. Read
Twenty-five poems
rev. by N. Heseltine; H. Howarth;
C. B. Spencer; J. Symons

Thomas, F. W.
Homo sap.
PP, 15 N39, 5 v

Thomas, Tom
The New Theatre League.
LR, ii 4 J36, 192 c

Thompson, Alexander Hamilton
The abbeys of Yorkshire.
HR, 4 1931, 11—15 c
Some remarks on English parish
churches.
HR, 7 1934, 12—15 c

Thompson, Denys
Extract from a text book:
'Between the lines'.
TO, i 3 Jy38, 19—22 c
Reviewers reviewed.
TO, i 1 J38, 28—30 c
Review [*African genesis,*
by L. Frobenius and D. C. Fox].
TO, i 3 Jy38, 31 r
Review [*Poetry and anarchism,*
by H. Read].
TO, i 4 Oc38, 24—25 r
Review [*Guide to culture,*
by E. Pound].
TO, ii 5 J39, 30—31 r
Reading and discrimination
rev. by S.H.V.A.
see also Leavis, Frank Raymond

Thompson, Peter
Basement fever.
NW, 5 Sp38, 126—31 p

Thomson, David Cleghorn
Scrutiny of 'Scrutiny', 2.
TC, vi 31 S—Oc33, 56—57 c
Some reflections on the drama in
Scotland.
MS, ii 1 A31, 45—52 c

Thomson, George Malcolm
The fight at Faughart.
MS, i 1 Sp30, 37—40 p

Thomson, Hector
Art, drains and Garbo.
LD, i 3 My37, 9—10 c
A Christmas tragedy.
FB, iii 7 25N37, 25 p
Confession I.
PR, 23 N37, 9 v
Confession IV,
B, 1 Su38, 16—17 v
Confession V.
B, 2 W38, 10—11 v
Food for thought.
LD, ii 3 F38, 6—7 c
Hermongrove.
FB, iii 7 25N37, 31 v

The replica.
LD, ii 2 D37, 5—6 p
A return to romanticism?
FB, iii 8 3M38, 56—57 c
Sappho and romanticism.
PR, 21 1M37, 14—16 c
Sentimental piece.
PR, 23 N37, 5 v
Sleeping out on fringe of city.
LD, ii 2 D37, 25 v
Three estates.
LD, ii 1 Oc37, 13, 15 p
Tischbein.
LD, ii 1 Oc37, 22 v
Winter.
LD, ii 3 F38, 26 v
see also Howarth, Herbert

Thomson, John
Where were you born?
LD, i 4 Je37, 9 v

Thorndike, Sybil
Greetings on May day.
LR, iii 16 My38, 962 c
Lecture.
R, i 1 N33, 6—8 c

Thornley, Thomas
An Aberdeen terrier; Retirement.
DD, viii 28 J—F31, 33 v
The four pilgrims.
DD, vii 26 S—Oc30, 382 v
Moss Eccles tarn; A lost home.
DD, vii 27 N—D30, 441—42 v
My pipe.
DD, vii 26 S—Oc30, 383—84 v
The ultra-modernist poet.
DD, vii 26 S—Oc30, 383 v

Thornton, Frances W.
With the Ledbury.
PQ, i 1 Sp39, 8 v

Thornton, Philip
Dead puppets dance
rev. by E. Waugh

Thornton-Duesbery, Julian Percy
The 'Oxford' groups defended.
NO, i 1 My33, 86—94 c

Thoroughgood, H. *see* Low, David

Thorp, Molly
Man overboard.
NS, ii 6 D36, 433—44 p

Thurber, James Grover
A night with the Klan.
ND, 22 25N37, 12—14 p

Thwaites, J. *and* **Thwaites**, M.
Surrealism and abstraction — the search

for subjective form.
AX, 6 Su36, 21—25 c

Tickel, Gilbert
Subtle technique.
LR, ii 8 My36, 386—90 p

Tiedeman, M. L. Seaton
The struggle for divorce law reform.
TC, ii 7 S31, 19—21 c

Tikhonov, Nikolai Semenovich
Morale, tr. by S. Garry.
NW, 4 Au37, 62—76 p
Nights in a Persian garden,
tr. by A. Brown.
NW, 2 Au36, 189—97 p
Story with a footnote.
tr. by S. Garry.
NW, ns1 Au38, 213—31 p
The tea-khan at 'The pond of the emir',
tr. by A. Brown.
NW, 1 Sp36, 87—106 p
Zeebrugge, tr. by A. Brown.
PP, 9 M39, 18—19 v

Tiller, L. M. N.
Triolet.
DD, viii 29 Su31, 80 v

Tiller, Terence R.
The double promise.
PP, 10 A39, 9 v
Lines to an eminent gentleman.
PP, 8 F39, 3 v
Poem.
FB, v 2 My39, 28 v

Tillotson, Arthur
As it is in heaven.
EX, 5 F30, 37 v
Suspicion.
EX, 5 F30, 28 v

Tillotson, Geoffrey
Two poems at New college chapel.
F, 4 D30, 30 v

Tilsley, Frank
Devil take the hindmost
rev. by J. Lindsay
I'd do it again
rev. by G. West

Timbron *pseud.*
Armaments.
LR, ii 15 D36, 827—28 p

Ting Ling
One day.
NW, 5 Sp38, 236—40 p

Titterington, John
Workless.
PP, 5 N38, 16—17 v

Todd, John Murray
Colour.
FB, iv 10 N38, 15 v
Cosmopolitan fare: 'Seven'.
FB, iv 10 N38, 11—12 r
Hang-over.
TH, 3 24F39, 2 v
Poem.
FB, iii 9 6 Je38, 70 v
'Tendebantque manus . . .'
FB, iv 10 N38, 1—2 p
Two ladies.
FB, iii 9 6Je38, 78 v

Todd, Judith
'Aristocrats' as a film.
LR, iii 3 A37, 189 r

Todd, Ruthven
Checklist of books and articles by
Wyndham Lewis.
T, 9 M38, 21—27 b
Christopher Wood.
PL, i 2 A39, [21] v
The commanding feather.
PR, 14 19F36, 6—7 v
Comments on a critic.
T, 6/7 N37, [36—38] c
Day's content.
C, ii 30 18Jy36, 15 v
Do you believe in geography?
NV, i 1 J39, 12 v
Drawings for 'Guernica'.
LB, 8/9 J39, 59 v
Evasion.
C, ii 38 12S36, 83 v
For Joan Miro.
LB, 13 15A39, 10 v
For John Piper.
LB, 6 Oc38, 27 v
From an outpost.
CV, 5 M36, [19—20] v
Gods, ghosts and heroes.
T, 10 My38, 36—38 v
The idiot.
C, i 16 21M36, 127 v
It was easier.
T, 15/16 F39, 147—48 v
Legend.
NV, i 1 J39, 6 v
The Little Review, 1.
T, 15/16 F39, 159—62 c
Migration.
VS, i 3 D38—F39, 22 v
Northward the islands.
T, 8 J38, [12] v
Offering for November; Poem for F.M.
T, 1 J37, [9] v
Paul Klee.
LB, 12 15M39, 18 v

Poem.
NV, 25 My37, 15 v
Poem. (For C.C.).
T, 9 M38, 15 v
Poem.
SV, 1 Su38, 19 v
Poem.
W, 5 Su38, 164—65 v
Poem.
NV, 29 M38, 11 v
Review [Surrealism,
ed. by H. Read;
The Scots week-end,
ed. by D. and C. Carswell;
The year's poetry,
ed. by D. K. Roberts;
Best poems of 1936,
ed. by T. Moult;
Reading the spirit,
by R. Eberhart;
Time in the rock,
by C. Aiken].
LT, i 10 D36, 32, 38, 43 r
Review
[Art and life in New Guinea,
by R. Firth;
New directions, 4].
LT, i 11 J37, 38—39, 40 r
Rhyme for the time, or 100% Arisch.
NV, i 1 J39, 16 v
Sometimes ghosts.
T, 5 S37, [16] v
Time was my friend.
NV, i 2 My39, 35—36 v
Two wars and Mr Campbell
[Journey to a war,
by W. H. Auden and C. Isherwood;
Poems for Spain,
ed. by S. Spender and J. Lehmann;
Flowering rifle, by R. Campbell].
T, 17 A39, 20—21 r
Unleavened bread
[Revaluations, by F. R. Leavis].
T, 2 M37, [14—15] r
Various places.
T, 14 D38, 129 v
Worm interviewed.
CPP, 3 Jy36, 54—55 v
Writings by W. H. Auden.
NV, 26/27 N37, 32—46 b
Over the mountain rev. by
J. Symons
see also Breton, A.; Eluard, P.;
Mesens, E. L. T.

Toller, Ernst
The German youth movement,
tr, by H. Ould.
DV, 2 A32, 36—39 c
The blind goddess
rev. by C. C. Doggett
Masses and men
rev. by C. C. Doggett
Seven plays rev. by B. Nixon

Tolstoy, Alexei
Art and happiness.
LR, iii 3 A37, 133—36 c

Tomalin, Miles
Empire builder.
LR, iii 13 F38, 779 v
Let's get sensible, what?
LR, iii 7 Ag37, 427 v

Tomkins, A. G.
Artist and crafstman.
LR, ii 2 N35, 79 c

Tomlin, Eric Walter Frederick
The bankruptcy of political thought.
AR, i 2 Jy37, 116—26 c
Classicism and the philosophy of
Bergson.
TO, i 3 Jy38, 27—30 c
The Criterion.
TO, ii 6 A39, 13—15 c
I. A. Richards and belief.
T, 10 My38, 46—51 c
Marxist economics.
AR, i 3 Oc37, 176—86 c
The philosopher-politician.
T, 6/7 N37, [32—36] c
Plea for poetry in the theatre.
R, i 6 Oc34, 7—8 c

Tomlinson, G. A. W.
Coal miner rev. by L. Jones

Tomlinson, Henry Major
All our yesterdays
rev. by F.H.

Tomlinson, Vera
A fallen pine tree.
JG, 13 Su30, [13] v
Nature.
JG, 15 W30, [27] v
Promise.
JG, 16 Sp31, [25] v

Tomorrow's money
rev. by A. Goldschmidt

Tompkins, John
Sea wall.
PQ, i 1 Sp39, 18 v

Tonge, John
The arts of Scotland
rev. by H. Macdiarmid

Toogood, Harry
John Smith; The worker.
PP, 9 M39, 7—8 v

Toppin, Isabel Whitehouse
They shall not pass.
PQ, i 2 Su39, 41 v

Topping, H. M.
Annal for the third decade.
LS, i 3 N34, 55—56 v
Pensioners be.
LS, i 1 F34, 19 v

Toros *pseud.*
The American artists' congress.
LR, ii 8 My36, 381—84 c
Cross section of English painting at the
Wildenstein gallery.
LR, iii 16 My38, 1007—9 c
The naive and the sophisticated.
LR, iii 15 A38, 927—30 c
Seventeenth century painting at
Burlington House.
LR, iii 13 F38 801—4 c

Torr, Dona
Marx: man and fighter
[*Karl Marx,*
by B. Nicolaievsky and O. Maenchen—
Helfen].
LR, ii 15 D36, 842 r
Ralph Fox and our cultural heritage.
LR, iii 1 F37, 5—6 c
Starting points
[*Friedrich Engels,*
by G. Mayer;
Karl Marx,
by F. Mehring].
LR, ii 13 Oc36, 713—14 r
Tom Mann rev. by T. A. Jackson

Towards the Christian revolution
rev. by H. Holorenshaw

Townsend, Irene
Mrs Parsons-Portal.
LD, ii 2 D37, 19, 21 p

Townsend, R. Uniacke
To what porpoise.
RM, 2 D34, 60 v

Toynbee, Arnold Joseph
A study of history, vols. 1—3
rev. by R. P. Arnot

Toynbee, Theodore Philip
Break-up.
LD, ii 3 F38, 29—31 p
Correspondence.
LD, i 4 Je37, 26—27 c

Tracy, Henry Chester
On individualism.
TC, iii 16 Je32, 8—10 p
Way of escape.
TC, iv 20 Oc32, 13—17 c
Way of escape, 2.
TC, iv 21 N32, 16—19 c

Traditional country ballads,

collected by A. L. Lloyd.
CPP, 10 Au37, 2—12 v

Transition [periodical] no.23
rev. by G. A. Hutt

A transport officer visits the General
Motors factory in Barcelona.
LR, ii 16 J37, 870—72 p

Traversi, Derek Antona
Marxism and English poetry.
AR, i 3 D37, 199—211 c
A note on Alfred Noyes.
AR, i 2 Jy37, 106—11 c
The novels of E. M. Forster.
AR, i 1 A37, 28—40 c
Review [*Look, stranger!,*
by W. H. Auden].
AR, i 1 A37, 64—65 r
Review
[*Drama and society in the age of Jonson,*
by L. C. Knights].
AR, i 3 Oc37, 248—50 r
'The winter's tale'.
AR, i 4 J38, 301—14 c

Treadgold, Paul
A note on Gertrude Stein.
PR, 8 19Je35, 12—13 c
Poem.
PR, 5 17My35, 16 v
Review [*Rats of Norway,*
by J. K. Winter].
PR, 2 12F35, 11 dr
The stage.
PR, 1 1F35, 6 dr
Surréalisme.
PR, 11 27N35, 4—7 c

Trease, Robert Geoffrey
A charter for youth: peace.
TC, vi 33 D33—J34, 172—74 c
Prelude to the English revolution.
TC, ii 9 N31, 21—23 c
Review [*The history of peace,*
by A. C. F. Beales].
TC, i 6 Ag31, 25 r
Review [*Aphrodite,*
by R. de Pomerai]; Letter.
TC, i 5 Jy31, 25, 27—28 r
The short path to peace.
TC, i 2 A31, 22—23 c

Treece, Henry
Angels and monsters
[*Poems,* by F. Garcia Lorca,
tr. by S. Spender and J. L. Gili;
The garden of disorder, by C. H. Ford;
Sequence on violence, by H. Roskolenko;
Don Quixote,
by D. S. Savage;
I have seen monsters and angels,
by E. Jolas].

SV, 6 Au39, 30—33 r
Dylan Thomas and the surrealists.
SV, 3 W38, 27—30 c
Poem.
VS, i 4 M—My39, 23 v
Poem; The three selves; Three poems.
SV, 4A Sp39, 26—30 v
Poem.
SV, 7 C39, 26 v
Some notes on poetry now.
VS, ii 1 Je—Ag39, 7—10 c

Tremayne, Herbert
The little red bullock.
DD, viii 28 J—F31, 34 v
The singing wood.
DD, viii 30 Au31, 104 v

Tremlett, Freda
The controversy.
F, 4 D30, 9 i
Wood engraving.
F, 1 F30, 63; F, 2 Je30, 81; F, 2 Je30,
131; F, 4 D30, 63; F, 5 F31, 112 i

Treneer, Anne
Charles Doughty
rev. by NV, 17 Oc35, 21

Tretiakov, Sergei Mikhailovich
Chinese testament
rev. by D. A. Willis

Trevelyan, Julian
The catfield staithe; Still life.
V, 5 F30, 232 i
John Tunnard.
LB, 12 15M39, 9—10 c
Squarcione today.
EX, 5 F30, 38—40 c
Statement in painting.
EX, 6 Oc30, 37—38 c

Trevelyan, Robert Calverley
Selected poems
rev. by A. Morgan

Trevor, D.
Poets of the Spanish war.
LR, iii 8 S37, 455—60 c, v

Trevor, Rose
Anticipation.
JG, 28 Sp34, [30] v
Retrospect.
JG, 63 W37, [30] v

Trimmer *pseud.*
Interlude.
OB, i 4 Je35, 50—57 p

Triolet, Elsa
Mayakovsky: poet of Russia,
tr. by J. Rodker.
NW, ns3 C39, 215—30 c

Trotsky, Leon Davidovich
Communism and world chaos.
TC, iii 14 A32, 1–6; TC, iii 15 My32,
6–10 c
My life rev. by C. R. Jones

Trott, F. H.
Roar, machines.
VS, i 3 D38–F39, 23 v

Trotter, Alys Fane
The game of chess.
CA, 3 Oc30, 60 v
Mors janua vitae.
CA, 5 M31, 114 v

Tsao Yu
Thunder-storm [excerpt from Act III].
LR, iii 12 J38, 730–36 d

Tschichold, Jan
On Ben Nicholson's reliefs.
AX, 2 A35, 16–18 c

Tschiffely, Aimé Felix
Don Roberto rev. by E. Waugh

Tuck, J. P.
English criticism and the Soviet writers'
congress.
CL, ii 1 Au34, 4–13 c

Tucker, Eisdell
Rogation days.
P, 4 1938, 87 v
Stony ground rev. by G. Grigson

Tunon, Raul Gonzalez
see Gonzalez Tunon, Raul

Tureck, Ludwig
The life and death of my brother Rudolf,
tr. by J. Morris from the French of
André Gide.
TU, 3 Je34, 7–13 p
A worker speaks,
tr. by J. Morris.
NO, ii 2 J35, 119–24 p

Turnell, G. Martin
Annabella.
AR, i 1 A37, 26–27 c
Marxism and the arts.
AR, i 3 Oc37, 195–98 c
Our debt to Chesterton.
AR, i 2 Jy37, 73–79 c
Review [*Illusion and reality,*
by C. Caudwell].
AR, i 3 Oc37, 250–52 r
Review
[*Les écrivains diaboliques de France,*
by M. Rudwin].
TO, ii 8 M39, 9–10 r
Review

[*Bagatelles pour un massacre,*
by L–F. Céline].
TO, ii 7 Ag39, 21–22 r
Review
[*Ce qui meurt et ce qui naît,*
by H. Daniel-Rops;
The novel and the people,
by R. Fox].
AR, i 1 A37, 61–64 r
Soviet films.
AR, i 3 Oc37, 229–33 c
Surrealism.
AR, i 3 Oc37, 212–28 c
Wit and humour in the poetry of Donne,
T. S. Eliot and the Symbolists.
V, 6 Je30, 300–8 c
Poetry and crisis
rev. by G. Grigson

Turner, David
Children of Spain.
LR, iii 12 J38, 703–4 c

Turner, Denis
The four blessings; Quid pro quo.
DD, xi 47 S–Oc34, 85 v
Meleager on love; Carpe diem.
DD, x 41 S–Oc33, 86 v
The poet's dream.
DD, x 42 N–D33, 104 v

Turner, James Ernest
Man-woman.
PE, 4 N36, 107–18 p
Mass of death, I–IV.
PE, 1 Ag36, 20–30; PE, 2 S36, 43–61;
PE 3 Oc36, 77–99; PE 4 N36, 123–34 p

Turner, Margery
Beauty from vanishing.
LS, i 1 F34, 21 v
World ended.
LS, i 2 My34, 59 v

Turner, Tom
Communion.
HR, 5 1932, 22 v
Gifts.
HR, 4 1931, 47 v
Love's renewal; Riches.
HR, 7 1934, 15, 23 v
Triolet; To my lady.
HR, 6 1933, 16, 49 v

Turner, Walter James
Comment on Auden.
NV, 26/27 N37, 30 c
W. B. Yeats.
AW, Su39, 17–19 c
Songs and incantations
rev. by G. Knowland

Tuwin, Juljan
Wisdom, tr. by P. Selver.

SM, 4 1933, 110 v
Two whiffs of Lewsite
[*Noah and the waters,*
by C. Day Lewis;
Poems of strife,
by J. Lipton].
NV, 21 Je36, 17–19 r

Tyler, Parker
American letter.
LB, 11 M39, 18–19 p
American letter.
SV, 4 Su39, 40–42 p
American periodicals.
TO, ii 5 J39, 28–29; TO, ii 6 A39, 11 c
Beyond surrealism.
CV, 4 1935, 2–6 p
Letter to Charles-Henri Ford.
LB, 17 15Je39, 21–22 c
The metaphor in the jungle.
SV, 6 Au39, 26–29 v
Mock trial.
SV, 3 W38, 6–7 v
New York letter.
LB, 8/9 J39, 60 p
The poetic athlete.
SV, 4A Sp39, 20–25 c
Review
[*The garden of disorder,*
by C. H. Ford].
TO, i 4 Oc38, 26–27 r
Words and blood
[*Contemporary legends,*
by S. Salt].
CV, 5 M34, [26–27] r

Tylor, E. Thornton
A cafe: a man thinks.
RM, 2 D34, 64 p

Tzara, Tristan
Ten poems, tr. by F. Scarfe.
CPP, 10 Au37, 32–42 v

U

Ubsdell, A. P.
Lines; On some day in June.
DD, vii 27 N–D30, 448–49 v
Of these I would sing; The pool.
DD, viii 29 Su31, 65 v

Uhl, J.
Four poems.
AR, i 4 J38, 298–300 v

Uhse, Bodo
Bread and water,
tr. by J. Cleugh.
NW, 2 Au36, 63–70 p

Uloth, A. W.
Birds and men.
DD, vii S—Oc30, 398 v

Umpleby, Arthur Stanley
At Cambridge.
G, 38 Au36, [30] v

Underwood, Leon
The cathedral.
, i 1 15Je31, 4 p, i
Lines written in Mexico; Oil painting.
, i 4 15D31, 110—11, p, i
Reflections on E1 Greco at an exhibition
of his paintings.
, i 1 15Je31, 20—21 c
Sculptural convictions; The dove returns
with a leaf.
, i 2/3 15S31, 40—44 p, i
The ship 'Freewill'.
, i 2/3 15S31, 90 v, i

Ungaretti, Giuseppe
Three poems,
tr. by J. Purves.
MS, v 3 Oc34, 188—92 v

Unik, Pierre
The manless society,
tr. by D. Gascoyne.
NV, 6 D33, 9 v

Uraon dance poem — for the Karam
festival,
tr. by W. G. Archer.
NV, 8 D36, 147—48 v

Uraon marriage sermon,
tr. by W. G. Archer and E. Kujar.
NV, 22 S36, 12 p

Upward, Edward Falaise
The border-line.
NW, 1 Sp36, 171—92 p
The island.
LR, i 4 J35, 104—10 p
The tipster.
NW, 3 Sp37, 124—27 p

Urquhart, Fred
The Christ child.
P, 2 1938, 70—93 p
The heretic.
NW, 3 Sp37, 154—64 p
Those things pass.
LR, iii 2 M37, 96—102 p
Tomorrow will be beautiful.
NW, ns1 Au38, 89—97 p
We never died in winter.
P, 4 1938, 13—30 p

U.S.S.R. handbook
rev. by R. Bishop

V

V., J.
The Stratford 'Troilus and Cressida'.
FB, i 3 9My36, 62—63 dr

Vachon, Hayden M.
Aspiration.
CA, 3 Oc30, 49 v

Vail, Laurence
January 21.
CV, 4 1935, 18 p
A selection from 'Off'.
SV, 2 Au38, 8—9 p
Selection from 'Off'.
SV, 3 W38, 23—25; SV, 4 Su39,
19—23 p
Scirocco.
TO, i 3 Jy38, 7 v

Valéry, Paul
From 'Eupalinos',
tr. by W. M. Stewart.
MS, ii 3 Oc31, 228—33 d
Regards sur le monde actuel
rev. by G. Pendle

Valle Inclan, Ramon Maria del
Luck, tr. by E. Richardson.
EQ, i 1 My34, 18—21 p

Valois, Georges pseud.
War or revolution
rev. by W. N. Warbey

Van Doren, Mark
Answers to an enquiry.
T, 12/13 Oc38, 107 p

Van Gyseghem, André
A letter from Moscow.
LR, i 7 A35, 269—73 c
Okhlopkov's realistic theatre.
NW, ns2 Sp39, 121—28 c
Mr Priestley and time: Shaw re-writes
Shakespeare
[Time and the Conways;
I have been here before;
both by J. B. Priestley;
Cymbeline].
LR, iii 11 D37, 671—74 c
Moscow theatre.
LR, ii 3 D35, 108—12 c

Vann, Gerald
Creators of the modern mind, II:
Thomas Hobbes.
AR, i 4 J38, 282—97 c

Vara, Madeleine
An address to an international audience.
WW, 1 Au35, 134—43 c
The exercise of English.
EP, 2 Su36, 134—36 c
George Sand.
EP, 2 Su36, 243—49 c
The theme of fame.
EP, 3 Sp37, 75—99 c
Convalescent conversations
rev. by A. Hodge
see also Riding, L.; Riding, L. and others

Varda, Jean
A lesson from China.
ND, 2 8Jy37, 10 p
More about the gay nineties.
ND, 24 9D37, 18—19 p
Publicity.
ND, 7 12Ag37, 22—23 p

Vassie, Edith A.
Bare trees.
PQ, i 1 Sp39, 16 v

Vaughan-Thomas, Arthur Spencer
Love on the dole.
W, 8/9 Ag39, 239 v

Vazov, Ivan
A literary party,
tr. by J. Lavrin.
EQ, i 3 N34, 197—203 p

Verrinder, Eileen
Footsteps.
NS, i 3 Je34, 221—27 p
The vale.
NS, ii 1 F35, 54—59 p

Verschoyle, Derek
The English novelist
rev. by K. Allott

Vesey-Fitzgerald, Brian
Blessed above women.
P, 3 1938, 7—16 p

Vickridge, Alberta
Black-out.
JG, 71 W39, [33] v
Blue day.
JG, 24 Sp33, [26] v
Cloud fabric.
JG, 70 Au39, [33] v
The comrades: story the third.
DD, vii 26 S—Oc30, 369—75 v
Consuming fire.
JG, 20 Sp32, [28] v
Country singers.
JG, 64 Sp38, [32] v
Dedicatory hymn.
JG, 13 Su30, [5—6] v
During snow.
JG, 31 W34, [30] v
Enif in Pegasus.
JG, 41 Su37, [38] v

Vickridge, Alberta (cont.)
Ephemera.
JG, 22 Au32, [28] v
Flowering aloe; A satirist.
JG, 30 Au34, [31] v
Godmother's wish; Watcombe.
DD, viii 30 Au31, 88 v
Godmother's wish.
HR, 5 1932, 20 v
The great seas.
HR, 6 1933, 50 v
Heaven's rebel; Martha at sunset.
HR, 7 1934, 43, 45 v
Identity.
JG, 26 Au33, [30] v
In a time of desolation.
JG, 67 W38, [34] v
Jupiter rising.
JG, 29 Su34, [30] v
Language.
JG, 23 W32, [23] v
Lost magic.
HR, 4 1931, 27 v
Lost magic; Forgotten stars;
Wonder street.
DD, viii 29 J—F31, 25—26 v
Maestro.
JG, 35 W35, [34] v
Moon craters.
JG, 32 Sp35, [33—34] v
Nasturtiums in a window box.
JG, 33 Su35, [32] v
Night ride.
JG, 18 Au31, [16] v
Numbers.
JG, 36 Sp36, [33] v
Objectivity.
JG, 69 Su39, [33] v
Of trees.
HR, 5 1932, 33—35 p
The poet and the crocus.
JG, 40 Sp37, [34] v
The Pole star.
JG, 39 W36, [32—33] v
Relativity.
JG, 28 Su34, [30] v
The rider.
JG, 65 Su38, [29—30] v
Salute to the New Year.
JG, 16 Sp31, [5] v
Sand.
JG, 21 Su32, [27—28] v
Schroter.
JG, 68 Sp39, [34] v
Sea serpent.
JG, 34 Au35, [32—33] v
Soap bubbles.
JG, 15 Au30, [16] v
A song for the hungry.
JG, 27 W33, [27—28] v
Sonnets in November.
JG, 19 W31, [24—25] v
Spices.
JG, 37 Su36, [31—32] v

Star-coming.
JG, 15 W30, [28—29) v
Transplanted.
JG, 63 W37, [33—34] v
Unsolved.
JG, 66 Au38, [33] v
A vision.
JG, 17 Su31, [6] v
The visionary.
JG, 42 Au37, [34] v
Weather glass in a wet summer.
JG, ?8 Au36, [33—34] v
Whit-Monday in the garden.
JG, 25 Su33, [27] v

Vidaković, A.
Memories, pleasant and unpleasant.
MS, v 3 Oc34, 156—58 c

Vidal, Lois
Magpie rev. by Jaques *pseud.*

Viereck, Peter
Liverpool.
B, 1 Su38, 16 v
We stared in silence through the wire
netting.
LD, ii 2 D37, 19 v

Viertel, Berthold
Comment on Auden.
NV, 26/27 N37, 25—26 c
Hollywood keeps abreast.
NW, ns2 Sp39, 129—44 c
The showman.
NW, 5 Sp38, 77—83 p

Vigilantes *pseud.* [*i.e.* K. Zilliacus]
Abyssinia rev. by J. Strachey

Vildrac, Charles *pseud.*
Return to yesterday
rev. by B. Nixon

Villa, J. M. *see* Moreno Villa, J.

Vince, S.
The watch.
JG, 63 W37, [15—16] v

Vines, Sherard
Hopes for economic change; Imposed
and spontaneous cultures.
PR, 4 5M35, 3—4 v
Writers international.
LR, i 3 D34, 75—76 c
Writers international.
LR, i 6 M35, 222 c

Vinogradov, Anatoly Kornelevich
The black consul
rev. by N. Cunard

Virta, Nikolai Evgenevich

On a journey.
NW, ns3 C39, 231—37 p

Visiak, E. H. *pseud.*
The old roof-tree.
DD, ix 36 N—D32, 99 v

Viveur, John
The A.D.C. Julius Caesar.
FB, i 3 9My36, 53—54 dr
G. K. Chesterton.
LD, i 1 J37, 5, 7 c
What hope for poetry?
FB, i 2 3M36, 32—34 c

Vladimir in the Taiga: an Evenk
folk tale.
NW, ns2 Sp39, 193—97 p

Vogel, Joseph
Harps upon the willows.
P, 2 1938, 189—99 p

Vogler, Sidney
David.
NS, ii 4 Ag35, 252—57 p
Old Anna.
NS, ii 5 Oc35, 321—27 p
The old woman.
NS, i 2 A34, 161—64 p
Poem.
LR, ii 2 N35, 80 v
Proletarian.
LR, ii 2 N35, 56 v
Spent savings.
LR, ii 2 N35, 88 v

Voller, Harry Colworth
Sunshine house
rev. by J. Garrett

The voyage of the Chelyuskin,
tr. by A. Brown.
rev. by A. Williams-Ellis

Vrchlicky, Jaroslav
Symphony of the winds,
tr. by P. Selver.
SM, 1 Je31, 58 v

W

W., A. S.
The Rome visit.
PP, 10 A39, 9 v

W., L.
Money from death
[*The private manufacture of armaments*

by P. N. Baker;
The profits of war,
by R. Lewinsohn].
LR, ii 15 D36, 849—50 r

W., R.
The theory and practice of democracy.
TU, 3 Je34, 31—38 c

W., R. S.
The prosperous.
SM, 2 S31, 9 v

W., S. T. [Shelley Wang?]
Concert of Soviet music.
LR, i 9 Je35, 384 c

Waddell, Helen Jane
Sylvester's discourses.
LQ, i 1 N36, [1—7] p
see also Abelard, Peter

Waddington, Ethel
The real sun-bathing.
TC, i 4 Je31, 22—24 c

Wade, H. O.
Reminiscences of the 6th Battalion of
the West Yorkshire Regiment.
HR, 4 1931, 50—53 p

Waffle *pseud.*
Bargains for all.
FB, iii 9 6Je38, 70 v
Eerie in the stillness.
FB, iii 7 25N37, 32—33 p
The whispering knights.
FB, iii 6 21Oc37, 17—18 d

Wainwright, Vera S.
The old man.
C, i 28 27Je36, 225 p
The water-diviner.
C, ii 35 22Ag36, 55 p

Wakefield, Jessie Hare
Amulet.
JG, 32 W34, [13] v
The elf arrow.
JG, 40 Sp37, [18] v
Eskdale.
JG, 38 Au36, [20] v
The estuary.
JG, 66 Au38, [26—27] v
A gorge near Adelboden.
JG, 16 Sp31, [14] v
If.
JG, 24 Sp33, [9] v
The immanent.
JG, 19 W31, [17] v
In a northern city.
JG, 26 Au33, [23] v
In an alpine forest.
JG, 17 Su31, [18] v

Nocturne.
JG, 20 Sp32, [13] v
On a windy morning.
JG, 21 Su32, [10] v
On the lake.
JG, 35 W35, [29] v
Orselina.
JG, 15 W30, [14] v
Palais des Nations.
JG, 69 Su39, [20] v
The priest on the digue.
JG, 25 Su33, [7] v
Rivers.
JG, 31 W34, [13] v
San Michele del Monte.
JG, 34 Au35, [18] v
Ships.
JG, 33 Su35, [19] v
The silver birch.
JG, 70 Au39, [24] v
The summit.
JG, 18 Au31, [17] v
Treasure.
JG, 30 Au34, [24] v
Vignette.
JG, 68 Sp39, [19] v
Yser.
JG, 42 Au37, [20] v

Walden, Herwath
Poem, tr. by H. Baerlein.
DD, ix 35 S—Oc32, 67—69 v
Poem.
DD, x 39My—Je33, 42 v

Wales, Nym *pseud. see* Chou wen

Wales [periodical], no.1
rev. by J. Symons

Walker, A. Danvers-
see Danvers-Walker, A.

Walker, Elsie M.
Noontide.
DD, vii 26 S—Oc30, 389 v

Walker, Frank Stead
Customer.
C, i 14 7M36, 107—8 p

Walker, G. E. H.
A Yorkshire trustee in Central Africa.
HR, 7 1934, 63—64 p

Walker, J. R.
The first of May.
PP, 11 My39, 2 v

Walker, L. C.
Writing a thriller.
ST, i 2 A33, 30—31 c

Walker, Mary
Cressida's room.
F, 6 Je31, 170 v

Walker, Mary Kelly
Another song, tr. from V. Hugo.
CA, 3 Oc30, 59 v

Walker, Nigel
Fox trot.
PR, 23 N37, 14 v

Walker, Patrick Chrestien Gorden-
see Gordon-Walker, Patrick Chrestien

Wallace, James William
The widow from Spain
P, 4 1938, 105—10 p

Wallace, Michael
In defence of fascism.
OB, i 1 M—A34, 27—29 c

Waller, Edmond
Go, lovely rose.
LQ, ii 1 My37, 15 v

Waller, John Stanier
Before the arras.
FB, iii 7 25N37, 35 v
The boy on the Bankside.
FB, iii 8 3M38, 52—55 p
A brave New Year!
K, i 2 D39—J40, 35—36 c
The Castle of Perseverance (as presented
by the Oxford University Experimental
Theatre).
B, 2 W38, 13—14 dr
De Quincey the surrealist.
FB, v 1 F39, 16—19 c
Do you believe in fairies?
FB, ii 8 3M38, 41—42 p
Editorial.
B, 1 Su38, [1—2] c
Editorial: Ho! Ho! Jollie Christmas.
FB, iii 7 25N37, 21—22 c
Editorial: What every mad student
should know.
FB, iii 6 21Oc37, 1—2 p
The end.
B, 3 Sp39, 15 v
Farewell seventeens.
B, 2 W38, 5 v
Fog.
FB, iii 9 6Je38, 79 v
Full fathom five.
K, i 2 D39—J40, 59 v
In this dream kingdom.
K, i 1 17N39, 29 v
Juan who dreamed of the moon.
FB, iii 9 6Je38, 71—73 p
Orchids or poppies?
K, i 1 17N39, 3—4 c
The O.U.D.S. 'The duchess of Malfi'.

Waller, John Stanier (cont.)
FB, v 1 F39, 20 dr
Per ardua.
FB, iv 10 N38, 2 v
Rocking horse.
B, 1 Su38, 11 v
A rook in the cherry tree
[*Songs from a cherry tree,*
by A. Rook].
B, 3 Sp39, 16 r
Subject matter and technique.
B, 2 W38, 1—2 c
Tu-whoo! Tu-whoo!
FB, iv 10 N38, 3—5 p
The wall.
PR, 21 1M37, 13 v
War not averted
[*On the frontier,*
by W. H. Auden and C. Isherwood].
B, 2 W38, 15—17 r
Young orange: a reply to an Old Blue.
FB, ii 5 5M37, 33—34 c
see also Burke, Patrick

Waller, Robert B.
Ballad.
NW, ns1 Au38, 87—88 v
Lines.
Y, i 2 My39, 68 v
The man who quacked.
NW, 5 Sp38, 110—13 p
Part of a longer poem.
J, 2 My36, 9 v
Poem.
J, 1 J36, 30 v
Poem.
NW, ns2 Sp39, 183 v

Waln, Nora
Reaching for the stars
rev. by D. U. Ratcliffe

Walpole, Hugh Seymour
Comment on Auden.
NV, 26/27 N37, 30 c

Walsh, Elizabeth J.
Dreams.
PQ, i 1 Sp39, 14 v
The incentive of progress to the
creative mind in poetry.
PQ, i 2 Su39, 33—35 c

Walsh, Kenneth R.
Abstraction as a weapon.
AX, 5 Sp36, 23—26 c
Background.
AX, 8 W37, 9—10 c

Walsh, Robert Patrick
The means test is unjust.
AR, i 4 J38, 328—30 c

Walter, Ethel
Blessed are . . .
JG, 70 Au39, [20] v
The child scholar.
JG, 32 Sp35, [23—24] v
The dance band.
JG, 41 Su37, [40] v
First thoughts: September 3rd.
JG, 71 W39, [16] v
The goit side.
JG, 40 Sp37, [17] v
In the woods.
JG, 67 W38, [33] v
An incident.
JG, 64 Sp38, [22—23] v
Memories of holidays.
JG, 66 Au38, [25] v
Morning in town.
JG, 33 Su35, [24] v
A motorist's prayer.
JG, 39 W36, [36] v
Some fell upon stony ground.
JG, 29 Su34, [20] v
A suburban street.
JG, 37 Su36, [27] v
Thunder rain.
JG, 42 Au37, [22] v
The visitation.
JG, 35 W35, [31] v
Wuthering heights.
JG, 34 Au35, [16—17] v

Walters, Meurig
Age.
WR, ii 3 Oc39, 142 v
Rhondda poem (No.5).
W, 10 Oc39, 273 v

Walton, William
Dawn.
DD, x 40 Jy—Ag33, 65 v
Windows five.
DD, xi 44 M—A34, 31 v

Wang, Shelley
Advertising mice,
tr. by J. Field.
LR, iii 9 Oc37, 528 v
China's struggle on four fronts.
LR, iii 12 J38, 717—21 c
The eagle, tr. by J. Field.
LR, iii 12 J38, 721 v
Night at the village inn, tr. by J. Field.
LR, iii 12 J38, 716 v
What China really is
[*Understand the Chinese,*
by W. Martin; *A house divided,*
by P. S. Buck].
LR, i 7 A35, 284—85 r
Writers' international.
LR, i 5 F35, 182—83 c

Warbey, William Noble
About it and about.

TC, iv 23 J33, 22—23 c
A charter for youth.
TC, vi 33 D33—J34, 170—72 c
Death of the Fabians.
TC, v 28 Je33, 240—45 c
Fascism and the middle classes.
TC, vi 34 M34, 236—39 c
Hunger marchers of hungry England
[*Hungry England,*
by A. F. Brockway].
TC, iv 21 N32, 26—27 r
Marxism revisited
[*What Marx really meant,*
by G. D. H. Cole].
TC, vi 35 Je34, 297—301 r
Mathematics for militarists.
TC, i 6 Ag31, 20—21 c
Neo-Fabianism and the revolution.
TC, v 30, Ag33, 367—70 c
Review
[*Soviet trade and world depression,*
by H. R. Knickerbocker;
The United States and disarmament,
by B. H. Williams].
TC, ii 11 J32, 26—27 r
Review
[*Comment réaliser le socialisme,*
by V. Alter].
TC, iii 16 Je32, 29—30 r
Review
[*War or revolution,*
by G. Valois].
TC, iii 17 Jy32, 27—28 r
Review
[*The coming struggle for power,*
by J. Strachey].
TC, iv 22 D32, 24—25 r
Review
[*Democracy in crisis,*
by H. J. Laski;
Where stands socialism today].
TC, v 25 M33, 47—48 r
Review
[*Nationalism in the Soviet Union,*
by H. Kohn].
TC, v 26 A33, 121—22 r
Review
[*Moscow dialogues,*
by J. F. Hecker].
TC, v 29 Jy33, 315—16 r
Review
[*The menace of fascism,*
by J. Strachey].
TC, vi 31 S—Oc33, 58—60 r
Review
[*Capitalism, communism and the
transition,*
by E. Burns;
Communism and religion,
by J. F. Hecker].
TC, vi 33 D33—J34, 182—83 r
Review [*Plan or no plan,*
by B. Wootton].
TC, vi 34 M34, 246—47 r

Review
[*Fascism and social revolution,*
by R. P. Dutt;
Will Roosevelt succeed?
by A. F. Brockway].
TC, vi 36 S34, 371—74 r

Warburg, Joan
The arks.
NS, ii 4 Ag35, 286—87 p

Warburton, Edward
Is the means test unjust?
AR, i 4 J38, 323—27 c

Ward, Barbara
César.
LS, i 1 F34, 50—54 p

Ward, Veronica M.
Club hymen.
PR, 3 19F35, 8 v
The dark room.
LS, ii 1 My35, 32—34 p
The question.
PR, 6 31My35, 1—2 p
Review [*Poem,* by G. Barker].
PR, 6 31My35, 16 r
Review
[*Murder in the cathedral,*
by T. S. Eliot].
PR, 8 19Je35, 14—15 r

Wareing, Alfred
Anniversaries.
HR, 5 1932, 21 c

Warman, Erik
Anti-babel.
DV, 1 M32, 5—7 c
Harvest.
DV, 2 A32, 35—36 c
Thunder on the left wing.
DV, 2 A32, 46—49 c

Warner, Alan
A note on modern tragedy.
CM, ii 1 Su35, 207—13 c

Warner, Rex E.
Arms in Spain.
LR, iii 3 A37, 139 v
The dinner party.
NW, ns3 C39, 127—35 p
Extract from a letter.
T, 6/7 N37, [43] c
The football match.
NW, 2 Au36, 210—16 p
Four poems.
NV, 15 Je35, 12—14 v
Fur and wire.
LR, iii 7 Ag37, 405 v
Jonathan Swift: defender of liberty.
LR, iii 5 Je37, 266—72 c

Pacifists.
LR, i 10 Jy35, 396 v
Sonnet; Truth.
T, 1 J37, [8] v
The tourist looks at Spain.
NW, 4 Au37, 229—31 v
Poems rev. by R. Fuller; G. Grigson;
S. Spender
The wild goose chase rev. by A. West

Warner, Sylvia Townsend
Barcelona.
LR, ii 15 D36, 812—16 p
Benicasim.
LR, iii 14 M38, 841 v
Competition in criticism.
LR, ii 4 J36, 178—79 c
An English fable.
LR, iii 7 Ag37, 406 p
In this midwinter.
LR, i 4 J35, 101 v
Red front.
LR, i 7 A35, 255—57 v
Some make this answer.
LR, ii 5 F36, 214 v
Underlying morality
[*New writing,* no. 3].
LR, ii 6 Jy37, 367—68 r
We are gentlemen
[*Spanish testament,*
by A. Koestler].
LR, iii 12 J38, 745—47 r
More joy in heaven
rev. by G. West
Summer will show
rev. by A. L. Morton

Warren, A. Highfield
What clever men!
FB, iii 8 3M37, 64 p

Warren, Phyllis
The Tower of London.
PQ, i 1 Sp39, 22 v

Warren-Dow, Alexander
The decline of standards in art.
CA, 3 Oc30, 45—47 c
Representations of God with brush
and pen.
CA, 9 1931, 283—84 c

Warwick, Phyllis Dulce
Despair.
DD, x 41 S—Oc33, 82 v
Pearls.
PQ, i 2 Su39, 45 v

Waters, Ivor
A dream.
JG, 32 Sp35, [5—6] v
Gleam in darkness.
JG, 16 Sp31, [6] v
In the orchard.

JG, 31 W34, [10] v
Paul Verlaine.
JG, 33 Su35, [8] v

Watkin, Bruce
It sounded like Sunday school.
LD, ii 1 Oc37, 9—11 p
Review
[*Out of the rhubarb tree,*
by K. Allott and S. Tait].
PR, 23 N37, 16 r
see also Downs, Barbara

Watkins, Vernon
The collier.
W, 6/7 M39, 205—6 v
Empty hands; The dancer in the leaves;
The turning of the leaves; The sunbather;
Indolence.
W, 2 Ag37, 61—64 v
From my loitering; La vie.
W, 4 M38, 148—49 v
Griefs from the sea; Triton time.
W, 1 Su37, 21—22 v
Review [*In parenthesis,*
by D. Jones].
W, 5 Su38, 184 r
Sonnet: pit-boy.
W, 10 Oc39, 272 v
Yeats's tower.
W, 3 Au37, 86—87 v

Watkinson, Margaret
At the shirt factory; Poppies;
Government job.
PP, 13/14 Jy—Ag39, 4—5 v
Eggs hatching; Gas-masks are given out.
PP, 13/14 Jy—Ag39, 6—7 p, v

Watkinson, Raymond
Illustration to Keats's 'Hyperion'.
P, 3 1938, 117 i
Poem.
P, 3 1938, 203—5 v
The roadmakers.
P, 4 1938, [133] i

Watson, Edmund Henry Lacon
Dedication.
DD, ix 35 S—Oc32, 75 v
My lady's dress.
DD, xi 47 S—Oc34, 82 v

Watson, Edward James
George Ambrose Burton.
CA, 9 1931, 285 v

Watson, Francis
The deserted village.
HR, 7 1934, 26—29 p
The impressionable passenger.
ND, 5 29Jy37, 8—9 p
No escape.
HR, 6 1933, 53 v

Watson, Francis (cont.)
The pioneer.
HR, 5 1932, 36 v

Watts, Doreen C.
Dreams.
JG, 71 W39, [23] v
The knight.
PQ, i 2 Su39, 38 v

Watts, E. Hyde
Macbeth.
OO, x 51 F30, 397 i

Watts, S. G.
Father's fancy woman.
K, i 2 D39—J40, 57—59 p

Waugh, Evelyn
All memory gone
[*The man who started clean,*
by T. O. Beachcroft].
ND, 19 4N37, 24—25 r
Art from anarchy
[*A date with a duchess,*
by A. Calder-Marshall].
ND, 12 16S37, 24—25 r
Bloomsbury's farthest North
[*Letters from Iceland,*
by W. H. Auden and L. MacNeice;
Dead puppets dance,
by P. Thornton].
ND, 7 12Ag37, 25—26 r
Bonhomie in the saloon bar
[*Sing holiday,* by P. Chamberlain].
ND, 4 22Jy37, 24—25 r
Companion to Fleming
[*Forbidden journey,*
by E. K. Maillart].
ND, 10 2S37, 26—27 r
Crusader manqué [*Don Roberto,*
by A. F. Tschiffely].
ND, 25 16D37, 25—26 r
Edith Sitwell's first novel
[*I live under a black sun,*
by E. Sitwell;
To have and to have not,
by E. Hemingway].
ND, 17 21Oc37, 28—29 r
Edwardian baroque [*Pepita,*
by V. Sackville-West;
Orientations, by R. Storrs].
ND, 21 18N37, 28, 30 r
Folkestone, for shame
[*Middle mist,* by N. Muskett]!
ND, 8 19Ag37, 24—25 r
For schoolboys only
[*The mind in chains,*
ed. by C. Day Lewis].
ND, 2 8Jy37, 24—25 r
The great incomprehensibles
[*Men of mathematics,*
by E. T. Bell].
ND, 6 5Ag37, 23—24 r

International list.
ND, 20 11N37, 23 r
Juvenilia.
F, 2 Je30, 88 v
Love among the underdogs
[*World's end,* by P. H. Johnson].
ND, 15 7Oc37, 29 r
More barren leaves
[*Ends and means,* by A. Huxley].
ND, 26 23D37, 24—25 r
A mystic in the trenches
[*In parenthesis,* by D. Jones].
ND, 1 1Jy37, 32—33 r
An old liberal says his say
[*Men and things,* by J. A. Spender].
ND, 13 23S37, 24—25 r
A parnassian on Mount Zion
[*Continual dew,* by J. Betjeman].
ND, 22 25N37, 24—25 r
Peter Pan in politics
[*The changing scene,*
by A. Calder-Marshall].
ND, 11 9S37, 25—26 r
Popes and peoples
[*Pope Pius XI and world peace,*
by Lord Clonmore].
ND, 23 2D37, 24—25 r
Saint's-eye view
[*Diary of a country priest,*
by G. Bernanos].
ND, 18 28Oc37, 24—25 r
The soldiers speak
[*Vain glory,* ed. by G. Chapman].
ND, 5 29Jy37, 24—25 r
Strange rites of the islands
[*May the twelfth,*
by Mass Observation].
ND, 16 14Oc37, 28, 30 r
A teuton in Tudor England
[*Thomas Platter's travels in England,*
ed. by C. Williams].
ND, 14 30S37, 26, 28 r
Uplift in Arabia
[*Triumphant pilgrimage,*
by O. Rutter].
ND, 3 15Jy37, 25—26 r
Uplift in the highball
[*No pockets in a shroud,*
by H. McCoy;
The crooked coronet,
by M. Arlen].
ND, 9 26Ag37, 26—27 r
Viceregal gothic
[*Helen's tower,*
by H. Nicolson].
ND, 24 9D37, 27—28 r

Wearing, Eric Paul
Come to me, death.
JG, 16 Sp31, [23] v
Dyserth, North Wales.
JG, 18 Au31, [18—19] v
Estrangement; Launcelot.
DD, viii 29 Su31, 69 v

The Law courts, Strand.
DD, vii 29 Su31, 59 v
Memories.
DD, viii 30 Au31, 101 v
Pirates.
JG, 23 W32, [16] v
Roundaway hill; To a lady counsel;
An old gown.
DD, viii 28 J—F31, 36 v
Ships.
DD, viii 30 Au31, 100 v
Sonnet.
JG, 26 Au33, [21] v
Strange haunts.
JG, 17 Su31, [15] v
When all the joys.
JG, 22 Au32, [27] v
When we are dead.
JG, 19 W31, [14] v

Webb, Sidney *1st baron Passfield*
Life in the U.S.S.R.
[*Soviet democracy,* by P. Sloan].
LR, iii 6 Jy37, 356 r
Soviet communism
rev. by R. Bishop

Webbe, Denis
Henry Swannel retires.
NS, i 6 D34, 439—43 p
The man who wanted a child.
NS, ii 7 F36, 541—52 p
The vegetable maidens.
NS, ii 6 D36, 473—80 p

Webster, Michael
Love's elegy.
JG, 71 W39, [22] v

Weiskopf, Franz Carl
Seven frontiers,
tr. by C. Ashleigh.
NW, ns2 Sp39, 232—48 p

Weissman, Martin
Epic.
PR, 15 1M36, 14 v

Welbank, Joseph
Escape from reality.
LR, iii 7 Ag37, 400—4 p

Weldon, Thomas Dewar
Modern greats.
NO, i 2 N33, 198—207 c

Well met.
CPP, 9 Sp37, 26—27 v

Wellard, James Howard
In defence of free verse.
BB, vii 2 M30, 27—32 c

Wellesley, Dorothy Violet
Deserted house
rev. by L. MacNeice

Wells, Elizabeth Temple
Who is she?
PQ, i 2 Su39, 44 v

Wells, Herbert George
Comment on the basis of the
Sexology group.
TC, iv 21 N32, 22 c
After democracy
rev. by G. West
The Bulpington of Blup
rev. by G. West
An experiment in autobiography
rev. by R. Fox
The shape of things to come
rev. by G. West
Star-begotten
rev. by S. Blumenfeld
*The work, wealth and happiness of
mankind*
rev. by A. J. Henderson; G. West

Wenzelides, Arsen
The Balkans and the peace of Europe.
EQ, i 4 F35, 209—14 c

Wescher, Herta
John Piper, 1935.
AX, 4 N35, 12, 13 c
New work in Paris.
AX, 6 Su36, 27—29 c
Paris notes.
AX, 3 Jy35, 28—29 c

West, Alick
Ben Jonson was no sentimentalist
[*Drama and society in the age
of Jonson*,
by L. C. Knights].
LR, iii 8 S37, 468—75 r
Chiboo tson [*Lifer*,
by J. Phelan].
LR, iii 15 A38, 946—47 r
Communism and Christianity
[*Christianity and the social revolution*,
ed. by J. Lewis *and others*].
LR, ii 4 J36, 174—76 r
The detective story.
LR, iii 12, J38, 707—10; LR, iii 13 F38,
795—98 c
Marx House.
LR, i 12 S35, 497—99 c
Marxism and modern thought
[by N. I. Bukharin *and others*].
LR, ii 1 Oc35, 44—47 r
Mirsky's one-sided picture
[*The intelligentsia of Great Britain*,
by D. S. Mirsky].
LR, i 8 My35, 324—28 r
New novels [*Sleep in peace*,

by P. Bentley; *Promised land*,
by C. Belfrage].
LR, iii 15 A38, 944—46 r
The 'poetry' in poetry.
LR, iii 3 A37, 164—68 c
A reply to Eric Gill.
LR, i 10 Jy35, 410—11 c
Shakespeare: a revaluation
[by A. A. Smirnov].
LR, ii 16 J37, 906—9 r
Surréalisme in literature.
LR, ii 10 Jy36, vi—viii c
Three novels [*The big firm*,
by A. Williams-Ellis;
No middle way, by J. Marston;
Red planes fly east,
by P. Pavlenko].
LR, iii 16 My38, 1014—16 r
Wild goose chase [by R. Warner].
LR, iii 10 N37, 630—31 r
Crisis and criticism
rev. by J. Lindsay

West, Anthony
No revolution.
AX, 8 W37, 17, 19 c

West, Edward Sackville-
see Sackville-West, Edward

West, Geoffrey *pseud.*
About it and about.
TC, ii 10 D31, 24—25; TC, ii 12 F32,
24—26; TC, ii 13 M32, 25—26 c
Anti-classicist — anti-catholic.
TC, ii 11 J32, 6—9 c
Basis.
TC, i 6 Ag31, 10—11 c
Beginning.
TC, vi 34 M34, 209—11 c
Capitalism in America.
TC, iii 18 Ag32, 16—18 c
Death.
SM, 2 S31, 5—8 p
The emigrant.
TC, i 5 Jy31, 7—9 p
God save the King!
TC, i 4 Je31, 1—3 c
Hitler and war
[*Young Oxford and war*,
by M. Foot *and others*;
The hour of decision,
by O. Spengler;
Hitler over Europe, by E. Henri;
Socialism's new start, by 'Miles';
The tragedy of a nation,
by H. Loewenstein].
TC, vi 35 Je34, 286—90 r
I for one.
TC, i 1 M31, 1—2 c
Lionel Britton's 'Hunger and love'.
TC, i 2 A31, 20—21 c
New novels
[*Kneel to the rising sun*,

by E. Caldwell;
The beauties and the furies,
by C. Stead; *We are betrayed*,
by V. Fisher; *Duke street*,
by M. Campbell; *I'd do it again*,
by F. Tilsley].
LR, ii 10 Jy36, 522—24 r
New novels [*Eyeless in Gaza*,
by A. Huxley; *The secret journey*,
by J. Hanley; *The coolie*,
by M. R. Anand; *Salka Valka*,
by H. Laxness;
Children with fire,
by A. Smith].
LR, ii 11 Ag36, 585—87 r
The new Wells
[*The work, wealth and happiness of
mankind*,
by H. G. Wells].
TC, ii 13 M32, 28—29 r
A note on James Joyce.
TC, iv 19 S32, 21—22 c
Pacifism, real and false.
TC, vi 31 S—Oc33, 23—27 c
Pigs with wings
[*The prospects of humanism*,
by L. Hyde].
TC, i 3 My31, 17—18 c
Political obligation.
TC, vi 33 D33—J34, 149—53 c
Review [*Boy*, by J. Hanley].
TC, ii 11 J32, 27—28 r
Review [*Chaos is come again*,
by C. Houghton].
TC, ii 12 F32, 30—31 r
Review
[*Post mortem on politicians*,
by D. Garman;
Pacifists in peace and war,
by D. Goldring;
A war museum, 1914—18,
by H. Miles;
Authors and the book trade,
by F. Swinnerton].
TC, iii 15 My32, 30—31 r
Review [*This surprising world*,
by G. Heard].
TC, iii 15 My32, 34 r
Review [*Under the fifth rib*,
by C. E. M. Joad].
TC, iii 16 Je32, 28 r
Review [*The necessity of communism*,
by J. M. Murry].
TC, iii 14 A32, 25 r
Review
[*Rhys Davies: a critical study*,
by R. L. Megroz].
TC, iii 17 Jy32, 29 r
Review [*Ebb and flood*,
by J. Hanley; *Aria and finale*,
by J. Hanley].
TC, iv 19 S32, 27 r
Review [*Spacetime inn*,
by L. Britton].

West, Geoffrey (cont.)
TC, iv 21 N32, 28—29 r
Review [*After democracy,*
by H. G. Wells].
TC, iv 22 D32, 21—23 r
Review [*Inferno,*
by H. Barbusse;
The red hills, by R. Davies;
Young man's testament,
by J. Arrow].
TC, iv 22 D32, 26—27 r
Review
[*The Bulpington of Blup,*
by H. G. Wells; *Ann Vickers,*
by S. Lewis].
TC, iv 24 F33, 30—32 r
Review
[*Guide to modern thought,*
by C. E. M. Joad].
TC, v 25 M33, 44—47 r
Review
[*Upton Sinclair presents William Fox*
by U. Sinclair;
Manssas, by U. Sinclair].
TC, v 27 My33, 190—91 r
Review
[*Germany puts the clock back,*
by E. Mowrer;
Spotlight on Germany,
by E. Roll; *The German paradox,*
by A. Plutynski;
Germany under the treaty,
by W. H. Dawson; *Modern France,*
by C. Hamilton].
TC, v 29 Jy33, 321—22 r
Review
[*Philosophers on holiday,*
by A. Robertson].
TC, v 30, Ag33, 377 r
Review [*The way out,*
by U. Sinclair].
TC, v 30 Ag33, 380 r
Review
[*The shape of things to come,*
by H. G. Wells].
TC, vi 32 N33, 112—13 r
Review [*Tender advice,*
by R. Wilson].
NS, ii 4 Ag35, 318 r
Review
[*O. Henry memorial award prize short
stories,*
ed. by H. Hansen].
NS, ii 4 Ag35, 319—20 r
Review [*Cut and come again,*
by H. E. Bates;
Tuesday afternoon,
by L. A. G. Strong;
Fierce and gentle,
by H. A. Manhood].
NS, ii 7 F36, 559—60 r
Review [*The laburnum tree,*
by J. Laver; *More joy in heaven,*
by S. T. Warner;

To blush unseen, by V. Dobrée].
NS, ii 6 D36, 481 r
Review
[*The best short stories of 1935,*
ed. by E. J. O'Brien].
NS, ii 6 D36, 482 r
H G. Wells rev. by J. P. Hogan
The problem of Arnold Bennett
rev. by J. P. Hogan

West, Keith
Br.dge at the tennis club.
FB, iii 8 3M38, 61 v
Confucius and the bee.
FB, iii 8 3M38, 47—49 p
Etching.
FB, iii 8 3M38, 50 v
Morning service.
K, i 2 D39—J40, 54 v

West, Rebecca
The dualism of Scott.
MS, iii 2 Ag34, 121—23 c
Review [*The three bottles,*
by E. Muir].
MS, ii 1 A31, 85—87 r

West, Victoria Mary Sackville-
see Sackville-West, Victoria Mary

Westerby, Robert
Militia man.
LR, ii 13 Oc36, 689—92 p

Wexley, John
They shall not die
rev. by C. C. Doggett

Wharton, Michael
Falling downstairs.
Y, i 1 M39, 4—8 p
Gathering samphire
Y, i 2 My39, 77—81 p

Wheatley, Vera
Afterwards.
JG, 13 Su30, [20—21] v
Births, marriages, deaths.
JG, 29 Su34, [10—11] v
Chimera.
JG, 30 Au34, [6—7] v
Convalescence.
JG, 16 Sp31, [9—10] v
Decision.
JG, 37 Su36, [18] v
Drawn curtains.
JG, 21 Su32, [12] v
Enigma.
JG, 31 W34, [18—19] v
For Nancy.
JG, 63 W37, [26] v
Friendship.
JG, 25 Su33, [17] v

Illusions.
JG, 17 Su31, [13] v
Loss.
JG, 67 W38, [8] v
Make-believe.
JG, 36 Sp36, [22—23] v
Making friends — a memory.
HR, 6 1933, 30—31 p
The meeting.
JG, 22 Au32, [11] v
Misunderstanding.
JG, 24 Sp33, [17] v
Nightfall.
JG, 27 W33, [8] v
Peace in our time.
JG, 71 W39, [32—33] v
Pity our simplicity.
JG, 34 Au35, [29] v
Portrait of the author.
JG, 17 Su31, [7] v
Prayer.
JG, 15 W30, [11] v
Reading in search of beauty.
JG, 32 Sp35, [11—12] v
Renaissance.
JG, 28 Sp34, [21] v
The riddle.
JG, 41 Su37, [24] v
Thoughts in Spring.
JG, 33 Su35, [30] v
To my mother in illness.
JG, 14 Au30, [20—21] v
To the man of God.
JG, 39 W36, [20] v
To the poets' club from an absent
member.
JG, 18 Au31, [31] v
To those who do not understand.
JG, 18 Au31, [17] v
Two kisses.
JG, 20 Sp32, [12—13] v

Wheelwright, John
Venus and Bacchus; Minus.
PR, 13 5F36, 10 v

Wherrett, B. I.
Genesis or the birth of revolt.
ST, i 2 A33, 8—9 p

Whistler, Laurence
A bed in starlight.
NO, ii 2 J35, 168 v
Dead lips.
NO, ii 1 My34, 26 v
Death of Pan.
F, 5 F31, 99—101 v
Dialogue.
LS, i 1 F34, 20—21 v
Eyes.
NO, i 1 My33, 106 v
Heat-wave.
F, 6 Je31, 174 v
October call.

PL, i 2 A39, [4] v
Poem.
NO, i 2 N33, 228 v
Renaissance.
F, 6 Je31, 198—99 v
A Sheraton table.
NS, i 6 D34, 469—83 p
Two love poems.
PR, 7 12Je35, 2 v
A window to movement.
PL, i 1 F39, [5] v
The emperor heart
rev. by H. B. Mallalieu
Four walls
rev. by G. Grigson; A. Hope

Whitaker, Malachi
Sometimes life is long.
TC, vi 34 M34, 193—99 p
Spring day at Salter's end.
HR, 5 1932, 66—69 p
The white line.
NS, i 5 Oc34, 325—34 p
Five for silver
rev. by A. Bristow

White, Antonia
The Agamemnon.
GTP, 3 S36, 2 c
At the theatre.
ND, 13 23S37, 29 dr
The crest.
LB, 3 Je38, 2 v
L. R.
CPP, 8 D36, 159—60 v
Review
[*Le quatuor en ré majeur,*
by A. Perlès].
SV, 4A Sp39, 51—52 r
Those stately homes: Horsley Towers.
ND, 20 11N37, 25—26 c

White, B. D.
Modern greats.
TU, 4 F35, 25—28 c

White, D. G.
'The rock' [by T. S. Eliot].
R, i 5 Je34, 7 dr

White, Eric Walter
The honest lovers.
NS, ii 6 D36, 464—72 p
Marie and the journeyman.
NS, i 3 Je34, 165—76 p
Realist reels.
Y, i 2 My39, 89—91 c
The warm brother.
NS, ii 4 Ag35, 274—77 p

White, J. B.
In the audience.
R, i 3 A34, 10—11 c

White, J. R.
The position in Ulster.
LR, ii 7 A36, 301—3 c

White, Patrick Victor Martindale
The house behind the barricades.
NV, 30 Su38, 9 v
Happy valley rev. by J. Symons

White, Terence Hanbury
Blake and Keats.
LT, i 8 Oc36, 11—13 c
Dialogue between unemployed and
intellectual; Song of an unemployed
labourer.
LT, i 2 A36, 8, 48 v
Forest storm.
LD, i 4 Je37, 18—19 p
Song of possible comfort.
LT, i 3 My36, 8 v
Song through space and other poems
rev. by R. P.-O.

Whitehead, Alfred North
Adventures of ideas
rev. by G. Sainsbury

Whitlock, Brand
Little lion rev. by R. Macaulay

Whitman, E.
Christe hys masse.
DD, viii 29 Su31, 74 v

Whittaker, Nancie
Cloth caps make working men.
LR, iii 4 My37, 227—28 p
Schooldays.
LR, ii 7 A36, 306—8 p

Whittock, Michael
The old man died.
LR, iii 8 S37, 461—62 p
Testament.
PP, 15 N39, 4 v

Whitworth, Geoffrey
Amateurs and the theatre.
R, i 7 N34, 8 c

Whyte, H. O.
Goodbye to a' that
[*He's got a million,*
by V. Krymov; *The calf of paper,*
by S. Asch; *Under Moscow skies,*
by M. Hindus].
LR, ii 14 N36, 790—91 r

Whyte, J. H.
The catholic Irish in Scotland.
MS, v 4 J35, 222—29 c
The drift south.
LR, ii 14 N36, 759—61 c

Editorial.
MS, ii 3 Oc31, 192—95; MS, ii 2 Jy31,
100—6 c
Editorial notes.
MS, ii 4 J32, 266—69; MS, iii 1 A32,
4—8; MS, iii 2 Ag32, 92—97; MS, iii
3 Oc32, 192—97; MS, iii 4 J33, 282—86 c
A letter to a middle-aged novelist
[Walpole].
MS, iii 3 Oc32, 243—49 c
The modern movement: a painters'
symposium.
MS, vi 3 Oc35, 244—57 c
Nationalism in the east.
MS, ii 3 Oc31, 218—21 c
Poetic justice
[*The Georgiad,* by R. Campbell].
MS, ii 4 J32, 343—44 r
Post-war Scotland.
MS, v 1/2 Je34, 5—19 c
The Royal Scottish Academy in 1933.
MS, iv 2 Jy33, 118—22 c
S. J. Peploe and seven others.
MS, vi 4 J36, 348—50 c
Scottish nationalism.
MS, iv 1 A33, 4—11; MS, iv 2 Jy33,
94—99; MS, iv 3 Oc33, 178—84;
MS, iv 4 J34, 270—76 c
Sigrid Undset.
MS, v 3 Oc34, 178—83 c
Socialism in transition.
MS, vi 2 Jy35, 95—100 c
Socialists and credit reform.
MS, vi 1 A35, 3—8 c
The theatre [*Dream island,*
by R. Millar].
MS, i 2 Su30, 11 dr
'This affligit realm'.
MS, vi 3 Oc35, 187—91 c
Upton Sinclair — puritan and socialist.
MS, iii 2 Ag32, 149—55 c
see also Crémieux, B.; Giono, J.;
Romains, J.

Wicksell, Johan Gustav Knut
Lectures on political economy,
vol. 1 rev. by B. Pritchard

Wicksteed, Joseph Hartley
The challenge of childhood
rev. by E. Capon

Wigham, W. S.
The case against out-and-out pacificism.
TC, vi 31 S—Oc33, 47—49 c

Wildman, Carl
Jean Cocteau, calembouriste; Poème.
OO, xi 54 M31, 37—43 c, v
Sonnet; Night; Morning.
F, 4 D30, 31 v

Wilenski, Reginald Howard
French painting rev. by W. Martin

[*The voyage of the Chelyuskin*, tr. by A. Brown].
LR, ii 2 N35, 95—96 r
The big firm
rev. by A. West

Williams-Ellis, Amabel *and*
Fisher, F. J.
Introduction to English history
rev. by A. L. Morton

Williams-Ellis, Clough
Soviet architecture.
LR, iii 10 N37, 588—93 c

Williams-Parry, R.
Pagan.
W, 6/7 M39, 202 v
Three poems, tr. by G. Williams.
WR, ii 2 S39, 77 v

Williamson, George C.
Aubrey Beardsley: a few memories.
CA, 9 1931, 278—80 c

Williamson, Hugh Ross
Some notes on theatre.
J, 2 My36, 16, 18 c
The theatre faces a new world.
R, i 8 D34, 5—6 c

Willis, D. A.
New China [*Chinese testament*, by S. Tretiakov].
LR, i 2 N34, 46—47 r
New life for the novel.
VP, i 1 A—Je34, 12—14 c
Novel review
[*Rhondda roundabout*, by J. Jones; *Under the wheels*, by J. Lawson; *Haunting Europe*, by M. Slater].
VP, i 2 Jy—S34, 49—51 r
Review [*Walls of glass*, by A. S. J. Tessimond].
VP, i 2 Jy—S34, 56 r

Wilson, A. D. L.
Sparrows and bread.
BB, vii 2 M30, 82 v

Wilson, Albert Edward
Harlequinade.
R, i 8 D34, 6—7 c
Margate's famous theatre.
R, i 4 My34, 16 c

Wilson, A. S.
Soil.
PP, 13/14 Jy—Ag39, 14 v

Wilson, Edward Merton *tr.*
see Gongora y Argote, Luis de

Wilson, G. M.
Channel crossing.
FB, v 2 My39, 39 v
Poem.
B, 2 W38, 6 v
Poem.
B, 2 W38, 18—19 v

Wilson, George Louis Rosa
New colour.
JG, 41 Su37, [37] v

Wilson, John H.
Towards integration.
LD, i 1 M37, 23 c

Wilson, Margaret
Review [*Out of the picture*, by L. MacNeice].
PR, 23 N37, 15—16 r

Wilson, Norman
Scotland and the cinema.
NA, i 1 Au39, 78—82 c

Wilson, Robert McNair
The ledger and the cross.
LS, i 3 N34, 16—34 c

Wilson, Romer *pseud.*
Who killed Cock Robin?
NS, i 1 F34, 27—48 p
Tender advice rev. by G. West

Wilson, Stanley
The coal tip.
LR, ii 14 N36, 772—74 p

Wilson, T.
I pellegrini.
LD, i 4 Je37, 22—23 p

Winocour, Jack
Claimant's reply.
LR, i 7 A35, 265—66 v
Draft for a hunger marcher, by J. J.
TU, i 2 1934, 41—43 c
Politics and jazz.
TU, 1 1933, 29—35 c
Spanish gentlemen.
TU, 3 Je34, 28—30 v
Suite in the Spanish manner.
NO, ii 2 J35, 113—18 v
The university and social freedom.
NO, ii 1 My34, 9—25 c
William Morris, by J. J.
TU, 3 Je34, 43 c
The wind.
TU, 4 F35, 55 v

Winser, David
Irrational protest to the scientists.
FB, ii 5 5M37, 40 v

Poem.
FB, ii 5 5M37, 44 v

Winslow, Walker
Pyramid.
CV, 4 1935, 7 v

Winter, Freda M.
Man and dog.
P, 6 1939, 146—57 p

Winter, John Keith
Rats of Norway
rev. by P. Treadgold

Winters, Yvor
Answers to an enquiry.
T, 12/13 Oc38, 111 p
The cremation; Much in little.
T, 12/13 Oc38, 98 v

Winterton, Paul
Russia — with open eyes
rev. by R. Jardine

Wintle, Irene
Compensation.
JG, 17 Su31, [16] v
The Cornish fisher-girl's song.
JG, 14 Au30, [22—23] v
The elusive god.
JG, 19 W31, [20] v
Spring song.
JG, 13 Su30, [6] v

Wintringham, Thomas Henry
Artists in uniform.
LR, i 5 F35, 151—60 p
Artists international.
LR, i 2 N34, 40—41 c
As to an eagle's eye
[*The correspondence of K. Marx and F. Engels*;
Anti-Duhring, by F. Engels;
Socialism victorious;
Dimitrov, by S. D. Blagoyeva:
Chapayev, by D. Furmanov].
LR, i 7 A35, 278—83 r
British medical unit.
LR, ii 16 J37, 873 v
Clerks and class struggle
[*Clerical labour in Britain*, by F. D. Klingender].
LR, ii 1 Oc35, 48 r
Contempt of court.
LR, i 1 Oc34, 26 v
Empire air day 1936.
LR, ii 10 Jy36, 502 v
First love.
NW, 1 Sp36, 65—68 p
The floating republic
[by G. E. Manwaring and B. Dobrée;
Storm warning, by I. Soboleff].

149

Wintringham, Thomas Henry (cont.)
LR, i 10 Jy35, 421–23 r
Heil and farewell
[*Heil! a picture book;*
Hitler re-arms,
ed. by D. Woodman;
British imperialism in India,
by J. Beauchamp] ?
LR, i 4 J35, 142–43 r
The immortal tractor.
ST, i 1 F33, 17–18 v
It's a bohunk.
NW, ns2 Sp39, 54–60 p
Lightness is all
[*The new book of English verse,*
ed. by C. Williams] .
LR, ii 5 F36, 237 r
Monument.
LR, iii 9 Oc37, 517–19 v
Mutiny.
LR, i 11 Ag35, 441–46 p
Rakosi.
LR, i 6 M35, 233 v
The road to Caporetto.
LR, ii 2 N35, 63–65 c
Soviet science
[by J. G. Crowther] .
LR, ii 9 Je36, 470 r
Speaking concretely:
a reply to C. Day Lewis.
LR, i 2 N34, 34 v
War is also an art.
LR, ii 5 F36, 194–96 c
War scholars
[*Cambridge University and war;*
Labour's way to peace,
by A. Henderson;
Arms and the clergy,
by G. Bedborough] .
LR, i 10 Jy35, 431 r
We have been scared
[*We have been warned,*
by N. Mitchison] .
LR, i 9 Je35, 381–83 r
Who is for liberty?
LR, i 12 S35, 482–87 c
Writers' international.
LR, i 6 M35, 223–25 c
The coming world war
rev. by A. L. Morton
Mutiny
rev. by L. E. O. Charlton; A. Hodge;
A. L. Morton

Wise, Marjorie
English village schools
rev. by K. Arnold

Witham, Karen M. T.
London fog.
JG, 65 Su38, [18] v

Withers, Carmel
Loneliness.

CA, 2 S30, 16 v
The model.
CA, 3 Oc30, 55 v
The moment.
CA, 8 1931, 253 v
Resurrection.
CA, 5 M31, 126–27 v

Wodehouse, Pelham Grenville
Blandings castle
rev. by NS, ii 3 Je35, 240

Woledge, Geoffrey
The deserter.
JG, 14 Au30, [17–18] v
For a house.
JG, 16 Sp31, [17] v
Muse and Lar.
JG, 26 Au33, [16–18] v
A portrait of Roman Ilkley.
HR, 4 1931, 41–43 c
To Apollo.
JG, 21 Su32, [4] v
The traditional architecture of
western Yorkshire.
HR, 6 1933, 37–41 c

Wolf, Friedrich
Professor Mamlock
rev. by J. B. Harvey
Sailors of Cattaro
rev. by C. C. Doggett

Wolfe, Ann
Poems after the Japanese.
PR, 1 1F35, 14 v
Poems from the Japanese.
PR, 2 12F35, 6 v
see also Olyesha, Y.

Wolfe, Humbert
Consola.
HR, 4 1931, 32 v
I died before you came.
WW, i 4 Oc30, 92 v
Early poems
rev. by C. B. Spencer
Notes on English verse satire
rev. by V. O. Neuberg
X at Oberammergau
rev. by LR, i 10 Jy35, 431–32

Women in Germany, by One of
them.
LR, iii 9 Oc37, 537–39 c

Wood, Raymond G.
The caves of South Wales.
WR, ii 2 S39, 84–90 c

Wood, Wendy
We will fight no more in England's
wars.
VS, i 1 Je–Ag38, 15–17 c

Woodburn, Frances
Experience.
DD, xi 47 S–Oc34, 74 v

Woodcock, George
Insular poem; Barbizon;
The announcer's speech.
T, 17 A39, 10–11 v
The island.
T, 14 D38, 124 v
Landore.
W, 8/9 Ag39, 239–40 v
Memorandum from Arcadia; Panegyric.
NV, 30 Su38, 10–11 v
Snow; Gods.
T, 15/16 F39, 155 v

Woodhouse, Frances
Walking on the beach.
NS, ii 1 F35, 8–12 p

Woodman, Dorothy
World crisis: armament firms.
TC, v 27 My33, 178–79 c
Hitler re-arms
rev. by T. H. Wintringham

Woodman, Mary
The child of sin.
SV, 4A Sp39, 44 v

Woods, Margaret
The mourners.
DD, ix 32 M–A32, 18 v

Woods, Sydney John
Bric-a-brac.
ND, 23 2D37, 14 p
Time to forget ourselves.
AX, 6 Su36, 19–21 c
Who's been frightened by the big bang?
LB, 11 M39, 13–15 c

Woolf, Hal
Twenty-four hours.
NS, i 4 Ag34, 253–69 p

Woolf, Leonard Sidney
After the deluge
rev. by I. Berlin

Woolf, Virginia
Why?
LS, i 2 My34, 5–12 c
Letter to a young poet
rev. by G. Pendle
A room of one's own
rev. by F.H.
Walter Sickert
rev. by H. Burnett
The waves
rev. by A. D. Hawkins; S. Spender

Wootton, Barbara
Plan or no plan
rev. by W. N. Warbey

Woozley, Anthony Douglas
Propagandist cinema.
NO, i 3 F34, 307−15 c
Review [*New stories,*
vol. 1, no. 1].
LS, i 1 F34, 57−58 r
Review [*India's coral strand,*
by R. Oke].
LS, i 3 N34, 72−73 r
Stream.
TU, 1 1933, 28 p

Worrall, Ralph Lyndal
Footsteps of warfare
rev. by T. Lincoln

Worsley, Thomas Cuthbert
A boy's love.
NW, 4 Au37, 150−60 p
The crest.
NS, i 6 D34, 444−51 p
The dance and the steps.
P, 5 1939, 113−33 p
The flight from Malaga.
LR, iii 3 A37, 137−39 p
Malaga has fallen.
NW, ns2 Sp39, 36−52 p
see also Auden, Wystan Hugh

Worts, Frederick Robert
The gleaming paradox.
HR, 4 1931, 45−47 c

Wray, Cyril
When we were very green.
SM, 2 S31, front. i

Wren, Mary
God in the night.
DD, xi 48 N−D34, 97 v
The houses of ivory shall perish.
DD, x 42 N−D33, 100 v
Saturday night; Strangers in
conversation.
DD, xi 45 My−Je34, 49 v
The weeders.
DD, x 41 S−Oc33, 82 v

Wrench, Margaret Stanley-
see Stanley-Wrench, Margaret

Wright, Basil
Film group.
GTP, 2 Ag36, [2] c
The Russian cinema.
NW, ns3 C39, 238−49 c
Soviet theatre.
LR, iii 10 N37, 584−86 c

Wright, Ralph
'Mother' by M. Gorki, as dramatized
by B. Nixon].
LR, ii 3 D35, 143−44 r
New novels [*The olive field,*
by R. Bates;
Three of the three million,
by L. Frank; *The exile,*
by P. S. Buck].
LR, ii 7 A36, 337−39 r
New novels [*Strange glory,*
by L. H. Myers; *South riding,*
by W. Holtby; *To tea on Sunday,*
by L. Halward].
LR, ii 8 My36, 399−401 r
New novels
[*Seven red Sundays,*
by R. J. Sender; *Studs Lonigan,*
by J. T. Farrell;
The bad companions,
by M. L. Richardson;
Let us pray, by J. Gray].
LR, ii 9 Je36, 459−61 r
The new tradition
[*Proletarian literature in the United
States: an anthology*].
LR, ii 6 M36, 276−77 r
Nobody loves them but H. G. Wells
[*The fate of the middle classes,*
by A. Brown].
LR, ii 8 My36, 408 r
Plays of the month
[*Storm in a teacup,*
by J. Bridie; *Red night,*
by J. L. Hodson].
LR, ii 7 A36, 350 r

Wright, Ralph *and others*
Left Theatre competition.
LR, ii 2 N35, 87−88 c

Wrighton, Basil
The actuality of Cardinal Newman.
AR, i 1 A37, 11−18 c
Thoughts on Kierkegaard.
AR, i 4 J38, 315−22 c

The writer in a changing world
[American Writers' Congress, 1937]
rev. by E. Rickword

Writers' International, British Section
Draft statement.
LR, i 1 Oc34, 38 c

Wyatt, H. E. M.
As yet undreamed.
DD, x 40 Jy−Ag33, 73 v

Wyatt, Honor
Death makes life.
SV, 3 W38, 22 v
Poems.
EP, 2 Su36, 137−38 v

Poems.
EP, 2 Su36, 137−38 v
A story: to die in a story.
EP, 3 Sp37, 100−6 p

Wyatt, Robert Elliott Storey
Youth v. the New Zealanders.
LD, i 4 Je37, 30−32 c

Wyatt, Woodrow Lyle
Father dies.
LD, ii 1 Oc37, 6−7 p
Our first birthday.
LD, ii 3 F38, 3 c

Wylie, Ida Alexa Ross
Everything in the window.
P, 2 1938, 57−69 p
Witches' sabbath.
P, 1 1938, 9−39 p

Wyllie, Thomas Hunter Steen
Too sweet the fruits.
LD, ii 2 D37, 13 v

Wyndham-Lewis,
Dominic Bevan
The scarecrow on the lawn.
CA, 1 Ag30, 14−17 c

Wynne, R.
Nightfall in the vale of Ewyas.
CA, 7 Je31, 200 v

X

X *pseud.*
Crucifix; Mulberry tree.
PR, 5 17My35, 7 v
Different mixtures
[*The disappearing castle,*
by C. Madge;
Calamiterror, by G. Barker].
NV, 28 J38, 20−21 r

Y

Y., E. G.
Dawn.
DD, xi 46 Jy−Ag34, 68 v

Y., S. B.
Fancy free.
MS, v 4 J35, 268−70 c

Yajnik, Ramanlal Kanaiyalal
In the Indian theatre
rev. by Jaques *pseud.*

Yang Hsien-yi *see* Mellor, B.

Yang Vei-tsen
Whither Chinese youth?
TC, i 4 Je31, 20—22 c

Yao Hsin-nung
Chinese literature and the
united front.
LR, iii 12 J38, 722—26 c

Yaroslavsky, Emelyan
Emelyanovich *pseud.*
History of anarchism in Russia
rev. by R. Jardine

Yasoshima, Minoru
A battle of roses.
TO, i 1 J38, 8 v

Yates, L. J.
Poem.
NW, ns1 Au38, 232 v

Yeats, William Butler
On the boiler.
OTB, 1 1939, p
Essays, 1931 to 1936
rev. by G. Grigson
A full moon in March
rev. by L. MacNeice
The herne's egg
rev. by G. Grigson
New poems
rev. by T. R. Barnes
*The Oxford book of modern
verse* rev. by G. Grigson;
C. Day Lewis
A vision rev. by G. Grigson
The winding stair
rev. by G. Grigson

Yeats-Brown, Francis Charles
Claydon
Dogs of war
rev. by T. Lincoln; F. Meynell

Yeaxlee, Joan
Poem.
PR, 6 31My35, 11 v
Poem.
PR, 7 12Je35, 15—16 v

Yeh Chien-yu
How Triumph Van went back
to the army.
NW, ns1 Au38, 195—207 p
The yellow spot
rev. by I. Olden

Yendell, Norman C.
Argument.
DD, xi 44 M—A34, 32 v
Destiny.
JG, 21 Su32, [10] v
The flower.
DD, ix 36 N—D32, 101 v
The road.
JG, 26 Au33, [24] v
The skylark.
DD, ix 34 Jy—Ag32, 62 v
Sleep.
JG, 24 Sp33, [11] v
Song of triumph.
JG, 31 W34, [7—8] v
The student.
JG, 20 Sp32, [19] v
*Reply to reason and other
poems* rev. by A. Morgan

Yorke, Henry
Savernake.
NO, i N33, 210—20 p

Yorke, Roland
The people one meets at the
universities.
FB, iii 6 21Oc37, 8—9 c

Young, Albert
A rude rhyme;
Farringdon market.
SM, 1 Je31, 59—62 v
To Liam O'Flaherty.
SM, 3 1932, 100 v

Young, Allan
The economics of planning.
TC, vi 36 S34, 355—70 c

Young, Andrew John
Culbin sands.
P, 1 1938, 84 v
Newlands corner; At Oxford.
SV, 1 Su38, 10, 18 v
The nightingales;
The house-martins;
A prehistoric camp;
Hibernating snails;
Drought in the fens.
SV, 2 Au38, 5—7 v
Overtaken by mist;
Morning in the combe.
FB, iv 10 N38, 15 v
Two poems:
Reflections on the river;
A brimstone butterfly.
P, 2 1938, 55 v
Walking in mist; A dead mole.
NV, 28 J38, 8—9 v
Nicodemus
rev. by K. Allott

Young, B. M. G.
A mystic on poetry.
PR, 13 5F36, 12—16 c

Young, Joan R.
Londoner's recompense.
LS, i 3 N34, 54 v
The return rev. by F. T. Prince

Young, Kathleen Tankersley
Apology for love.
CV, 1 Su34, 8—9 v
Two poems.
CV, 5 M36, [12] v

Young, Robert *tr.*
see Pasternak, B.

Young, Sidney
Abdication.
P, 2 1938, 146—49 p

Young, Terence
The great disillusion.
FB, iii 8 3M38, 46 p

The young hunting.
CPP, 6 Oc36, 115—17 v

Youth and peace.
LR, ii 15 D36, 818—19 c

Z

Zak, William
Eugene Potter.
LR, iii 16 My38, 991—95 c

Zamiatine, Evgeny Ivanovich
Comrade Chourigine has the
floor,
tr. by E. Bentley-Mott.
CPP, 10 Au37, 12—23 p

Zangwill, Oliver
Psychology in relation to the
novel.
CM, ii 1 Su35, 225—28 c

Zech, Paul
The pioneer, tr. by P. Selver.
SM, 5 1934, 118—19 v

Zhdanov, A. *and others*
Problems of Soviet literature
rev. by M. Slater

Zoschenko, Mikhail Mikhailovich
The housing crisis,
tr. by S. Garry.
NW, 5 Sp38, 163—65 p
A point of view, and
Nervous people,
tr. by F. Polanovskaya.
EX, 7 Sp31, 43—46 p

Zozulya, Efim Davidovich
Romance sans paroles.
tr. by A. L. Lloyd.
CPP, 9 Sp37, 28—33 p

Zukertort, Ivan *pseud.*
Why I dislike communism.
PR, 7 12Je35, 3, 5 c

Zweig, Stefan
The tower of Babel.
LR, i 1 Oc34, 6—11 p
Die Heilung durch den Geist,
rev. by P. Sedgwick